Theatre for Youth
TWELVE PLAYS WITH MATURE THEMES

Theatre for Youth
TWELVE PLAYS WITH MATURE THEMES

Edited by Coleman A. Jennings
and Gretta Berghammer

 University of Texas Press, Austin

Copyright © 1986 by the University of Texas Press
All rights reserved
Printed in the United States of America

First edition, 1986

Requests for permission to reproduce material from this work should be
sent to:

Permissions
University of Texas Press
Box 7819
Austin, Texas 78713

Library of Congress Cataloging-in-Publication Data

Main entry under title:

Theatre for youth.

Bibliography: p.
Contents: The Honorable Urashimo Taro / dramatized
by Coleman A. Jennings—Courage! / dramatized by
Ed Graczyk—The Odyssey / dramatized by Gregory A.
Falls and Kurt Beattie—[etc.]
1. Young adult drama, American. 2. Children's
plays, American. [1. Plays—Collections]
I. Jennings, Coleman A., [date]. II. Berghammer,
Gretta, [date].
PS625.5.T46 1986   812'.54'0809282   85-26515

ISBN: 978-0-292-78085-9

Contents

Foreword

by Jed H. Davis

The quest to increase the stature of theatre for young audiences as a profession has been led by playwrights exploring new directions, by publishers willing to take chances with unproved concepts, and by producers, both amateur and professional, energetically pursuing fresh production modes. The present volume, so insightfully assembled by Coleman A. Jennings and Gretta Berghammer, is an important document of one of the new directions in playwriting for young people. Twenty—even ten—years ago such a collection would have been impossible. Those of us who work in this field will hail its appearance as an important step forward.

Ever since the theatre for children and young people began in this country, producers have been bemoaning the scarcity of scripts suitable for audiences who have passed beyond the age of interest in adventure stories of the classic tradition. There was a gap in the repertoire, and everyone saw it. Most existing plays suited the younger set well enough. But after age twelve, the young person, entering a period of important discoveries about life, rejected most material that was intended to keep him or her interested in theatrical fare. Some were content to play a wait-and-see game. Some, in their frustration, turned to inappropriate adult plays, found them beyond their comprehension, and lost interest entirely. Many others didn't even try. They simply assumed the theatre held nothing for them, and pursued other amusements. So the notion of connections between theatre attendance as children and attendance as adults was upset by the gap at junior high age—twelve to fifteen. The need for plays to interest this age group has been pointed out by practitioners in numerous articles, convention sessions, and symposia; and here at last is a volume to address that need.

What is a "mature theme"?

A theme, of course, is a statement of universal truth derived through the action of a play. It is the rule of life and living that one carries away after the play is over. It goes beyond the play's subject matter, but is, of course, tied to it. It is the distillate that remains after the nonessentials have been stripped away. A mature theme is one that requires of the interpreter a rather advanced reasoning power, one that allows a universal truth to emerge from apparently unhappy, disastrous, or immoral occurrences. The simple reasoning of younger children must eventually give way to awareness of complexities, to precise associations of causes and effects, to connections between premises and outcomes. The good-bad morality concepts so prevalent in children need to be augmented by consciousness of degrees of goodness and badness found in real people, so that the "greater good" or the "lesser evil" can be admitted in judging the events. An ability to project the play's happenings into future time comes with increasing age and experience; so perceptions of themes as they relate to ultimate, rather than immediate, ends can afford greater pleasure and meaning to the youthful psyche. It takes mature judgment for one to see that Hamlet's personal tragedy and death ultimately result in straightening out the rotting state of Denmark. The rightness of causes—even those that result in death for the protagonist—determine how poetic justice is served in the long run.

Such reasoning is possible as young people reach what Piaget identified as the cognitive stage of "formal operations." At that point, one seeks out the kinds of activities and stimuli that challenge the intellectual capacities being developed. Young adolescents reject subjects that seem childish; they have gone beyond that. A play that reminds them of that stage through which they have successfully passed will be met with marginal tolerance if not open derision. But one such as those in this volume, which require challenging intellectual activity as well as emotional involvement through their subject matter, will be a delight.

I will leave detailed analysis of these plays to the readers and producers. However, of special interest to me and, I suspect, to the youth for whom these plays are intended, is the particular mix of fantasy and realism represented. Some of the plays, such as *The Honorable Urashima Taro*, are largely fantasy, taking place in an unreal world in which creatures of many kinds are endowed with unusual powers. In this case, a very human fisherman gets caught up in the dream world under the sea, and when he returns to the natural world of living human beings he finds that he is a very old man and most of his lifetime has been spent; but he will find contentment in the few days he has left in the bosom of his descendants. A similar blend of fantasy and reality maintains in *The Arkansaw Bear*, in which the beginning and ending occur in the context of an Arkansas home where Grandpa is dying and the middle is a fantasy involving a dancing bear from a circus. In the guise of a futuristic fantasy, Ray Bradbury, master of that genre, has fashioned an allegory of human history called *The Martian Chronicles*, showing Earth man's invasion of Mars in four successive waves, bringing with him not only the disease that kills off the native population but the hope of a promising second chance for humankind's survival. Also on the futuristic side is the fantasy of *The Code Breaker*, in which a computer named Ruby keeps inquisitive teenagers in line to prevent their discovery of the free world outside their cubicles. Another allegory, *Noodle Doodle Box*, pits two universal character types against each other, holding fast to their individual territories until an opportunist cons them out of their possessions, forcing them to act cooperatively to restore order. Included in this group would have to be the classic *Odyssey*, which shows a famous Greek band of warriors confronting every terror conceivable in man's versatile imagination, yet emerging triumphant.

At the realism end of the scale we find *Doors*, in which a boy finds ways to avoid the growing conflict that will lead his parents to divorce. It is a very real world that Jeff occupies, as is the Civil War world engulfing the Boy/Young Man of *Courage!*, even though we seem to step easily between external happenings and those taking place within his mind. *The Boy Who Stole the Stars* and *The Boy Who Talked to Whales* are also placed in a real world where believable people encounter plausible contemporary problems and work through down-to-earth solutions without supernatural help. Music provides a theatricalized framework for the unique *My Days as a Youngling*, yet its characters and episodes are right out of small-town life experiences.

The three Oscar Wilde stories that comprise *Broken Hearts* in a sense epitomize the fantasy-reality link. In a historically real sixteenth-century Spain, *The Birthday of the Infanta* is celebrated. The last one, *The Happy Prince*, is a fantasy about a Swallow who carries out a series of commands given by the statue of a repentant, self-centered ruler, while in between is the cynical story of *The Devoted Friend*, whom no one should have even as an enemy!

It should be apparent from the above that the plays in this volume exemplify not only mature themes but also very sophisticated dramaturgy. Playwrights have taken note of the natural interest in fantasy continuing into the teen years, and have not hesitated to employ mixtures of fantasy and reality in the same play. As the reader examines them, the plays will be found to employ a wide range of theatrical devices carefully selected to encourage acceptance and understanding of the premises being examined. Our playwrights have come a long way from the early simplistic days. Authors represented here have demonstrated that a new era is at hand, not only in dealing with mature themes, but in pointing the way toward a mature art form.

They and the editors deserve our thanks.

Theatre for Youth
TWELVE PLAYS WITH MATURE THEMES

Introduction

Since the beginning early in this century of the theatre for youth movement in the United States, the majority of plays written in the genre have been fairy tales. Characters were clearly defined as representative of either good or evil, and their conflicts were resolved so that all received their just desserts. The serious exploration of mature subjects such as prejudice, man's inhumanity to man, aging, and death was seldom a consideration of children's theatre. Rare were the playwrights who intended their young audiences to question values, make judgments about a character who showed a combination of both good and bad traits, or openly discuss traditionally "adult" themes such as death and dying, adolescence, maturation, sexuality, and divorce. "Restrictions that parents, psychologists and educators imposed on children's theatre stifled its creative genius."[1]

By the decade of the sixties, the winds had begun to shift. Society had begun to change its attitude toward children. The earlier child-rearing philosophy of "barring anything disagreeable that would cause a child to shudder or shed a tear" had been replaced by a growing tendency on the part of parents and teachers to have children face rather than avoid the more difficult truths of existence.[2] This, in turn, has opened the theatre to new and previously unsuitable subjects, themes, and characters for the young audience.

The first play of major importance in showing the way along the new paths was *Reynard the Fox*, in 1962, by Belgian playwright Arthur Fauquez. Reynard, an immensely likeable rogue-hero who, in making mischief, exposed the hypocrisy that was rife among his society's leaders, was such a radical departure from past heroes that Sara Spencer, the editor and publisher of the Children's Theatre Press, included a justification for this new direction in children's plays in the catalogue that first announced its publication. She wrote:

Does Good Always Win?

"The first real story in the Bible," says Arthur Miller, "is the murder of Abel. Before this drama, there was peace, because man had no con-

---

1. William H. Kingsley, "Happy Endings, Poetic Justice, and the Depth and Strength of Characterization in American Children's Drama: A Critical Analysis." Unpublished dissertation, University of Pittsburgh, 1964, p. 324.

2. Helen S. Noble, "The Importance of Make-believe in the Life of a Child," *Theatre Magazine* (September 1919), pp. 199–200.

sciousness of sex or his separateness from plants or other animals. Presumably we are being told that the human being becomes himself in the act of becoming aware of his sinfulness.

"After all," he goes on to say, "the infraction of Eve is that she opened up the knowledge of good and evil. She presented Adam with a choice. So that where choice begins, Innocence ends. For what is Paradise but the absence of any need to choose? And two alternatives open out of Eden. One is Cain's alternative—to express without limit one's unbridled inner compulsion, in this case to murder, and to plead unawareness as a virtue and a defense. The other course is what roars through the rest of the Bible and all of history—the struggle of the human race through the millennia to pacify the destructive impulses of man, to express his wishes for greatness, for wealth, for accomplishment, for love, but without turning law and peace into chaos."

For sixty years the children's theatre has worked overtime to keep our children in the Garden of Eden, in this beautiful state of innocence, where good is always pretty or handsome, and evil is always ugly, and there is no necessity to choose, because good always wins. Shakespeare tells us that the purpose of playing is to hold the mirror up to nature, and this is what the adult theatre has concerned itself with for two thousand years—but it has never occurred to us to apply this to the children's theatre—and yet, who needs it more?

Outside the theatre, hard lessons are waiting for our children. Life is going to teach them that good and bad take many forms, and that good never really wins. It only strives, through our efforts, to stay ahead of evil—and it does not always succeed in that.

Is it so hard to say this to children? Yes, it is. We all know it is, and we all shrink from it, cowering behind our fairy tales. Nobody likes to put an end to innocence. There will be time enough, we say. But actually, what better way is there to bring children to a true understanding of good and evil, than through the unfolding of a play? What better place is there than the theatre to speak the truth to children? Is it not better they should learn some of the bitter things from the experience of actors on a stage, than at first hand? And especially, for our purposes, is it not well to let them know that they can look to the theatre not only for beauty, and fun, and adventure, and illusion, but for truth as well? And isn't this what we should be asking of our playwrights?

It is this line of thinking that has led us to expand our repertoire in a new direction, requesting our playwrights to speak to children sincerely, even though in comedy terms, on matters of broad application to all generations—such as the use of time, such as setting ourselves up in judgment over others, such as the place for nonsense in our many-faceted world. Themes like these depart from the traditional fairy-tale concept, and undertake to remove some of the insulation with which we have tried to protect our children. Life itself is stripping the insulation ruthlessly away—and surely the best way to protect our children is to prepare them for it.

We pray the time will never come when we shall cease to offer fairy tales to our children. But interspersed among them, let us dare to offer an occasional play that touches their innocence with awareness, and presents them with the necessity of choice. It is not only man who must learn to pacify his destructive impulses, to express his wishes for greatness, for accomplishment, for love. It must begin with children, mustn't it? [3]

Since the publication of *Reynard the Fox*, which is available in several anthologies and the acting edition, a growing number of children's theatre playwrights have been following suit, ignoring standard social restrictions and other established traditions of writing for children.

These new directions are exemplified by the scripts selected for this volume and those in the annotated bibliography. These plays deal with mature themes and are from both American and foreign playwrights. Drawing from traditional sources such as history, biography, and fantasy, these plays take problems and themes familiar and timely to the older sector of the youth audience and present them in a style that is challenging to them. The playwrights of these texts are no longer asking members of the audience to sit back and view the adventures of a two-dimensional good or evil character. Rather, this new genre of theatre for youth more than ever before reflects the trends of contemporary adult theatre, and demands that its audience examine a whole area of grey.

The twelve full-length plays contained within this anthology cover a wide range of topics, including the problems of aging, death and dying, friendship, courage, conformity, maturation, sexuality, and struggles with moral judgements. They have been chosen not only for their mature themes, but also for their professional integrity, the delicacy with which they handle their subject matter, and their respect for their intended audience. Realism and fantasy are also blended in the twelve scripts that follow.

In addition to these twelve plays, the fifty-six scripts listed at the end of the text have made substantial contributions toward new directions in dramatic literature for children and youth. These scripts, with their theatricality, honesty, and maturity, are plays that should be part of the existing performance repertory, to be shared by older youths and their parents for generations to come.

---

3. Sara Spencer, "Does Good Always Win?" *Children's Theatre Press* (now Anchorage Press) *Catalogue*, 1964.

The Honorable Urashima Taro

Japanese folk tale

Dramatized by Coleman A. Jennings

The Honorable Urashima Taro (1971)

The Honorable Urashima Taro is Coleman A. Jennings' fantasy adaptation of two Japanese folktales.

The play begins with the arrival of an Old Sea Turtle on a beach near a small fishing village. Taro, a poor fisherman, saves the Turtle from three boys who are taunting and beating it with sticks. Taro's kindly action convinces the Turtle that Taro is someone to be trusted, and he coerces him into leaving his family and journeying to the bottom of the sea. Beneath the sea, in a world of indescribable beauty, Taro uses his bravery and knowledge to destroy an evil Sea Scorpion and restore peace once more to the Sea Princess' kingdom. In doing so, Taro unknowingly spends his entire life beneath the sea. Upon his return to the beach, he discovers eighty years have passed, and that his wife is dead and his son is now an old man. Taro is now faced with an important decision: should he return to a life beneath the sea where eternal youth awaits him, or face impending death by living his last years as an old man on earth? Taro eventually chooses the latter, deciding that the chance to share love with other human beings cannot be surrendered. The Turtle returns beneath the sea, and Taro begins a new life on earth with his son and grandchildren.

CHARACTERS

Old Turtle

Three Young Boys, ages ten to fifteen

Urashima Taro, twenty-eight years old

Kimo, Taro's eleven-year-old son

Michiko, Taro's wife

The Sea Creatures

The Sea Princess

The Four Seasons

The Sea Scorpion

A Woman

Sentaro, Taro's great-grandson, age seven

SETTING
The shore of Shikoku, an island of Japan, near a little fishing village and the mountains and valleys of the ocean depths.

TIME
Long ago.

Note. "Urashima Taro" is pronounced without accenting any of the syllables: oo-ra-shee-ma tah-ro.

The Honorable Urashima Taro

Scene: Long ago. The shore of Shikoku, an island of Japan, near a little fishing village and the mountains and valleys of the ocean depths.

Japanese music is playing as the audience enters the theatre. There is no curtain, only screens upstage, painted to suggest a beach locale. As the house-lights dim, the Japanese music cross-fades to ocean sounds. The Turtle is "washed" ashore, settles at stage C, his back to the audience. The Three Boys run on stage, excited about going to the beach.

BOY 3. The boats will be back soon!

BOY 1. Hurry!

BOY 2. I'll race you to the water!

BOY 3. Look!

BOY 2. Look what's on the beach! *(The Boys gather around the Turtle.)*

BOY 1. I wonder how long he's been here?

BOY 3. He must have been washed ashore.

BOY 2. Look, how big he is!

BOY 1. Yes, he is.

BOY 3. Let's play with him.

BOY 2. Watch out!

BOY 1. Hit him!

BOY 3. Let's take him to the village.

BOY 1. No. No.

BOY 2. *(Picking up a stick.)* Let me hit him!

BOY 1. Make him stick out his head.

BOY 2. Watch out, he'll bite you!

BOY 3. How old is he?

BOY 2. Who cares?

BOY 1. Let's kill him.

BOY 3. No, just turn him on his back.

BOY 2. Wait! Here comes a boat.

BOY 1. Who is it?

BOY 3. It looks like Urashima Taro.

BOY 1. It is Taro!

BOY 3. *(Starting to leave.)* Let's go!

BOY 2. Wait. I'm not afraid of Urashima Taro.

BOY 3. But he will be angry with us!

BOY 2. It's none of his business what we do. Who cares what he says?

BOY 1. Does Taro own the sea or the beach?

BOY 2. No. No!

BOY 3. No, but he does care for the animals and sea creatures!

(Taro and his son, Kimo, are now near the shore.)

BOY 2. If he is so kind to sea creatures, why does he catch fish every day?

BOY 3. He catches fish for his family to sell in the marketplace. *(Taro and Kimo leave their imaginary boat in the shallow water and approach the boys.)*

TARO. Boys, what are you doing?

BOY 2. Nothing.

TARO. What do you have there?

BOY 2. A turtle we found on the beach!

TARO. But, what are you doing with it?

BOY 1. Nothing. Just playing!

TARO. You have a strange way of playing. Why are you so cruel?

BOY 2. We can do whatever we like! We found him. He's ours now.

TARO. *(Crossing to the Turtle.)* The turtle belongs to the sea.

BOY 2. He should stay in the ocean if he doesn't want to be caught. He belongs to us, and we can kill him, if we want.

TARO. Why would you be so unkind to a poor creature?

BOY 1. Look at your baskets! You catch and kill fish every day. Why shouldn't we kill an old turtle?

TARO. It is right to take the turtle if you are hungry, but you are teasing and hurting him.

BOY 1. Look at him; he's old. Who cares if he lives?

TARO. You needn't kill him just because he is old. Think what a wonder it is to live so long—maybe even as long as three men!

BOY 3. Yes, let's *not* kill him.

TARO. You do not need the turtle for food. Let's make a trade. We will give you some fish for him. Kimo, the fish. *(Kimo brings a small net of fish to Taro.)*

BOY 1. We could use the fish.

BOY 2. Why are you listening to him?

BOY 1. We will do what we please. Leave us alone.

BOY 2. Move out of the way!

(As the argument builds, Boy 2 attempts to strike the Turtle with the stick. Boy 3 grabs his arm and holds him.)

TARO. *(As he covers the Turtle with his body.)* Wait! You must not kill him!

BOY 2. Get away! He belongs to us!

TARO. *(Angrily.)* He belongs to no one. Now go home. *(Pause, then firmly, but kindly.)* Boys! Here are fish for your family. *(Pause.)* Go on. *(Boy 2 puts the stick down and exits with Boy 1, without accepting any fish. Boy 3 remains with Taro and Kimo.)*

BOY 3. I'm sorry. I hadn't meant to be so cruel. *(Turns to leave.)*

KIMO. I wonder how deeply he can swim.

BOY 3. Maybe he's been on this beach before.

TARO. Let's help him return to his home.

KIMO. *(As they help the Turtle into the "water.")* He *is* big.

(Note: The actors never touch the Turtle. Keeping their hands approximately six inches from him, they create a stylized effect of grasping the shell. The Turtle retains complete freedom of movement.)

TARO. Yes, my son, and he is handsome, too. Now he will be free. Be on your way, ancient one!

KIMO and BOY 3. *(To the Turtle as he begins to exit into the sea.)* Good-bye.

TARO. *(As Boy 3 starts to exit, calling him back.)* Wait. *(Offering him some fish.)* Take these to your family.

BOY 3. All of these?

TARO. Take them, and go along.

BOY 3. Thank you for the fish. Good-bye, Kimo. Good-bye, Urashima Taro.

TARO and KIMO. Good-bye.

> *(When Taro and Kimo are left alone, Taro starts cross to the boat area.)*

KIMO. How old was that turtle?

TARO. Over a hundred years old, I think. What a glorious creature! Listen! I thought I heard him call. *(Pause.)* I wonder why he came to this part of the beach.

KIMO. Do you think the turtle can swim out as far as we were today?

TARO. Even farther. *(Returning to reality.)* Now Kimo, help me with the boat. *(As they begin to pantomime pushing the boat ashore.)* Push, Kimo, push.

WIFE. *(Offstage.)* Taro. Kimo.

TARO. We are here. *(To Kimo.)* Push harder.

> *(Wife enters.)*

WIFE. Why, Taro, you are late. Have you just now returned?

TARO. Yes, Michiko.

WIFE. Where's Kimo?

KIMO. Here, Mother.

WIFE. I didn't see you. Were you a help to your father today, Kimo?

KIMO. I hope so. Father and I rowed out farther than we've ever gone.

WIFE. Did you have a good catch?

TARO. Three baskets. The water was very clear and blue. We could almost see the bottom. It reminded me of the old legend about the Princess and the Sea Palace. Michiko, you remember that old story.

WIFE. You are a dreamer, my husband. You are more interested in legends of the sea than in catching fish for your parents to sell.

TARO. We always have enough fish.

WIFE. When you come home so late everyone buys fish from the others. No one needs our fish. We must hurry. *(As she inspects the catch.)* Taro, this basket is almost empty.

TARO. I gave some to a boy.

WIFE. *(Looking around.)* What boy?

TARO. He's gone.

WIFE. Why did you give him our fish?

TARO. He helped me return an old turtle to the sea.

KIMO. You should have seen that turtle. He was this big—*(Spreading his arms apart to indicate the length of the Turtle.)*—and his feet were like huge oars. I would like to have him for a pet.

WIFE. You are so much like your father, always wanting to keep every animal you see. I suppose you'll soon be dreaming of ocean legends, too.

TARO. Try to understand . . .

WIFE. I do understand. A boy helped you, and being a kindly man, you wanted to repay him. But we need every fish you can catch.

TARO. It is so.

WIFE. Hurry to the marketplace with these fish, Kimo. Your grandparents are waiting for them.

TARO. *(As Kimo starts to leave.)* Stay a moment. *(To Michiko.)* I need the boy to help me with the boat and the nets.

WIFE. *(As Taro looks out into the ocean, as if listening to something.)* Then I shall take some fish to them. *(She picks up the fish to go, but pauses as she notices Taro moving toward the ocean.)* Taro? *(Pause.)* My husband, what is wrong?

TARO. *(Ignoring Michiko.)* Why did we send him away so quickly? Perhaps the Old Turtle had something to tell me. Old One! We're still here. Come back!

WIFE. Forget the ocean for a little while. You must stop this dreaming. Come home, now.

TARO. I think I can hear him now—pleading with me to come into the ocean. I must know why he came here. Turtle, Old Turtle!

WIFE. Taro? *(Pause. Taro continues to stare out into the ocean. To Kimo.)* I have never seen your father like this. Help him home. I will take these to the marketplace and then meet you at home.

KIMO. Yes, Mother.

WIFE. *(To Taro, as she exits.)* I will prepare something for us to eat. Try not to be late. *(Taro remains silent.)*

KIMO. *(Quietly.)* Do you want to clear the nets now, Father?

TARO. *(Not moving.)* What a magnificent creature he was!

KIMO. *(Still trying to reach Taro.)* I'll help you with the boat.

TARO. *(Noticing Kimo again.)* Yes . . . yes. *(Moving to the boat.)* Where is your mother?

KIMO. She took some of the fish to the marketplace. She will meet us at home.

TARO. Good. Help me with the boat and the nets.

KIMO. *(As he helps pantomime pushing the boat ashore, and later straightening the nets.)* Tomorrow, let's go out farther than we have ever been!

TARO. Perhaps. We'll see. We must clear the nets now.

KIMO. Remember the time you told me about the old legend you heard as a boy? Would you tell me again?

TARO. Your Mother just told you—told us—we must stop thinking so much about those old stories.

KIMO. I can't help it. When we are so far out in the ocean and it's quiet and still—the stories seem more real than ever.

TARO. Hand me the small net.

KIMO. *(Handing Taro the small net.)* Sometimes I can almost see the evil sea scorpions of the ocean mountains. Which is more powerful, a sea creature or a man?

TARO. I don't know, Kimo.

KIMO. What if a man could really meet a sea scorpion? Do you think they would fight?

TARO. Perhaps, if the man thought his life were in danger.

KIMO. Remember that old story about how the man used water from his mouth to destroy the sea scorpion?

TARO. Yes.

KIMO. But how can water from a man's mouth be so powerful under the sea? Tell me that story again.

TARO. Not now. Tomorrow . . . when we are out in the boat. Get the fish.

TURTLE. *(Calling from offstage.)* Taro. Taro.

TARO. Listen!

KIMO. What was that?

TURTLE. Taro. Urashima Taro!

KIMO. *(Frightened.)* Who is that?

TARO. Who calls? *(Looking about on the beach.)* Who calls "Urashima Taro"?

(Turtle enters.)

TURTLE. Taro! Out here in the ocean . . .

KIMO. The turtle! Over there! *(Pointing toward the Turtle.)*

TURTLE. I'm the turtle whom you rescued a few minutes ago.

KIMO. How can that be? Turtles cannot talk.

TURTLE. Taro, those boys almost destroyed me.

TARO. I'm glad we found you in time. From now on, Old Turtle, you'd better remain in the sea.

TURTLE. I shall, but I've come back to thank you for saving me. You were very kind to help. When the boys caught me, I was on my way to find you.

TARO. *(Astonished.)* Me?

TURTLE. Yes, we of the Palace of the Sea have often heard you speak kindly of us. Many times when you and your son were far out to sea, we heard you tell him the old ocean legends.

TARO. I have wondered about your world so much. Is it true that the Princess' Sea Palace is more glorious than any place in all of Japan?

TURTLE. It is lovelier than a thousand setting suns. Few men know anything of it. Would you like to see our world for yourself?

TARO. I cannot go. I am not a turtle or a sea creature who can swim so deeply under water.

TURTLE. That is true, but it will be different if you are with me. You'll be able to breathe under water as easily as you do now. Wade into the water, Taro, and climb on my back. I'll take you to the Sea Princess this very moment.

TARO. How I would like to go! *(Taro starts toward the Turtle, but stops as Kimo calls.)*

KIMO. May I go, too?

TARO. My wife and parents are waiting for me to bring these fish to sell.

TURTLE. You may return as soon as you wish.

KIMO. Is he a real turtle?

TARO. Yes, he's real.

KIMO. Can't we go with him?

TARO. Just imagine—getting to visit the Sea Princess! Let me go to the market place first and tell my family. It will take only a few moments. The village is not far from here. *(Taro starts to exit.)*

TURTLE. A voyage to visit the Sea Princess would take even less time. Let the boy tell your family where you have gone.

TARO. What am I thinking of? I cannot go with you. I must stay here with them. Good-bye, Old One, and thank you for inviting me. *(Taro picks up nets to leave.)*

TURTLE. Urashima Taro, we need you to come to the sea kingdom. You are a good man and we trust you. We must have such a man to help us. We live in dread fear of——

TARO. In fear of what?

TURTLE. I'm sworn to secrecy. Only in the Sea Palace may you be told. Come with me!

TARO. But how can I?

TURTLE. We know that you, above all fishermen, understand and love us. That is why the Princess sent me to find you.

TARO. *(Humbly.)* And if I do not come?

TURTLE. The sea world is in great danger of being completely destroyed.

TARO. Destroyed? How? What can I do?

TURTLE. I can say no more. We have a plan, but we must have a man to help.

TARO. The ocean has been kind to my family and our ancestors for a long, long time. We have depended upon you for our living.

TURTLE. Now we are depending on you to save our kingdom. It may take many days, but you must help or there will be no ocean creatures left in all of the sea.

TARO. My family and the sea are linked together. I will come. *(To Kimo.)* Hurry to your mother and grandparents with the fish. Tell them what you have seen. I will try to return tonight.

KIMO. *(Starting to go.)* Yes, Father. *(Stopping.)* Would you take me with you? Please! I could help you.

TURTLE. Not this time, my child. My back can carry only one. Listen! *(Pause.)* The Princess calls. The Princess of the deep. Her call may never come again. Come, now!

TARO. Good-bye, son. I'll be back tonight.

TURTLE. Quickly then, climb onto my back, and we'll be off.

(Taro stands closer to the Turtle's back, holding his arms up as if grasping his shell, but he never touches the Turtle. Remaining approximately six inches from the Turtle, Taro retains a freedom of movement, while establishing the stylized trip to the ocean depths.)

KIMO. *(Pleading for Taro to stay.)* Father, wait!

TARO. Good-bye. *(The Turtle and Taro should convey the idea of moving out into the ocean as they exit.)*

KIMO. Good-bye. Hurry back, Father! I'll be waiting for you. *(One last call.)* Father! He's gone. *(Kimo collects the fish and nets, then after a final look toward the ocean, runs off, calling:)* Mother. Mother!

(A gong sounds. The upstage screens revolve to reveal the underwater designs. Music to enhance the mood begins. Two or four Sea Creatures enter with lengths of blue billowing fabrics which help create an underwater effect. The remaining Sea Creatures enter and through their movement and actions help establish the underwater locale.)

TARO. *(From offstage.)* Oh, Turtle, this is amazing! It's as if we were flying.

TURTLE. *(Offstage.)* Hold on, Taro, we'll soon be there.

TARO. *(Offstage.)* I can't see the beach. How far out into the sea are we going?

TURTLE. *(Offstage.)* We are ready to descend now. Hold on tighter.

(The Turtle and Taro enter. The Sea Creatures rush about the stage, reacting to each movement of Taro and the Turtle; at times making their journey easier, at other times making it more difficult.)

TURTLE. Down, down we go to the floor of the ocean.

TARO. What a ride! I'm not getting wet and I can breathe under the sea!

PRINCESS. *(Far away, a chant or song-like quality, or an echo chamber effect.)* Turtle, Royal Turtle.

TURTLE. Listen, it is the Princess!

PRINCESS. *(As before.)*
Turtle, Old Turtle,
You must
You must bring
Bring an earthly creature.
An earthly creature,
A compassionate, brave man.
A man, a man,
To help, to help.
Hurry, Royal Turtle, hurry.

TURTLE. *(Calling, answering the Princess.)*
He comes, Princess, he comes

At last.
A brave man,
A brave man has been found.
Urashima Taro, Taro,
Urashima Taro comes.

PRINCESS.
Echo, echo through the deep.
A brave man comes.

SEA CREATURES. A brave man comes.

PRINCESS. Urashima Taro.

SEA CREATURES. Urashima Taro.

PRINCESS. Prepare, prepare.

TURTLE. Look ahead and you will see the Palace.

TARO. Yes. I see it. This is like a dream.

TURTLE. Here we are!

SEA CREATURES. Urashima Taro, welcome to the deep. The Sea Princess expects you.

TARO. Am I dreaming, Turtle? I have never seen such beautiful glittering stones, and so many rainbows.

TURTLE. It is no dream, but an uncommon privilege for man to experience.

TARO. The rainbows are moving—coming closer.

TURTLE. They are not rainbows. You are seeing the creatures of the deep. You are seeing us at home.

TARO. My eyes, my eyes. The creatures, the stones, the coral, even the sand is changing colors. The brightness, the colors are blinding me. You must take me back to the beach, Turtle.

TURTLE. Wait a moment. You are not accustomed to seeing things under water. Everything is more brilliant here. You will see. *(As the gong sounds.)* The Princess!

SEA CREATURES. The Princess!

(The Sea Princess enters.)

PRINCESS. Welcome, kind one from Japan. Welcome to the Sea Palace, Urashima Taro.

TARO. *(Bowing to his knees.)* Thank you, Princess, I am honored.

PRINCESS. Once again we have heard of your kindness. Some of our creatures saw you rescue our turtle from the boys. All of us thank you for helping a creature from the deep.

SEA CREATURES. A creature from the deep.

(Taro bows to the Princess.)

PRINCESS. It has been a long time since a man has been invited to our world. You know that you are here not only because of your kindness, but because we have an urgent request to make of you.

TARO. What is your request, Princess?

PRINCESS. For centuries, our domain has been a land of peace and beauty, where sorrow never came. But for many years now we have lived in terror.

TURTLE. It is this terror which I spoke of on the beach.

PRINCESS. We want you to help us.

TARO. What is it you fear?

PRINCESS. Our agony began one night when we heard a thunderous, rumbling sound. As it grew louder the waters began to churn and we were blinded by two huge flaming lights.

TURTLE. As the glowing balls of fire came toward us, we saw that they were the eyes of a gigantic Sea Scorpion.

PRINCESS. The horrible monster came nearer and nearer. Everyone tried to hide in the palace, but we could not bear the noise and the blinding light. As we tried to escape, the Sea Scorpion caught hundreds of our sea horses and devoured them before our eyes!

TURTLE. Then the Sea Scorpion turned his huge, ugly body away and left us. But a few seasons later he returned——

PRINCESS. He returned and took hundreds of our turtles. He has returned many times to devour more of our creatures. We never know when he will come back.

TURTLE. If it goes on like this much longer, we shall lose everyone who lives in the sea. The Princess herself will fall victim to the monster.

TARO. But he must be stopped.

PRINCESS. At first we thought that we could destroy him, and for years we tried to defeat him, but we have been powerless.

TARO. I have often heard of the sea scorpions of the deep. There must be a way——

TURTLE. The crabs told us about seeing men who use bows and arrows to destroy animals.

PRINCESS. We hoped we could destroy the beast in the same way. For months we all searched the ocean and beaches for arrows and bows. Three arrows were found, and after a long while, the swordfish guard found a bow. But we quickly discovered that not one of us was able to shoot arrows from a bow. For that we needed a man!

TURTLE. And so, for years, we looked for a brave, compassionate man to help us. Even though men often take our creatures for food, they have never tried to destroy us completely, as the Sea Scorpion is doing.

PRINCESS. Old Turtle searched many shores for such a man. One day we heard the voice of a fisherman in a boat far from shore. He was telling his son stories about us with great sympathy and understanding. And we knew he loved the sea and its beauty. Maybe he would be willing to save it. You, Taro, are that fisherman.

TURTLE. And today, when I came to find you on the beach of Shikoku, I soon learned that you are a man of courage.

PRINCESS. Urashima Taro, will you help us rid the ocean of our mortal enemy, the Sea Scorpion?

TARO. It was easy to help Old Turtle against some small boys. But how can I face the evil Sea Scorpion with only a bow and three arrows?

TURTLE. Our creatures will help you. Please do not refuse us, Taro.

PRINCESS. We await your answer.

TARO. *(After a pause.)* All right, I will try. Where are the arrows and the bow?

TURTLE. They are guarded day and night by our swordfish. The bow is large and the arrows are strong.

TARO. Where can we find the Sea Scorpion? Direct me, and I will go now!

TURTLE. No, you must wait. You cannot attempt to fight him alone. He lives on the ocean islands, just beyond the palace. Before you go, we must send word to all the sea creatures to come and join you.

PRINCESS. Messengers, go to all parts of our kingdom. Sound the call that each creature must come to follow the brave young Urashima Taro, who will lead us against the Sea Scorpion. *(To Taro.)* It is wonderful to have you with us. Everyone, let us have a festival for our friend, Urashima Taro. *(A gong sounds.)*

TARO. Princess, I have not even seen the Sea Scorpion. Maybe I will not be able to defeat him. Let me search for him now, since I have so little time. Bring the arrows and bow.

TURTLE. The arrows, the bow!

(One Sea Creature brings the bow, while another brings imaginary arrows. Taro accepts the bow and "arrows," accompanied by drum beats, and prepares for battle.)

PRINCESS. You cannot go without the warriors.

TARO. I must go now.

PRINCESS. Then our turtles and swordfish will accompany you. Royal Turtle, summon your fellow creatures and watch over our Taro.

TURTLE. *(Sounding a strange, shrill cry.)* Meet brave Taro at the palace gates.

TARO. Quickly, Old One. Which way?

TURTLE. I will lead you. We will find our other companions as we leave the palace.

PRINCESS. *(Quietly.)* May you have great courage, Urashima Taro. *(Taro, the Turtle, and several Sea Creatures leave the palace. The Princess and other Sea Creatures exit the opposite side of the stage.)*

(The Turtle and Taro enter again, accompanied by all the Sea Creatures. The journey toward the Sea Scorpion's area is difficult, slowing both Taro and the Sea Creatures in their movement. After Taro and the Creatures make two large counterclockwise movements, the mountain is sighted, offstage.)

TARO. How far have we yet to go?

TURTLE. We are here. *(Everyone stops. The Sea Creatures kneel around the Turtle and Taro, who remain standing.)* Look, there is the mountain where he lives.

TARO. It's very high.

TURTLE. It is said that the only entrance to his cave is near the top.

TARO. Then we must go there. *(The journey continues.)* Let me climb on your back and we'll swim near the top of the mountain. From there, it should be easy to shoot the Sea Scorpion as he comes from the cave. *(Rumbling sounds are heard.)* What's that?

SEA CREATURES. The Sea Scorpion's not in his cave! He's come out already. He's at the base of the mountain! The Sea Scorpion is stirring! He must know that someone is near. *(The rumbling sounds increase in volume.)*

TURTLE. Quickly, Taro, shoot the arrows!

SEA CREATURES. We're too far away! The arrows can't reach the Sea Scorpion from here. We must escape while there is still time.

TURTLE. There is no hope.

SEA CREATURES. We haven't a chance.

TARO. *(Attempting to shoot the offstage Sea Scorpion.)* I can't hold the bow—my hands are burning! *(The blinding red lights of the Sea Scorpion's eyes search the stage.)*

TURTLE. He is opening his eyes!

TARO. I can't see—the flame is blinding me!

TURTLE. The other way! Look the other way!

TARO. Help! Ohhhhhh. *(Screams as if severely burned, then falls to the ocean floor. Mournful, mysterious music begins and continues until Taro is returned to the palace.)*

TURTLE. Fish, turtles, horses, cover Taro! Hide him. *(All the Sea Creatures fall upon the motionless body of Taro.)* Do not move! Maybe the Sea Scorpion will not see us. *(The red, glowing "searchlight" eyes of the Sea Scorpion pass.)*

SEA CREATURES. *(After a few seconds of silence.)* He didn't see us. He's going back to sleep. We must return immediately to the palace.

TURTLE. We must take our earthly one back to the Princess.

(The Sea Creatures lift the prone body of Taro to their shoulders and start their sad journey. The Turtle picks up the bow and "arrows." Following behind Taro and the Sea Creatures, he keeps watch for the Sea Scorpion. The music echos the somber mood of the Creatures as they work their way to the palace. Their movements are continuous from the mountain site to the palace. Once in the palace, the Creatures place Taro on the floor at stage C. One Creature holds his head in her lap, all others move away from him. The Princess enters.)

PRINCESS. *(Running to the Turtle as she sees the prone and almost lifeless Taro.)* Taro! Is he dead?

TURTLE. He has been burned by the gaze of the Sea Scorpion.

PRINCESS. *(Crossing to Taro.)* Taro.

TURTLE. Our enemy was out of his cave, sleeping at the base of the mountain when we first saw him. He must have heard us approach, for he awakened.

A SEA CREATURE. We were too far away for Taro to shoot the arrows. He could not avoid the blinding light shining from the Sea Scorpion's eyes and he fell wounded.

TURTLE. When all was quiet once more, we carried Taro home.

PRINCESS. *(Kneeling at Taro's side.)* We must help him. *(Suddenly, she has an idea.)* We'll call forth the seasons of the year. Let each one bring its healing gifts to Taro. First is Spring!

(The gong sounds. As the Four Seasons enter and begin to move, the Princess crosses to the Turtle, watching Taro carefully. As Taro begins to stir, the healing power should seem to emanate from the movements of the seasons. One or four different actors should suggest each of the seasons. Japanese fans should be used by the actors. Different music may be used to identify each season.)

PRINCESS. Summer! Autumn! And last, Winter! *(As the movements of Winter ends, Taro speaks.)*

TARO. Where are the arrows?

PRINCESS. *(Crossing to Taro and kneeling at his side.)* Seasons, suspend! Taro speaks.

TARO. *(Sitting up.)* Turtle, the arrows! The arrows! Where am I?

PRINCESS. You are in the Palace of the Sea. You have been very ill.

TARO. Have I been dreaming?

TURTLE. It was no dream. You were burned by the gaze of the Sea Scorpion, but now you are well.

TARO. I remember—we were near the mountain of the Sea Scorpion. But how did we escape?

SEA CREATURES. The eyes of the Sea Scorpion passed over us. He did not see us, and so went back to sleep.

TURTLE. We carried you back here.

TARO. The Sea Scorpion. I must find him! *(Rises.)* We must go now to the mountain to destroy him.

PRINCESS. Later, later. Now—a celebration! A celebration for your recovery and for your courage to face the Sea Scorpion. *(Shouts of joy and approval from all of the Sea Creatures. The gong sounds.)*

TURTLE. The festivities in honor of Urashima Taro now begin!

(Two Sea Creatures exit and return immediately with trays of food and drink for Taro.)

TARO. *(Kneeling near the Princess, upstage from the food.)* I hope I shall deserve such rewards. You have seen that I am only a man with no special powers. I fear I will be helpless against the Sea Scorpion.

PRINCESS. No, Taro, you will find a way. You must save us! You are our only hope. *(After offering Taro another cup of tea, the princess silently calls the Turtle to her side and whispers to him. He nods and speaks.)*

TURTLE. Urashima Taro, we of the sea world have one other request.

TARO. What is it?

PRINCESS. Would you stay with us here in the ocean forever?

TARO. Princess, this is a remarkable place, but I must go back to my home. I long to see my family and they will be anxiously awaiting my return.

PRINCESS. I understand. It is to be expected that one who is considerate of others would feel as you do. When you succeed in destroying the evil Sea Scorpion, we will once again know the peace of this land of eternal youth. Perhaps then you will realize that you are not needed upon the earth.

TURTLE. *(As the gong sounds.)* In honor of Urashima Taro!

SEA CREATURES. *(Bowing low to Taro.)* In honor of Urashima Taro! *(Suddenly the palace is shaken by what sounds like a marching army. The Sea Creatures scream and rush about.)*

ALL. *(Except Taro.)* The Sea Scorpion! The Sea Scorpion! The monster! Run! Hide! Leave the palace! *(The Princess and the Turtle stay near Taro.)*

PRINCESS. He's coming for us!

TURTLE. Taro, don't look at his flaming eyes!

TARO. Where are the arrows and the bow?

TURTLE. *(To one of the Sea Creatures.)* Go! Get them! Hurry!

TARO. *(Looking offstage.)* Over there, what is that moving?

PRINCESS. The legs of the monster.

TURTLE. Sea Creatures, help Taro and the Princess!

(As the Sea Creatures gather around Taro and the Princess, they form two groups. The Sea Princess' group is always farther away from the Sea Scorpion than Taro's group. A Sea Creature returns with the bow and "arrows" and gives them to Taro.)

SEA CREATURES. He's winding his way around the hills, coming closer and closer to the palace gates.

PRINCESS. Oh, he's almost here!

(The stomping, swaying Sea Scorpion enters and begins to chase Taro and the Sea Creatures.)

PRINCESS. *(Attempting to pull Taro out of the palace.)* Taro!

TARO. No. I shall stay. You hide while I try to destroy him. *(After taking careful aim, Taro shoots the first imaginary arrow. A gong sounds.)*

TURTLE. You've hit him! *(Throughout this scene, all Sea Creatures ad lib appropriate reactions.)*

PRINCESS. But look! . . .

SEA CREATURE. The arrow fell to the ground!

PRINCESS. It didn't even pierce his skin!

SEA CREATURE. He's still coming!

PRINCESS. He'll devour us all! We must hide!

TURTLE. He's coming closer.

TARO. The other arrow! *(Taro shoots the second "arrow." The gong sounds.)*

TURTLE. It missed him again. What will we do? We are finished! *(The sound of the Sea Scorpion increases to a deafening volume, as the stage "burns" from the fire of his eyes.)*

PRINCESS. The Sea Scorpion has never been so angry! The noise, oh, oh . . . *(The Princess attempts to cover her eyes and ears.)*

TARO. Wait! There's an old legend that says water from a man's mouth is deadly to Sea Scorpions. Do you think it can be true, Princess?

PRINCESS. Maybe, but how can that help us?

TURTLE. Do not think of legends now. We will all perish!

TARO. *(To the Princess and the Turtle.)* You go now! Find one last hiding place.

TURTLE. What will you do?

TARO. *(As the Turtle and others start to run away.)* I'll follow you after I try the last arrow.

PRINCESS. Be careful.

TARO. *(Thinking aloud.)* Water from a man's mouth. It has to work. *(Taro takes the last "arrow" and draws the end of it from side to side in front of his mouth, as if licking it. After carefully aiming, he shoots it. The gong sounds.)*

(A piercing scream from the Sea Scorpion is heard. The fiery light changes to a dull glow, and then goes out. Thunder rolls and lightning flashes. It should appear as if the sea world were coming to an end. The Sea Scorpion begins his death on stage but exits after the climax of his death movements.)

ALL SEA CREATURES. You have destroyed him! We are saved! You have freed us! The Sea Scorpion is dead! We have nothing to fear!

SEA CREATURES. *(After the Sea Scorpion's exit.)* Honor to Urashima Taro! The sea legend was true, a Sea Scorpion can be destroyed by water from a man's mouth. *(All bow to Taro.)*

PRINCESS. Urashima Taro, due to your bravery, we can continue to live. Without your help the Sea Scorpion would have destroyed us all! Urashima Taro, we honor you, the bravest warrior in all of Japan! We of the sea are all your servants.

SEA CREATURES. *(Shouting.)* Urashima Taro. The bravest warrior in all of Japan!

PRINCESS. You must remain with us forever.

TURTLE. Yes, stay here in the ocean! *(Shouts of "yes," etc. from all the creatures.)*

TARO. I am sorry, but I cannot stay.

PRINCESS. You have seen so little. Now we can show you all the wonders of the everchanging waters. You will be surrounded by beauty always. We want you to stay. Please. *(All listen for Taro's reply.)*

TARO. Life would be filled with beauty here, but I must say no. My home is on the earth and my thoughts are filled with memories of it. I shall go back. Will you help me find the way to the beach, Turtle?

PRINCESS. Of course, he will. Before you go, see for one last time the beauties that healed your wounds—Spring, Summer, Autumn, Winter.

TARO. I have only a few minutes. My family will be searching for me.

PRINCESS. It will take only a little time.

TARO. To see all of the seasons?

PRINCESS. Just watch, Taro.

(The Princess commands the Seasons, which are interpreted simultaneously here. If only one actor is used to portray the Four Seasons, he should change from one season to the other as rapidly as possible. The movements, with appropriate music, should last approximately forty seconds, as the swirl of the seasons builds to a climax.)

PRINCESS. The Seasons: Spring. Summer. Autumn. Winter.

TARO. Princess, the ocean is a beautiful place. How is it possible for the seasons to change so quickly here?

PRINCESS. If you stay with us you will learn many of the mysteries of the sea. And each time, the seasons are lovelier than before. They are always new.

TURTLE. There is much more to see, Taro.

PRINCESS. All of this is yours to enjoy if you remain with us.

TARO. You have been so kind to me, and I am happy here, yet I can stay no longer! Although the beauties of my village are ordinary compared to those of the ocean, I long to go back. *(Bowing low before the Princess.)*

PRINCESS. To us it seems as if you have been here only a short time.

TURTLE. In the sea we measure time differently than men do on the earth.

TARO. Don't you see? Earth is where I belong—where I am needed. The people I love are there. *(Pause.)* I must go back to them.

PRINCESS. I understand.

TARO. I'm ready to go back to the beach now, Turtle.

PRINCESS. You are always welcome here. We will be expecting you to visit us again some day.

TARO. It will be a privilege, Princess. I look forward to returning.

PRINCESS. Then, here is a token to help you remember us. *(A gong sounds. The Four Seasons hand the box to the Princess, who gives it to Taro.)*

TARO. A gift from you, after all the many favors I have received? . . .

PRINCESS. We want you to have it, Taro.

TARO. Thank you, my friends. *(Kneels, looking at the box.)*

PRINCESS. *(As Taro starts to untie the cord.)* Not now, Taro.

TARO. I will always keep the box as a reminder of you and of my stay here in the sea. Who knows? Some day in the years to come—*(Taro rises.)*—especially in the winter, when the earth is barren and cold, this gift may lead me back to you and to the mysterious beauty of the sea.

PRINCESS. Perhaps. Perhaps. *(To the Turtle.)* Take our brave friend home. *(To Taro.)* We shall never forget you. Thank you, brave one! Remember us!

TARO. I will. Good-bye, Princess. *(Waves to all.)* Good-bye!

SEA CREATURES. Good-bye! Good-bye, Urashima Taro. *(As the entire court wishes him good-bye, the Turtle and Taro exit, moving the same way as when they arrived in the ocean depths. The Sea Creatures slowly exit. Some watch longer after Taro and the Turtle. The Princess, the last to leave, continues to look toward the area where the Turtle and Taro were last seen.)*

(The gong sounds. The upstage screens revolve, showing the beach designs again.)

TURTLE. *(Offstage.)* We are almost there.

TARO. *(Offstage, as an old man.)* Yes. Here is the bay I know so well.

(Turtle enters with Taro "on his back.")

TURTLE. And the beach where we first met. Here you are, Taro!

(Note: When Taro appears we realize that he is doubled with age, his hair snowy white, and his face wrinkled. Offstage he has exchanged his kimono for a ragged and torn one of duplicate design. He wears a gray wig and is made up as an old man. Taro is an old man in body and voice.)

TARO. Thank you for a swift journey home.

TURTLE. We will remember you always, Urashima Taro. Don't forget us!

TARO. Never, Turtle, never. Good-bye, and tell the Sea Princess——But he is gone. Down, down, down. Good-bye, Ancient One. Good-bye, my friend. *(Kneels.)* How good the dry sand feels! *(Pause.)* What time can it be? How long was I gone? I must get home. I wonder if those boys are still around. What a story I have to tell them about the old turtle they were tormenting! *(Calling toward his offstage home.)* Ho! Ooooooora! Is anyone here?

(A Woman, carrying a large straw basket, enters and passes, not noticing Taro.)

TARO. Good woman, do you live around here?

WOMAN. *(Starting to exit.)* I have lived here on the beach of Shikoku for many years. Who are you? Have you just come to our village, old sir?

TARO. Old sir? What do you mean? I am Urashima Taro. Everyone here knows me.

WOMAN. You may or may not be called Urashima Taro, that I do not know. The only Urashima Taro from our village was a man who lived over eighty years ago. He was a good fisherman who was drowned at sea.

TARO. Drowned?

WOMAN. Yes, so the story goes.

TARO. What of his wife and parents?

WOMAN. They perished long ago.

TARO. Did he have a son?

WOMAN. Yes, his son is called Kimo.

TARO. *(Quietly.)* Kimo.

WOMAN. He lives just down the beach with his elder son and grandchildren. He used to be a fisherman, too.

TARO. What is he like?

WOMAN. He's full of tales of the sea. Even today in his old age, he still tells the story of his father, Urashima Taro, who went off to sea on the back of a giant turtle.

TARO. *(To himself.)* But it was only yesterday that I——

WOMAN. Not long ago the old man began coming down to the beach every day to call out for his father, just as they say he did as a child, for many weeks after his father was drowned.

TARO. It cannot be.

WOMAN. Life is filled with fantastic tales, old man.

TARO. Fantastic tales. Me, an old man? I am only twenty-eight.

WOMAN. *(In disbelief.)* Twenty-eight years old?

TARO. *(To himself.)* My son, an old man, with sons and grandchildren of his own—no, no. *(To the Woman.)* I am Urashima Taro, the young fisherman!

WOMAN. Urashima Taro was drowned long ago. *(As she starts to exit.)* Good-bye, old man. *(Woman exits.)*

TARO. This is like a strange dream! I must have been gone for several days. *(Rushing to the edge of the ocean.)* Turtle! Oh, Turtle, help me! *(Pause, then convincing himself.)* I am Urashima Taro, the fisherman, and I live here. *(Once again, he looks out toward the ocean.)* Turtle, oh Turtle of the deep, please, help me. Princess! The gift . . . the box from the Princess! Yes, it will have the answer to this riddle. *(Taro kneels, unties the cord. As he opens the box there is a flash of light; wind chimes sound.)* Ohhh. Only a mirror. Look at my hands, my face, my hair. I am an old man. Maybe the Princess was right, I should never have left the ocean. I want to go back. I'm afraid to stay here. If only I could return. I'll call the Turtle. Maybe he'll hear. Please come, Turtle! Help me! Can you hear me? *(After receiving no response from the Turtle, Taro picks up the box, crosses to the rock, and sits, staring at the box. Then, as if from the box, we hear the following vocal collage. All voices have an echo effect.)*

VOICE OF THE PRINCESS. Urashima Taro, the box will remind you of the sea, the land of eternal spring, and of your glorious adventures there.

VOICES OF THE SEA CREATURES. The Sea Scorpion! The Sea Scorpion! Run! Hide!

VOICE OF THE TURTLE. Taro, don't look at his flaming eyes!

VOICE OF THE PRINCESS. See how he winds around the mountain!

VOICE OF THE TURTLE. Taro. You've hit him!

VOICE OF A SEA CREATURE. The arrow fell to the ground! He's still coming!

VOICE OF THE PRINCESS. Don't look directly at his eyes!

VOICE OF THE TURTLE. Don't think of legends now. We shall perish!

VOICE OF THE PRINCESS. Urashima Taro, we honor you, the bravest warrior in all of Japan! We of the sea are your servants. *(Taro remains seated, looking out toward the ocean.)*

(Kimo, now an old man, enters with his grandson, Sentaro.)

SENTARO. Isn't the sea beautiful today, Grandfather? Look, you can see fishing boats out there.

KIMO. Where could he be?

TARO. *(Looking toward Kimo.)* Who can that be?

KIMO. *(Slowly moving toward the ocean.)* Turtle! Turtle, bring Urashima Taro back! Come home, my father!

TARO. Kimo? *(Standing.)* It is my son. Kimo, it is you!

KIMO. *(Crossing to Taro.)* Father! Father! Is it really you? *(Embracing his father.)* How long it has been! I knew you would come back some day. Are you well?

TARO. Yes, yes.

KIMO. No one ever understood when I told them about the turtle.

TARO. *(Looking at the frightened Sentaro.)* Who is this?

KIMO. My grandson, Sentaro. *Your* great-grandson.

TARO. "Sentaro," that's a good name. What a fine boy you are!

KIMO. I've told him about that day on the beach long ago.

TARO. Remember, Kimo, how so few people believed the old legends of the sea? *(Turning to Sentaro.)* One day as your grandfather was helping me pull in the nets we met the Turtle of the Deep.

KIMO. Yes.

TARO. The turtle called to us from far out in the water. It wasn't long before I was on his back—gliding out to the middle of the ocean. Then we started down. Down, down, down—we went. I could breathe under the water.

KIMO. Did he take you to the Sea Princess?

TARO. I saw her in the underwater land of great mountains and valleys. She was as beautiful as the sea waves on a calm day.

(Turtle enters.)

TURTLE. *(As he enters.)* Taro, Taro!

TARO. You've returned.

TURTLE. I've come to take you back to the Sea Palace.

KIMO. No, Father . . .

TURTLE. You will be young again.

TARO. But, Turtle, why am I old? I don't understand.

TURTLE. You went on one of the greatest adventures of all time, and now your life is spent.

TARO. But that cannot be. I was with you only a few days.

TURTLE. No, Taro, you were with us for many seasons, many years. You saved our kingdom. You were our hero!

TARO. But to keep me with you in the deep for a lifetime——

TURTLE. In the deep we have no sense of earthly time. We live suspended. Years are like minutes. Come back to us! Come back to the seasons. Life will be as it was before. You will be young again!

TARO. But, Turtle . . .

TURTLE. If you stay on earth, you will remain an old man with only a few years to live. You can see your family's life has changed. You no longer have a place with them.

KIMO. *(To the Turtle.)* You are wrong. His home is with us. *(To Taro.)* You will always belong here.

TURTLE. You will never find peace again out of the deep.

TARO. You can't understand, Turtle, for you are not a human being. I will not return to the sea.

TURTLE. And what if your grandsons want to venture out into the deep?

TARO. I would tell them to go, to live life to its fullest—to take the adventures. . . .

TURTLE. And what of you? Was it worth it, Taro?

TARO. Yes. But I cannot continue to live suspended. Surely no man finds more beauty and adventure in life on earth than I had in the sea. My memories are rich. Your sea kingdom had everything; everything except the chance to share love with other human beings. Now I will have that, too.

TURTLE. For the last time then, good-bye, old man.

TARO. Not old. With a son and grandchildren, my life is beginning anew.

TURTLE. Good-bye, Urashima Taro. *(As he exits.)* Good-bye!

TARO. Good-bye, Turtle! *(Pause.)*

KIMO. Come, Father.

TARO. *(Joining Kimo.)* Sentaro. *(Taro, with Kimo at one side and Sentaro at the other, exits.)*

(The box, which was left on stage, takes on a glowing brilliance. We hear, as if from the box:)

VOICES OF THE SEA CREATURES. Everlasting honor to Urashima Taro, the bravest warrior in all of Japan! Urashima Taro, the bravest warrior in all of Japan!

(Sentaro rushes back on stage, picks up the box, and studies it briefly.)

KIMO. *(Offstage.)* Sentaro!

(Sentaro exits hurriedly as the lights dim and the play ends.)

(Curtain.)

Courage!

From *The Red Badge of Courage*
by Stephen Crane
Dramatized by Ed Graczyk

Copyright, 1973, Pickwick Press

Courage! (1973)

Courage! is playwright Ed Graczyk's powerful historical play based on Stephen Crane's novel *The Red Badge of Courage*. Although today Graczyk is best known for his plays and screenplays for adults, such as *When You Coming Back to the Five-and-Dime, Jimmy Dean, Jimmy Dean*, he has written many plays and musicals for the youth audience.

Set in the Civil War, *Courage!* is a composition of scenes, images, and impressions that unite to form a character study of a young soldier who discovers himself through his cowardice, and eventual "courage" in battle. By juxtaposing the character of the young soldier with the character of the young boy who represents "the child and conscience" of the young soldier, we witness externally the inner adolescent struggles of a boy/soldier waiting and learning to be a man.

Graczyk exemplifies this struggle through the reoccurring question "What is courage?" After the young soldier finally admits that "he is afraid of becoming a man," he and the audience learn that true courage is not something you wear like a badge, but rather is something only the individual bearer can see, because it is worn inside.

The universality of the play is extremely important. While the main focus is on the Civil War, a feeling of all wars should be made evident through the slides, costumes, and music the script relies on, and these elements should be used by the director to comment on the action of the play, and help the audience visualize better the production's scope and timeliness.

CHARACTERS

Young Man (Henry Fleming)	Trumpet
Young Boy (Henry Fleming)	Banjo
Mother	Drum
Tall Soldier	Flute
Loud Soldier	Wounded Soldier
Tattered Soldier	Friendly Soldier
Lieutenant	Scared Soldier
Decayed Soldier	Glum Soldier
Cheery Soldier	Singing Soldier
Harmonica	Townspeople

SETTING
America.

TIME
The Civil War.

Courage!

ACT I

The set, revealed as the audience enters, is a stark unit center stage, composed of sweeping ramps and platforms elevated by tall wooden posts. These posts rise far above the top level of the platform, reaching high for the sky. The center platform in the unit is reached by two steep sweeping ramps on either side. A small set of stairs reaches from this platform to the right of it. Another smaller one to the left rear is also reached by a ramp in the back. The entire unit must be airy and spacious, not heavily burdened with bracing and supports, to allow easy movement in, around and about. The towering posts should suggest giant trees and the ramps and platforms, paths and hilltops. The wood they are constructed of is old and weathered and firmly embedded into the earth. On either side of the unit are hanging sections of grey scrim that will be used for the projection of slides. As the houselights dim we hear the distant sound of drums and bugles. The Young Man enters from up the rear ramp to the center platform. He carries a milk bucket and pauses to wipe his brow. He hears the sound and looks about for its source. The Young Boy, dressed exactly the same as the Young Man, runs on from the right, also carrying a bucket. It is important that it be clear from the beginning that the Young Boy and the Young Man are one and the same person, the Young Boy being the child and conscience of the Young Man.

BOY. Do ya hear? . . . Do ya hear the sound of the drums?

YOUNG MAN. It's comin' from town . . . hear tell there's a recruitin' rally this afternoon.

BOY. What are they recruitin'?

YOUNG MAN. Soldiers! . . . For the war . . . President Lincoln's called for 300,000 recruits.

BOY. Do ya think they'd let me join up?

YOUNG MAN. They need *men* for the war . . . Haven't you ever seen pictures in books? . . . Heroes are men, not boys.

BOY. Why ain't you down there joinin' up, 'stead of totin' milk buckets from the barn?

YOUNG MAN. I've been a-thinkin' about it . . . saw a poster nailed to the fence over yonder an' it sure looks excitin' . . . bright shiny uniforms, drums, bugles . . .

[Slide: recruiting poster, colorful and inviting to the imagination.]

and it says my country needs *me.*

[Slides, quick succession: enlistment posters from many wars.]

BOY. Wish I was grow'd enough to join up and be a hero . . . you sure are lucky.

YOUNG MAN. A lotta the guys from town my age are goin' . . . hate to be left outta my share of the medals.

BOY. They may even write books about yeh like all those heroes I've read about.

[Slides, quick succession: knight poised over dragon; Revolutionary War soldiers; storybook soldiers. All are brightly colored. The slides continue to flash as they speak.]

YOUNG MAN. An' when I got back from the war with my chest all loaded with medals and my head all bandaged up from the fightin' . . . the whole town would turn out to cheer and yell out my name.

BOY. They might even name the town after yeh.

YOUNG MAN. Never can tell. (Thinks.) Sure would be swell to be a hero.

BOY. Yeh could get killed.

YOUNG MAN. Heroes don't get killed . . . only cowards get killed!

VOICE OF MOTHER. Son! . . . Are you out there dreamin' 'stead a doin' your chores?

YOUNG MAN AND BOY TOGETHER. No, Ma . . . just thinkin'!

MOTHER. (Entering.) Well, what are yeh thinkin' of?

BOY. (Crossing to Mother. Young Man remains, staring at them.) Thinkin' about volunteerin' for the war, Ma.

MOTHER. Nonsense, Son, you're too young.

YOUNG MAN. (From his spot.) No I ain't, Ma, lots are joinin' up that are my age.

MOTHER. I need yeh here, Son . . . What with yer pa gone, I need yeh all the more than ever. Yer confusin' yer thinkin' with dreamin'. War's a dangerous thing, Son. You could get yourself serious hurt.

BOY. *(Crossing to Young Man.)* She doesn't want me to be no hero.

YOUNG MAN. *(Crossing down ramp toward Mother.)* It ain't so, Ma, the country needs me too. I hear tell we're losin' bad . . . Mr. Lincoln needs all the help he can get.

MOTHER. You're just a boy.

BOY. No I ain't, Ma . . .

MOTHER. Don't yeh be a fool now, Son . . . Carry that milk outta the sun before it spoils, and get yourself washed up for lunch.

YOUNG MAN. But, Ma!

MOTHER. *(To Boy.)* I don't want to hear no more talkin' of war and joinin' up . . . You can do a great service to yer country right here on the farm by providin' food for everyone.

BOY. They don't make heroes outta farmers . . .

YOUNG MAN. Yeh need to be in the action, yeh need to be fightin' . . . fighters is what they're needin', not farmers.

MOTHER. Wash up . . .

   (She exits.)

YOUNG MAN. She treats me like a boy . . . like I have no sense of my own . . .

BOY. She doesn't want me to be a hero.

   (Sound: a bright rousing march, recorded: "The Battle Cry of Freedom." At first very dim.)

YOUNG MAN. This is the opportunity of my life . . .

BOY. . . . . Castles and crowns, slaying dragons by the dozens . . .

YOUNG MAN. . . . . There may never ever be another war . . . I've got to join up before it's too late.

BOY. An' be a hero like in all the books! . . .

YOUNG MAN. They'll not leave me behind to be forgotten.

   [Slides: a combination of the recruiting posters and the story-book heroes.]

(Sound: the march builds slowly.)

YOUNG MAN. I'm comin', Father Abraham! . . .

MOTHER. *(Off.)* Did yeh hear me, Son?

BOY. I'm comin'. . . .

YOUNG MAN. I'm comin' to join yer war . . .

MOTHER. Hurry up now, it's gettin' late.

YOUNG MAN. *(To poster.)* That bright blue coat's gonna be on me
. . .

BOY. I'll wear it all the time, for everyone to see.

YOUNG MAN. Drums and bugles callin' out . . . callin' out for me to
join the fight.

BOY. I'll show yeh! . . . You'll be proud of me, all dressed up in
bright blue and brass. I'll slay that grey dragon singlehanded.

YOUNG MAN. With drums and bugles blaring out my name.

*(Sound: the march builds to a crescendo as Soldiers march on
up the back ramp; Townspeople enter waving small flags and
cheering. The Young Man and Boy move into the Crowd.)*

*[Slides: crowds cheering passing soldiers, and various other
bright and colorful views of the glorious soldier from many
wars.]*

*(The Crowd ignores the Young Man and Boy as they cheer the
Soldiers. At the end of the song the Soldiers stand at attention
up and down the ramps. The Crowd gives one last cheer and
freezes.)*

BOY. *(Pointing to Tall Soldier.)* Look, there's one of my friends from
school . . .

YOUNG MAN. *(To Loud Soldier.)* . . . And there's another . . . they're
already joined up.

BOY. They got a uniform before I did.

YOUNG MAN. Tell me what to do. How do I join up too?

BOY. I have a right to a gun and some cheers too.

WOMAN IN CROWD. *(Breaks freeze.)* Let's give a cheer for the new
recruits!

BOY. *(To Crowd.)* I want one of them bright blue suits!

(Drum roll.)

SOLDIER. Give that boy a bright blue suit!

(Cheer and drum roll as the Townspeople put a coat, brighter than all the others, on him.)

YOUNG MAN. How about some shiny black boots?

(Drum roll.)

SOLDIERS. Give that boy some shiny black boots!

(Cheer and drum roll as the Crowd gathers around him removing his farm pants. His blue pants and boots are underdressed.)

BOY. Can I have me a gun that shoots?

(Drum roll.)

SOLDIERS. Give that boy a gun that shoots!

(Sound of guns. The Crowd cheers and hands him a rifle.)

BOY. What else do I need to be a hero?

(No sound.)

TOWNSPEOPLE. What else does that boy need to be a hero?

(Drum roll.)

SOLDIERS. Give that boy a sword!

(Crowd cheers and gives him a toy wooden sword.)

Give that boy a cap!

(Crowd cheers and does.)

YOUNG MAN. *(Entering dressed in blue like the other Soldiers.)* Give that boy a word! . . .

(Drum roll as they all turn to the Young Man.)

SOLDIERS AND CROWD. Courage!

(Sound: a reprise of "The Battle Cry of Freedom" from the crescendo as everyone crowds around the Young Man. The Loud Soldier and the Tall Soldier slap him on the back congratulating him, etc. Two other Soldiers carry the Boy on their shoul-

ders up the left ramp, leaving the Young Man below. As they reach the bottom on the other side where the Young Man is, the Mother enters and the music stops.)

YOUNG MAN. Ma, I've enlisted.

MOTHER. *(After short silence.)* The Lord's will be done, Son.

(She crosses stage right. The Crowd and Soldiers back off slowly, leaving the Young Man and Boy.)

BOY. She's crying . . . she's not proud of what I've done.

YOUNG MAN. I'm sure she is . . . she has to be.

BOY. She never mentioned my bright new uniform.

MOTHER. *(As she sits quietly on the edge of the right ramp.)* You watch out, Son, and take good care of yourself in this here fighting business—you watch out, an' take good care of yerself.

BOY. *(Crossing in to her.)* But, Ma . . .

MOTHER. Don't go a-thinkin' you can lick the whole Army at the start, because yeh can't. Yer just one little feller amongst a whole lot of others, and yeh've got to keep quiet an' do what they tell yeh. I know how you are, Son.

(The Boy crosses to a box under the platform and carries it away from them, left. As she continues to speak he takes out dozens of toy soldiers—about one foot high—and places them in a small group, arranging them in a regiment.)

I've knit ye eight pairs of socks, Son . . . to be used fer the winter . . . but I suppose yeh will be needin' 'em more now. I'll pack ye a bundle an' put in all yer best shirts. I want my boy to be jest as warm and comf'table as anybody in the Army. *(During the above she pantomimes packing a bundle.)* Whenever they get holes in 'em, I want yeh to send 'em right away back to me so's I kin darn 'em. *(Hands imaginary bundle to him and crosses slowly to the Boy, not talking to him, but is near to him.)* Ye be careful now, Son . . . there's lots of bad men in the Army. The Army makes 'em wild, and they like nothing better than the job of leading off a young feller like you, as ain't never been away from home much. I don't want yeh to ever do anything that yeh would be 'shamed to let me know about. Jest think as if I was a'watchin' yeh. If yeh keep that in mind allus, I guess yeh'll come out about right. I don't know what else to tell yeh, Son, excepting that yeh must never do no shirking, child, on my account. If so be a time comes when yeh have to be kilt or do a mean thing, why, Son, don't think of anything 'cept what's right 'cause there's many a woman has to bear up 'ginst sech things these times, and the Lord'll take keer of us all. *(Turns to Young Man.)* Don't fergit to send yer socks to me the minute they git holes in 'em, and here's a little Bible I want yeh to take along with yeh. *(Hands him imaginary Bible.)* I don't presume yeh'll be a-sittin' reading it all day long, child, ner nothin' like that. Many a time yeh'll fergit yeh got it, I don't doubt. But there'll be many a time too, Son, when yeh'll be wantin' advice, and all like that. And there'll be nobody around, perhaps, to tell yeh things. *(Crosses back to her spot.)* Don't fergit about the socks an' the shirts, child, and I've put a cup of blackberry jam with yer bundle because I know yeh like it above all things . . . Good-bye, Son . . . Yeh may think of yerself as a man, but yeh've still got a lot of the boy within yeh.

(The Boy rises and starts to run to the Mother.)

BOY. Ma!

(The Young Man stops him. Together they turn, the Young Man's arm about the Boy's shoulder, and walk back to the army of toy soldiers. They turn back to the Mother who rises, and with her back to them, wipes her eyes with a corner of her apron.)

BOY. I'm scared. . . .

YOUNG MAN. Too late now for any turnin' back . . .

TALL SOLDIER. *(Rushing in.)* Come on, the regiment's formin' up in the square to move out. Are yeh through sayin' yer farewells?

YOUNG MAN. Suppose so.

TALL SOLDIER. Then get a-movin' afore yeh get left behind . . .

(As he exits.)

. . . Don't want to be labeled a coward afore ye even begin, do yeh?

YOUNG MAN. I ain't no coward! . . . I'll fight 'long side the best of yeh . . . you'll see.

(Sound: recorded, "We Are Coming, Father Abraham," coming from the distance, building to the foreground, then fading out. The Young Man exits, leaving the Boy, who sits among the toy soldiers arranging them into rows.)

[Slides: the toy soldiers marching in rows and various quick closeups of the uniform, cap, drum, etc. . . . as the music plays.]

(At the end of the song lights come up on Young Man, Loud Soldier, and Tall Soldier being served food by village ladies.)

LOUD SOLDIER. Wow, this is the life, ain't it? . . .

TALL SOLDIER. Ever tasted such fancy cookin'?

YOUNG MAN. Sure treat us boys in blue like kings . . . cheer at us every town an' village we pass through.

LOUD SOLDIER. Did yeh get a look at the girls in the last town? . . . Yahoo, they sure took a lookin' at us.

TALL SOLDIER. One singled me out from all the others and gave me a wink.

LOUD SOLDIER. Ah, g'wan!

TALL SOLDIER. Ain't lyin' . . . *(To Young Man.)* You saw her, didn't yeh?

YOUNG MAN. I thought she was winkin' at me.

(Tall Soldier and Loud Soldier laugh hysterically as the lights fade. Sound: recorded, "Hold On, Abraham.")

[Slides: toy soldiers marching, this time adding toy cannons and quick closeups of the flag, buttons, buckles, etc.]

(After the song the lights come up on the same group a bit wearier than before.)

LOUD SOLDIER. *(Rubbing his feet.)* Sure wish they'd stop all this marchin' and settle down in one spot for a while . . . my feet have nearly marched through the bottoms of my boots.

TALL SOLDIER. Aw, yeh ain't happy 'less yeh have somethin' tuh complain about.

LOUD SOLDIER. Sure saw yeh limpin' mighty heavy last day or so.

TALL SOLDIER. Had a stone in my boot.

LOUD SOLDIER. Musta' been that loose one's been rollin' aroun' in yer head. *(Laughs.)*

YOUNG MAN. Is that all there is to war is marchin'? . . . When's the fightin' start?

TALL SOLDIER. We'll be gettin' there soon enough . . . just keep yer pants on.

LOUD SOLDIER. What's yer big hurry . . . Plan to lick the whole Rebel Army singlehanded in an afternoon so's yeh can be back home fer supper? *(Laughs.)*

YOUNG MAN. Jest aim tuh do my part . . .

LOUD SOLDIER. Jest make sure that's all yeh do. Save some for us. *(He laughs.)*

LIEUTENANT. *(From off.)* All right, everyone fall in . . . rest's over . . . time to march on!

LOUD SOLDIER. *(Groaning.)* Easy fer him tuh say; he gets to ride a horse.

LIEUTENANT. Quit all the moanin' and groanin' like a bunch of little boys.

TALL SOLDIER. . . . Heard tell the Lieutenant's pushin' pretty hard for camp in two days.

LOUD SOLDIER. No rest, no sleep . . . no nothin' till we get there.

LIEUTENANT. Sound the call! . . . We're movin'!

(Bugle call and all the Soldiers begin to rise, groaning. Recorded music will only be used from here on for special sound effects. All singing will be done live to the occasional accompaniment of a Harmonica, Snare Drum, Banjo, Flute and Trumpet, which are played by the Soldiers. The lights on the marching Soldiers are dim, the spot on the Boy and the toy soldiers a bit brighter. The Drummer starts the beat of "John Brown's Body," the Flute follows in, and the Boy sings the first line. The other Soldiers follow to the end. They will march in one spot, getting wearier as the song progresses.)

BOY. John Brown's body lies a-molderin' in the grave.

SOLDIERS. John Brown's body lies a-molderin' in the grave,
John Brown's body lies a-molderin' in the grave,
His soul is marchin' on . . .
We'll hang Jeff Davis to a sour apple tree,
We'll hang Jeff Davis to a sour apple tree,
We'll hang Jeff Davis to a sour apple tree,
As we go marching on.

[Slides: muddy boots, closeups of mud-spotted blue uniforms, missing buttons, etc.]

(The Drummer slows his tempo and the Boy and Young Man sing slowly.)

BOY AND YOUNG MAN.
Mine eyes have seen the glory of the coming of the Lord;
He is trampling out the vintage where the grapes of wrath
are stored.
He hath loosed the fateful lightning of his terrible swift sword.
His truth is marching on.

(The Soldiers sing slowly as they begin to set up camp below the platform.)

SOLDIERS. Glory! Glory Hallelujah! Glory! Glory Hallelujah!
Glory! Glory Hallelujah! His truth is marching on.

(They repeat the chorus until only the Boy is left singing amid his toy soldiers. A sentry is on the small tall platform playing "Jeanie with the Light Brown Hair" on his Harmonica while leaning back against a post. Several others lie back against posts, some writing letters, others sleeping, playing cards, etc.)

[Slide: a Union camp.]

LOUD SOLDIER. *(Entering from under the platform.)* Anyone seen Conklin tonight?

SOLDIER. Over by the river doin' some washin'.

LOUD SOLDIER. *(To Young Man.)* Well, yeh couldn't wait for us to get here . . . and here we are . . . two months now an' jest a-sittin' an' a-waitin'.

YOUNG MAN. What are we waitin' for? . . . When are we gonna move in on 'em?

LOUD SOLDIER. Someone aroun' here's gotta have some answers.

(The Tall Soldier rushes in waving a shirt.)

TALL SOLDIER. We're goin' t' move t'morra—sure. . . . We're goin' way up the river, cut across an' come around in behind 'em.

LOUD SOLDIER. It's a lie! . . . That's all it is—a thunderin' lie!
(Walks away with his hands in his pockets.) I don't believe the derned old Army's ever gonna move. I've got ready to move eight times in the past two weeks, and we ain't moved yet.

TALL SOLDIER. Well, yeh kin believe me or not, jest as yeh like. I don't care a hang. *(He exits.)*

YOUNG MAN. It could be true . . . t'morrow could be the day. *(To boy.)* Are yeh ready?

BOY. I don't know. . . . I want it to come, but I'm kinda afraid of it too . . . afraid when the battle comes I'll run.

YOUNG MAN. *(Crossing to Boy.)* What makes yeh think you'll run?

BOY. Dunno. Things ain't turnin' out like I imagined 'em to be.

YOUNG MAN. Sure ain't the kinda war I hoped for. I gotta admit I'm kinda at a loss here, like a stranger . . . sure glad I got you around.

(Tall Soldier enters, followed by the Loud Soldier.)

TALL SOLDIER. That's all right, you can believe me or not, jest as you like. All you got to do is sit down and wait as quiet as you can, then pretty soon you'll find out I was right.

LOUD SOLDIER. Well, yeh don't know everything in the world, do yeh?

TALL SOLDIER. Didn't say I knew everything in the world.

YOUNG MAN. Goin' to be a battle sure, is there?

TALL SOLDIER. Of course there is, of course there is. You jest wait till tomorrow and you'll see one of the biggest battles ever was. You jest wait.

BOY. Thunder!

TALL SOLDIER. Oh, you'll see fightin' this time, what'll be regular out-and-out fightin'!

LOUD SOLDIER. Huh!

YOUNG MAN. Jim!

TALL SOLDIER. What?

YOUNG MAN. How do you think the regiment will do?

TALL SOLDIER. Oh, they'll fight all right, I guess, after they once get into it. There's been heaps of fun poked at us 'cause we're new and young and all that, but they'll fight all right, I guess.

YOUNG MAN. Think any of the boys'll run?

TALL SOLDIER. Oh, there may be a few of 'em run but there's them kind in every regiment, 'specially when they first goes under fire. Of course, it might happen that the hull kit and kaboodle might start and run if some big fightin' came first off. And then again they might stay and fight like fun. But you can't bet on nothin'. Of course, they ain't never been under fire yet and it ain't likely they'll lick the hull Rebel Army all-to-oncet the first time, but I think they'll fight better than some, if worse than others. That's the way I figger.

LOUD SOLDIER. Oh, you think you know!

TALL SOLDIER. Well, I sure know better'n you . . .

LOUD SOLDIER. You don't know nothin'!

YOUNG MAN. *(Interrupting.)* Did you ever think you might run yourself, Jim? *(Laughs suddenly, as if he meant it to be a joke.)*

TALL SOLDIER. Well, I've thought it might get too hot for Jim Conklin in some of them scrimmages, and if a whole lot of boys started and run, why, I suppose I'd start and run. And if I once started to run, I'd run like the devil! But if everybody was a-standing and a-fighting, why, I'd stand and fight. By jiminey, I would . . . I'll bet on it.

LOUD SOLDIER. Huh!

YOUNG MAN. *(To Boy . . . his conscience.)* See that there . . . they all got the same feelin' you do.

BOY. Still don't answer my question.

YOUNG MAN. What's that?

BOY. Will *I* run like a coward or fight like a hero an' maybe die?

YOUNG MAN. Guess only time will tell . . . Are yeh afraid of dyin'?

TALL SOLDIER. *(Answering.)* Ain't thought much about it . . . all depends, I guess. If it happens quick-like so's I don't know about it, guess I won't mind . . . but if it's goin' tuh linger on tuh make me think about it, guess I'd prob'ly mind a lot.

YOUNG MAN. Don't yeh want tuh die a hero?

TALL SOLDIER. Jest want tuh do my best . . . If it turns out they make me a hero for doin' it . . . sure would make my ma proud . . . wouldn't make *me* no never mind . . . wouldn't be here to get the medal anyhow.

LOUD SOLDIER. Not likely you'll die anyhow . . . Yer too darned stubborn.

(Sound: "Taps," played by Trumpet on the tall platform.)

TALL SOLDIER. I'll outlast you, I'll bet . . . Come on, let's get us some shut-eye . . . gotta be ready fer the fightin' t'morra. *(Starts to exit.)*

LOUD SOLDIER. Huh! I'll believe it when I see it. *(Exits.)*

BOY. *(To Young Man.)* Do yeh think he's right? . . . About the fightin'?

YOUNG MAN. Hope so. . . . *(Picks up Guitar and strums lightly.)* Sure would like tuh know what it's like.

BOY. Been thinkin' a lot about Ma . . . Wonder how she's gettin' along without me.

YOUNG MAN. Not gettin' homesick, are yeh?

BOY. Suppose I never see her again? . . . Suppose I die t'morra and never see her again.

YOUNG MAN. *(Picking out the chords of "Just Before the Battle, Mother" on the Guitar.)* Funny, ain't it, 'bout how she had it all figured out right?

BOY. *(Singing softly to the accompaniment of the Young Man's playing. The Harmonica also joins in.)*
Just before the battle, Mother,
I am thinking most of you,
While upon the field we're watching,
With the enemy in view.

(Young Man joins in.)

Comrades brave are round me lying,
Filled with thoughts of home and God;
For well they know that on the morrow,
Some will sleep beneath the sod.

(The Soldiers join in softly.)

Farewell, Mother, you may never
Press me to your heart again;
But, O, you'll not forget me, Mother,
If I'm number'd with the slain.

(The Harmonica plays another chorus and the Soldiers hum during the following.)

BOY. Maybe I'll get wounded and wear a white bandage to show off my bravery. What good's courage if yeh can't show it?

YOUNG MAN. What happens if it turns out you're a coward? What'll yeh wear then?

BOY. *(No answer.)*

YOUNG MAN. I don't have an answer either.

(The lights fade slowly with the singing, leaving only the slides. Then abruptly the sound of a Trumpet. The slides change quickly to scenes of sunrise through trees and a spot comes up on the Soldier and his Trumpet on the highest level. The other lights fade up revealing the Soldiers waking and moving into line. The Boy is arranging his toy soldiers in the same formation.)

LOUD SOLDIER. *(To Tall Soldier as they move into line.)* Well, it's t'morra. Where's all that fightin' yeh was promisin' us?

TALL SOLDIER. They were supposed tah move in durin' the night.

LOUD SOLDIER. Told yeh it weren't nothin' but another of yer lies.

TALL SOLDIER. Weren't no lie! . . . I heard it!

LOUD SOLDIER. From Lincoln himself, I suppose!

YOUNG MAN. Yeh mean there ain't goin' to be any fightin'?

TALL SOLDIER. If this here loudmouth don't shut up, there will be.

LOUD SOLDIER. I'll show yeh a fight if yeh want one! *(Starts after Tall Soldier. Several Soldiers pull him away.)* Leave me be, he's long overdue for a good sluggin'!

LIEUTENANT. *(Off.)* Prepare to move out!

LOUD SOLDIER. Move out?!

HARMONICA. More marchin'?!

LOUD SOLDIER. *(As the line breaks up to gather their belongings.)* I can't stand this much longer. I don't see what good it does to make us wear out our legs for nothin'.

BANJO. I suppose we must go reconnoitering around the coun-
tryside jest to keep 'em from getting too close, or to develop
our muscles, or something.

LOUD SOLDIER. Huh!

SINGING SOLDIER. I'd rather do anything 'most than go tramping
'round the country all day doing no good to nobody and jest
tiring ourselves out.

LOUD SOLDIER. So would I. It ain't right. I tell you, if anybody with
any sense was a-runnin' this Army it . . .

TALL SOLDIER. Oh, shut up! . . . You little fool! You little damn
cuss, you ain't had that there coat and them pants on for two
months, and yet you talk as if . . .

LOUD SOLDIER. Well, I wanta do some fightin' anyway. I didn't come
here to walk. I could've walked at home . . . 'round and 'round
the barn if I jest wanted to walk. *(He crams things in his sack.)*

GLUM SOLDIER. They say we're catchin' it over on the left. They say
the enemy drove our line intuh a devil of a swamp an' took
Hannises' Battery.

HARMONICA. No sech thing. Hannises' Battery was 'long here jest
last night.

GLUM SOLDIER. I met one of the 148th Maine boys an' he says his
brigade fought the hull Rebel Army fer four hours over on the
turnpike road an' killed about five thousand of 'em. He sez one
more sech fight as that an' the war'll be over.

LOUD SOLDIER. The war'll be nothin' but a memory before we see
any action . . . durn it all anyhow!

LIEUTENANT. *(Off.)* All right, men, let's move on out.

*(The band begins the music to "Marching through Georgia" as
they again begin to march in their spots.)*

*[Slides: roads, paths, forests from all over the world, inter-
spersed with slides of toy soldiers. The slides should encom-
pass several days . . . morning sunrise to noon to setting sun
to night.]*

SOLDIERS. *(Sung.)*
Bring the good old bugle boys,
We'll sing another song.

Sing it with the spirit
That will start the world along.
Sing it as we used to sing it,
Fifty thousand strong,
While we are marching through Georgia.
Hurrah, hurrah, we bring the jubilee . . .
Hurrah, hurrah, the flag that makes you free,
So we sing the chorus from Atlanta to the sea
While we are marching through Georgia.

Yes, and there were Union men,
Who wept with joyful tears
When they saw the honored flag
They had not seen for years.
Hardly could they be restrained
From breaking forth in cheers
While we are marching through Georgia.
Hurrah, hurrah, we bring the jubilee . . .
Hurrah, hurrah, the flag that makes you free,
So we sing the chorus from Atlanta to the sea
While we are marching through Georgia.

*(As they finish it is night and they collapse, set up camp, etc.
The Young Man settles near the Boy and his soldiers.)*

BOY. It feels like I was home again makin' the rounds from the
house to the barn . . .

YOUNG MAN. From the barn to the fields . . .

BOY. From the fields to the barn . . .

YOUNG MAN. And from the barn to the house.

BOY. I'd trade in my bright blue uniform and all its brass buttons if I
could just go back home . . . I ain't like them. I ain't cut out to
be their kind of soldier.

YOUNG MAN. The darkness seems to be sharin' my feelin's tonight.

(Laughter from the Soldiers.)

BOY. Listen to 'em laughin' . . . They ain't even like the heroes in
my books.

YOUNG MAN. Ain't no way I could ever join in with 'em; they can't
understand things like I do.

BOY. I understand yeh.

YOUNG MAN. You're different. You're so much a part of me by now, ain't no way I'd ever be able to shake yeh loose.

BOY. *(Excited.)* We could run away . . . they'd never even miss us. They'd think we just got lost along the way.

YOUNG MAN. Couldn't run back home . . . folks would call us cowards. No, I could never face 'em.

(Loud Soldier moves in.)

LOUD SOLDIER. What are ye doin' way over here by yourself?

YOUNG MAN. Oh, thinkin'.

LOUD SOLDIER. *(Sitting down.)* You're actin' kinda blue . . . What the dickens is wrong with yeh?

YOUNG MAN. Oh, nothin'.

LOUD SOLDIER. *(Changing the subject and being very excited.)* We've got 'em now. At last, by the eternal thunders, we'll lick 'em good.

YOUNG MAN. I thought you were objectin' to this march a little while back.

LOUD SOLDIER. Oh, it wasn't that. I don't mind marchin' if there's goin' to be fightin' at the end of it, and I got me a feelin' in my bones we're goin' to be seein' it right soon. *(Rises and moves about, almost show-offy.)* Gee rod! How we'll thump 'em! Yes siree, we'll thump 'em real good!

YOUNG MAN. Oh, you're going to do great things, I suppose!

LOUD SOLDIER. Oh, I don't know . . . I don't know. I s'pose I'll do as well as the rest.

YOUNG MAN. How do you know you won't run when the time comes?

LOUD SOLDIER. Run? . . . Run? . . . Of course not! *(Laughs.)*

YOUNG MAN. Well, lots of good-a-nough men have thought they were going to do great things before the fight, but when the time came they skedaddled.

LOUD SOLDIER. Oh, that's all true, I s'pose. But *I'm* not going to skedaddle. The man that bets on my runnin' will lose his money, that's all.

YOUNG MAN. Oh, shucks! . . . You ain't the bravest man in the world, are yeh?

LOUD SOLDIER. No, I ain't . . . an' I didn't say I was the bravest man in the world neither. I said I was going to do my share of fighting . . . that's what I said. And I am too. Who are you anyhow? You talk as if you thought you was Napoleon Bonaparte! *(Storms away.)*

YOUNG MAN. Well, yeh needn't git mad about it. *(To Boy.)* See what I mean? They ain't like me . . . we ain't alike in no way.

BOY. He don't seem to be 'feared of runnin' at all.

YOUNG MAN. Sure certain of himself . . . wish I was so certain, one way or the other. Even if it weren't true certain, at least I'd know somethin'.

(Harmonica begins to play "All Quiet Along the Potomac.")

BOY. Look! Across the river yeh can see the red dots of the enemy's campfires . . . like lightnin' bugs yeh can reach out an' cup in yer hand, holdin' them prisoner till yeh choose to let 'em go.

YOUNG MAN. The quiet's spooky tonight . . .

BOY. Are you tryin' to scare me?!

YOUNG MAN. Not intentional . . . it's a quiet kind of quiet, the kind of quiet you hear just before a thunderstorm . . .

BOY. I'm scared of thunder.

YOUNG MAN. Is there anything you're not scared of?

BOY. I'm not scared of you.

YOUNG MAN. *(Pause.)* I am.

(Sound: the screech of a shell shattering through the silence and landing in an explosion, followed by whistling bullets.)

LIEUTENANT. On your feet . . . Prepare for attack!

(The Soldiers grab their rifles and take places behind posts, platforms, etc.)

LOUD SOLDIER. A fine time to attack . . . I ain't ready for 'em . . . sneakin' devils.

DRUM. I can't see 'em in the dark.

HARMONICA. Then they can't see us either.

GLUM SOLDIER. I can't see what I'm shootin' at.

FLUTE. Just keep shootin'. You're bound to hit somethin'.

(The Boy with his toy rifle crouches in the center of his toy army. The Young Man crouches near him behind the ramp.)

HARMONICA. They certainly ain't got much sense attackin' in the pitch dark.

(The shooting ceases.)

DRUM. They stopped firin'.

LOUD SOLDIER. Probably jist tryin' tuh scare us.

BOY. *(Panicked.)* Where are you? . . . Don't leave me alone.

YOUNG MAN. I'm here. Quiet! . . . Don't let 'em know you're scared . . . Try to be brave.

SCARED SOLDIER. What do we do now?

SINGING SOLDIER. They could outnumber us by hundreds.

FLUTE. If we could just see 'em.

(Loud Soldier rushes to Young Man.)

LOUD SOLDIER. Are yeh okay?

YOUNG MAN. Fine . . . the fightin' took me unexpected.

LOUD SOLDIER. Me too. It's my first and last battle . . .

YOUNG MAN. What?

LOUD SOLDIER. It's gonna be my first an' last battle . . . gotta feelin'. Somethin' tells me I ain't gonna see another.

YOUNG MAN. Don't be . . .

LOUD SOLDIER. Here . . . I want yeh to take these here things . . . to . . . my . . . folks. *(Hands him an envelope.)*

YOUNG MAN. Why, what the devil! . . .

LOUD SOLDIER. It's got my gran-pa's gold watch and . . .

SINGING SOLDIER. Somethin's movin' there in the bushes . . .

(Gunshot.)

LOUD SOLDIER. I gotta get back . . . careful with it now. *(He returns to his spot. A Soldier enters from under the platform.)*

TALL SOLDIER. It's Jackson, yeh shot Jackson. *(He rushes to him and helps him to a spot under the platform.)*

LOUD SOLDIER. Fine Army we got here . . . shootin' their own men.

TALL SOLDIER. Shut up an' give me a hand here bandagin' him up . . . he's bleedin' bad in the arm.

(Loud Soldier helps the other one bandage the Soldier.)

WOUNDED SOLDIER. Stupid fool! Now I'll never be able to fight . . . waited all these months for the fight, to be shot by one of my own.

YOUNG MAN. They don't know what they're doin' . . . the whole bunch is crazy.

DRUM. Think they'll come back?

CHEERY SOLDIER. Sure of it. They know we're here now.

LIEUTENANT. All right men, cozy into where yeh are an' be alert . . . they'll be back, an' you be ready for 'em . . . Jackson, yeh fool . . .

BOY. It was an accident. He didn't mean to hurt him . . . he'll be all right tomorrow.

LIEUTENANT. You're gonna have tuh fight anyhow. We need everyone we can get.

HARMONICA. I'm sure they'll wait till sun-up and come up on us full blast.

BOY. *(To Young Man.)* Let's run . . .

YOUNG MAN. *(To Soldiers.)* Let's clear out before they come . . . Why are we waitin' around just to be shot at?

TALL SOLDIER. They must have a reason.

BOY. How do yeh know they're right? . . . We've got to run or we'll be killed.

SINGING SOLDIER. Yeh was lookin' for fightin', weren't yeh? Better here than marchin' somewhere else to get it.

TALL SOLDIER. We'll be ready for 'em when they come back.

SCARED SOLDIER. Give us a chance to prepare.

LOUD SOLDIER. Again it's waitin' . . . waitin' . . .

BOY. I can't wait till it's over.

YOUNG MAN. All this waitin's makin' it worse.

BOY. I wanna gather up everythin' an' go back home . . . they ain't doin' it right.

YOUNG MAN. Wait . . . Wait an' see what happens next . . . I've got to find out what all this waitin' was for.

[Slide: sunrise.]

(The lights brighten. Gunshots.)

TRUMPET. Here they come!

[Slide: a fiery dragon.]

(Sound: a trumpet blast followed by music and battle sounds. The battle is in slow motion and pantomimed. Only the Young Man and Boy will break the pace and the quick flashing of the slides. The slides will show the toy soldiers in various stages of destruction. . . . The stage after the first blast blacks out and spots of light pop up, revealing individual Soldiers. A light remains up on the Young Man and Boy at all times.)

YOUNG MAN. There are hundreds of them . . . We'll never be able to hold them off.

BOY. They're expectin' too much of me.

(Spot on Tall Soldier tying red handkerchief around his neck.)

TALL SOLDIER. Oh, we're in for it now . . . we're really in for it now.

LIEUTENANT'S VOICE. Reserve your fire, boys . . . Don't shoot till I tell you . . . save your fire . . . wait till they get close up . . . don't be damned fools!

(The Young Man feverishly waits. He wipes his eyes with his coat sleeve. He lifts his rifle into position and fires. There follow other gunshots blending into the sound of fireworks.)

BOY. The fireworks are getting too close. . . . I'll get hurt. . . . I'll get hurt.

[Slide: a fireworks display.]

(Sound: the spots will pop up to reveal a Soldier. A recorded sound or phrase will correspond with the Soldier. Following their initial exposure the sounds will begin to blend, forming a chant, and the spots will cross blend, like a pinball machine at victory.)

SOLDIER 1. *(Muffled.)* Please, God, don't let me die.

SOLDIER 2. Rotten Rebs!

SOLDIER 3. Yea! . . . Got yeh, damned devil!

SOLDIER 4. Our Father, who art in heaven. . . .

SOLDIER 5. *(Heavy breathing.)*

SOLDIER 6. They got Pete Johnson in the head.

SOLDIER 7. *(Muttering.)* Be brave . . . be brave . . . be brave.

TALL SOLDIER. I ain't a liar . . . I said there'd be fightin'.

LOUD SOLDIER. Die, you stinkin' devils!

SOLDIER 8. Dear Lord, don't leave my side.

SOLDIER 9. I'm afraid . . . I'm afraid.

[Slide: a toy soldier with broken off arm, followed by slides of other toy soldiers with broken legs, head, torso, etc.]

BOY. Stop it! . . . You ain't playin' fair . . . You're breakin' 'em . . . You're breakin' 'em!

(Sound: the chant begins to increase in tempo, a swirl of mismatched words. The Boy covers his ears. The Young Man swirls in all directions as a spot stops on a Soldier who clutches his head, which is dripping red. It moves to another who clutches his stomach and falls to his knees, to another whose knee is splashed with red. He drops his rifle and clutches a post and cries out in silence. The Boy rushes to the Young Man and pulls at him.)

BOY. Come on, you've got to run . . . You can't stay here. You'll be killed . . . Run! . . . Run!

(Young Man rises and the Boy pulls him off up the ramp. The chanting combined with the music and battle sounds continues. They reach the center top platform and the Young Man

*stops and stands on the edge, teetering. He catches himself
and turns and runs down the back ramp pulled by the boy.
The lights fade to black except for the slides.)*

*[Slides: toppled over broken toy soldiers, a battlefield of
strewn bodies, a closeup of a broken toy soldier, a closeup of a
dead soldier, a picture of a beautiful forest with red dripping
down it.]*

*(Sound: chant fading to the distant sound of battle. The lights
come up on the right ramp to reveal the Young Man and Boy
running on. They are breathing heavily.)*

YOUNG MAN. I can't run any more.

BOY. You've got to . . . It will catch us.

YOUNG MAN. Why didn't the others run, the fools . . . Didn't they
see what was happening? The stupid fools will be killed! They
were as stiff as toy soldiers waiting for a giant hand to lift them
out of there.

BOY. *(Crossing to toy soldiers.)* They're all broken. They're no good
any more . . . but you are, and I am . . . We're at least alive . . .

YOUNG MAN. Yes, I'm still alive to be used again . . . Someone had
to live to tell about it.

BOY. You're the only one alive to be a hero . . . to tell stories about
it.

[Slide: toy soldier with huge oversized medal.]

(Sound: Soldiers' voices cheering in the distance.)

YOUNG MAN. Listen.

BOY. What is it?

YOUNG MAN. Sounds like cheering . . . Ssh, someone's coming . . .
Hide over here. *(They hide behind ramp.)*

SOLDIER. *(Far off.)* They did it! . . . They did it. They walloped the
bee-jeezus out of 'em.

SOLDIER. The 304th?

SOLDIER. Sure 'nuf did . . . We'll take 'em for sure now. The war's
nearly over.

(The distant cheering continues.)

YOUNG MAN. They beat 'em. Those fools beat 'em! *(He rises and rushes to the tall platform to see.)* Look, he's right . . . They beat 'em. I ran! . . . You made me run! *(Grabs Boy.)* You stupid fool, you made me run!

BOY. *(Crying.)* I had to. You're the only friend I have . . . I had to save you.

(The cheering fades.)

YOUNG MAN. Why? . . . What good am I now? . . . I could never go back . . . I'm a coward . . . I ran . . . just like I thought I might.

BOY. No, you were right . . . It's them who are the fools . . . They're all broken into a million pieces.

YOUNG MAN. They may be broken, but they ain't dead. They can be patched back together. They'll have proof of their courage. They'll wear their bandages like medals of courage. Look at me . . . I ain't even got a scratch to prove I was there.

BOY. They'll know you were there.

YOUNG MAN. How? . . . Are you gonna tell 'em? A silly kid . . . Who'd even believe yeh? I can't wait till I get rid of yeh. It's you who's keepin' me from bein' a hero.

BOY. No, I want to help!

YOUNG MAN. I don't want your help. I can do it by myself. Go play with your toys and leave me be.

(Sound: battle sounds and chant.)

The fightin's started up again. The sound shames me . . . I've got to run and hide. *(He starts to run. The Boy follows. He stops.)* Where you goin'? . . . I said leave me be.

BOY. I'm scared . . . Take me with you.

YOUNG MAN. You're goin' to destroy me!

BOY. Please, just for a little longer . . . please!

YOUNG MAN. *(Pause.)* Well, I guess I can't keep yeh from following me . . . *(Grabs his head.)* That sound! . . . I've got to find some place quiet to think this all out! Tell those voices to stop!

(Sound: the voices stop abruptly, replaced by sounds of nature—birds, etc. Shafts of light as if filtering through trees pour down.)

[Slides: trees with rays of sun.]

YOUNG MAN. What happened? . . . The voices stopped. I'm . . . *(Looks around.)* I'm somewhere else.

BOY. We've been wandering through the woods for hours . . . I'm gettin' tired. Let's rest here for a spell.

YOUNG MAN. Where are we? . . .

BOY. It's as quiet as a church.

(Sound: organ music, very subdued.)

YOUNG MAN. The quiet's like a hazy wall shielding out all the awful sounds of life.

BOY. *(Quickly.)* Look! . . . There's a squirrel . . . *(He throws a pine cone at him.)* Look. Look at him run. *(Laughs.)*

YOUNG MAN. He runs from fear of death . . . and he's just an ordinary squirrel, not a man like me. Nature prepared him to run. It's not cowardly for him to run from fear and the unknown. Does anyone shame the squirrel for running from attack? . . . Then why should they shame me?

BOY. You were right to run . . . just like the squirrel. You did what you had to at the time.

YOUNG MAN. Yes . . . I had to . . .

BOY. Come on, let's run and play . . . Chase me. *(Starts to run.)*

YOUNG MAN. I'm too tired for games.

BOY. Please? . . .

YOUNG MAN. All right, but be careful where you run.

(Boy runs up one ramp and down the other, then under the back of the platform. He trips over something . . . a body. The body is leaning against a post, rotted and forgotten. A skeletal arm hangs loose from the sleeve of a once-blue uniform, now faded to a pale blue-grey. The Boy falls in such a way that he lays across it. He looks up and is face to face with the "once" Soldier and freezes. The Young Man enters and, seeing the Boy, freezes momentarily into a statue. He finally pulls the Boy from the body.)

BOY. Who was he? . . . Was he a soldier like us?

YOUNG MAN. Quiet. Don't disturb his peace.

BOY. Did he run away too? . . . He seems lost.

YOUNG MAN. Leave him to his secrets.

BOY. *(Crying.)* Did anyone tell his mother? . . . Does anybody know?

YOUNG MAN. You see, there's no running away from it . . . It will follow us wherever we go. *(Pulls Boy.)* Let's get out of here . . . Stop crying . . . He's happy . . . he's dead! He knows his end.

(Boy runs up the ramp.)

BOY. Wait! Wait for me. Don't leave me here alone with him.

(Sound: distant singing. "Battle Cry of Freedom" sung by the Soldiers, which stops the Boy on the center platform.)

YOUNG MAN. Stop! . . . Listen, it's singin' . . . it's comin' this way.

BOY. It's soldiers. They're comin' to drag us back. Let's run.

YOUNG MAN. There's no place left to run. Wherever we run we'll be haunted.

BOY. You ain't goin' back, are yeh?

YOUNG MAN. How else will I become a hero? . . . I don't want to die and lie rottin', a forgotten hero. Gotta let folks know I was a part of this whole thing. Gotta patch up the broken past an' move on.

BOY. It'll just be more of the same.

YOUNG MAN. Might not, but I've gotta stop runnin' some time before I run my whole life away.

[Slide: toy soldiers all pieced back together with bandages.]

BOY. *(Looking down the back ramp.)* They're all bloody an' hurt . . . They're comin' this way, at us.

YOUNG MAN. We'll just follow 'em. Maybe they'll lead us back to our camp.

(The wounded Soldiers enter up the back ramp. Their uniforms are those of many wars. They are bloodied and bandaged and a terrible sight. They will cross down the right ramp and settle below the center platform around the body.

Sound: a funeral procession. Suggest: "Lincoln's Funeral March.")

SINGING SOLDIER. *(Hopping on one leg, singing.)*
Sing a song a' vic'try,
A pocket full a' bullets,
Five an' twenty dead men
Baked in a . . . pie.

FLUTE. *(Shot in the arm.)* Durned General . . . If he knew how tuh run an army, never woulda been hit.

(Two Soldiers carry a limp body on a stretcher. Another helps a Soldier who can hardly walk.)

GLUM SOLDIER. Don't joggle me so, Johnson, yeh fool. Think m'leg is made of iron? If yeh can't help me decent, leave me be an' let someone else do it. *(As they move down the ramp.)* Say, make way there, can't yeh? Make way, dickens take it all!

SOLDIERS. *(As they pass.)*
—Think yeh're the only one hurt?

—Watch who you're shovin'! . . .

—If I had my arm back, I'd show yeh! . . .

—Careful who yeh're trompin' on!

(They bump into a Soldier walking in a daze, completely unaware of anyone or anything. They knock him down, off the ramp. A Tattered Soldier helps him to sit up with his one good arm.)

YOUNG MAN. Yeh see anyone from our regiment in the lot?

BOY. They're so patched up, couldn't tell if there was.

YOUNG MAN. They're like a funeral procession marchin' to their graves. . . .

BOY. If they lost their bandages they'd fall apart into a million pieces. *(They walk slowly down the ramp looking over the mass of men.)* They all know his secret grave now. *(Referring to the body.)*

YOUNG MAN. He'll have to move over to make room for more.

(They settle on the ramp near the Tattered Soldier, who looks up at them.)

TATTERED SOLDIER. Was a pretty good fight, wasn't it?

YOUNG MAN. What?

TATTERED SOLDIER. Was a pretty good fight, wa'n't it? Dern me if I ever seen fellers fight so. Laws, how they did fight! I know'd the boys'd fight when they oncet got square at it. The boys ain't had no fair chancet up t' now, but this time they showed what they was. I know'd it'd turn out this way. Yeh can't lick them boys. No sir! They're fighters, they be. I was talkin' with a boy from Georgia oncet, an' that boy, he sez, "Your fellers'll all run like hell when they oncet hear a gun," he sez. "Mebbe they will," I sez, "but I don't b'lieve none of it," I sez, "an' by jiminey," I sez to 'im, "mebbe yer fellers will run like hell when they oncet hear a gun," I sez. He laffed. Well, they didn't run t'day, did they, hey? No, sir! They fought an' fought an' fought!

(The Young Man stands and starts to move.)

Where yeh hit?

YOUNG MAN. What?

TATTERED SOLDIER. Where yeh hit?

YOUNG MAN. Why, I . . . I . . . that is . . . why . . . I . . . *(Fidgets with a button on his coat. Boy grabs his hand and pulls him away.)*

BOY. C'mon . . . Let's set over here in the shade.

(They move to the other side of the stage.)

YOUNG MAN. It shows! . . . Even that old man could see right through me . . . They're all lookin' at me. They can see it burned on my face . . . Coward!

BOY. They look happy with their wounds . . . all torn and broken, but proud. I wish I had a wound like theirs . . . a red badge of courage.

YOUNG MAN. They make me feel guilty . . . but I'm not. I'm not guilty . . . I ran . . .

BOY. Like the squirrel, I ran. With all of the wounded, they'll need me now. They have only me left to fight.

(The dazed soldier moves his head toward us and we see he is the Tall Soldier. He recognizes the Young Man and makes his way toward him.)

YOUNG MAN. Someone had to run, to run and come back later . . . I did right. They'll see.

(The Tall Soldier places his gory hand on the Young Man's shoulder. The Young Man turns slowly.)

Gawd! Jim Conklin!

TALL SOLDIER. *(Slight smile.)* Hello, Henry.

YOUNG MAN. *(Helping him to sit.)* Oh, Jim . . . Jim . . .

TALL SOLDIER. *(Monotonous voice.)* Where yeh been, Henry? I thought mebbe yeh got keeled over. There's been thunder t' pay t'day. I was worryin' about yeh a good deal.

BOY. Jim! . . . Gawd, not Jim. He's the best one of the bunch.

TALL SOLDIER. Yeh know, I was out there. An', Lord, what a circus! An' by jiminey, I got shot . . . I got shot. Yes, by jiminey, I got shot.

BOY. I'm afraid . . . I'm afraid!

TALL SOLDIER. *(Clutching Young Man's shoulder and whispering.)* I tell yeh what I'm 'fraid of, Henry . . . I'll tell yeh what I'm 'fraid of. I'm 'fraid I'll fall down . . . an' then, yeh know . . . they likely as not'll tramp right over me. That's what I'm 'fraid of.

YOUNG MAN. *(Crying out.)* I'll take care of yeh, Jim! I'll take care of yeh! I swear t' Gawd I will!

TALL SOLDIER. Sure . . . Will yeh, Henry?

BOY. *(Crying.)* Yes . . . yes . . . I tell yeh . . . I'll take care of yeh, Jim!

TALL SOLDIER. *(Weakly falling into the Young Man's arms.)* Please . . . please don't let 'em run all over me . . . promise me. I was allus a good friend to yeh, wa'n't I, Henry? I've allus been a good fella, ain't I? An' it ain't much t' ask, is it? Jest t' pull me along outer the road? I'd do it fer you, wouldn't I, Henry?

(Young Man cannot answer for the held-in sobs. Sound: the funeral march begins again as the wounded men slowly get up, grumbling, and begin to move off. The Tall Soldier sees them and begins to rise.)

YOUNG MAN. Here, lean on me.

TALL SOLDIER. *(Shaking his head, protesting.)* No . . . No . . . No . . . Leave me be . . . Leave me be . . .

YOUNG MAN. You're weak. You need help.

TALL SOLDIER. No . . . No . . . Leave me be . . . Leave me be.

(Tattered Soldier moves in.)

TATTERED SOLDIER. Ye'd better take 'im outta the road, son. He's a goner anyhow in about five minutes . . . yeh kin see that. Ye'd better take 'im outta the road. Don't know where the blazes he gits his stren'th from.

YOUNG MAN. Lord knows!

(Grasps shoulders of the Tall Soldier, who has been wandering around aimlessly.)

Jim! Jim! Come with me.

TALL SOLDIER. *(Weakly attempting to wrench himself free.)* Huh? *(He stares at the Young Man, then dimly realizing.)* Oh! Inteh th' fields? Oh! *(He starts blindly toward the ramp.)*

TATTERED SOLDIER. Gawd! He's runnin'!

YOUNG MAN. *(Rushing to him.)* Jim! . . . Jim, what are you doing? You'll hurt yourself.

TALL SOLDIER. *(Gazing up toward the center platform.)* No . . . No . . . Don't tech me . . . Leave me be . . . Leave me be.

YOUNG MAN. Where yeh goin', Jim? . . . What are you thinkin' about? . . . Tell me, won't yeh, Jim?

TALL SOLDIER. *(Nearly in tears.)* Leave me be, can't yeh? Leave me be for a minnit.

YOUNG MAN. Why, Jim? . . . What's the matter with you?

(He pulls forward, releasing himself from the Young Man's grasp and struggles forward to the center platform where he clings to a post. His chest begins to heave. It increases . . .)

BOY. No! . . . No! . . . Don't take him away! . . . He didn't do no harm to nobody! . . . Stop! . . . Stop! . . . Don't take him!

(Young Man starts up the ramp.)

YOUNG MAN. Jim! . . . Jim!

TALL SOLDIER. *(Quietly gesturing.)* Leave me be . . . Don't tech me . . . Leave me be.

(He grasps the pole and with several gasps, slithers to the ground. The Young Man rushes to the body and kneels. He touches his shoulder and then with livid rage shakes his fist at the battlefield.)

[Slide: a dead body.]

YOUNG MAN. Hell! . . .

[Slide: a grave marking.]

TATTERED SOLDIER. *(Moving up the other ramp with the Boy.)* Well, he was a reg'lar jim-dandy fer nerve, wa'n't he? *(Softly.)* A reg'lar jim-dandy. *(Pokes one of the hands with his foot.)* I wonder where he got his stren'th from? I never seen a man do like that before. It was a funny thing. Well, he was a reg'lar jim-dandy.

(Young Man rises and, unable to screech out, grabs a post and clutches it, sobbing. The Tattered Soldier watches for a moment.)

Look-a-here, son. He's up an' gone, ain't 'e, an' we might as well begin t' look out fer ol' number one. This here thing is all over. He's up an' gone, ain't 'e? An' he's all right here. Nobody won't bother 'im. An' I must say I ain't enjoyin' any great health m'self these days. *(Crosses to Young Man.)* There ain't no use in us stayin' aroun' here. He'll be jest fine.

BOY. He picked the spot hisself . . . he and the other feller here will keep each other company.

YOUNG MAN. 'Tis the quietest spot around.

TATTERED SOLDIER. Well, he were a jim-dandy, weren't he?

YOUNG MAN. *(Walking down ramp.)* A jim-dandy.

TATTERED SOLDIER. *(Weakly.)* I'm commencin' t' feel pretty bad . . . I'm commencin' t' feel pretty damn bad.

BOY. Are yeh goin' t' die like Jim?

TATTERED SOLDIER. Oh, I'm not goin' t' die yet! There's too much dependin' on me fer me t' die yit. No, sir! Nary die! I *can't!* Ye'd oughter see th' swad a' children I've got, an' all like that.

(The Young Man turns to see him smile. The Tattered Soldier and Boy come down the ramp.)

Yeh know Tom Jamison, he lives next door t' me up home. He's a nice feller he is. An' we was allus good friends . . . smart too. Smart as a steel trap. Well, when we was a-fightin' this afternoon, all of a sudden he begin t' rip up an' cuss an' beller at me. "Yer shot, yeh blamed infernal!" . . . he swear horrible . . . he sez t' me. I put up m' hand t' m' head an' when I looked at m' fingers, I seen, sure 'nough I was shot. I give a holler an' began t' run, but before I could get away another one hit me in the arm an' whirled me clean 'round. I got skeered when they was all a-shootin' behind me an' I run t' beat all, but I catch it pretty bad. I've an idee I'd a' been fightin' yit, if 'twasn't for Tom Jamison . . . I don't believe I kin walk much further.

BOY. Set for a minute . . . Yeh ain't lookin' good at all.

TATTERED SOLDIER. *(To Young Man.)* Yeh look pretty peaked yourself . . . I bet yeh got a worser wound than yeh think. Ye'd better take keer of yer hurt. It don't do t' let sech things go. It might be inside mostly, an' them plays thunder. Where is it located?

YOUNG MAN. Why don't yeh not bother me?

BOY. He's jest tryin' to be nice . . . He's a nice man.

TATTERED SOLDIER. I seen a feller git hit plum in th' head when my regiment was a-standin' at ease oncet. An' everybody yelled out to 'im, "Hurt, John? Are yeh hurt much?" "No," sez he. He looked kinder surprised, an' he went on tellin' 'em how he felt. He sed he didn't feel nothin'. But, by dad, the first thing that feller knowed he was dead. Yes, he was dead . . . stone dead. So, ye want to watch out. Yeh might have some strange kinda hurt yerself. Yeh can't never tell. Where is your'n located?

YOUNG MAN. *(Crying out.)* Oh, don't bother me! *(In pain.)* Don't bother me!

TATTERED SOLDIER. Well, Lord knows I don't want to bother anybody. Lord knows I've gotta 'nough m' own t' tend to.

(Loosens Boy's hand. Boy walks away.)

BOY. Good-bye.

TATTERED SOLDIER. Why . . . Why, boy, where yeh goin'? *(He begins to act dumblike, his thoughts floundering about in his head.)* Now . . . now . . . look . . . a . . . here, you. Tom Jamison . . . now . . . I won't have this . . . this here won't do. I . . . I see through you, boy . . . where . . . Where yeh goin'?

YOUNG MAN. *(Pointing vaguely.)* Over there.

TATTERED SOLDIER. Well now, look . . . a . . . here . . . now . . . this thing won't do now, Tom Jamison. It won't do. I know yeh, yeh pigheaded devil. Yeh wantta go trompin' off with a bad hurt. It ain't right . . . now . . . Tom Jamison . . . it ain't right. Yeh wantta leave me take keer of yeh, son. It ain't right . . . it ain't fer yeh t' go . . . trompin' off . . . with a bad hurt . . . it ain't . . . ain't . . . ain't right . . . it ain't . . .

(Falling to his knees beside the Decayed Soldier, he delivers his final lines clutching him.)

YOUNG MAN. *(To Boy.)* Come on . . . We gotta find our way back.

TATTERED SOLDIER. Yeh need me tuh take keer of ya.

BOY. *(To Young Man.)* We can't leave him here . . . he's hurt bad . . . he needs us.

YOUNG MAN. Well, I don't need him botherin' and pesterin' at me no more . . . Yeh decide . . . him or me . . . I'm leavin'.

(He starts up the ramp and down the back.)

TATTERED SOLDIER. Look . . . a . . . here now, Tom Jamison . . . now . . . it ain't . . .

(The Boy runs after the Young Man as the lights fade. Sound: wind, lonely.)

[Slides: deserted graves.]

(The lights come up on the right ramp as the Young Man and Boy enter.)

BOY. How could yeh jest leave 'im there tuh die? . . . What'd he ever do tuh you?

YOUNG MAN. He knew, he knew I was a coward . . . He could see right through me. Yeh heard him say it.

BOY. It ain't right . . . It ain't right to desert him.

YOUNG MAN. If yeh care so much, why don't yeh go back? . . . If he means that much to yeh . . . a complete stranger, go on ahead. Be glad to get rid of yeh anyhow . . . It's your fault I'm in this mess.

BOY. Yer jest as much tuh blame as me.

YOUNG MAN. Go! . . . Get out of my life! Get out! Without yeh I can be what I want . . . Without yeh, I'll be a man. There's no room in me for you any more.

BOY. Yeh really mean that? . . . Yeh don't want me around no more?

YOUNG MAN. *(Falling to his knees, sobbing.)* I don't know . . . I don't know *what* I am any more.

BOY. Then I'll leave . . . I'll leave . . . then you'll see. *(Starts to run up the ramp.)*

YOUNG MAN. No! . . . Don't leave me alone . . . I didn't mean it.

BOY. Yah, yeh did . . . I know yeh. I know yeh did. *(He runs off.)*

YOUNG MAN. *(Shouts.)* You don't know me at all . . . Nobody knows me!

(Sound: gunfire, explosions.)

[Slides: soldiers running.]

I'm hungry . . . thirsty and hungry. That's all it is. *(Stands and dizzily moves about. He covers his ears.)* That noise . . . the gunfire's blowing my head apart! Stop it! . . . Stop this war! . . . I give up. You win! I surrender to you. *(The lights fade slowly to a circle of light around him.)* I can't run another step . . . Somebody find me.

(Sound: recorded voices.)

"Where's Henry Fleming?"

"He run, didn't he?"

"He run like a coward, he, did."

MOTHER: Henry, don't run, you'll fall.

"What are yeh 'fraid of, Henry?"

YOUNG MAN. Somebody find me . . . I surrender.

(Soldiers begin to run through, passing the circle of light. The Soldiers are the same as in previous scenes. They wear the same jackets, but solid light-colored trousers to indicate they are from another regiment. They bump into him, knocking him about as they pass.)

HARMONICA. There's hundreds of 'em in there . . . C'mon man, run.

BANJO. Where's the way out of here?!

YOUNG MAN. No, yeh can't run . . .

SCARED SOLDIER. We're outnumbered . . .

YOUNG MAN. Don't run . . . I'll help you. I'll help you . . . Stay!

GLUM SOLDIER. *(To Young Man.)* Get outta the way . . . run, yeh fool . . .

TRUMPET. *(Screaming.)* Gawd, it's the walls of hell fallin' in . . .

YOUNG MAN. *(Grabbing Soldier by the arm and swinging him to him.)* Why? . . . Why? . . .

TRUMPET. Let me go! . . . Let me go! *(Heaving and panting, he struggles, pulling the Young Man along.)* Let me go! . . . Let me go!

YOUNG MAN. Why? . . . Why?

TRUMPET. Well then!

(He swings his rifle around and crashes the butt on the side of the Young Man's head. The Young Man falls to the ground and the Soldier runs off. The second the rifle strikes, the sound whirls like a plug pulled on a phonograph and the slides blur. They heighten, then blur and fade along with the light on the Young Man to black.)

ACT II

The slides and sound slowly fade up to where they were at the end of Act I. A light fades up on the Young Man. A bloodstain is now on the side of his head. He clutches his head as he stands and weaves unsteadily on his feet. The sound develops into a recorded eerie, haunting version of "Battle Cry of Freedom."

YOUNG MAN. The drums an' bugles are callin' me . . . They're callin' me to fight . . . *(Cries out.)* I don't know the way . . . I don't know the way to run.

(Spot up on Boy.)

BOY. Run to the castle and bolt all the doors . . . the dragon won't get you there . . . run to the castle.

(Spot up on the Decayed Soldier, who rises.)

DECAYED SOLDIER. Run to the grave and bury your secret beneath . . . Kill your confusion . . . Put your running to rest. Run to the grave.

(Spot up on Tall Soldier.)

TALL SOLDIER. The war's in your hands now, Henry . . . Yer fightin' fer the both of us now . . . Get in there an' show 'em how a war is run.

(Spot up on Mother.)

MOTHER. I told yeh yeh'd get bad hurt if yeh played that fightin' game . . . Run inside, Son, an' wash off that blood.

(Spot up on Tattered Soldier.)

TATTERED SOLDIER. Hold onto yer head . . . hold on fer dear life . . . death is fer the dead . . . don't let it run away with ye, son.

YOUNG MAN. I'm bleeding! . . . My head is lying open . . . Everyone get out! . . . Get out!

BOY. You can't get rid of me that easily . . .

MOTHER. Don't forget what I said, Son . . .

TALL SOLDIER. Don't let what I started go undone.

TATTERED SOLDIER. You can't escape what you are, boy.

DECAYED SOLDIER. I'll always be in your thoughts . . .

YOUNG MAN. Get out! . . . Get out! *(He starts to run, but bumps into them.)*

BOY. Run to the castle!

MOTHER. Run inside an' wash off the blood.

TALL SOLDIER. Show 'em how a war is run!

TATTERED SOLDIER. Don't let it run away with yeh, son.

DECAYED SOLDIER. Put your running to rest!

BOY. *(Sing-song.)* Henry's a coward . . . Henry's a coward.

MOTHER. Yeh gotta be brave to be a hero, Son.

TALL SOLDIER. Where's yer courage, Henry?

TATTERED SOLDIER. Ain't no place for cowards here.

DECAYED SOLDIER. Cowards die a thousand deaths.

YOUNG MAN. *(Falling to his knees. A piercing vibration as the spots fade and the Young Man cowers in pain.)* Somebody help me! . . . Please! . . . Somebody point me in the right direction!

(The Cheery Soldier, who has been watching in the background, walks up behind him.)

CHEERY SOLDIER. Yeh seem t' be in a pretty bad way, boy.

YOUNG MAN. *(Not looking up.)* Uh!

CHEERY SOLDIER. *(Taking his arm.)* Well, I'm goin' your way. The whole gang is goin' your way. An' I guess I kin give yeh a lift. *(Lifts him up, putting his arm around him to steady him.)* Yeh seem mighty troubled 'bout somethin' . . . been watchin' yeh. Oh, you'll make it . . . you'll make it jest fine. Fightin's a little harder fer some than fer others . . . Pretty nearly everybody got their share of fightin' t'day. By dad, I give myself up fer dead any number of times.

(They move into different light areas as they make their way up one ramp and down the other.)

There was shootin' there, an' hollerin' there in the durn darkness until I couldn't tell t' save my soul which side I was on. It was the most mixed up dern thing I ever seen. These here hull woods is a reg'lar mess. How'd yeh get way over here anyhow? Well, I guess we can find yer way okay. Yeh know, there was a boy killed in my comp'ny t'day that I thought the world an' all of. Sure was a nice feller. By ginger, it hurt like thunder t' see ol' Jim jest git knocked flat. We was a-standin' purty peaceable fer a spell, though there was men runnin' ev'ry way all 'round us, an' while we was a-standin' like that, 'long comes a big fat fellow. He began t' peck at Jim's elbow, and he sez, "Say, where's the road to the river?" Jim was a-lookin' ahead all the time tryin' t' see the grey comin' through th' woods, an' he never paid no attention t' this big fat feller fer a long time, but at last he turned 'round an' he sez, "Ah, go t' blazes an' find the road to the river!" An' jest then a shot slapped him bang on the side of the head. Them was his last words.

(Sound: faint strains of "Tenting Tonight," sung by the Soldiers offstage and played by Harmonica.)

SOLDIERS. *(Sung.)*
We're tenting tonight, on the old camp ground.
Give us a song to cheer
Our weary hearts, a song of home
And friends we love so dear.
Many are the hearts, that are weary tonight
Wishing for the war to cease.
Many are the hearts, looking for the right
To see the dawn of peace.
Tenting tonight . . . tenting tonight,
Tenting on the old camp ground.

YOUNG MAN. Where are yeh takin' me?

CHEERY SOLDIER. Leadin' yeh to where yeh belong, jest like yeh asked.

YOUNG MAN. How do yeh . . . ?

CHEERY SOLDIER. Funny how yeh get instincts 'bout some things . . . Jest take it easy now . . . I'll help yeh find yer way.

(They move off into the darkness as the Soldiers enter, their song building as they arrange themselves around the camp. The Boy is spotted near his toy soldiers.)

[Slides: a peaceful camp with fires, etc. A homelike and inviting picture.]

(At the end of the song the Harmonica continues and the Young Man and Cheery Soldier enter up the rear ramp.)

CHEERY SOLDIER. Ah, here yeh be! . . . See, they're all waitin' fer yeh 'round the fire. You'll be jist fine now. Willin' to bet all I own on it too. Good-bye, ol' boy, good luck to yeh.

(He rests him by a post, then turns and cheerfully strides away, whistling.)

YOUNG MAN. Wait . . . I don't know who you are . . . I never saw yer face. *(He clutches onto the post.)* Why did you bring me here?

(From below the Loud Soldier grabs a rifle and starts up the ramp toward him.)

LOUD SOLDIER. Halt! . . . Halt!

YOUNG MAN. *(Recognizing the voice.)* Wilson? . . . You . . . You here?

LOUD SOLDIER. *(Moving in closer.)* That you, Henry?

YOUNG MAN. Yes, it's . . . it's me.

LOUD SOLDIER. Well, well, ol' boy, I'm glad to see yeh! I give yeh up for a goner. I thought yeh was dead sure enough.

YOUNG MAN. *(Clutching even stronger to the post.)* I've . . . I've had an awful time. I've been all over. Way over on the right. Terrible fightin' over there. I had an awful time. I got separated from the reg'ment.

(Spot up on Boy.)

BOY. We ran . . . we ran till we was clean outta breath.

YOUNG MAN. No! . . . Got separated! . . . Over on the right. I got shot . . . in the head.

(Spot up on Mother.)

MOTHER. Son, I taught yeh never to lie . . . Tell the truth now, Son . . . Tell the truth.

YOUNG MAN. I got shot!

(Light pops out on Mother.)

In the head! I never seen sech fightin'. Awful time. I don't see how I coulda got separated from the regiment.

BOY. Yes yeh do . . . yeh ran . . . like the squirrel.

YOUNG MAN. I got shot too.

BOY. Ma told yeh never to lie.

(Spot out on Boy.)

LOUD SOLDIER. What? Got shot? Why didn't yeh say so first?

LIEUTENANT. *(Coming up the ramp.)* Who yeh talkin' to, Wilson? Yer the darndest sentinel . . . Why I . . . *(Sees Young Man.)*

Henry! . . . Why, I thought you was dead four hours ago. Where was yeh?

YOUNG MAN. Over on the right. I got separated . . .

LOUD SOLDIER. Yes, an' he got shot in the head. We'd best see to him right away. *(Puts his arm about him.)* Gee, it must hurt like thunder!

YOUNG MAN. Yes, it hurts . . . hurts a good deal . . .

LIEUTENANT. *(Taking Young Man's arm.)* Come on, son. I'll take keer o' yeh. *(Starts to lead him down the ramp.)*

LOUD SOLDIER. Put 'im to sleep on my blanket. Look at his head by the fire an' see how it looks. May be its a pretty bad 'un. When I git relieved in a coupla minutes, I'll be over an' see t' him.

LIEUTENANT. *(Leading him to fire by the Boy and his toy soldiers.)* Now, let's have a look at yer ol' head.

(The Young Man sits down and the Lieutenant fumbles through his hair, spots the wound, and lets out a long whistle.)

Ah, here we are! Jest as I thought . . . yeh've been grazed. It's raised a strange lump jest as if some feller had lammed yeh on the head with a club. It stopped bleedin' long time ago. The most about it is that in the mornin' yeh'll feel that a number ten hat wouldn't fit yeh . . .

(Spot up on Mother.)

MOTHER. An' your head'll be all het up an' feel as dry as burnt pork. An' yeh may get a lotta other sicknesses, too, by mornin'. Yeh can't never tell. Still, I don't much think so. It's jest a hit on the head, Son . . . nothin' more . . . Yer always gettin' in some sort of scrap . . . always fightin' . . . Be a good boy, Son, and stop all this fightin' . . . Be a man . . .

(Spot out.)

LIEUTENANT. Now, you jest sit here an' don't move. I'll send Wilson t' take keer a' yeh.

(He exits up the ramp and relieves Wilson.)

BOY. Yeh sure have 'em all fooled.

YOUNG MAN. I thought yeh left . . . preferred that tattered soldier t' me.

BOY. He's dead . . . died soon after I got to him. Yeh don't have to worry 'bout him . . . he won't say nothin' to no one . . . his suspicions died with him.

YOUNG MAN. Where was yeh when I needed yeh? . . . When I got hit.

BOY. Proves yeh can't get along without me.

YOUNG MAN. I don't need anyone but me.

(The Loud Soldier comes forward, carrying a canteen.)

LOUD SOLDIER. Well now, Henry, ol' boy, we'll have yeh fixed up in jest about a minute. *(Sits down and hands him the canteen.)* Here, drink some of this hot coffee. *(Pours water from another canteen into a white scrap of cloth and ties it around the Young Man's head.)*

BOY. They'll really take note of yeh back home now . . . a red badge of courage . . . Wow!

LOUD SOLDIER. Yeh sure are a brave one, Henry . . . Yeh don't holler ner say nothin'. Most men would a' been in the hospital long ago. A shot in the head ain't foolin' business.

(Young Man makes no reply but fidgets with the buttons on his coat.)

TALL SOLDIER. *(Entering.)* I died fer doin' an honest deed . . . Yer makin' a fool a' me, Henry . . . Yer lies are laughin' at me.

TATTERED SOLDIER. *(Entering.)* You ain't foolin' me none . . . I see right through yeh, an' soon enough they all will see through too.

MOTHER. *(Entering.)* I raised yeh better than that, Son . . . I'm ashamed of yeh . . . I'm ashamed to call yeh my own.

YOUNG MAN. *(Frantically pulling on Loud Soldier.)* Tell 'em to go away . . . Tell 'em to leave me alone.

LOUD SOLDIER. Who? . . . What are yeh talkin' about? . . . Ain't no one there . . . jest darkness. That's all that's out there.

YOUNG MAN. They're haunting me . . . the darkness is . . .

LOUD SOLDIER. Calm yerself down now . . . yer jest tired . . . yeh need rest. Good night's sleep'll do yeh jest fine. *(Lays him back on the ground and covers him with a blanket.)* Tomorrow everythin'll be jest like before. *(He rises and exits.)*

MOTHER. Tell the truth, Son.

BOY. Tell 'em yeh was only foolin'.

TALL SOLDIER. Let me die in truth, Henry.

TATTERED SOLDIER. Yer only foolin' yerself, son.

YOUNG MAN. I'll show yeh what courage I got in me . . . you'll see! *(He becomes weaker and weaker but he grasps for strength. Finally he falls back into sleep.)* You'll see! . . . You'll . . . you'll . . . you . . .

(Mother comes to him and kneels.)

MOTHER. Sleep well, my son . . . rest.

BOY. *(Moving in.)* We can start all over again tomorrow.

TALL SOLDIER. Let me rest in peace, Henry.

TATTERED SOLDIER. *You* have another chance . . . Try again in truth, my son.

(The lights fade on them, but remain up on the Boy and his soldiers.)

BOY. One little, two little, three little soldiers . . . four little, five little, six little soldiers . . . seven little, eight little, nine little . . . ten little soldiers . . . dead!

(He furiously topples them all over.)

[Slide: a mound of bodies.]

Dumb toys! . . . Stupid game! . . . Where have all the dragons gone? . . . Castles are for kids . . . Heroes are for storybooks . . . Courage is a word for showoffs! *(Starts to cry.)* I'm afraid of becoming a man!

(The light fades on him. Sound: hollow rumble of drums and a distant bugle sounding faintly.)

[Slide: a new day.]

(The lights fade up slowly. The Young Man rises slowly and yawns.)

YOUNG MAN. Thunder! . . . Mornin' already.

LOUD SOLDIER. *(Crossing to him.)* Well, Henry, ol' man, how do yeh feel this mornin'?

YOUNG MAN. I feel pretty bad.

LOUD SOLDIER. I hoped ye'd feel all right this mornin'. Let's see the bandage . . . I guess it's slipped.

(He begins to fumble rather crudely with it.)

YOUNG MAN. *(Pulling back.)* Gosh-dern it! You're the hangdest man I ever saw! You wear muffs on yer hands? Why in good thunderation can't you be more easy? I'd rather yeh stand off an' throw rocks at it. Now, go slow, an' don't act as if you was nailin' down a carpet.

LOUD SOLDIER. Sorry . . . Come now an' git some grub. Then maybe you'll feel better.

(They move to a fire where a group of Soldiers are pouring coffee.)

BANJO. How yeh be, Henry?

HARMONICA. Welcome back . . . Sorry yeh got shot up.

CHEERY SOLDIER. Try to fight the whole war yerself?

GLUM SOLDIER. Some guys'll do anythin' to get themselves a badge fer courage. *(Laughs.)*

SINGING SOLDIER. Prob'ly jist fell an' hit his head on a rock while he was runnin'. *(Laughs. Tattered Soldier enters.)*

TATTERED SOLDIER. They see right through yeh, son.

YOUNG MAN. *(Turning sharply to him.)* You . . . You're dead! . . . You're dead . . . What do you know?

TATTERED SOLDIER. I'm dead . . . What do *you* know?

BANJO. *(Confused.)* Who yeh talkin' to, Henry? . . . Got yerself a dead ghost?

(They all laugh.)

YOUNG MAN. *(To them quickly.)* Jim Conklin's dead!

LOUD SOLDIER. What? . . . Is he? . . . Jim Conklin?

YOUNG MAN. Yes. He's dead. Shot in the head.

CHEERY SOLDIER. Yeh don't say so. Jim Conklin . . . poor cuss!

GLUM SOLDIER. One more gone . . .

TALL SOLDIER. *(Entering.)* Don't let 'em chalk me off as jest another number . . .

BOY. *(Counting Soldiers around the fire.)* One little, two little, three little soldiers . . . four little, five little, six little . . .

YOUNG MAN. *(Quickly.)* He died real brave like . . . with courage!

HARMONICA. Courage ain't no good to a dead man.

LOUD SOLDIER. Gonna be hard to fergit ol' Jim.

YOUNG MAN. He was a hero! . . . With courage . . . He had no fears at all.

HARMONICA. Them's the kind always gettin' themselves killed . . . It's the cowards who live on to tell 'bout it. *(Laughs.)*

YOUNG MAN. *(Mad.)* It ain't so! . . . I ain't no coward! You take that back or I'll kill yeh! . . . I ain't no coward! I got shot. Ain't that proof 'nuf fer yeh?

LOUD SOLDIER. *(Quieting him down.)* Whoa there, Henry . . .

SINGING SOLDIER. Awf'lly touchy, ain't yeh, Henry?

BANJO. Can't yeh take a little ribbin'?

LOUD SOLDIER. Ain't no one callin' yeh a coward . . . Cheer up . . . Have some hard crackers . . . That'll take yer mind off from things.

CHEERY SOLDIER. Take yer appetite away too.

BANJO. Hard crackers an' coffee . . . 'nough to make yeh crave goober peas an' mush.

GLUM SOLDIER. They say an army travels on its stomach.

SINGING SOLDIER. Well, my innards have taken a mighty punishment.

HARMONICA. My stomach lost the battle months ago. *(Hands cracker to Young Man.)* Have yourself a jaw breaker, Henry . . . Keep yer jaws busy on somethin' else fer a spell.

(Banjo plunks several strings. Harmonica joins in.)

SOLDIERS. *(Sung.)*
> Let us close our talk of cowards.
> Take our tin cups in hand.
> While we gather round the cook tent's door
> Where dried bundles of hard crackers are given to each man.
> Oh, hard crackers come again no more.
>
> 'Tis the song and the sigh of the hungry
> Hard crackers, hard crackers
> Come again no more.
> Many days have you lingered upon
> Our stomachs sore . . .
> Oh hard crackers, come again no more.

(They all laugh as they move away.)

LOUD SOLDIER. Well, Henry . . . What d'yeh think the chances are? Do yeh think we'll wallop 'em?

YOUNG MAN. Day b'fore yesterday you would've bet you'd lick the hull kit-an'-boodle all by yourself.

LOUD SOLDIER. Would I? . . . Well, perhaps I would. *(Stares into fire.)*

YOUNG MAN. Oh, no you wouldn't either.

LOUD SOLDIER. Oh, yeh needn't mind, Henry . . . I believe I was a pretty big fool in those days . . . All the officers say we've got 'em in a pretty tight box. *(Clears his throat.)* They all seem t' think we've got 'em just where we want 'em.

YOUNG MAN. I don't know about that . . . What I seen over on the right makes me think it was the other way about. From where I was, it looked as if we was gettin' a good poundin' yesterday.

LOUD SOLDIER. D' yeh think so? . . . I thought we handled 'em pretty rough yesterday.

YOUNG MAN. Not a bit . . . Why, Lord, man, you didn't see nothin' of the fight like I did.

LOUD SOLDIER. Fleming.

YOUNG MAN. What?

LOUD SOLDIER. *(Putting his hand to his mouth, coughing and beginning to fidget.)* Well, I guess yeh might as well give me back that envelope.

YOUNG MAN. All right, Wilson . . . *(Producing it from his jacket and handing it to him.)*

LOUD SOLDIER. *(Embarrassed.)* Thanks, Henry, fer carryin' it fer me . . . Guess I can handle it myself now. *(Walks away.)*

YOUNG MAN. *(To himself.)* Too bad! Too bad! The poor devil, it makes him feel tough.

BOY. How do *you* feel?

YOUNG MAN. A mite stronger than yesterday . . . Poor ol' Wilson seems a bit jealous a' my courage.

BOY. Yeh mean yer beginnin' tuh believe it yerself?

YOUNG MAN. How do you know? You weren't there! . . .

BOY. What's happenin' to yeh? . . . I don't know yeh at all any more. Yeh can't go on livin' a lie . . . Admit it . . . at least to yerself.

YOUNG MAN. The whole regiment knows who I am fer the first time . . . They know me by name. Before, I was jest one of the hundreds of thousands . . . but now I'm somebody . . . I can't . . . I can't admit it! I feel part of this whole thing fer the first time . . . Don't take that away from me.

BOY. You're cheating . . . it ain't fair.

YOUNG MAN. Nothin' about this war is fair . . . Look at ol' Jim Conklin. What was fair 'bout him dyin'?

BOY. He died honestly . . . he *lost* fairly . . . if yeh can't be truthful to yerself, be truthful fer Jim.

YOUNG MAN. I can't! . . . I can't! . . . He's gone. I'm still here . . . I've gotta think of me now.

BOY. You'll never win, yeh know . . . Someone somewhere'll see right through yeh . . . jest like that tattered soldier.

YOUNG MAN. He's dead! . . . Yeh jest want tuh take my courage away . . . It was you who made me run.

BOY. Yeh can't go on blamin' me for yer mistakes forever.

YOUNG MAN. No! Yer trickin' me . . . tryin' tuh get me to confess.

BOY. Yer trickin' yerself . . . I'm goin'. *(Starts to pick up toy soldiers.)*

YOUNG MAN. You can't . . . you can't go till I tell you to.

BOY. I'm ashamed I was ever a part of you. *(Pleads.)* Why don't yeh become a man an' let me go away feelin' proud? . . .

YOUNG MAN. I don't know what yer talkin' about . . . Yer jest a crazy kid with a sackful of toys playin' a war game. It ain't real! . . . This! . . . This is real! They don't topple over . . . They die!

BOY. An' lie?

YOUNG MAN. So do those storybooks yeh read . . . It ain't like that here . . . There are no knights an' shiny white horses . . . Here there ain't none of that . . . They lied too.

BOY. They were fer me tuh read an' believe in . . . not you.

YOUNG MAN. Go then . . . I'll do jest fine without yeh. You'll see things my way some day.

(The light fades on the Boy and the Young Man talks to the darkness.)

This ain't a storybook war . . . This is real! When are yeh goin' to realize it? . . . Yeh dumb, stupid, idiot kid!

(Loud Soldier walks up to him.)

LOUD SOLDIER. What's the matter, Henry? . . . Talkin' to yerself is supposed to be some sign of guilt, yeh know.

YOUNG MAN. Jest had tuh get rid a' somethin' on my chest, that's all.

LOUD SOLDIER. Well, is it gone?

YOUNG MAN. Disappeared . . . Don't know if it's gone, though.

LOUD SOLDIER. Wanta tell me about it? . . . I'm still yer friend, ain't I?

YOUNG MAN. I'll be fine . . . Thanks though, Wilson.

LOUD SOLDIER. Well, if yeh change yer mind yeh know where tuh find me . . . How's yer head?

YOUNG MAN. Fine . . .

LOUD SOLDIER. Good. *(He exits.)*

YOUNG MAN. *(To where Boy was.)* That dumb little kid's changed roles on me . . . He's suddenly made me into the boy an' he's walked away the man.

(Mother walks into the Boy's light.)

MOTHER. Yer such a bad boy, Henry.

YOUNG MAN. Ma . . . Ma, yer goin' to be real proud of me, Ma . . . Look, I got shot . . . a badge of courage.

MOTHER. Courage ain't somethin' yeh wear like a badge, Son. Courage is somethin' only you can see . . . It's worn inside, outta sight.

YOUNG MAN. But I . . .

MOTHER. What do yeh have tuh prove, Son . . . except to yerself?

YOUNG MAN. I want *you* tuh be proud.

MOTHER. I always was, Son . . . Yeh don't need tuh win a badge fer me . . . Yeh don't need tuh lie fer me.

YOUNG MAN. He told you, didn't he? . . . That little . . .

MOTHER. This war yer fightin's in yerself, Son . . . You can win over it . . . with truth!

(The light fades on her.)

YOUNG MAN. I want to belong . . . to be part. Try an' understand, Ma, it's the only way.

(Light up on Decayed Soldier.)

No, I don't want to die! . . . Don't hang around waitin' fer me . . . You ain't gettin' me like yeh got Jim . . . Ain't yeh got enough by now? . . . What do yeh hang around lurkin' at me for?! Take those yeh already got and go away! *(He turns and begins to run toward the right ramp.)* I can run faster than you . . . I'll manage to stay a step or two ahead!

(The light fades on the Decayed Soldier. Sound: cannons and guns. Lights flash and flicker. The Soldiers rush to their spots.)

LOUD SOLDIER. Take cover, Henry . . . Protect yerself!

YOUNG MAN. What's happening? . . .

TRUMPET. Yer in a war, boy . . . Show yer courage!

YOUNG MAN. *(Dazed.)* Show my courage. . . . Show my . . . *(Shouts.)* It's here! . . . See! . . . See my red badge of courage.

FRIENDLY SOLDIER. Prove it!

YOUNG MAN. I have proof . . . See it . . . See the bandage.

HARMONICA. Live up to it then! *(Throws him a rifle.)* Here, put yer courage into action.

YOUNG MAN. Yes! . . . Yes, I'll prove it to you all . . . I'll show you.

(Spot up on Mother.)

MOTHER. Show yerself, Son.

(Spot up on Boy.)

BOY. Let me walk away proud.

LIEUTENANT. I was willin' t' bet they'd attack as soon as the sun got fairly up.

YOUNG MAN. *(Showing off.)* Good Gawd! We're always bein' chased around like rats! It makes me sick. Nobody seems to know where we go or why we go. We jest get fired around from pillar to post an' get licked there, an' nobody knows what it's done fer. It makes a man feel like a durn kitten in a bag . . .

LOUD SOLDIER. It'll turn out all right in th' end.

YOUNG MAN. Oh, the devil it will! You always talk like a dog-hanged parson. Don't tell me! I know . . .

LIEUTENANT. You boys shut up! . . . You've been jawin' like a lotta old hens. All you've got to do is fight. Less talkin' an' more fightin' is what's best for you boys. I never saw sech gabblin' jackasses.

(Sound: battle roar settling into a single long explosion.)

[Slides: Civil War battle photos interspersed throughout the following scene.]

(The Young Man cowers behind a post, as do the other Soldiers stationed about the unit. A spot comes up on the Boy.)

BOY. Why are you drawing me back? . . . I left . . . Let me stay gone.

YOUNG MAN. I can't do it alone . . . I'm still afraid.

BOY. You're going to ruin everything . . . everything. Think for yourself. You don't need a boy to talk to any more . . . Talk it out with the man.

YOUNG MAN. *(As he speaks the Decayed Soldier appears behind the Boy. The Boy smiles up at him and takes his hand. The Boy's spot slowly dims.)* I don't know what to do. I can't let them see I lied . . . They're all watching to see . . . Their eyes are all glued to me, digging into me to find the truth.

BOY. Don't let them see it . . . Don't let them see me . . . Do something!

YOUNG MAN. *(Looking out, searching for the Boy.)* What? Tell me what!

BOY. Quickly . . . This is your moment of truth. Tell yourself, Henry.

YOUNG MAN. *(As he speaks his voice fades into a recording. The recording, played over the sound system, becomes his new-found self. No longer is the Boy his conscience. He has become a man.)* My moment of truth . . . my moment of proof. *(He begins to rise unconsciously.)* What's happening? . . . I'm being pulled up . . . A giant hand is lifting me like a toy soldier. I have no control. The hand is moving me. *(He starts to move down the ramp without control. He stumbles and falls.)* I've been shot! In the arm? . . . In the head? . . . Where? *(He rises.)* Where are you, death? *(He searches for the Decayed Soldier.)* He's gone . . . I'm still here . . . I managed to slip through his boney fingers. *(He rushes down the ramp and takes refuge beside it.)* You won't get me like yeh got Jim . . . All right, yeh stinkin' devils, yeh ain't gonna take me! I'll fight yeh till my arms fall off . . . *(He continually pumps cartridges into his rifle.)* I'll show yeh I ain't no coward . . . I'll get eight of you for every Jim of ours yeh took . . . *(He becomes a mad man.)* Run! . . . Run back, yeh dragons of death. . . . *(He moves out, standing in the open.)* Look at 'em! . . . What's the matter, are yeh afraid? . . . Run! . . . Run! . . . Run, ya stinkin' fools!

(Everyone has stopped firing but him. They stare at him in amazement.)

TRUMPET. *(Laughing.)* Yeh infernal fool, don't yeh know enough t' quit when there ain't anythin' t' shoot at? Good Gawd!

(The Young Man turns, the only one out front. They are all staring at him. He turns front again, seeing a deserted ground.)

YOUNG MAN. Oh.

(He returns to the group and sits.)

LIEUTENANT. By Gawd, if I had ten thousand wildcats like you, I could tear the stomach outta this war in less'n a week!

LOUD SOLDIER. *(Crossing to Young Man.)* Are yeh all right, Fleming? Do yeh feel all right? There ain't nothin' the matter with yeh, Henry, is there?

YOUNG MAN. No.

BANJO. By thunder, I bet this Army'll never see another reg'ment like us!

FLUTE. You bet!

HARMONICA. A dog, a woman, an' a walnut tree. The more yeh beat 'em, the better they be!

SCARED SOLDIER. That's like us.

WOUNDED SOLDIER. Lost a pile of men, they did. If an ol' woman swept up the woods, she'd get a dustpanful.

GLUM SOLDIER. Yes, an' if she'll come aroun' ag'in in 'bout an hour she'll git a pile more.

(Sound: rolling clatter of musketry.)

YOUNG MAN. *(Recorded.)* Yer wantin' more, are yeh? . . . Well, come on, quit hidin' like a bunch of scared boys . . . Show yerself! . . . Fight like men. Let us have it! . . . We'll give it back to yeh ten times better.

(The stage brightens suddenly in vibrant red. A Soldier falls. Others shield their eyes.)

Good Gawd, it's suddenly turned into the fires of hell!

(The men seem paralyzed. They lower their guns and stare bewilderedly at the sight.)

What's wrong with 'em? . . . They're frozen . . . Come on, raise those rifles and let 'em have it . . . Yeh durn fools, yer actin' like a bunch of rundown toy soldiers . . . Wind yerselves up or they'll charge in and trample yeh into the ground.

YOUNG MAN. *(Live.)* Come on, yeh fools! . . . Come on! Yeh can't jest set there like a bunch of wooden men. Come on!

(They stare blankly at him. The Loud Soldier rushes down, raises his rifle and shoots. The shot seems to awaken them and they come alive.)

YOUNG MAN. *(Recorded.)* Good goin', Wilson . . . Fire death right back in their faces . . .

(The color bearer rises to the top level.)

Raise that flag high. Show 'em what we're fightin' for . . . the reason we're here riskin' our lives. *(Quietly, as if suddenly realizing.)* The reason . . . the flag . . . of course that's what this is all about . . . the purpose. A flowing flag of truth and honesty. A badge of courage.

(The color bearer is hit and falls to his knees.)

It's been hit! . . . It's falling!

YOUNG MAN. *(Live.)* The flag! . . . Someone grab the flag. It's been hit!

(They ignore his cry.)

YOUNG MAN. *(Recorded.)* It's falling like Jim Conklin into a coward's grave . . . For Gawd's sake, someone save it! *(He starts up the ramp to the flag.)* That flag is the real meaning of all this fighting nonsense . . . Don't let it fall into a lie. *(He reaches the flag and pries it from the dying Soldier. He holds it as if it were made of precious china.)* Here, here is the real badge of my courage. *(Suddenly he rises and waves it frantically over the men.)*

YOUNG MAN. *(Live.)* Look! . . . Look, all of you . . . Here is what we're here for . . . This is what we're fightin' for . . . Ripped and shredded it still holds together . . . Fight like the flag, men . . . Fight for the right of the flag!

YOUNG MAN. *(Recorded.)* They see it . . . seems to be callin' to them like it called to me . . . Look at those bullets fly . . . Wahoo! Show 'em, men . . . Show 'em what this war is all about . . . Looky there, they're runnin' . . . They're runnin' like hell . . . We won 'em . . . We won 'em!

LOUD SOLDIER. *(Rushing to the Young Man.)* I can't believe it . . . We did it . . . We did it! We fought like thunder! Yeh jest oughtta heard.

YOUNG MAN. Heard what?

LOUD SOLDIER. The Colonel . . . The Colonel, he says to Simpson, he says, "Who was that lad that grabbed the flag?" Yeh hear that, Henry? . . . An' Simpson, he says, "Why, that was Fleming, Sir, he's a real courageous lad." "He's a good un," says the Colonel, "a real brave lad he is." Put that in a letter an' send it home to yer mother, Henry.

YOUNG MAN. Yer lyin', Wilson.

LOUD SOLDIER. No, I swear to yeh, Henry . . . it's the truth . . . Yer a hero!

YOUNG MAN. Yeh mean, with all those men fightin' out there, they saw me?

LOUD SOLDIER. Sure 'nough did . . . Sure made me feel proud I knew yeh.

YOUNG MAN. *(Shouting out.)* Yeh hear that, Boy . . . Yeh hear what Wilson's sayin' 'bout me?

LOUD SOLDIER. Who yeh yellin' at?

YOUNG MAN. A boy I knew before I became a man.

LOUD SOLDIER. Well, yeh sure took hold a' that flag like a man. Heard 'em talkin' about us joinin' up with the 265th. They're needin' help bad.

YOUNG MAN. So soon? . . . Ain't we goin' to get a rest?

LOUD SOLDIER. Movin' out right away . . . Heroes don't rest. Don't yeh read yer storybooks? *(He laughs.)* Can I walk beside yeh, Henry?

YOUNG MAN. Yeh mean it?

LOUD SOLDIER. Sure, we're ol' school buddies, ain't we?

YOUNG MAN. Sure.

LOUD SOLDIER. Meet yeh on the road. *(He runs off.)*

YOUNG MAN. Did yeh hear that, all of yeh? I ain't no coward . . . I've erased my lie . . . I'm a man . . . Yer all outta me now, back where yeh belong . . .

(The spot fades up on the body of the Tall Soldier where he died.)

Yeh can rest in peace now, Jim. . . .

(Spot up on body of Tattered Soldier.)

Yeh were right, ol' timer . . . I don't need to run no more.

(Spot up on body of Decayed Soldier.)

Your secret's safe with me, dead man . . . You've got others to keep you company now . . . Share your deaths with each other.

(Spot up on Boy lying dead, a blood spot on his head. The sack of toy soldiers is spread about the ground around him.)

You! . . . No! . . . Not you . . . I didn't mean for you to die. *(He runs to him.)* I just wanted you to leave. *(Holds body in his arms.)* You didn't have to die to make me a man . . . Or did you?

(The musicians begin to play "When Johnny Comes Marching Home.")

Do yeh hear the drums and bugles? . . . *(Brushes dirt from the Boy's uniform.)* Yer new blue coat's gotten dirty . . . What's Ma gonna say? *(Holds him tightly.)* I'll miss yeh. The castle will be lonely without yeh.

(Loud Soldier rushes in.)

LOUD SOLDIER. Come on, Henry, it's time to move on.

YOUNG MAN. Comin'.

LOUD SOLDIER. Another dead one? . . . Did yeh know him?

YOUNG MAN. Used to play war with him when I was a kid.

LOUD SOLDIER. Come on! . . . We've got a real war to win now.

(They join the others as the Soldiers in dim light begin to sing and march up the right ramp, down the left and off slowly. The spots remain up on the bodies.)

SOLDIERS. *(Sung.)*
When Johnny comes marchin' home again,
Hurrah! Hurrah!
We'll give him a hearty welcome then,
Hurrah! Hurrah!
The men will cheer, the boys will shout,
The ladies they will all turn out,
And we'll all feel gay
When Johnny comes marching home.

Get ready for the jubilee,
Hurrah! Hurrah!
We'll give the hero three times three,

Hurrah! Hurrah!
The laurel wreath is ready now
To place upon his loyal brow
And we'll all feel gay
When Johnny comes marching home.

(As they march off, the spots on the bodies fade slowly and die as the song fades to silence.)

(Curtain.)

The Odyssey

By Homer

Dramatized by Gregory A. Falls and Kurt Beattie

Copyright, 1978, Anchorage Press, Inc.

The Odyssey (1978)

The Odyssey is Gregory A. Falls' and Kurt Beattie's adaptation of Homer's epic poem. Like many of the plays in this anthology, it is an ensemble piece that combines narration, song, sound effects, pantomime, and masks to create the continuous action of the play.

The Odyssey is a play of high adventure and courage that traces Odysseus' efforts to return home with his band of men following their victory over Troy. We see the adventures through a series of flashbacks, which are narrated in part by a mysterious Old Man who has arrived at the home of Odysseus' wife, Penelope. These flashbacks include Odysseus' confrontations with Cyclops, Circe, and the Sirens. Intermingled within the plot, the theme of survival of honor, on both a personal and national level, is woven.

CHARACTERS

(Doubling pattern in order of speaking)

Actress 1: Pallas Athena, Old Man, Aeolous' Attendant, Circe, Siren, Apollo

Actor 1:   Ktessipos, Peremides, Teiresias

Actor 2:   Eurymachus, Perites, Poseidon, Aeolous' Attendant, Hylax, Dead Soul

Actor 3:   Leodes, Perites, Hermes, Old Man, Dead Soul

Actress 2: Penelope, Old Man, Circes' Attendant, Anticlea, Siren

Actor 4:   Antinous, Eurylochus, Dead Soul

Actor 5:   Telemachus, Cyclops, King Aeolous, Dead Soul, Zeus

Actor 6:   Odysseus, Old Man

SETTING
Ancient Greece.

TIME
Long ago.

The Odyssey

OPENING

A loud steady bass drum beat begins with a parade of the god masks. The Hermes, Poseidon, Zeus, Apollo, and Athena masks come down across the stage and exit behind it. The last, Athena, is introduced with music; one actor supports her mask behind her, then hangs it on the back wall. After each god appears in the play, his mask, too, is hung on the back wall, where they watch the proceedings.

PALLAS ATHENA.
    I, Pallas Athena, speak of Odysseus
    Whom the whole world knows
    Because of his famous journey.

    (Each character enters as introduced* by Athena, forming a tableau.)

    I tell the story of resplendent Penelope,*   *(Tinkle.)*
    And of the many young suitors*   *(Clacker.)*
    Who demand that she marry.

    I tell the story of wandering Odysseus*   *(Three wood bells.)*
    Whom father Zeus calls the cleverest man alive.

    Ten years of war against the mighty Trojans
    Nine years of wandering and captivity
    Even to the point of despair
    Until I, Pallas Athena, lead him home.
    Home to Ithaca, to his wife Penelope,
    to his son Telemachus*   *(Wood bells.)*
    to wreak vengeance on the spoilers.   *(Wood bells.)*

    (Exit Odysseus.)

    Even now, I go there myself, disguised
    As an old poet, singing my songs and begging food,
    While Odysseus struggles in vain
    to sail back to his home.

    (Exit Pallas Athena.)

    (Laughter as The Tableau activates.)

KTESSIPOS. More wine! I die of thirst. Would you like some wine, Eurymachus?

EURYMACHUS. You die of drink, not thirst, Ktessipos.

KTESSIPOS. I die of waiting for the lady to make up her mind which of us she will marry.

LEODES. Fair Penelope, we know this weaving is only a trick to put us off.

PENELOPE. Young princes, I tell you again, I cannot think of marriage until I have finished this winding sheet for my husband's father. He is very old and near death.

EURYMACHUS. You do not fool us anymore. We have discovered that while you weave cloth by day, you unravel it by night.

ALL. Yes!

ANTINOUS. It is only a way to avoid choosing one of us to be your husband.

PENELOPE. I see.

ALL. Choose!

(The Suitors all press around Penelope at the loom when Old Man enters, masked.)

OLD MAN. Peace! To all travellers in this land.

PENELOPE. Telemachus, take this cup and give it to the stranger who now enters our door. Tell him not to be shy, for he may freely beg from these suitors.

TELEMACHUS. Old stranger.

OLD MAN. May Lord Zeus make you a happy man.

TELEMACHUS. You are welcome here. My mother makes you this gift: go round and beg at your pleasure.

ANTINOUS. Penelope, may I ask why you let this old beggar in to pester us?

PENELOPE. Zeus forbid that we should not welcome a stranger to our house.

KTESSIPOS. He stinks so he will ruin my exquisite sense of taste!

ANTINOUS. Telemachus, don't you already have enough guests eating up your father's wealth?

TELEMACHUS. I appreciate your fatherly concern, Antinous, but he is welcome here. Give him something yourself.

OLD MAN. A small coin, sir; you look to be a king and can afford a generous gift. There was a time when I, too, was lucky, and rich, lived in a house, had many servants and went. . . .

ANTINOUS. What god has inflicted this talking plague upon us, to spoil our dinner. Stand off, you leech!

(Antinous kicks him away.)

OLD MAN. Ah . . . I was wrong about you. You eat freely from another man's table and yet you will not give even a crust to a beggar!

EURYMACHUS. Watch your tongue, old man, and get out of here. Next time I will drag you out of here by the leg. Ha!

(Eurymachus grabs the Old Man's arm and flings him out.)

TELEMACHUS. Gentlemen! This is not a public inn, but Odysseus' palace. Though I am young, I know right from wrong. . . . You are many and strong, and so I must . . . but if. . . .

(Suitors threaten Telemachus.)

KTESSIPOS. My friends, my friends! Let us not bully Telemachus. I feel that he speaks prudent . . . prudent . . . hic . . . URRRRP!

(Suitors laugh.)

LEODES. Then I shall speak prudently, and to fairest Penelope.

PENELOPE. Speak, Leodes, I shall listen.

LEODES. As long as there was any hope that your husband would return, none of us could blame you for waiting.

EURYMACHUS. Daughter of Icarus, the time for waiting is over. Odysseus is gone forever. All the men in Argos will fill this house, for in beauty there is no one to match you.

PENELOPE. Alas, all beauty that I had was destroyed when Odysseus embarked for Troy. Now I am alone and my house cursed with strangers.

ANTINOUS. Madam, your husband has been gone for nineteen years. Some wave has washed him into the sea. He is either dead or lost forever. Therefore, you must pick the best, most generous of your suitors, marry him and go live in his house. Then Telemachus can enjoy his natural inheritance.

KTESSIPOS. It is the custom, fair Penelope.

PENELOPE. The custom? None of you observe the custom! Surely it is the oldest of customs for suitors to entertain the lady, bring her gifts, not carouse at her expense.

ANTINOUS. You speak true. That is our custom, but we shall not leave your palace until you agree to choose a husband.

SUITORS. Aye . . . Aye . . . We shall not . . . etc.

PENELOPE. I see. Very well, you have driven me to this moment. Antinous, we must both observe the custom. If all the suitors will bring their traditional matrimonial gifts to the palace, I shall select one to be my husband. Will you accept my choice?

ANTINOUS. I will! Do you all agree with the lady?

SUITORS. We do! Come . . . a fine proposal . . . etc.

(Suitors exit, Antinous last, bowing graciously to Penelope and nodding to Telemachus.)

PENELOPE. If I had my way, there's not a man among them who would see tomorrow's dawn.

TELEMACHUS. I hate them all . . . especially Antinous, who is the most treacherous.

PENELOPE. May Apollo strike him, even as he did that old man. Go, my good son, ask the old man to come here that I may greet him and ask if he has any news of Odysseus.

(Telemachus exits.)

Unless my husband returns soon and purges our house of these terrible men, I must bid farewell to it forever, although in my dreams I shall never forget it.

(Telemachus enters with Old Man.)

TELEMACHUS. And so, if you speak the truth she will give you a warm cloak to protect you from the cold.

OLD MAN. Royal Madam.

PENELOPE. Peace, old man! Where is your home? Have you any news of Odysseus?

OLD MAN. I have, fair Queen.

I am from the land in the dark blue sea called Crete, a mighty island. My grandfather, King Minos, once reigned there, and long ago, nine years ago, Odysseus himself touched our shores. It happened thus.

(Seven notes sound as Penelope and Telemachus exit. Odysseus and his men push the prow on stage, set the mast, kneel with their oars in a ready position, Odysseus at the helm.)

After the burning of Troy, all the finest Greeks set sail for their homes, carrying their rich booty. All reached their homes safely, except Odysseus. A mighty gale blew his ship off its course to my island Crete.

I took him to my home and made him welcome for thirteen days, until the winds fell and he bade us thanks and farewell.

(Odysseus waves good-bye to the Old Man, a bass drum beat begins, and the men start to row.)

And so he left my country, his sailors raising their sails and pulling their oars. I have heard that he sailed into unknown seas, even to the land of the giant Cyclops.

(Old Man exits. Rowing stops, the ship lands and Odysseus leaps to the shore.)

ODYSSEUS. Good sailors, we must go onto this shore. Make fast the ship. *(Ship prow and mast are pushed aside.)* Well, we shall soon see whether these Cyclops are lawless savages, or a god-fearing people who are bound by Zeus' laws.

(The sailors are Eurylochus, Peremides, Perites, and Polites, who later becomes Hylax. They step ashore and begin exploring the island, accompanied by jungle sounds.)

EURYLOCHUS. Although I am no coward, I have a foreboding about this place.

PEREMIDES. Watch carefully then. Be ready.

PERITES. Look!

EURYLOCHUS. Where?

PERITES. Here, a cave. And look at the size of the opening.

PEREMIDES. Why, it's large enough for a giant.

POLITES. He's a shepherd. Look at all these lamb and goat pens.

ODYSSEUS. Come, let's go in the cave and see. *(They mime entering and exploring the cave.)*

POLITES. Oh, look, cheese! Goat cheese!

PERITES. Polites, I have never seen a wedge of cheese as large as this.
(Sheep bells.)

PEREMIDES. What's that?   *(Sheep sounds.)*

ODYSSEUS. Quiet. The shepherd is coming back. He may be friendly
but we'd better be careful. Let's hide.

*(While the men hide, the Cyclops enters, herding his sheep
into the cave and rolling a big stone across the opening. We
created a large Cyclops head with one eye that could be
pushed in out of sight. The head was attached to an ankle-
length tunic and strapped to the actor who looked through the
mouth. The arms were extended with sticks and gloves. Because he must be able to move freely, we opted not to elevate
him on stilts; his height did not seem to worry the children.)*

CYCLOPS. In goats . . . in rams, in sheep for the night . . . there in,
sheep. Now I roll the big stone in front of the mouth of the
cave so you can sleep safely until the morning. There . . . over
there, big ram, sheep. Wait! Who else is here? Strangers? And
who may you be?

ODYSSEUS. We are Greeks. A contrary wind has driven us to your
island.

CYCLOPS. Are you not roving pirates come to rob me of my sheep?

ODYSSEUS. No. we are Greek soldiers returning home from our great
victory over Troy. We hope for hospitality from you, remembering Zeus' great edict binding all to give hospitality to travellers.

CYCLOPS. Ha, ha, ha! Strangers, you are either fools, or have come
very far afield. We Cyclops care not a jot for Zeus' law nor any
of the gods. But, tell me where you have moored your ships.

EURYLOCHUS. *(Whispering.)* Captain, he is trying to trick us.

ODYSSEUS. Softly . . . I know. Cyclops—

CYCLOPS. My name is Polyphemus.

ODYSSEUS. Polyphemus, our ship is wrecked upon your shore. We
desperately need food.

CYCLOPS. So do I! I am hungry too, so I think I shall eat you, pirate
sailor!

PEREMIDES. Look out! He's got Polites!

ODYSSEUS and EURYLOCHUS. Help us!

(Polyphemus reaches out and grabs one of the sailors by the neck, who is rescued only when several sailors combine to pull him from the strong Cyclops. This leads to a chase accompanied by drums, clackers, and other noises. We used tumbling rolls and flips by the men trying to avoid the slower Cyclops. Eventually the Cyclops catches Polites. The sailors rush the Cyclops. During the struggle, Polites puts his cloth cowl partially in the Cyclops' mouth. With a mighty movement the Cyclops throws the sailors to the side of the stage. The actor playing Polites goes with them and exits unnoticed. The Cyclops puts his hand to mouth as he goes upstage to sit and eat Polites.)

EURYLOCHUS. He's eating him! He is eating him! We must kill him before he eats us all.

PERITES. I'll stab him with my sword.

EURYLOCHUS. No, wait. Let's all rush him together. Ready? Now.

ODYSSEUS. Hold, hold fast. If we kill him now, we may be trapped inside this cave forever. That is a heavy stone across the door. Eurylochus, men, come help me try to move it. *(They mime trying to move the great stone, even using an oar as a lever, but they cannot budge it.)*

EURYLOCHUS. It's no use. We can't move it, and he is not likely to move it for us. I would rather die killing this monster than be eaten.

ODYSSEUS. Maybe he would do it for us! I have a plan. Give me that wineskin.

(Odysseus takes wineskin and goes to the Cyclops.)

Cyclops! Polyphemus, here, have some Greek wine to wash down your meal of human flesh. Come, take it in your hands. It will be the finest wine you ever tasted.

(He places the wineskin between the two hands of the Cyclops, who drinks the wine.)

CYCLOPS. Hmmm. Ahh. This wine is delicious. A pleasure to drink. . . . Tell me your name, sailor, and I will reward you for giving me this good wine, it tastes like nectar and ambrosia. What is your name?

ODYSSEUS. My name is "Nobody."

CYCLOPS. *(Little tipsy now.)* Whatsch that?

ODYSSEUS. "Nobody." That is the name my father gave me: "Nobody."

CYCLOPS. *(Yawning now.)* Ahhhhh . . . Well, then, Nobody, your reward shall be this: I shall eat you last. Ahhhh . . . Eat all the others first. I am getting schleeepy from this good wine . . . so very schleepy. . . .

(Now drunk, the Cyclops sits down and sleeps as his eye closes.)

ODYSSEUS. Success. The wine's made him sleepy. Peremides, take that staff. Perites, sharpen it with your sword. Now put it in that fire to harden it. Good, now lift it up and aim it for his eye. Now drive it home. Take that, you cannibal!

(The sailors mime the action described by Odysseus, using an oar for the staff, a red cloth for the fire. Then they take the staff and start toward the sleeping Cyclops. He almost wakes but then mumbles and lays his head on his other hand. The sailors guide the staff to the eye and, with a big push, force the eye into the mask, leaving only the eye hole showing. They scramble to one side as the Cyclops roars and stands up.)

CYCLOPS. Help, neighbors! Cyclops, neighbor Cyclops! I am being attacked!

VOICES. *(Off stage.)* Who is attacking you, Polyphemus?

CYCLOPS. Nobody!

VOICES. If nobody is attacking you, you must be dreaming. Leave us alone. We must drive our sheep out to pasture. It is morning already.   *(Sheep noises and bells.)*

CYCLOPS. Oh . . . Oh . . . it is morning already. I must let my sheep out to graze. I must roll away this big stone. Out, sheep!

(The Cyclops rolls the stone aside and Odysseus' men try to sneak out, but the Cyclops blocks the entrance with his hands, and mimes feeling the backs of his sheep as they pass through the opening. Enter the Old Man.)

But I must not let those men escape.

OLD MAN. And he passed his hand over the back of each sheep as it went through, to make sure that none of Odysseus' men escaped. But, clever Odysseus tied his men to the bellies of the largest sheep, and he himself clung to the belly of the largest ram.

(Odysseus puts a sheepskin on the back of each of his men, who crawl past the Cyclops as he feels the wool on their backs. Odysseus is the last to start crawling out, but the Cyclops stops him.)

CYCLOPS. Ho! Big Ram, why are you last? You who never lagged before, are you grieved for your master's eye, blinded by these wicked men?

(The Cyclops lets Odysseus through. Meanwhile the men have reassembled the ship so that when Odysseus escapes, they are ready to sail away.)

ODYSSEUS. Cyclops!

CYCLOPS. They have escaped.

ODYSSEUS. We men are not as weak as you thought. For your great crime of eating your guests, Zeus has punished you! If anyone should ask, tell them Odysseus of Ithaca put out your eye.

OLD MAN. So angry was the Cyclops that he seized a mountain top and hurled it at Odysseus' ship.

PEREMIDES. Look out!

OLD MAN. It fell right in front of the ship and almost drove it back to shore.

(The Cyclops mimes throwing a huge stone that goes over the top of the boat, lands just ahead, almost swamping it.) (Whistle, drum, cymbals.)

CYCLOPS. Father Poseidon, Father Poseidon, if I am your son, grant that Odysseus never reach his home in Ithaca.

POSEIDON. *(Entering.)* I hear your prayer, my son. I will never let this impudent Odysseus go unpunished. Rise, Great Sea, buffet them about: Rock them side to side. They shall not escape my vengeance.   *(Storm noises.)*

(A storm rises and rocks the ship mightily as Poseidon and the Cyclops exit.)

OLD MAN. And the seas raged, Poseidon's mighty waves tossed Odysseus' ship to and fro, almost drowning the sailors. At last the sea began to calm and Odysseus cried out,

ODYSSEUS. Landfall! At last some relief from these angry seas.
(Storm noises fade.)

(He leaps ashore and finds it spongy, like walking on rubber.)

What's this? This island is floating on the water! Now I know
where we are. This is the floating island of King Aeolous who
is the keeper of all the winds. These wild winds have blown us
here to their master. And he can tame them.

(King Aeolous and two Attendants enter to an airy tune
played on a recorder. He is masked and the Attendants each
carry a flag made of many colored ribbons which flutter in the
wind when they are moved.)

KING AEOLOUS. La, la, la, la. Clever Odysseus, your black-prowed
ship survived Poseidon's rough sea. You are welcome here with
me and my children. Come, tell us of your adventures. We long
to hear them.

OLD MAN. And Odysseus stayed with his kind host for a month,
and he told him of the Greeks' great victory over the walled
city of Troy, and all things else that had transpired.

(Odysseus mimes the battles of Troy.)

KING AEOLOUS. What exciting news, Odysseus. Now, in recompense
what may we do for you?

ODYSSEUS. King Aeolous, my men and I have been away from our
homes in Ithaca these nineteen years and more. Despite all we
have suffered, the winds and the seas thwart our return. Can
you help us?

KING AEOLOUS. I can. I will. Come with me. Here, take this large
pouch. In it I have imprisoned all the rough winds and gales so
they cannot bother you any more. Keep this strong cord tightly
around the pouch because these winds are so powerful they
could blow your ship apart.

(King Aeolous gives Odysseus a large round bag tied with a
cord, which seems to float in the air. Odysseus stows it on his
ship and waves goodbye.)

Farewell now. To drive you safely home, here is a gentle west
wind.

(King Aeolous now opens a small bag and one of the Attendants imitates a gentle wind with her flag, taking the wind so

it strikes Odysseus' sails gently and he sails away. King and Attendant fade to side of the stage.)

OLD MAN. King Aeolous' west wind blew them kindly on the seas, toward Ithaca. Along the way they stopped at many ports, where Odysseus was welcomed, as became his reputation, and he was given many costly gifts. In a short time, the ship hove to in sight of land.

(Odysseus mimes greeting people at various ports and then lies down to rest and sleep. Hylax rushes to prow and stares ahead.)

HYLAX. Land ahead! Ithaca!

PERITES. Is it?

HYLAX. Rocky Ithaca! We're home! We're home!

(They dance for joy.)

HYLAX. I'll wake Odysseus.

EURYLOCHUS. No, don't wake him yet. It will be at least an hour before we reach shore.

HYLAX. I can't wait.

EURYLOCHUS. Then start bringing our cargo on deck.

PERITES. Well, this is the biggest pouch.

(He has the large bag King Aeolous gave them.)

PEREMIDES. Wherever we go they always gave him costly treasures, but they never gave anything to us. We ought to have a share in all these treasures.

HYLAX. If we want any of this we had better take it for ourselves— and now!

(They all open the sack, which begins to tremble and make an increasingly loud humming sound until it whirls all them about, wakes Odysseus and they are in a terrible storm, all clinging to the mast, which almost blows over. At the same time, King Aeolous and the Attendant each take up a larger flag of ribbons which they use to lash the sailors and the ships. They exit as the storm subsides.)

OLD MAN. Out blew all those terrible, wild winds, raging into a mad tempest, driving them farther and farther away from

Ithaca. Six days, six nights! Driving them into seas unknown, even to the strange enchanted Island of Aeaea: home of the strange goddess, Circe.

ODYSSEUS. Hear my words, men. We are fortunate to escape from those winds but they have blown us I-know-not-where. We are lost. I cannot even tell which is east and which is west.

EURYLOCHUS. Well, the land may look inviting but. . . .

ODYSSEUS. Look! There's smoke rising from that dense wood. There must be inhabitants here. Maybe they can help us.

PEREMIDES. They might be Cyclops, too. Maybe they could eat us!

ODYSSEUS. Peremides, we have no choice. We must divide into two groups, one to explore that dense wood and seek help, the other to secure the beach.

PEREMIDES. Oh, great Odysseus, let us take our chances on the sea with Poseidon.

ODYSSEUS. Which way would we sail? We are lost and would soon starve to death at sea. Come now, bravely. Half with Eurylochus, and half with me. Draw, Eurylochus.

(Odysseus holds straws for Eurylochus to draw, who loses. Odysseus exits with Perites.)

Come Perites, this way.

PERITES. Peremides, good luck.

(As they explore with drawn swords, strange music begins, like the rustling of the wind in the trees, reflecting the enchantment of the island and the spirits there.) (Tinkle and small drum sounds.)

PEREMIDES. Why am I the one that always has to go on these expeditions?

(Wind voices off echo and fade "Aeaeaeae . . .")

EURYLOCHUS. Quiet, listen. . . .

HYLAX. It's only the leaves rustling.

WINDS. *(Off-stage voices.)* Beware. . . . Beware. . . .

EURYLOCHUS. I hear words! It is as if the wind is speaking. . . .

HYLAX. No, the whole forest is quiet as death. Ooooh, why did I have to mention death?

WINDS. *(Echoing.)* Death. . . . Death. . . . Death. . . .

PEREMIDES. Oh, there! What do I see?

WINDS. See, see, see.

HYLAX. Ah! A huge wolf came right at me!

PEREMIDES. Ah! Lions! Oh, help us Athena, goddess with the bright eyes.

HYLAX. Trapped. Wolves and lions.

(Off stage, Circe begins to sing her song accompanied by enchantment music and sounds.)

EURYLOCHUS. No, wait, shipmates, look. Look at them carefully. They are not attacking. They are wagging their tails.

HYLAX. Like dogs. . . .

PEREMIDES. I don't like this. . . .

HYLAX. Neither do I but what a wonder. They fawn at our feet like dogs.

EURYLOCHUS. Strange how gentle they are.

(Circe enters.)   *(Finger cymbals.)*

CIRCE. *(Singing.)*
    Sweetly, sweet, let darkness come,
    Sad night sings in hollow tones,
    Rest is near and sorrow gone.
    Lay thy swords upon the earth,
    Voyager, whose weeping wakes
    The forest with thy human tale.

(During the scene, whenever she moves her hands close to their faces they follow her movements in a hypnotic trance until she stops or snaps her finger cymbals. Eurylochus, who was farthest from her, breaks her spell and hides, watching what happens.)

PEREMIDES. Have mercy upon us, goddess or woman, whichever you are.

CIRCE. Strangers, you are welcome to the Island of Aeaea.   *(Echo: "Aeaeaeaeae. . . .")*

HYLAX. Thank you, lovely lady. We are Greeks searching our way home to Ithaca. And I ask, who are you?

CIRCE. I am the goddess, Circe. My father is the Sun who lights the earth and my mother is Perse, Daughter of the Ocean. You are welcome, refresh yourselves from your journey with this honey-wine in its golden bowl.

(To accomplish their conversion into pigs, we used cloth pig masks combined with their cowls. As they began to change, they pulled them up as hoods. When Circe touched them with her wand and they dropped on all fours, they appeared to be men with pig heads.)

HYLAX. Hmmm. What a splendid taste. Oink, oink.

PEREMIDES. *(Giggling and drifting into oinks.)* This is delicious. Hylax, your nose. It's beginning to look just like an oink—I mean a pig!

HYLAX. Well, oink yourself, you old oink, oink, oink, oink.

(Circe touches them with her wand and they drop on all fours. Eurylochus exits.)

CIRCE. And now, sailors, my powerful drug steals away your memory of home in Ithaca. You are pigs! You grunt like pigs, but your minds are human. You eat like pigs, some acorns, eat, acorns. Come piggies, follow me. . . .

(They follow her off, squealing like pigs as the enchantment music rises, then stops. Eurylochus enters with Odysseus.)

EURYLOCHUS. And then they all followed her to the pig sty. They were crying like men, but grunting and rooting like pigs. Both of them!

ODYSSEUS. Quick, we must go help them! This way.

EURYLOCHUS. *(Falling to his knees.)* My king, leave me here. Don't force me to go back there. You will never return yourself, nor save a single man. This island is bewitched! We must escape now while we have the chance and with what men we have left.

ODYSSEUS. Eurylochus, I am their leader. I must go to them. You stay here and guard the ship.

(Eurylochus exits while Odysseus draws his sword and begins warily to hunt for his men. Hermes and his mask enter. They

follow Odysseus, who senses something is wrong, but Hermes, the trickster, never lets himself be seen until he has some fun with Odysseus.)

ODYSSEUS. *(Whirling and drawing his sword.)* Ha! Who are you!

HERMES. Wouldn't you like to know!

ODYSSEUS. Watch your tongue, man. *(Hermes sticks out his tongue to "watch" it.)* I do not like your insolence either. I have killed men for less.

HERMES. To kill me you would have to catch me. To catch me, you'd have to run to Mount Olympus and back as fast as this!

(Hermes makes as though he leaps into space at incredible speed; Odysseus' eyes follow this imagined journey with amazement. Finally, Hermes taps him on the shoulder.)

Hello, there. I'm back.

ODYSSEUS. I know who you are. You must be Hermes.

HERMES. *(Simultaneously with him.)* Hermes! Son of Zeus and his messenger on earth to you silly mortals.

ODYSSEUS. I heard you were something of a trickster.

HERMES. Ah, well, you need a master trickster, Odysseus, Circe will turn you into a pig, too.

ODYSSEUS. Please do, Hermes. Help me rescue my men.

HERMES. That is the reason Pallas Athena asked me to come to you. Well, all right, with this.

(He magically produces a flower.)

Take this flower-herb, called Moly, with its white flower and black root. It is the antidote to the drug Circe will give you.

(Circe begins singing off stage.)

Come closer, even the leaves in the forest have Circe's ears.

(Hermes mimes whispering to Odysseus that he must put the Moly into the goblet before drinking it or else he will be changed into a pig. Enchanted music.)

Now, do what I have told you and no harm will come to you.

ODYSSEUS. Hermes, guardian of the wayfarer, I thank you.

HERMES. Thank the goddess, Pallas Athena, she sent me and now, farewell.

(Hermes again makes as though to leap off rapidly into space; again Odysseus follows with his eyes. Hermes shrugs, grins and trots off stage. Circe's song continues as she enters.)

CIRCE. *(Singing.)*
Sweetly, sweet let darkness come,
Sad night sings in hollow tones.
Give up thy shield and helmet strong,
As life grows old thy dreams grow young.

Welcome stranger. You are welcome to the enchanted Island of Aeaea.   *(Echoes off stage: "Aeaeae. . . .")*

Refresh yourself from your journey with this honey-wine in its golden bowl.

(She begins to hypnotize Odysseus as she did the sailors with her hands and movements. He takes the goblet but when she moves behind him, he drops the Moly flower into the goblet and drinks.)

And now, my powerful drug turns you into a pig. Go and join the other swine in the sty!

(She taps him with her wand. Odysseus has a terrible struggle because her drug tries to pull him onto all fours. At last, he overcomes it, draws his sword and threatens her with it. She falls to her knees.)

ODYSSEUS. No, terrible goddess. You shall die on my sword!

CIRCE. No man has ever resisted my potion before, who are you? What parents bred you? What city claims you?

ODYSSEUS. I am the son of Laertes, from rocky Ithaca.

CIRCE. Ah, then, you must be Odysseus, the man whom nothing defeats! It has long been prophesied that you would come to me. Stay and live with me in my palace.

(Old Man enters. A drum begins.)

OLD MAN. And she had rich rugs laid, and a silver basin for him to wash himself with sweetly perfumed water. And she entertained him with dancing.

(An Attendant enters with a silver basin and cloth so Odysseus can wash his hands. Then he sits and Circe dances for him.)

So, Odysseus trusted Circe and stayed in the enchanted palace for a year, but always his thoughts longed for his wife and son in far away Ithaca.

CIRCE. Why do you sit there, speechless, neither eating nor drinking?

ODYSSEUS. Can any man eat and drink while his friends grunt and root the ground like pigs?

CIRCE. I will restore them to you. Come, pigs.

(They enter. She taps them with her wand and they transform back into men by removing their pig masks.)

HYLAX. What's happening?

PEREMIDES. My snout, the bristles are falling off. . . .

HYLAX. We are changing back into humans!

PEREMIDES. Now I remember, we were pigs! Odysseus, what has happened?

ODYSSEUS. Circe has released you from her secret drug. You are free to return to our ship.

HYLAX. Thank you, Odysseus! You have saved us!

PEREMIDES. Oh, great leader, if we ever are to escape this magic place, it must be now.

ODYSSEUS. You're right. I will ask Circe to free us all. Go make our ship ready.

(They go.)

Circe, I beseech you, let us leave this place in peace.

CIRCE. My beloved Odysseus, I cannot keep you here against your will. You are free. But, royal son of Laertes, hear this: before you reach your home you must take a strange and difficult journey.   *(Music: a drum heart beat begins.)*

ODYSSEUS. A strange and difficult journey? Where?

CIRCE. You must go to the dread kingdom of Hades.

ODYSSEUS. How can I leave this earth? How descend into hell? No man has ever sailed there and lived!

CIRCE. Have courage, my love. Go now. Do not fret about a pilot to guide you. Set your mast and sail. The north wind will blow you to the Waters of the River Styx, then to the great rock pinnacle at the confluence of the River of Flaming Fire and the River of Lamentation. There dig a pit and pour in it a drink offering of milk-in-honey. Then, take a cup of red blood—life-giving blood of an all-black ram, and draw your sword, because a multitude of dead souls and wraiths will come to you, begging to drink the life-sustaining blood. But you must seek out the blind prophet, Teiresias. He alone can tell you where you must go, how long it will take, and thus direct you home across Poseidon's seas.

(Using only the prow of the ship for the voyage, Odysseus quickly mimes the voyage as Circe describes. He leaps off the ship, and goes downstage center and mimes the sacrifice. He ends on his knees with a cup in one hand and his sword in the other. Music changes to strong drum and cymbal beats. Enter four wraiths, each completely covered with flowing black cloth. One carries a mobile of death masks on a long stick which floats over Odysseus' head while the others swirl like black clouds.)

VOICES OF THE DEAD. Brave Odysseus, give us a drink . . . blood is life, only a drop.

ODYSSEUS. Keep back!

VOICES OF THE DEAD. Don't hurt me with your sword . . . one sip of blood . . . blood . . . blood.

ODYSSEUS. No. I seek the blind prophet, Teiresias.

(Anticlea, dressed as a wraith, enters swirling, the other wraiths drop to the ground like pools of black water. She floats to and fro towards Odysseus.)

ANTICLEA. Noble son . . . Odysseus, my boy. . . .

ODYSSEUS. Who is it that calls my name?

ANTICLEA. I am your mother, Anticlea. Give me but one drink that I may speak with you.

ODYSSEUS. Alas, dear mother! Here, drink one sip and tell me what has brought you to this horrible place.

(She drinks a sip and when she lowers her cloth-covered head, the cloth slides down revealing her death mask.)

ANTICLEA. My son, it was no disease that brought me to this place of darkness. It was my longing for you to return from Troy that brought my life to an end.

ODYSSEUS. We are now reunited. Let me embrace you once more. Why do you avoid me? May I not hold you in my arms once more?

ANTICLEA. You can't. I am only a spirit now. It is the fate of mankind. I have no flesh, no bones. You must fly from this black place. It is no place for you, the living. Go back . . . go back . . . go back to the lighted world.

(She exits, whirling out like a wisp of black fog.)

ODYSSEUS. I cannot go until I see Teiresias. Oh, mother, please return. What a terrible place this is. Lord Hades, I beseech you send the blind prophet, Teiresias, that I may speak with him.

(Loud drum. Enter Teiresias, also covered with black cloths and wearing a blind death mask. Then, low drum beats under the scene. The other wraiths whirl, then drop.)

TEIRESIAS. I come. I come, great Odysseus, I come. Hold your sword aside so I can drink the blood and prophesy the truth to you.

(Odysseus holds the cup so Teiresias can drink from it.)

ODYSSEUS. Tell me, blind prophet, how I may get home to Ithaca?

TEIRESIAS. You must sail past the Isle of Thrinacia, where the Sun God, Apollo, pastures his golden cattle. If you do not harm them, you *may* reach your home. But if you do them harm, you and all your men may be drowned at sea! I have told you the truth.

ODYSSEUS. Thank you, blind prophet.

TEIRESIAS. One final warning: You must sail past the rocks of the Twin Sirens. Beware! Now I must return, return, return to the darkness . . . return. . . .

VOICES OF THE DEAD. Give me life . . . drink . . . Odysseus, help us . . . return . . . return. . . . Blood . . . help us . . . life . . . !

(As Teiresias leaves the sounds grow louder. The wraiths rise again from the floor and swirl even stronger. Then all the

wraiths leave except one who three times tries to take the goblet from him. At last the wraith seizes it from him, drinks the blood and floats off. Crescendo of music and sounds.)

ODYSSEUS. This is no place for the living! I must fly out of here. Ho, Sailors!

(The Sailors enter, set the prow and the mast.)

Raise the mast! Man the long oars, we fly out of Hades! Away, away! We are bound for Apollo's golden island of Thrinacia. We are going home to Ithaca!

SAILORS. Hooray! Yea!

(They begin to sail away as Eurylochus mans the tiller and Odysseus joins him.)

EURYLOCHUS. What an adventure, Odysseus! To descend alive into Hades and return safely! One death is enough for every man but now you will have two.

HYLAX. Reefs ahead! Beware, helmsman.

PEREMIDES. Rocks on this side, steer carefully.

(Using their oars the Sailors guide the ship off the reefs on both sides.)

PERITES. Reefs off there!

ODYSSEUS. Good sailors, hear me. We must sail through these treacherous rocks. But beware, the Sirens who live here sing so beautifully that every sailor is drawn to them, hypnotized, and their ship smashed on the rocks. Put this wax in your ears so that you cannot hear them.

(He gives them wax, which they put in their ears and then man their oars in a ready position.)

Eurylochus, come quickly! Tie me to the mast, for I shall hear the Sirens' song and live! And do not loose the bonds no matter how I beg until we are safely past. Do you promise?

EURYLOCHUS. I promise, Odysseus.

(Eurylochus has tied Odysseus to the mast.)

ODYSSEUS. Good. Now I am ready for them.

(Eurylochus puts wax in his ears and takes the tiller. The men begin to row; they neither see nor hear the Sirens, who enter and begin singing, while the men sing a low counterpart of "row, row" to the rhythm of their rowing. The Sirens move from the prow to the helm trying to catch the attention of the sailors.)

SIRENS. *(Singing.)*
Come here, come here,
Sailor so long on the sea.

ODYSSEUS. What a beautiful song. . . . I hear you, I will come!

SIRENS. *(Singing.)*
Come here, come near,
Following my song, come to me.

ODYSSEUS. Eurylochus, steer to the left. No, steer to the right. Do as I tell you!

SIRENS. *(Singing.)*
Sail here, don't fear.
Come here and rest close to me.

ODYSSEUS. Over there, please go over—I am trying, please, please. . . . I am coming to you, ohhhhh. . . .

SIRENS. *(Singing.)*
Come near, come near,
Follow my song and be free.

(As they exit, Odysseus tries to reach out to them and faints.)

EURYLOCHUS. Are we past them yet? Odysseus? He has fainted from the strain. I wonder if I can take the wax out of my ears yet.

(He does so.)

Rowers, you can take the wax out of your ears now!

(They don't hear, he speaks louder.)

Take the wax out of your ears!!!!

(They still do not hear him. He shows them in mime to take the wax out of their ears, while saying it softly. This time they understand.)

Take the wax out of your ears.

HYLAX. Those were terrible rocks . . . and the current . . . almost too strong. . . . What a horrible ordeal.

PERITES. Six days and nights of rowing! We have never rowed so hard and travelled so far without rest and no food for three days.

PEREMIDES. Wait! Look there, land! Steer in toward the shore.

PERITES. We can put ashore and find food. It's shallow. Ease her in.

HYLAX. *(Leaping ashore.)* I am not staying on this ship tonight. I shall sleep on land.

PERITES. *(Leaping ashore, followed by Peremides.)* Come on.

PEREMIDES. We can forage for food. What . . . look there, or is it a mirage?   *(Cow bell.)*

PERITES. No, it is cattle grazing.

HYLAX. Beautiful—golden in the sunlight, with long horns.

EURYLOCHUS. Wait, men. Don't touch those golden cows, they're sacred to the god Apollo.

HYLAX. We intend to kill and eat one of these cattle while we still have the strength. Join us—or, at least, don't try to stop us!

(Eurylochus attempts to draw his sword but they prevent him and threaten him with their weapons.)

EURYLOCHUS. All right . . . in another minute we'll be killing each other. Apollo forgive us: we starve.

HYLAX. Come on! Take that one! Haaa!   *(Cow bells sound.)*

(They mime killing a cow. The mask of Apollo comes forward and they freeze in a tableau.)

EURYLOCHUS. Odysseus has fainted from exhaustion yet he has heard the Sirens' song and is still alive.

APOLLO. No! Father Zeus, I, Apollo, call upon you to punish these wicked followers of Odysseus. They are killing my golden cattle. If you let them go unpunished, I will take my golden sun down into Hades to shine among the dead and leave this earth dark and cold forever.

ODYSSEUS. Oh, my friends, what are you doing? Oh no! A golden cow! Oh gods who live forever, why have you lulled me into a sleep while men offended Apollo? He will surely punish us. Come, we must leave this island quickly, although I fear it is already too late.

(They enter the ship, apprehensive of the danger they feel around them. The ship is configurized so that the prow faces downstage and the ship is sailing directly at the audience. Zeus is on one side, Apollo on the other.)

ZEUS. Apollo, continue to shine your sun upon the earth. I, Zeus, Lord of Olympus, will soon strike them with my thunderbolt, and scatter them on the wine-red sea. Now rise great waves! Rock their boat from side to side!

HYLAX. Man overboard!

ZEUS. Now, omnipotent thunderbolt, strike!

(With mime and manipulation of the prow, mast and tiller, the actors make the ship pitch up and down, then roll from side to side—even tossing a man overboard, who saves himself by clinging to the prow at water level. When Zeus calls for a thunderbolt, the ship breaks apart; the prow tumbles off stage, as does the tiller, the mast holder, and all the sailors, leaving Odysseus clinging to the mast, awash in the sea.)

ODYSSEUS. Swim, men, swim! Pallas Athena, help us! We are drowning!

(He, like the men, is then tumbled off stage. Drums and sounds throughout the scene. After the ship's break-up, the two gods pass each other and go upstage, bow to each other and their masks are hung on the wall. A gong sounds.)

ANTINOUS. *(Entering with all the Suitors.)* It is true! Odysseus was drowned in the sea by Zeus' great thunderbolt. He is dead. Now, Penelope, we have brought you our matrimonial offerings as is the custom. Now you must choose which one of us you will marry.

PENELOPE. *(Entering with Telemachus.)* I shall choose, Antinous. Telemachus, go fetch your father's bow from its accustomed place. I shall choose by challenge. He among you who can string Odysseus' great bow and shoot an arrow through those twelve axes as he did, shall have my consent. Will you accept the challenge?

EURYMACHUS. A fair challenge. He who can string the bow and shoot through the axes wins Penelope's hand.

ANTINOUS. Are we agreed then to take up this challenge?

SUITORS. Agreed!

(Telemachus returns with the bow.)

TELEMACHUS. Here is the bow. Try it if you dare.

SUITORS. *(Laughter.)* If we dare, . . . etc. . . .

ANTINOUS. Come, young princes, we shall go even as the wine is passed: from left to right.

KTESSIPOS. *(Tipsy.)* Me? Am I first? Give me the bow.

ANTINOUS. Ktessipos.

KTESSIPOS. Fair Penelope.

(Ktessipos tries to string the bow but fumbles with it and hits himself on the nose.)

This is a strong bow. . . .

EURYMACHUS. Did you say a strong drink, Ktessipos?

KTESSIPOS. Yes, I'll have one! I may not be able to string this bow, but I can drink these two goblets of wine in only one breath.

(He drinks two goblets of wine simultaneously.)

ANTINOUS. Leodes, son of Oenos. You are next.

(He tries but cannot string it.)

LEODES. Generous Queen, I have tried the strength of this bow and I shall never string it. Believe me, this bow will break the heart and be the death of many a champion here today!

EURYMACHUS. What a preposterous thing to say, Leodes. Surely there be men—or at least one—here today who can string this bow. Like this!

(With great strength, Eurymachus almost strings the bow, but cannot.)

ANTINOUS. Lo, mighty Eurymachus cannot even string Odysseus' bow! Then how can he shoot an arrow?

(Laughter and taunts from the suitors.)

EURYMACHUS. Here, Antinous, take this bow. This humiliates me and the disgrace sticks to my name.

ANTINOUS. There is no disgrace here today. Today should be a holiday—in preparation for a princely wedding! We shall call today a festival and tomorrow we can take up the challenge of this bow once again.

EURYMACHUS. No Antinous, you will try today.

SUITORS. *(General ad lib.)* No—today! You must try now!   *(Tinkle sound.)*

(Enter the Old Man.)

OLD MAN. Young princes, let me try the strength of these old arms and hands on that great bow.

ANTINOUS. Miserable old beggar, are you out of your senses? Are you not content to eat with your betters and be quiet? Now I warn you, you will come to harm. Stand off!

PENELOPE. Antinous, it is not common courtesy to be so rude to a guest in my house.

EURYMACHUS. And it is not proper behavior for you to let a miserable beggar compete for your hand in marriage.

TELEMACHUS. Peace, I say. *(Takes the bow from Antinous.)* No man in Ithaca has more right than I to give this bow. Though I am young I am still master of this house. I shall decide. Try it, old man.

SUITORS. *(Laughter, ad lib.)*

EURYMACHUS. Oh, the too young and the too old!

(The Old Man strings and mimes shooting an arrow past the Suitors, whose eyes and heads follow its flight. Drum roll and beat for arrow shot and hit.)

KTESSIPOS. A hit!

OLD MAN. And now I shall conclude my story of Odysseus. He returned to his home, disguised as an old beggar,

(He takes off the mask and hat.)

to meet again his beloved wife and his brave son.

(He embraces Penelope and grasps Telemachus' hand, then turns to the Suitors.)

And to find his home filled with corrupt suitors who would steal his wife, murder his son and dishonor the immortal gods. So the match is played and won. Odysseus is home!

ANTINOUS. It's Odysseus!

ODYSSEUS. Yes! And who is to say he should not rid his house of the vermin that infest it?

EURYMACHUS. Get your weapons! Attack him, everyone!

(The slaughter of the suitors is in slow motion. With Penelope on one side of Odysseus and Telemachus on the other, the family make a fortress. Telemachus mimes handing arrows to Odysseus, who then shoots each suitor: Antinous, Ktessipos, Leodes and Eurymachus. As they are hit by an arrow they bring a red silken handkerchief to the place of the wound and fall to the ground.)

ODYSSEUS. It is not yet finished! I have purged my house, but I fear the families of these dead suitors will rise up in arms for revenge.   *(Humming begins and grows.)*

PENELOPE. Is there to be still more slaughtering?

ODYSSEUS. Fair Penelope, only the gods of Olympus know. Telemachus, when we are in the heat of battle, I know you will not bring disgrace to our house.

TELEMACHUS. Father, I shall stand at your side, and you will see!

ODYSSEUS. I hear them coming even now. Ready!

(The Suitors begin an increasing hum and slowly rise, placing their red handkerchiefs over their heads and raising their swords. Odysseus, Penelope, and Telemachus take up a siege position. Athena enters between them.)

ATHENA. Stop, you Greeks! Lay down your weapons! *(They do.)* I, Pallas Athena, tell you! There will be no more bloodshed.

Odysseus, you shall make a treaty of mutual friendship with these noble families. You, Ithacan nobles, will make peace with his family. Salute each other, so that peace and prosperity will return to my beloved Greece. Now, let us all join hands as we celebrate the end of this Odyssey.

(They shake hands, then turn and bow.)

(The Suitors remove the red cloths and lay them down with their swords. One of them shakes hands with Odysseus, then all join hands with Pallas Athena in the center and, facing the audience, bow to them.)

(Curtain.)

Noodle Doodle Box

By Paul Maar

Adapted and translated by Anita and Alex Page

Copyright, 1979, Baker's Plays.

Noodle Doodle Box (1979)

Written in 1972 by West German playwright Paul Maar and translated into English in 1979, *Noodle Doodle Box* is an absurdist play that makes important social statements to its audience without portraying real-life situations, characters, or events.

Using only three characters and an essentially bare stage, Maar's plot retells the events of a day in the life of two delightful, clownish wags, Pepper and Zacharias. Pepper and Zacharias each possess a box that serves both as their house and their private space, which they refuse to share with each other. Their boxes are unique and interesting in their own peculiar ways, and reflect their personalities.

The play begins with Pepper and Zacharias testing the limits of their friendship; they consequently resolve to have little to do with each other. As the play continues, the two-dimensionality of the characters becomes more obvious and the audience easily begins to identify Zacharias and Pepper as authority/non-authority, parent/child, teacher/student, and bully/nonbully models.

The play continues with the appearance of a greedy, pompous Drum Major, who uses the selfish and competitive qualities of Zach and Pepper's friendship to deceive them out of their boxes and turn them against each other. The play concludes with Zacharias' and Pepper's discovery that the Drum Major was not a friend at all, and that the two of them need each other. At the end, the two clowns have discovered the friendship each holds for the other; it is this thin bond that at last brings them together.

CHARACTERS

Zacharias

Pepper

The Drum Major

SETTING
An empty stage.

TIME
Today.

Noodle Doodle Box

Setting: The stage is empty. In the Center, however, there are two large different-colored boxes; one is a little larger than the other.

At rise: For a while, nothing happens. Then a cock crows loudly: cock-a-doodle-doo. Zacharias appears out of the smaller box. Leisurely he takes his toothbrush from his pocket and brushes his teeth. Then he takes off his hat and brushes his hair with the toothbrush. He puts on his hat, disappears into the box and now reappears with one black and one white shoe. Now he brushes the shoes with his toothbrush. Meantime out of the other box rises Pepper. His hair is all uncombed. He yawns, stretches, and then starts to do kneebends. His head slowly disappears inside the box with each bend and then he rises up again.

ZACHARIAS. Pepper!

PEPPER. *(Stops his exercises. His head comes up just beyond the edge of the box.)* Yes?

ZACH. You're a pig! *(He spits on his toothbrush and keeps brushing his shoes.)*

PEPPER. Indeed! *(He continues his kneebends but speeds them up.)*

ZACH. *(Stops cleaning his shoes. Interested, he watches Pepper doing his kneebends. His head keeps time with Pepper. He stops and yells.)* Pepper!

PEPPER. *(He stops in the middle of moving.)* Yes?

ZACH. Don't you want to know why you are one?

PEPPER. One what?

ZACH. A pig.

PEPPER. *(Gently.)* Yes, Zacky. You can tell me.

ZACH. How many times do I have to tell you that my name is Zach-a-ri-as.

PEPPER. Your name is too long. *(Assuredly.)* Names that are too long can be shortened.

ZACH. Nothing is going to be shortened. I don't call you Pep.

PEPPER. You may call me Pep. I don't like Pepper anyway.

ZACH. *(Laughs smugly.)* Every person has the name that he deserves. *(He speaks grandly.)* Zach-a-ri-as. *(Then briefly and sharply.)* Pepper! *(He spits contemptuously on his shoes and continues to clean them.)*

PEPPER. *(After thinking briefly.)* Listen, Zack.

ZACH. Zacharias, you ass!

PEPPER. *(Unshaken.)* Listen, Zachariassss.

ZACH. What?

PEPPER. You were going to tell me why I am one.

ZACH. One what?

PEPPER. A piglet?

ZACH. Oh, yes, of course. You are a pig because you don't take care of yourself. Look at me; brushed my teeth, combed my hair, shined my shoes.
A sloppy Joe is not quite okay;
Big shots wash nearly every day.

PEPPER. Hey, Zacharias.

ZACH. What?

PEPPER. You've got strange shoes. One is black and one is white.

ZACH. *(Inspects them attentively.)* That's curious.

PEPPER. What does that mean?

ZACH. That's funny. That's even more curious.

PEPPER. What is it?

ZACH. Even more curiouser. Because here in the box, I actually have another pair like that. *(He holds the second pair of shoes up high.)*

PEPPER. There has to be a shoe sickness.

ZACH. *(Worried.)* You think so?

PEPPER. Maybe it's contagious. *(He descends into his box and rises with two huge black shoes. Triumphantly.)* My shoes haven't caught it yet. Don't come too close with yours, Zacky.

ZACH. *(Correcting him.)* . . . ariasssssss!

PEPPER. *(Thinking he is supposed to speak more quietly, whispers.)* Not too close, Zachary.

ZACH. *(Angrily and emphatically.)* sss ssss ssss!

PEPPER. *(Looks around anxiously and whispers.)* Don't be afraid. I won't tell anybody that you have infected shoes, Zacky.

ZACH. *(Throws all four shoes furiously to the ground in front of the box.)* Zacharias, you camel! Zacharias!

PEPPER. Today, you aren't being very nice to me. You just said I'm a camel. I don't think I like that.

ZACH. Don't start blubbering. Help me out of the box.

PEPPER. Okay, Zacharias. *(He climbs out of his box and runs in stocking feet to the other box. En route he stumbles over the shoes which Zacharias had thrown out earlier and pushes them instinctively together so that two black and two white shoes make two pairs next to each other. Then he slowly pulls up bulky Zacharias.)*

ZACH. Careful. Not so fast.

PEPPER. *(He has almost pulled Zacharias out of the box when he suddenly realizes that the correct pairs are lined up. Bewildered, he lets go of him. Zacharias falls back into the box with a loud racket. Pepper inspects the shoes from close up, quite untroubled.)* Hey, Zacky.

ZACH. *(Corrects Pepper, his voice muffled from inside the box.)* Zachariasss.

PEPPER. Hey, Zachariasss. Look at those shoes. They're healthy again.

ZACH. *(Wide-eyed, looks over the edge of the box.)* So it is. Fantastomatic.

PEPPER. I even know what made them healthy. The nose dive is what healed them. That's what I'm going to write in all the newspapers. "Pepper's cure for sick shoes, works triple A one, okay and quick."

ZACH. Don't talk such nonsense.

PEPPER. What?

ZACH. You don't even know how to write.

PEPPER. But I can read.

ZACH. So you can read! Then read something that's in the news-paper. *(He gets a newspaper out of the box and holds it in front of Pepper.)*

PEPPER. *(Pepper holds it upside down, opens it and mumbles to show that he is earnestly "reading.")* Hum, hm, mhm.

ZACH. *(Climbs out of his box and looks with interest over Pepper's shoulder, happily surprised.)* Read it louder!

PEPPER. *(Pushes him back a couple of steps and assumes a grand posture. Zacharias waits patiently in amazement. Pepper reads with expressive head movements and large gestures.)*
    Two frogs went on a Friday
    To the barber in the Mall
    For the very latest hairdo

(Noisily turns the page.)

    For a very important ball.
    The barber looked and cried:
    My, what a silly pair
    To ask for a fancy hairdo

(Turns the page.)

    And you don't have a single hair!

(At first Zacharias has listened attentively, moving his head in time to the rhythm of the lines. Suddenly he stops; his glance stays glued to the front page, he lowers his head and looks at it from closer up. Then he walks around Pepper, looks over his shoulder as he is reading and waits, furious, until he is finished. Pepper turns around and looks proudly at him. Zacharias very calmly takes the paper from Pepper's hands, folds it carefully together several times and hits Pepper over the head with it.) You phony! *(Hits him.)* You deceiver! *(Hits him again.)* You show-off! *(Hits him.)* You big mouth! *(Hits him twice.)* You can't read at all. You've said everything by heart. The newspaper is upside down. I could tell by the pictures!

PEPPER. *(Crying.)* You're mean. All day you've been bawling me out. First, I'm a pig, then a donkey, then a camel, then a big louse.

ZACH. Big louse! Big mouth I said and that's what you are. *(Pepper cries louder.)* Well, a small mouth. *(Pepper keeps on crying.)* A mini mouth.

PEPPER. And you've been hitting me too!

ZACH. But only with paper.

PEPPER. Hitting, all the same. I'm not going to be your friend any longer.

ZACH. Don't be so easy to insult. I'm going to give you a present.

PEPPER. *(Asks immediately, very businesslike.)* What is it?

ZACH. My handkerchief. You can use it to wipe the tears away. *(He pulls out an immense handkerchief full of holes and passes it to Pepper. He takes it and thrusts a finger through one of the holes and shakes his head. Finally, he folds it and wipes away his tears. But the holes bother him. He resumes crying.)*

ZACH. Why are you bawling again?

PEPPER. Your handkerchief has holes.

ZACH. Holes? Where?

PEPPER. Here.

ZACH. All you have to do is turn the hanky around.

PEPPER. *(Pleased, turns the handkerchief around. But his face saddens again.)* Here are also holes.

ZACH. Such a peculiar coincidence. Holes in back and holes in front.

PEPPER. That's the way it always is.

ZACH. What's always so?

PEPPER. Everything looks from behind exactly the way it looks from in front.

ZACH. What nonsense!

PEPPER. Here you go again—fighting.

ZACH. Naturally, if you say such nonsense. Since when are things the same in front as in back. I'm going to prove to you that you look different from behind than from in front. Stand there. *(He positions Pepper facing the audience.)* And now tell me what you see.

PEPPER. *(Looks at the audience. Shrugs his shoulders.)* Children.

ZACH. No, no, no! You're supposed to look at yourself, your front. What do you see there?

PEPPER. One button, another button, a tummy, two legs and two socks.

ZACH. *(Nods in agreement. Then he turns Pepper around so that his back faces the audience. Triumphant.)* Are you going to claim that you look from behind exactly as in front? Then tell me what you see now?

PEPPER. A button, another button, a tummy, two legs, two socks.

ZACH. Oh, you . . . *(Furious, he throws his handkerchief at Pepper. Pepper walks away hurt.)* Pepper!

PEPPER. *(Walks away, paying no attention. Zacharias runs after him and holds him by his coat.)*

ZACH. *(Flatteringly.)* I just want to show you something. Don't be hurt, little Pepper.

PEPPER. Show! *(Contemptuously.)* You just want to laugh at me. Show me how it works on your box.

ZACH. What?

PEPPER. That with a front and a back.

ZACH. Won't work.

PEPPER. Aha, won't work.

ZACH. Because it's too heavy.

PEPPER. Excuses, excuses.

ZACH. No. . . .

PEPPER. Yes.

ZACH. No.

PEPPER. Then turn the box around.

ZACH. Okay. Let's turn it on my side.

PEPPER. No, on my side.

ZACH. No.

PEPPER. Okay, your side.

ZACH. Let's go. Let's turn it around. Push! *(Zacharias takes a smaller box out of his larger one and puts it on the floor; then together they grab the large box, raise it and turn it around. Suddenly the green box is red. Zacharias and Pepper stare at it speechlessly. Zacharias is even more astonished by the new color than Pepper.)*

ZACH. Did you see? First it was green. Now it's red.

PEPPER. Fabulous.

ZACH. Fantastomatic.

PEPPER. Super, now let's turn my box around.

ZACH. Okay. Let's turn your box around. What are those funny holes on the side?

PEPPER. I sawed them in.

ZACH. What for?

PEPPER. So I can put out my hand and find out if it's raining.

ZACH. Such foolishness! *(Pepper bends over the edge of the box and pulls out all kinds of things: shoes, assorted objects, a half-filled water bottle. He gives it all to Zacharias, who makes a small pile of them. When an object pleases him especially, he polishes it with his sleeve and lets it disappear in his pocket. Then both grab hold of the box and turn it. This one doesn't change color.)*

PEPPER. Let's try again. *(They turn it over once again and again nothing changes.)*

ZACH. Foolish box.

PEPPER. Dummy! *(He kicks the box angrily.)*

ZACH. *(Standing before his box.)* Now there's a box. Come, we'll turn it around. *(They turn the box.)* You see? Green. *(They turn the box again.)* And now, red. That's big-time stuff. Fantastomatic.

PEPPER. Zacky.

ZACH. Zachariasss.

PEPPER. Zacharias, won't you give me your box?

ZACH. Have you a screw loose in your head?

PEPPER. Can we swap? Mine is bigger. *(Zacharias points to his head, indicating that Pepper is crazy.)*

PEPPER. Will you lend it to me?

ZACH. *(Picking up the handkerchief and wiping invisible spots from the box.)* A box isn't a rental car.

PEPPER. But I can step into it.

ZACH. With those dirty feet?!

PEPPER. I can put on my shoes.

ZACH. They haven't been cleaned.

PEPPER. If you don't let me in, I'm going to be really hurt. *(Zacharias won't have it. He spits on his hanky and energetically polishes the box.)* I'm going to find myself another friend.

ZACH. *(Still polishing. Offhand.)* With that box? *(He pulls his toothbrush out of his pocket and proceeds to clean the box with it.)*

PEPPER. I was kidding.

ZACH. *(Polishing.)* Sounded quite serious.

PEPPER. I was really just kidding, Zacharias.

ZACH. That kind of kidding I don't find at all funny.

PEPPER. You're right, Zacharias. It was silly kidding. You can do better than that. Pretend you're the fountain, like yesterday; that was lots of fun.

ZACH. For that, I must put on my shoes.

PEPPER. Let me get them for you, Zacharias. The black or the white?

ZACH. The white, naturally, idiot.

PEPPER. *(Hurries to get the shoes. Zacharias raises his leg. Pepper bends down and puts the shoes on Zacharias.)* And now we'll play fountain together, okay?

ZACH. Together won't do because only one can play fountain.

PEPPER. You may play fountain. I'll get the water.

ZACH. There is no water.

PEPPER. Yes, there is, a whole bottle half full. *(He gets the water bottle.)* I'll find a bucket.

ZACH. We don't need a bucket.

PEPPER. No bucket?

ZACH. Today we play an automatic fountain with electricity.

PEPPER. How does that work?

ZACH. You stand in front of the fountain. You say, please, water, please.

PEPPER. And then?

ZACH. Then you get some.

PEPPER. Where do I get it?

ZACH. You'll see.

PEPPER. Okay. Please, water, please.

ZACH. Wait. Not so fast. You have to go off a little way and then you come back and say it.

PEPPER. *(Eagerly takes a few steps. Zacharias is about to fill his mouth with water. Just as he raises the bottle, Pepper turns around and asks.)* Like this?

(Zacharias quickly hides the bottle behind his back, accidentally pouring water over his coat. He suppresses his anger. He says in a kindly way.) No, a bit further. *(While Pepper goes off further, he angrily shakes off the spilled water. He again raises the bottle. Pepper turns around a second time. Zacharias hides the bottle and again wets the jacket.)*

PEPPER. Should I come?

ZACH. Don't ask every three steps whether you should come or not. Go on, further.

PEPPER. Okay, Zacharias, I'm going.

ZACH. *(Fills his mouth with water and stands waiting with full cheeks. Pepper continues to walk and disappears off stage.*

Zacharias keeps waiting, bangs his foot on the floor impatiently. At last, he spits out the water in a high arc and yells.)
Pepper!

PEPPER. *(Comes running happily.)* Please, water, please.

ZACH. No, no, no. You do it all wrong. Let's do it over. Now you take ten paces, turn around and come back here to me. Got it?

PEPPER. Got it, Zacharias. One, two, three, four, six, five, eight, ten. Coming. *(Zacharias has his mouth full of water. Pepper stops in front of Zacharias, looks at him questioningly. Zacharias nods graciously.)* Please, water, please.

ZACH. *(Sprays the water into his face. He almost falls over from laughing so hard. He keeps thumping Pepper on his shoulder.)* Ho, ho, ho. That was some kidding, eh? Fantastomatic. Lots of fun. You should have seen your face when the water hit you— like a worm in a puddle. Ha, ha.

PEPPER. *(Wipes off his face with his sleeve. Barely controlling himself.)* So now I'm going to play the fountain and you get the water.

ZACH. *(Still laughing.)* You, the fountain?

PEPPER. Yes, me.

ZACH. I get the water?

PEPPER. Yes, you.

ZACH. So be it. I get the water. *(He thrusts the bottle into Pepper's hand and takes a few paces. Thirsting for revenge, Pepper takes a huge swallow and stands waiting with very bloated cheeks. Zacharias stops without turning around.)* Pepper?

PEPPER. *(Hastily spits out the water.)* What?

ZACH. *(Innocently.)* Are you ready, Pepper?

PEPPER. Yes, Zacharias. *(He quickly takes another swallow.)*

ZACH. Pepper?

PEPPER. *(Again spits the water out.)* What?

ZACH. So it's okay for me to come.

PEPPER. Ye-e-es! *(Takes another swallow.)*

ZACH. Pepper? *(At first, he gets no answer. Once again.)* Pepper?

PEPPER. *(Spits.)* What now?

ZACH. I'm coming. *(Pepper quickly takes another swallow. Zacharias approaches Pepper and stops before him. Pepper mumbles something incomprehensible with his mouth full.)* What are you trying to say?

PEPPER. *(Spitting out the water. Angrily.)* That's all wrong. You have to say it.

ZACH. What do I have to say?

PEPPER. *(Screaming.)* That with the water. You know what I mean. You just want to spoil my turn. *(He is so furious that he is unaware that Zacharias has taken the water bottle from him.)*

ZACH. What do I have to say?

PEPPER. Please, water.

ZACH. Please, what? *(He turns aside and takes a big swallow.)*

PEPPER. *(Very loud, very angry.)* Please, water, please.

ZACH. *(Sprays water into Pepper's face and bends over shaking with laughter.)* Please, ho, ho, ha, ha, water, he, he, please, ho, ha. Fantastomatic. *(He sings.)*
Please, water, please, please
Look, look how on his knees
He begs to be moister
Than a wet, soggy oyster.

(Pepper, highly incensed, yanks the bottle out of Zacharias' hand and tries to pour the water over his head. The bottle is empty. Zacharias has another attack of laughing.)

ZACH. It's empty. I've drunk it all. It's been a joke. A fantastomatic joke.

PEPPER. You're mean, really mean. I'm through being your friend.

ZACH. *(Stops laughing, almost threatening.)* You're through being *my* friend?

PEPPER. Because you sprayed water all over me. *(Less sure of himself.)*

ZACH. Through being *my* friend? *(Pepper nods.)* You mean to say, *I* am through being *your* friend. I don't want to have as friends people who can't take a joke and especially people with such a shabby box. *(He kicks Pepper's box contemptuously.)*

PEPPER. Don't touch my box. *(Zacharias kicks the box forcefully a second time. In response, Pepper runs over to Zacharias' box and kicks it triumphantly. A bitter fight breaks out in which each kicks, shoves, scratches, and spits at the other's box. Finally Pepper hits Zacharias' box very hard. He yells, jumps in pain in a circle and holds his foot. Zacharias laughs uncontrollably.)*

ZACH. *(Snorts.)* He jumps around like a bull frog! Fantastomatic! *(Pepper sticks out his tongue, climbs into his box and disappears entirely. Zacharias goes to his own box, tries to turn it around but can't do it himself. He tries a number of times, gives up and ambles near Pepper's box. Loud humming can be heard from it. Pepper is imitating the sound of airplanes. Fascinated, Zacharias steps closer.)* Hey, Pepper. *(No reply.)* Pepper!

PEPPER. *(Raises his head beyond the edge suspiciously.)* Yeh, what now?

ZACH. What are you doing in there?

PEPPER. I am playing airplane. *(He imitates an airplane motor and disappears again into the box.)*

ZACH. That's not how it is. Airplanes have to have wings.

PEPPER. *(Rising again.)* Wings?

ZACH. Yes, wings, like chickens and ducks.

PEPPER. My box doesn't have any wings.

ZACH. Then stick out your arms like this. *(He shows him how. Pepper copies him and adds the sound of motors. Then Zacharias, caught up in the game, begins to play airplane also.)* Hey, Pepper.

PEPPER. What?

ZACH. Put your arms through the hole. That will make it look more real.

PEPPER. Through the holes of the handkerchief?

ZACH. You idiot, through the holes in the box. *(Pepper sticks both hands through the holes. There appears on the right side a tiny arm, on the left a giant one. Zacharias screams in excitement.)* Pepper! *(He points to the big arm.)*

PEPPER. What's the matter?

ZACH. Your arm.

PEPPER. What about it?

ZACH. Huge like a giant. That's fantastomatic. Is the other one just as big? *(He runs to the other side of the box.)* It's small, quite small. How do you do that? *(Pepper pulls both arms out of the openings. He bends over the edge of the box and looks through the holes from outside in. Then he shrugs helplessly, glances suspiciously at Zacharias, who is beside himself with excitement.)* Stick your arms through the hole once again. Incomprehensible. And now the left. Unbelievable. *(Pepper glances over the edge and only now sees his two changed arms. He is frightened and pulls the arms back quickly. Then he rises, feels his arms which are entirely normal. Hesitantly, he tries once again and again one arm becomes huge and the other tiny.)*

PEPPER. *(With growing delight.)* It doesn't hurt at all. Absolutely, first rate. It's fantastic. In fact, fantastomatic. That's what I call a box, eh? None other like it.

ZACH. It's crazy. I have to find out if it works with me. *(He is about to climb into Pepper's box.)*

PEPPER. Hey, out of my box. That would be just like you. First, to spit at my box, then to climb in.

ZACH. That was just kidding. I didn't even hit it. I spat *next* to it, like this. *(Demonstrates.)*

PEPPER. I don't find anything funny in spitting.

ZACH. Don't be so touchy. Besides, I'm not doing it anymore. Besides, my mouth is completely dry. Look, nothing. *(He spits a number of times but nothing comes out.)*

PEPPER. All the same, you did spit on my box.

ZACH. I'll wipe it off, Pepper. We don't want to fight about a thing like that. *(He pulls out his handkerchief and wipes the box.)* Was it here?

PEPPER. No, there. *(He points to a spot on the outside which Zacharias wipes. Pepper points to another spot, very far removed.)* And there. *(Zacharias wipes there also.)*

ZACH. *(While he is wiping vigorously.)* I like it that we're getting along again. You don't have to be afraid. I'm going to be your friend for good. That was just a joke that I said then.

PEPPER. Zacky?

ZACH. *(First wants to correct him but controls himself.)* What?

PEPPER. Way down there. That's where you spat.

ZACH. *(Leans way down and wipes.)* If you would like to have my box for a while, we can swap. I'll be glad to lend you mine, if you want it.

PEPPER. A box isn't a rental car.

ZACH. Well, just a suggestion. *(He keeps wiping.)*

PEPPER. Zacky?

ZACH. What, Pepper?

PEPPER. I don't like your wearing your hat while you work.

ZACH. Should I take it off?

PEPPER. Yes, give it to me. *(Puts it on.)*

ZACH. May I now get in?

PEPPER. Later, Zacky.

ZACH. Why later?

PEPPER. First, we're going to play.

ZACH. Play what?

PEPPER. You know all kinds of interesting games.

ZACH. We can play Aggravation.

PEPPER. Don't want to.

ZACH. Or Blind Man's Bluff.

PEPPER. Don't like it.

ZACH. Or Leap Frog.

PEPPER. Nothing doing.

ZACH. Concentration?

PEPPER. Out of the question.

ZACH. Heads and Tails?

PEPPER. Boring.

ZACH. Four Squares?

PEPPER. No good.

ZACH. Going to Jerusalem.

PEPPER. Uninteresting.

ZACH. Ghosts?

PEPPER. Dull.

ZACH. Red Rover.

PEPPER. Childish.

ZACH. We can sing.

PEPPER. Silly.

ZACH. You are right.

PEPPER. How do you mean I'm right?

ZACH. Singing is silly.

PEPPER. Says who?

ZACH. You.

PEPPER. You must have heard wrong. Let's sing together and loud.

ZACH. You don't even know how to sing.

PEPPER. And you?

ZACH. How can we both sing together loud if you don't know how to sing?

PEPPER. We sing together like this. You sing loud while I listen loud.

ZACH. That doesn't make sense.

PEPPER. *(Snitty.)* Maybe not. *(He begins to play by himself. He reaches his arm through the hole in the box and says.)* Bang! *(He pulls it back. Says.)* Wham! *(Repeats several times.)*

ZACH. Honestly, doesn't this hurt?

PEPPER. What?

ZACH. When your arm gets that large?

PEPPER. Can't feel it at all. Bang, wham, bang, wham!

ZACH. Hey, Pepper.

PEPPER. What?

ZACH. We can try it.

PEPPER. Try what?

ZACH. Well, singing.

PEPPER. Don't feel like it.

ZACH. Why not, Pepper. Singing is beautiful. *(He takes a few steps and sings, Ta, ra, ta, ta, then steps and looks expectantly toward Pepper.)*

PEPPER. Okay, start off.

ZACH. What should I sing?

PEPPER. Maybe a song.

ZACH. That's obvious, but which?

PEPPER. A song with a box.

ZACH. A song with a box?

PEPPER. You heard me.

ZACH. There's no such thing.

PEPPER. Well, if there isn't, there isn't. *(He pushes his other arm through the other hole, saying wham, bang.)*

ZACH. Pepper.

PEPPER. What?

ZACH. *(Hastily.)* I'm going to make one up, especially for you.

PEPPER. Make up what?

ZACH. A song with a box. Wait, what rhymes with box? . . . A pair of sox are in a box.

PEPPER. I think this is super dumb. *(He resumes playing.)*

ZACH. Wait a minute, wait a minute, I've got something new. How do you like this? I rocks my box.

PEPPER. You can rock your box as much as you like, but you're not going to rock mine.

ZACH. Here's a good one.
　　　We nest in our box
　　　Safe from the crow and the fox.

PEPPER. Ha, ha, we nest. I'm not a bird.

ZACH. *(Very angry.)* No, you're not a bird, but you are coo-coo. You're super coo-coo. *(He jumps around the box, beats his arms as though they were wings and yells jeeringly.)* Cock-a-doodle-doo.

PEPPER. *(Furious, he throws his hat at Zacharias.)* You're not going to get into my box, even if you stand on your blockhead.

ZACH. What would I do in your silly box? It stinks like a monkey house.

PEPPER. Monkeys don't have houses.

ZACH. Well, what do they have?

PEPPER. Fleas.

ZACH. Then it stinks like a smelly cheese.

PEPPER. Not true.

ZACH. Is.

PEPPER. Isn't.

ZACH. Is.

PEPPER. No.

ZACH. Yes it does, yes it does.

　　(While they are arguing the Drum Major appears. He has a marching drum slung over his shoulder with cymbals attached to the top. He beats a catchy marching tune and sings with it. He marches past both of them without giving them a glance. Before they have recovered from their surprise, he has disappeared. Pepper climbs out of his box and stares after him.)

PEPPER. Did you see that? Did you see that? That's how he marched. *(He marches in an exaggerated way.)* Rum ta ta rum ta ta. *(Zacharias trips him, Pepper falls on his belly. Zacharias yells at Pepper on the ground.)*

ZACH. Rum ta ta. And it's your fault that he went off. Why didn't you talk to him?

PEPPER. Why should I talk to him. You're fatter.

ZACH. I'm fatter? Very funny.

PEPPER. We can measure that.

ZACH. By all means let us. *(He takes off his coat, measures his coat, measures his waist with his hand, and shows the distance.)* That's how thin I am. *(Then he walks over to Pepper, puts one hand on his shoes and extends the other to his head. He shows with extended arms.)* That's how fat you are.

PEPPER. Ha! You cheated.

ZACH. *I* cheated?

PEPPER. Of course. You first took off your coat. *(He also removes his coat.)* So I am also thin.

(At this moment, the Drum Major reappears. As before, he marches past the two, clear across the stage. Immediately after that he disappears. The two quickly put on their coats.)

ZACH. *(Whispering the whole time.)* Go on, speak to him. Go on, say something. Hurry. Speak to him. *(He kicks him.)* Now he's gone. You oaf.

PEPPER. *(Crying.)* You're always bawling me out. I don't have any idea how to speak to him.

ZACH. All right. We'll practice. *(He grabs Pepper by his shoulders and places him in front of himself. He steps back a few paces. He assumes a new demeanor, raises one finger and begins to imitate the Drum Major as he marches off with a rum ta ta. Pepper runs after him and marches alongside delighted. Zacharias, unnerved, makes a face, stops and puts his hand on his waist. Pepper bumps into him and continues to march in place.)*

ZACH. *(Yells at him.)* You're supposed to address me.

PEPPER. What am I supposed to say?

ZACH. Good morning, my name is Pepper.

PEPPER. Ha ha. Your name is Zacharias.

ZACH. *(Kicks him.)* But your name is Pepper. You hippo!

> *(For the third time, the Drum Major appears. Pepper and Zacharias shove each other in his direction. Neither dares to address him. Each pushes the other ahead. As the Drum Major is about to go off, Zacharias pulls himself together and stands determined in his path. He bows very low and remains there for a long time. The Drum Major stops and ceases to play. Zacharias continues to bow.)*

ZACH. *(Bent over.)* Good morning.

MAJOR. *(Very curt.)* Morning.

ZACH. *(Still bent over.)* Pepper wants to address you.

PEPPER. *(Whispering.)* Speak to him.

ZACH. *(Raising himself.)* What did you say?

PEPPER. Talk to him.

ZACH. *(Bending down again.)* Pepper wants to talk to you.

MAJOR. Well, then.

ZACH. *(Stands up, pushes Pepper before him, pushes Pepper's head down for a bow.)* Go on, say something.

PEPPER. Like this, I can't talk.

ZACH. What do you mean like this?

PEPPER. With the head down.

ZACH. But you are talking.

PEPPER. *(Resentfully.)* Good morning, my name is Pepper.

MAJOR. So much I know.

PEPPER. *(Straightens up and looks delighted at Zacharias.)* He knows me. *(He turns to the Drum Major and points to Zacharias.)* Do you know him too?

MAJOR. No.

PEPPER. He doesn't know you. That's Zacky.

ZACH. Zach-a-ri-asss!

PEPPER. We think it's nice the way you walk around, really nice, with ram tam tam. *(He starts to march.)*

ZACH. It's fantastomatic.

PEPPER. And that's a fine drum. Drums real nice. Ram ta ta ta. *(He imitates the march and infects Zacharias with it. Both march in a circle around the Drum Major.)*

MAJOR. *(Hits the cymbals and shouts.)* Quiet! Number one, that's not walking, that's marching. Number two, that's not an ordinary drum, that's a marching drum. Third, it makes me sick to look at you. That's how badly you march.

PEPPER. So show us how you munch.

MAJOR. *March!*

PEPPER. May we also hit the drum?

ZACH. And also the metal thing up there? Ping, ping, ping.

MAJOR. *(Hits the cymbals and shouts.)* Quiet! First we will march, then you may hit the drum once.

ZACH. Fantastomatic.

PEPPER. Really, super terrific.

MAJOR. Quiet! No talking in-between. All in step!

PEPPER. *(Puzzled.)* What are we supposed to step on?

ZACH. Don't know. On all he said.

PEPPER. You can't step on all.

ZACH. Then step a little bit. Go on before he starts yelling again. *(He pushes him with his elbow. Pepper raises his foot uncertainly several times. Then both stand and look at the Drum Major in order to discover what he could have meant.)*

MAJOR. *(Shouting.)* Line up!

ZACH. Oh, well.

PEPPER. You see. *(Neither makes a move.)*

MAJOR. What's the matter. I'm waiting.

ZACH. There is no line.

PEPPER. Nowhere.

MAJOR. One stand behind the other.

PEPPER. Oh, well.

ZACH. Why didn't he say that? *(Pepper takes a position in front of Zacharias.)*

ZACH. Hey, he said behind the other. You're standing in front of me.

PEPPER. Excuse me. *(He now goes behind Zacharias.)* Now you're standing in front of me. Now you have to stand behind me.

ZACH. I stay where I stay!

PEPPER. As you like. *(He steps again in front of Zacharias.)*

ZACH. Will you please go behind me, you wise guy. I am marching first.

PEPPER. That's what you think.

ZACH. We'll see about that. *(He stands now in front of Pepper.)* You think you can march first because you've got two holes in your box.

PEPPER. You're jealous. Because you can't make things big and small with your box.

ZACH. Big and small, big and small. My box is seventeen times better than yours.

PEPPER. Better? *(He turns to the Drum Major who has been listening impatiently.)* Come, I'll show you my box.

MAJOR. Now we'll march.

ZACH. No. My box. Come here to my box. Pepper, here, let's turn my box around. *(Pepper turns his back to him.)*

MAJOR. Go on, help him. So we can finally do our marching. *(Pepper and Zacharias turn the box over twice.)*

ZACH. Isn't this a magic box? You see it's green and now watch it. Red. Big time, eh? Fantastomatic.

MAJOR. *(Genuinely surprised.)* Amazing. Changes color as it's turned.

ZACH. Now I'll show you Pepper's box. You'll be amazed again. *(He prepares to climb into Pepper's box.)*

PEPPER. Leave my box alone. *(He pulls Zacharias away and climbs in himself.)* Now watch. *(He pushes the two different-sized arms out of the box.)* Wham, bang, wham, bang.

MAJOR. I'll be damned!

PEPPER. Bang, wham, bang, wham.

MAJOR. Extraordinary, remarkable! The most remarkable boxes I've ever come across.

ZACH. Which do you like best? Mine?

PEPPER. Mine, of course.

MAJOR. I like them both. Yes, both. *(He nods approvingly at both boxes.)*

ZACH. Who can march first?

MAJOR. What did you say? Oh, yes, marching. Let me think. Best thing is for each of you to practice by yourself. More likely to succeed that way. *(He hangs the drum around Zacharias' neck and gives him the drum sticks.)* Hit the drums and forward march. One, two, one, two. *(He pushes Zacharias off stage and shouts after him.)* Practice well and no stopping even after three hundred paces!

PEPPER. You let him march and you let him hit the drum.

MAJOR. *(Putting his hand on Pepper's shoulder.)* Leave him, you'll get your turn. Then the drum is going to sound much louder.

PEPPER. Much louder?

MAJOR. Of course, much louder. It's got to be warmed up or else I wouldn't have first sent Fatso off.

PEPPER. Who?

MAJOR. The fat one. Can't stand him, can you, that showoff? *(Pepper is about to gently contradict him but the Drum Major doesn't give him a chance.)* I get it, I get it only too well. A disgusting big talker. The way he treats you, really mean.

PEPPER. It's a fact. He never lets me shorten his name. He always says Zacharias.

MAJOR. You see, you see. He surely never lets you into his box, this
 Zacky. *(Pepper shakes his head self-pityingly.)* I could see that
 at first glance, the kind of guy he is. His box isn't much. Not
 much at all.

PEPPER. He always calls me animal names.

MAJOR. Animal names. Devilish. What a pig! I could see right away
 what you thought when he marched off.

PEPPER. *(Surprised.)* I?

MAJOR. You are right, absolutely right. He's got to be taught a
 lesson. We have to take something from him that he really
 likes.

PEPPER. How about his hat? He's always got it on, even when he
 sleeps.

MAJOR. Right. His hat, for example. But that we can't take away
 because he isn't here. What could we take away? *(Looks
 around, nothing occurs to him. He shrugs.)* If only he'd left
 something behind.

PEPPER. Only the box.

MAJOR. Right! This man can think, splendid. We'll take his box
 away from him. I'll make you my headmarcher. You may march
 behind me, immediately behind me. But not a word to Fatso.
 Okay? Now grab hold of the box.

PEPPER. But that isn't right. What's Zacky going to say?

MAJOR. You're not going to be a spoilsport, you're not going to be
 chicken? After all, it was your idea. Are you afraid?

PEPPER. What are you going to do with the box?

MAJOR. My truck is over there. A good hiding place. Grab hold of it.

PEPPER. What if Zacky is going to be angry?

MAJOR. Why should he be angry with you? He doesn't know that
 you've hidden his box.

PEPPER. But then we'll give it back to him. All right?

*(In the meantime, the drumbeats have become louder. Zacha-
rias is returning.)*

MAJOR. The elephant walrus is coming back. What are we going to do with the box? After all, yours is the bigger. Let's put his into yours. Quick, on the double. *(They put Zacharias' box into Pepper's.)* Not a word to Zacky. That's agreed. Best thing is— you be gone. Or else he'd be able to tell by your face. Don't look so dumb, Mr. Headmarcher. It's only a joke. You want to be part of a joke, don't you? *(They just manage to hide the box. Zacharias returns marching. He proudly keeps banging the drums and the cymbal. He's marking time in order to show Pepper how it's done.)*

ZACH. Surprised, eh? This is the right article. Fantastomatic.

MAJOR. Very expert. *(He removes the drum from him and puts it on Pepper.)* All right, now it's your turn. Pay attention to the beat. One, two, one, two, and so on.

ZACH. *(The expert.)* He's hitting it too fast. Much too excited. Slower, Pepper. More feeling. He just doesn't have the gift. *(Pepper is off.)*

MAJOR. Could be a fact. Doesn't compare to you.

ZACH. Really?

MAJOR. Can't get it through my head, how you can have a friend like that? With your talents. That dwarf, he isn't all there, is he?

ZACH. Well, now . . .

MAJOR. Not much of a friendship, I'm sure. More like acquaintances, I guess.

ZACH. Well . . .

MAJOR. Nor do I understand how a flea like him ever got a box like that. His is far superior to yours.

ZACH. That's not true. Mine . . . *(He realizes only now that his box is gone.)* My box! My box is gone. My box, where's my box?

MAJOR. Your box. You must be kidding.

ZACH. *(Looking everywhere.)* Somebody has swiped my box. It's been stolen. Didn't you see who took it? My box is gone.

MAJOR. Didn't see a thing. I've been listening to you. Still I have certain ideas. . . . If I were you, I'd put a few questions to your friend.

ZACH. Pepper? I'm going to clobber him if he did it. I'm going to get him.

MAJOR. And if he doesn't admit it? You've got to be smarter than that.

ZACH. So what shall I do?

MAJOR. You've got to force it. Put it to him this way: either you give me back my box or . . .

ZACH. Or?

MAJOR. I keep something of yours.

ZACH. Indeed, keep what?

MAJOR. Hmm, keep what?

ZACH. I don't have anything of his.

MAJOR. Then take something. Look around.

ZACH. I don't see anything.

MAJOR. And what is that?

ZACH. The box?!

MAJOR. That's it. Took you a good long time. You take my box, I'll take your box. That's clear and simple.

ZACH. Maybe it wasn't even Pepper.

MAJOR. Entirely unimportant. He's got to be taught a lesson. Such a wise guy and he keeps insisting that his box is better than yours. Marches like an orangutan and pretends to be a head-marcher.

ZACH. Is that true?

MAJOR. That's what he said. But he's in for a surprise. I've thought of someone else for that job. Got my meaning? Of course, this is strictly between you and me. We'll hide the box, over there on my truck. You may march directly behind me but it has to remain a secret as we said. He can keep looking for it for a long time, eh? That'll be a killer of a joke. Just imagine his dumb face. Attention! Pu-u-sh, push. Easy does it.

ZACH. *(Pushing against the box.)* It's good and heavy.

MAJOR. No problem for experienced marchers. Keep shoving.

(Slowly they push the box off stage. A few seconds later Pepper marching proudly returns. With the cymbal he strikes the drum and with the drumsticks he strikes the cymbal. He walks in a large circle on the stage. He hasn't realized that he is alone.)

PEPPER. *(Over his shoulder.)* Hey, Zacky, you haven't said a thing. Flabbergasted, eh? Great, eh? Bang, bang, ta ra. *(He turns around.)* Zacky, Zach-a-ri-asss. The box is gone. I'm all alone in the world. Zacharias! The box!

(Zacharias and Drum Major return. Zacharias tries to hide a little behind the Drum Major and looks at Pepper anxiously.)

PEPPER. My box is gone too! Someone has taken my box!

MAJOR. Has to be investigated. Carefully investigated. Look at yourself. Did you use that to hit the drum? *(He takes the cymbal from him.)* Go on, hit it! *(Pepper listlessly strikes the cymbal with the drum stick.)*

MAJOR. Incredible! About time that you march properly. Let me have it. *(He straps the drum on himself.)* Pepper, you march first. You like that, eh?

PEPPER. Nothing matters to me if I don't have my box.

MAJOR. Forget your box. That'll be carefully investigated. Right now let Fatty go first. Are you ready? When I say forward march, you march off. It's always one, two, begin with the left foot. Which is your left foot? *(Pepper points unenthusiastically to his left arm. Zacharias points eagerly to his right foot.)*

MAJOR. *(Steps on the left foot of each.)* That's the left foot. That's the one you start with. Forward, march. One, two, one, two, rum, rum ta ta. That's right, first class. Doing it right. *(Pepper and Zacharias march in a circle across the stage. Pepper is at first indifferent, but with praise from the Drum Major marches spiritedly. The Drum Major withdraws unnoticed from the stage. His praises and commands are still heard as he moves further and further away. Pepper and Zacharias fall out of step, then one can hear a truck starting and driving off in high gear. Pepper and Zacharias run to the edge of the stage.)*

ZACH. He's driving away.

PEPPER. Simply driving away.

ZACH. Such a dog!

PEPPER. What a meany!

ZACH. Such an ape! Such a hippo! Such a beast. I'll kick him in the behind if I ever get hold of him again.

PEPPER. He was no friend. He just pretended.

(Brief silence.)

ZACH. Hey, Pepper.

PEPPER. What.

ZACH. I have to tell you something.

PEPPER. What?

ZACH. You . . . your box . . .

PEPPER. What about my box?

ZACH. It's in his truck. *(Hurriedly.)* I just wanted to hide it. I would have returned it to you. Right away. He said you had to be taught a lesson. So I helped him . . .

PEPPER. You helped him?! A fine friend you turned out to be. The hell with you. *(He spits in front of him.)* I would never have believed it.

ZACH. I'm very sorry.

PEPPER. Sorry, sorry! That doesn't help me a bit. *(Pause.)* Zacky!

ZACH. *(Very sad.)* Zach-a-ri-ass.

PEPPER. Zachariass, I have to tell you something.

ZACH. Go on.

PEPPER. Something bad about your box.

ZACH. *(Grabbing hold of him.)* My box? What have you done with it?

PEPPER. He put it into mine.

ZACH. In yours?

PEPPER. He said it was just a joke. I meant to give it back to you. Right away. But how can I take it out if my box is gone too?

ZACH. You helped him. You worm.

PEPPER. Just a bit. He said you had to be taught a lesson. He turned me against you. *(Zacharias shakes him furiously until Pepper cries.)* If you hadn't carried off my box, yours would still be here too.

ZACH. *(Letting him go.)* You're right. He cheated both of us, the liar.

PEPPER. He said he was going to make me the headmarcher.

ZACH. You abandoned your friend, Zacharias, just so you could become a headmarcher.

PEPPER. You also wanted to march first. And besides you wanted to teach me a lesson too. You just said so.

ZACH. You, me, too. We're beginning to argue again. Everything that happened, happened because we didn't stick together.

PEPPER. It's our fault.

ZACH. We made it very easy for him. All he does is promise you something and right away you cheat your friend Zacharias.

PEPPER. And you your friend Pepper.

ZACH. It's our fault. *(They sadly sit down where their boxes formerly stood.)*

(Pepper begins to do gymnastic exercises. Zacharias takes out his toothbrush and brushes his hair and shoes.)

PEPPER. You're all right. At least, you still have a carton and a toothbrush.

ZACH. You still have a bottle.

PEPPER. It's empty.

ZACH. My carton, too. *(He listlessly keeps on brushing.)* I once knew someone who could blow on a bottle like a steamboat's whistle.

PEPPER. On a bottle?

ZACH. Yes, like this. *(He tries it but all that comes out is a sad hissing.)*

PEPPER. Let me try. *(He tries without success. In the meantime, Zacharias examines his carton.)*

ZACH. Looks actually like a truck. You just have to imagine the head-lights. And the wheels. *(Zacharias has stood up and pushes the carton along the ground. There is a rattling noise. Surprised, he stops. At that very moment, the noise stops too. He pushes it a little further and again there is a noise. Pepper gets up and watches, fascinated. Zacharias pushes the box across the stage behind the backdrop. When he reappears on the other side of the backdrop, the clatter has become louder and the carton bigger.)*

PEPPER. Hey, Zacharias, look!

ZACH. *(The noise ceases.)* What's the matter?

PEPPER. Your carton got bigger.

ZACH. Really?

PEPPER. Drive it around once more.

(Zacharias pushes the little box several times at increasing speed around the backdrop. Every time he reappears, the clatter becomes louder and the box larger. At last the box is as large as the old one. Exhausted, Zacharias stops center stage.)

ZACH. Pfgh. No more driving around. The carton has gotten too heavy. *(He wipes the sweat off.)*

PEPPER. What do you mean carton? This is an honest-to-goodness box. Just as big as the one that he swiped.

ZACH. *(Realizes it only now.)* Box! Man that's crazy, fantastomatic. *(He walks around the box, steps inside.)*

PEPPER. Hey, Zacharias.

ZACH. Absolutely first rate. Nice box, nice box.

PEPPER. Zacharias, that's our box isn't it? I mean it belongs to both of us. Doesn't it?

ZACH. Both of us? You've got to be batty.

PEPPER. But you'll lend it to me.

ZACH. *(Polishing the edge of the box.)* A box is not a rental car.

PEPPER. May I climb in just once?

ZACH. With those dirty feet?

PEPPER. If you don't let me, I'm not going to be your friend anymore. *(Zacharias continues to polish his box.)* I'm going to find myself another friend.

ZACH. Without a box?

(Pepper turns around and walks away angrily. Zacharias doesn't notice that Pepper has disappeared. After a while, he looks up and realizes that he is all alone.)

ZACH. *(Astonished.)* Pepper?

(Zacharias shrugs and keeps on cleaning his box but soon he loses interest and, annoyed, throws down his handkerchief. He stands inside the box and considers intently what he should do next. Then he climbs out of the box and tries to turn it around. But by himself, he can't do it. He furiously kicks the box and climbs back in. Now he begins to play airplane. It's no fun. His arms keep dropping lower and finally he cries out, "PEPPER." No reply. Zacharias climbs out of the box and starts looking for Pepper. Unsuccessful, he sits down in front of the box in complete despair. At that moment, Pepper returns because he has forgotten his bottle. He stumbles over Zacharias.)

PEPPER. What's the matter with you?

ZACH. You left me alone.

PEPPER. Left you alone, left you alone! This box was more important to you than a friend.

ZACH. It was only a joke, Pepper. This box belongs to both of us. We found out together how to make it bigger.

PEPPER. Now you tell me. But later you're going to say it's your box and kick me out.

ZACH. Never again. It's much too boring in that box alone. Come get in. It belongs to both of us.

PEPPER. Okay. *(He climbs into the box and helps Zacharias when he gets in.)* Wait I'll help you. A great box, our box. Really super, extra super. And so cozy.

ZACH. Before you said it was worm-eaten.

PEPPER. I was just kidding, because you annoyed me. This box is okay. Perfect for playing airplane. Really phenomenal.

ZACH. Phenomenal?

PEPPER. Yes, terrific. Or maybe it could be a motorcycle with a passenger seat on the side. One of us can sit on the edge like a
side-car passenger. *(Zacharias makes loud motor sounds and
Pepper joins in excitedly.)*

ZACH. Watch it. Curve! *(He sits on the edge of the box.)* Lean over!
*(He leans out so far that he almost falls out of the box. Pepper
pulls him back in.)* Fantastomatic.

PEPPER. You can do this only if there are two of us. If there are two
of us, playing in a box is better. Hey, we can also play police
car. Fa too ta too ta. Listen there's a song for a box. I just didn't
tell you before.

ZACH. What's it called?

PEPPER. Seven cops. That goes well with a police car.

ZACH. I know it.

PEPPER. Why didn't you sing it then?

ZACH. Because it's about cops.

PEPPER. And about boxes. *(He starts to sing and Zacharias sings
along.)*
>Seven thick, fat copses
>Who weighed almost a ton
>Fell into some boxes
>One by one by one.
>Their sergeant wrote a letter
>To the Chief Justice of the state
>To send slim men, maybe eight.

*(While they are still singing, one can hear drumbeats. The
Drum Major returns. He is wearing a different hat and a false
nose. It's impossible to tell whether he is the former one returning disguised or another Drum Major. Again he marches
arrogantly across the stage. This time however the two are so
deeply absorbed in their games that they don't notice him.
Unsuccessfully, he tries to get their attention. Then he speaks
to them.)*

MAJOR. Well, you two. Don't want to march with me. One, two,
one, two. Hut, hup, eh?

ZACH. Don't feel like it.

PEPPER. We're playing.

ZACH. Racing car, drr, drr, drrm. *(Pepper joins him in making racing car sounds.)*

MAJOR. Racing car? Ridiculous.

PEPPER. We like it.

MAJOR. *(To Zacharias.)* That shrimp's got a pretty big mouth. You're putting up with that?

ZACH. If that bothers you, you don't have to listen.

PEPPER. *(Triumphant.)* If you want to go, nobody's stopping you.

MAJOR. And that's what I'm going to do. . . . But seriously, a little marching would be good for both of you. Especially that fat gentleman. Then you'd have a little more room in the box, eh? *(He laughs loudly.)*

PEPPER. *(Cool.)* We've got enough room.

ZACH. Better fat than dumb.

MAJOR. All kinds of fancy ideas with your ratty box. Racing car and such. You're too stupid to learn how to march properly. Yep, that's it. You're childish. Racing car! *(He goes off furious.)*

ZACH. Beat it. Or we're going to help you out of here. *(Raises his arm threateningly.)*

PEPPER. Yes, on the double, one, two, one, two, you kangaroo. I gave it to him.

ZACH. We showed him. Fantabulous. What are we going to play now?

PEPPER. We'll sing.

ZACH. And what will we sing?

PEPPER. The second part.

ZACH. The second part is fine. Who starts off?

PEPPER. Both of us.

ZACH. Both of us. Right. *(They sing the second stanza together. As they sing, they slowly sink into the box. At the very end, they raise their heads one last time. Then they disappear for good.)*
Seven thick, fat copses
Who weighed almost a ton

Climbed out of the boxes
One by one by one.
The sergeant burnt the letter
Which he didn't have to send.
It turned out for the better,
Which brings us to the end . . .

(Curtain.)

The Arkansaw Bear

By Aurand Harris

Copyright, 1980, Anchorage Press, Inc.

The Arkansaw Bear (1980)

In his twenty-five plays for children Aurand Harris has continually shown a masterful understanding and appreciation of the child audience. He broke new ground in 1980 with a serious fantasy that focuses on a subject seldom discussed in detail with children, death. In *The Arkansaw Bear*, Harris skillfully combines spoken philosophies concerning death and dying with an actual event to remind his audience that death is a natural and inevitable part of life and living.

The play includes two separate but fundamentally related stories. The first concerns a young girl, Tish, who is trying to come to terms with her grandfather's eminent death. Through minimal exposition, it is revealed that Tish's mother is trying to shield her from this fact by forbidding her to see him. This only serves to add to Tish's confusion, fear, and frustration.

When Tish runs off to be alone, Harris introduces the second story of the play through the character of the World's Greatest Dancing Bear. Dancing Bear is an aged circus performer who is trying to escape the Ringmaster. Dancing Bear knows that once he succumbs to the Ringmaster he will be led to the great Center Ring—Harris' metaphor for death. Dancing Bear eventually realizes that his spirit can go on living forever if he teaches his dances to Little Bear, his "chip off the old block." It is through these actions by Dancing Bear that Tish learns the old bear's secret; life is a full circle and that although her grandfather may die, a part of him will live on—in her.

CHARACTERS

Tish

Star Bright

Mime

World's Greatest Dancing Bear

Little Bear

Voices: Mother

      Aunt Ellen

      Announcer

SETTING
Somewhere in Arkansas.

TIME
The present.

The Arkansaw Bear

As the house lights dim, there is a glow of light on the front cur-
tain. Over a loudspeaker a man's whistling of "O Susannah" is
heard. The curtains open. Tish walks into a large spot of warm
light at L. The whistling dims out. Tish is a little girl and carries
some hand-picked flowers. She listens to the voices, heard over a
loudspeaker, and reacts to them as if Mother and Aunt Ellen were
on each side of her, downstage.

TISH. I've come to see Grandpa.

MOTHER'S VOICE. No, dear. No. You can't go in.

TISH. But Mother—

MOTHER'S VOICE. No, Tish! You can't see Grandpa now.

TISH. I picked him some flowers. These are Grandpa's favorites.

AUNT ELLEN'S VOICE. *(She is Tish's great-aunt, elderly, gentle, and*
emotional.) Quiet, child.

TISH. But Aunt Ellen—

AUNT ELLEN'S VOICE. The doctor is here.

TISH. The doctor?

MOTHER'S VOICE. Tish, dear.

TISH. Yes, mother?

MOTHER'S VOICE. Grandpa had a turn for the worse. His heart—

AUNT ELLEN'S VOICE. Oh, it's the end.

(Cries quietly.)

TISH. The end?

AUNT ELLEN'S VOICE. The doctor said . . . no hope.

(Tish reacts.)

MOTHER'S VOICE. Don't cry, Aunt Ellen.

TISH. Is Grandpa going . . . to die?

AUNT ELLEN'S VOICE. Yes.

TISH. No! He can't.

MOTHER'S VOICE. We all have to die, dear.

TISH. I know. But not Grandpa.

(*Starts to move.*)

MOTHER'S VOICE. Stop. You can't go in.

TISH. Why can't he live forever!

AUNT ELLEN'S VOICE. You're too young to understand. Too full of life.

TISH. I have to tell him there's a circus coming. I saw a poster with a bear.

MOTHER'S VOICE. It doesn't matter now.

TISH. Yes, it does! Do something!

MOTHER'S VOICE. (*Firmly.*) We've done all we can.

TISH. But not enough! I . . . I didn't do enough!

AUNT ELLEN'S VOICE. Quiet. Quiet.

TISH. (*Softly.*) Yes, if I'd been quiet so he could sleep. And—Oh! Once when I was mad, I said . . . I wish he was dead. Oh, I didn't mean it, Grandpa. I didn't mean it.

MOTHER'S VOICE. Hush, dear. It's not your fault. Grandpa loved you.

TISH. Then why is he . . . leaving me?

(*Pulls away as if being held.*)

TISH. Oh, let me go!

MOTHER'S VOICE. (*Sharply, becoming edgy with emotion.*) Yes. Go put the flowers in some water.

TISH. He liked the pink ones. Now . . . he'll never see them. Oh, why . . . why does Grandpa have to die?

MOTHER'S VOICE. (*Sternly, trying to control and cover her grief.*) Run along, dear. Run along.

AUNT ELLEN'S VOICE. Keep away. Away from his door. Away . . . away.

(*The voices of Mother and Aunt Ellen overlap and mix together, as they keep repeating, "Run along," "Away," "Run . . . run," "Away . . . away," "Run," "Away," "Run . . . away; run . . . away." They build to a climax in a choral chant, "Run . . . away.")*

TISH. I will. I'll run away. Up the hill . . . to my tree . . . my tree.

(She runs, circling to the tree which is at R, and on which the lights come up. The circle of light on the first scene dims out, and the chanting of the voices stops. Tish stands alone by her tree in the soft light of evening. She brushes back a tear, shakes her head, and throws the flowers on the ground.)

(She sinks to the ground by the tree, hugs her knees, and looks up. She sees the first star, which is out of sight. Quickly she gets up, points to the star and chants.)

Star light, star bright,
First star I see tonight,
I wish I may, I wish I might,
Have the wish I wish tonight.
I wish . . . I wish . . . Oh, Grandpa . . . why?

(Goes back to tree.)

Why do you have to die?

(There is star music, tinkling with bells. From above, a small swing starts descending. Magic star light spots on it. Star Bright stands on the swing, which stops in mid-air. Music dims out.)

STAR BRIGHT. Repeat, please.

TISH. I wish . . . I wish . . .

STAR BRIGHT. I know you are wishing. That's why I'm here. But WHAT? Repeat, please.

TISH. *(Sees and goes near him.)* Who are you?

STAR BRIGHT. *(Slowly and proudly.)* I am the first star out tonight!

(Happily.)

I did it! I did it! I did it again!

(Excitedly.)

First star . . . first star . . . first star out tonight!

(To Tish.)

It's the early star, you know, who gets the wish. What is yours? Repeat, please.

TISH. Can you make a wish come true?

STAR BRIGHT. I've been making wishes come true for a thousand years.

TISH. A thousand years! You're older than Grandpa.

STAR BRIGHT. *(Sits on swing.)* Old? Oh, no. I'll twinkle for another thousand years.

TISH. And then?

STAR BRIGHT. *(Cheerfully.)* Then my light will go out.

TISH. Like Grandpa.

STAR BRIGHT. But there will be a new star. It's the great pattern . . .

TISH. I'll never have another Grandpa.

STAR BRIGHT. . . . the great circle of life. In every ending there is a new beginning.

TISH. *(Fully realizing it.)* I'll never see Grandpa again. I'll never hear him whistle.

(Begins to whistle "O Susannah.")

STAR BRIGHT. Your wish? What is your wish?

TISH. I wish . . . I wish Grandpa could live a thousand years!

STAR BRIGHT. *(Startled.)* What? Repeat, please!

TISH. *(Excited.)* I wish he'd never die. Nobody would ever die! Everyone live forever!

STAR BRIGHT. Oh, no, no, no! Think what a mixed up world it would be!

TISH. *(Speaks intently.)* I wish . . . I wish I knew why . . . why Grandpa has to die.

STAR BRIGHT. That is not a quick one-two-buckle-my-shoe wish. No. That is a think-and-show-it, then-you-know-it, come-true wish.

TISH. Please.

STAR BRIGHT. *(With anticipated excitement.)* Close your eyes. Whisper the words again. Open your eyes. And your wish will begin.

(Tish closes her eyes. Star Bright claps his hands, then motions. There are music and beautiful lights. Star Bright is delighted with the effect.)

Very good! Repeat, please.

(He claps and waves his hand. Again there are music and beautiful lights.)

Excellent! Thank you!

(The swing with Star Bright is pulled up and out of sight. The full stage is seen, lighted brightly and in soft colors. [Never is the stage dark, eerie, or frightening.] It is Tish's fantasy. There are the large tree at R, and open space with beautiful sky.

Mime appears at R. He is a showman, a magician and an accomplished mime who never speaks. He wears a long coat with many colorful patch pockets. He is NOT in white face, but his face is natural, friendly, and expressive. He enters cautiously, carrying a traveling box, which he sets down at C. On the side the audience sees is painted the word BEAR. On the other side is painted the word DANCING. He beckons off R. The World's Greatest Dancing Bear enters R. He is a star performer, amusing, vain, and loveable like a teddy bear. He does NOT wear an animal mask, nor is the actor's face painted, frightening or grotesque, with animal make-up. He wears his traveling hat. He hurries in, worried and out of breath.)

BEAR. I must stop and get my breath.

(Pants heavily.)

My heart is pounding.

(Looks about.)

Are we safe?

(Frightened.)

I don't see him. I don't hear him. Yes, we have outrun him.

(Motions and Mime places box for Bear to sit.)

Where . . . where in this wide whirling wonderful world . . . do you think we are? Switzerland?

(Mime makes pointed mountain with his wrist, runs his fingers up and down the "mountain," then shakes his head.)

You are right. No mountains. England?

(Mime opens and holds up imaginary umbrella, holds hand out to feel the rain, shakes his head.)

You are right. No rain. India?

(Mime leans over, swings one arm for a trunk, then other for his tail and walks.)

No elephants.

TISH. Excuse me.

(They freeze. She comes to them.)

I can tell you where you are. You are in Arkansas.

BEAR. Quick! Disguise. Hide.

(He and Mime hurry to R. Mime quickly takes from one of his pockets a pair of dark glasses and gives them to Bear who puts them on; then stands beside Bear to hide him.)

TISH. *(Recites with pride.)* Arkansas was the twenty-fifth state to be admitted to the union. It is the twenty-seventh in size, and the state flower is apple blossom.

BEAR. Who is it?

(Mime pantomimes a girl.)

A girl?

(Mime pantomimes a small girl.)

A little girl? Tell her to go away. To run away.

(Mime pantomimes to Tish. Bear hides behind tree.)

TISH. I have. I have run away. Have you run away, too?

(Mime nods.)

Why?

(Mime looks frightened off R, then puts finger to lips.)

Who are you?

(Mime takes a card from a pocket and presents it to her. She reads.)

"A Mime." You never speak.

(Mime shakes his head, and "walks" in one spot and tips his hat.)

"A Magician." You do tricks!

(Mime pulls handkerchief from sleeve.)

"Friend." You give help.

(Mime touches handkerchief under her eyes.)

Thank you. I was crying because my Grandpa . . . he's going to . . .

(Bear, without glasses, steps out from behind the tree, does a loud tap dance step, and poses. Mime turns the traveling box around and with a flourish points to the word painted on that side of the box. Tish reads it with amazement.)

Dancing.

(Mime turns box around again. She reads.)

Bear.

(Mime motions to Bear who steps forward.)

I've never met a bear. I've never seen a DANCING bear.

BEAR. *(To Mime.)*
Should I?

(Mime nods.)

Shall I?

(Mime nods.)

I will! My Spanish hat.

(Mime jumps with joy and gets hat from box. Bear motions to Tish who sits on the ground.)

Be seated, please.

(Mime holds up handmirror, which he takes from a pocket, holds it up for Bear to look at himself, and fixes the hat.)

To the right . . . to the right . . . Ah, just right!

(Mime motions and a spotlight comes on. An announcer's voice is heard over a loudspeaker.)

ANNOUNCER'S VOICE. Ladies and Gentlemen: Presenting in his spectacular, special, Spanish dance, the World's famous, the World's favorite, the World's Greatest Dancing Bear!

(Mime motions and Spanish music is heard. Bear steps into the spotlight. He dances with professional perfection a Span-

ish dance, but he does not finish. At a climactic moment, he stops, holds his hand against his heart, and speaks with short breaths.)

BEAR. Stop the music.

(Mime motions. Music stops.)

Dim the light.

(Mime motions. Spot dims out.)

TISH. What is it?

BEAR. *(Breathing heavily.)* He is near. He is coming.

TISH. Who?

BEAR. He is almost here. Hide. I must hide. He must not find me.

(Mime points to tree.)

Yes, the tree. Hurry!

(Mime helps Bear to tree.)

TISH. Who? Who is coming?

BEAR. The box. Cover the box.

(He disappears behind the tree. Mime sits on traveling box. Bear's head appears.)

Talk.

(Mime mime-talks with hands and face.)

Louder!

(Bear's head disappears. Mime motions for Tish to talk.)

TISH. Talk? What about?

BEAR. *(Head appears.)* Arkansas.

(Head disappears.)

TISH. *(Recites nervously.)* Arkansas has mineral springs, natural caves, and . . . and . . . diamond mines.

(Looks off R and whispers, frightened.)

I don't hear anyone. I don't see anyone.

(Mime motions for her to talk.)

Arkansas was first known as the state of many bears.

(Looks and whispers mysteriously.)

There isn't anyone. Nothing. Just quiet, nothing. Who is he running away from?

(Mime motions "Sh," then runs L to R and looks, then motions for Bear to come out.)

BEAR. *(Comes from behind tree.)* He didn't find me. I escaped . . . this time.

(Pleased, but short of breath.)

My traveling hat. We must go on.

(Mime takes Spanish hat and gives Bear traveling hat.)

TISH. Where? Where will you go?

BEAR. *(Looks off R, afraid.)* I must keep ahead of him.

TISH. Ahead of who? Who!

BEAR. *(Cautiously.)* Never speak his name aloud.

(Looks around.)

He may be listening, and come at once.

(Mime gives him hat.)

Oh, my poor hat. You and I have traveled together for many a mile and many a year. We are both beginning to look a little weary.

(Puts hat on.)

TISH. Grandpa has an old hat.

BEAR. Perhaps, if it had a new feather. Yes! A bright new feather!

TISH. I think your hat is very stylish.

BEAR. *(Pleased.)* You do?

TISH. And very becoming.

BEAR. *(Flattered.)* Thank you. You are a very charming little girl. What is your name?

TISH. Tish.

BEAR. Tish-sh-sh! That is not a name. That is a whistle. Ti-sh-sh-sh-sh!

TISH. It's short for Leticia. It was my Grandmother's name.

BEAR. Leticia. Ah, that is a name with beauty.

TISH. Grandpa calls me "Little Leticia."

BEAR. I shall call you . . .

> *(Rolling the "R").*

> Princess Leticia.

TISH. Princess?

BEAR. All my friends are important people. Kings and Queens. . . . Command performances for Ambassadors and Presidents . . .

> *(To Mime.)*

> The velvet box, please.

> *(Mime takes from a pocket a small box.)*

> I will show you my medals, my honors.

TISH. My Grandpa won a medal.

BEAR. Ah?

TISH. He was the best turkey caller in Arkansas.

BEAR. Turkey caller?

TISH. He won first prize!

BEAR. *(To Mime.)* Pin them on me so she can see. And so that I can remember . . . once again . . . all my glories.

> *(Royal music begins and continues during the scene. Mime puts ribbons and jeweled medals on Bear as Voice announces each decoration. Two are pinned on. One is on a ribbon which is fastened around Bear's neck.)*

ANNOUNCER'S VOICE. The Queen's highest honor, the Royal Medallion.

BEAR. I danced in the Great Hall. It was the Queen's birthday party.

ANNOUNCER'S VOICE. The Diamond Crescent of the East.

BEAR. Fifteen encores. Fifteen encores and they still applauded.

ANNOUNCER'S VOICE. The Royal Ribbon of Honor for Distinguished Service.

BEAR. It was during the war. I danced for the soldiers.

ANNOUNCER'S VOICE. And today, a new decoration. Her Royal Highness Princess Leticia presents, in honor of her Grandfather, the highest award in the State of Arkansas—the Turkey Feather.

(Mime takes a bright feather from a pocket and gives it to Tish. Bear parades to her, with a few dance steps, and she puts the feather in his hat. Royal music stops.)

BEAR. Thank you. A party! We will celebrate my new honor!

(To Mime.)

Food and festivities! Honey bread!

(Mime nods.)

Thick with honey spread!

(Mime nods twice, then makes magic motions toward Bear. Suddenly Mime turns and points to Leticia. She puts out her hand which, magically, holds a honey bun.)

TISH. *(Delighted.)* O-o-oh! It looks delicious.

BEAR. *(Mime turns and points to Bear who puts out his hand which, also magically, holds a colorful honey bun.)*

A-a-ah! It IS delicious.

(Bear puts finger in it, then licks finger. Mime raises his hand.)

Yes, give us a toast.

(Bear and Tish hold honey buns up. Mime pantomimes "A toast . . ." holds up his hand; "to the winner . . ." clasps his hands and shakes them high in the air; "of the turkey feather," walks like a turkey, bobbing his head, then Mime pulls out an imaginary feather from his hip.)

Thank you.

TISH. What did he say?

BEAR. You didn't listen.

TISH. How can I hear when he doesn't speak?

BEAR. You listen with your eyes, and then YOU say the words. Listen. He will repeat the toast.

TISH. *(Mime pantomimes the toast again. She watches and speaks aloud.)* "Toast . . . to the winner . . . of the turkey feather!"

BEAR. Thank you. Now entertainment!

(To Mime.)

You tell us a story.

(To Tish.)

You listen and say the words.

TISH. Me?

BEAR. And I will eat!

(Wiggles with excitement and sits on box.)

TISH. *(Mime pantomimes a story which Tish, watching him, repeats in words.)* "Once there was . . . a princess . . . a beautiful princess!"

BEAR. Named.

(Sings it.)

Leticia.

(Takes a bite.)

TISH. "One day . . . in the woods . . . she met . . .

(Doubtful.)

. . . a cat?"

(Mime shakes his head. Mimes again.)

A . . . goosey-gander?

(Mime shakes his head. Mimes again.)

TISH. A . . . bear!

BEAR. The World's Greatest Dancing Bear!

(Seated, he makes his own vocal music and dances with his feet.)

TISH. "Under a spreading tree . . . they had a party . . . with honey bread, thick with honey spread."

BEAR. *(Licks his five fingers, one on each word.)* Yum . . . yum . . . TO . . . the . . . last . . . crumb.

(Licks his hand and picks and eats crumbs from his lap.)

TISH. "Now honey bread, thick with honey spread . . . made the bear . . . very . . . sleepy. He yawned."

(Bear follows action of the story and goes to sleep.)

". . . gave a little sigh . . . and took a little nap."

(Bear snores.)

He's asleep. Who . . . who is he running away from?

(Mime goes to sleeping Bear, puts his finger to his lips, then mimes.)

"The World's Greatest Dancing Bear . . . is old and tired . . . and his heart . . . is tired."

(Herself.)

Like Grandpa.

(Speaking for Mime.)

"He is running away from . . ." Who? "Someone is coming to take him away . . . forever." Does that mean if he's caught, he will die?

(Mime nods.)

TISH. Is he running away . . . from death?

(Mime nods.)

Oh! I'll help him. Yes, I'll help him.

(Faint music of a calliope is heard, Bear stirs.)

He's waking up.

BEAR. *(Slowly wakes up.)* Music . . . the calliope . . . circus music . . . of the Great Center ring!

(Rises.)

The Ringmaster is coming!

TISH. *(To Mime.)* Death?

(Mime nods.)

BEAR. He is near. I hear the music.

TISH. I don't hear it.

(To Mime.)

Do you?

(Mime shakes his head.)

BEAR. Only I can hear him. Only I can see him. He is coming for me. Quick! We must go.

TISH. Yes, I'll help you.

BEAR. This way. Hurry!

(Mime carries box. Led by Bear they start L, but stop when the music becomes louder.)

No! No! The music is here. Quick! Turn! Run the other way.

(They rush to R and are stopped by music becoming louder.)

No! The music is coming from here. It is all around us! Here! There! Look!

(He points off R.)

TISH. What?

BEAR. The Great Ringmaster. He is there! He is coming . . . for me!

(Ringmaster enters slowly from R. He wears an ornate ring-master's jacket, boots and a tall hat. He has a friendly face, a pleasant voice, but walks and speaks with authority. He stops. Music stops.)

Quick! Hide me! Hide me!

(Bear runs to L. Tish and Mime follow. He quickly hides behind them when they stop. Bear peeks over Tish's shoulder.)

Tell him to go away.

TISH. I can't see him. Where is he?

BEAR. There.

(Hides.)

TISH. *(Bravely speaks, facing front talking into space.)* Excuse me . . . sir. This is my secret place . . . by the big tree. You must leave at once. Go away. Now.

(Whispers to Bear.)

Did he go?

BEAR. *(Peeks.)* No.

(Hides.)

RINGMASTER. *(Distinctly and with authority.)* I have come for the Dancing Bear. I have come to take him to the Great Center Ring.

BEAR. Tell him he has made a mistake.

TISH. Excuse me . . . sir. You have made a mistake.

RINGMASTER. *(Opens book.)* No. It is written plainly in the book. The date is today. The name is . . . the Dancing Bear.

BEAR. *(Who was hidden by Mime at the side, now steps into view, wearing boxing gloves and a sport cap.)* You HAVE made a mistake. I am a BOXING bear.

(Mime blows a whistle and continues to blow it, as Bear shadow boxes, comically, with a few dance steps and kicks thrown in. He ends in a heroic pose.)

Goodbye.

RINGMASTER. A boxing bear?

(Looks in book.)

There has never been a mistake.

TISH. *(Whispers.)* Have you tricked him? Outwitted him?

BEAR. *(Nods, then calls loudly.)* Yes. Training time. On your mark; get set; ready—talleyho!

(Starts jogging off R.)

RINGMASTER. *(Reads.)* The book says: His father, born in Russia, a dancing bear.

BEAR. *(Stops, indignant.)* Correct that. He was Russia's most honored dancing bear.

RINGMASTER. His mother, born in Spain, also a dancing bear.

BEAR. She was the prima ballerina bear of all Spain!

RINGMASTER. He, only son—

BEAR. Is the World's Greatest Dancing Bear!

RINGMASTER. Then you are the one I have come for!

BEAR. Yes!

RINGMASTER. Then we will have no more tricks or games.

(Bear realizes he has revealed himself.)

Come. Take my hand.

(Bear always reacts with fear to the Ringmaster's white gloved hand.)

I will show you the way to the Great Center Ring.

BEAR. No! No!

TISH. What is he saying?

BEAR. He is going to take me away.

RINGMASTER. Come. You must. And it is easier if you go quietly.

BEAR. No! I will not go with you. I will fight!

(Holds up boxing gloves.)

TISH. Fight him! I'll help you!

BEAR. I have fought all my life. Battled my way to the top. Look at my medals. I will fight to the end.

RINGMASTER. This, my friend, is the end.

BEAR. No! No! Not for me. Not yet! Stay away! I have new dances to do.

RINGMASTER. Today you will take your last bow.

BEAR. No! No.

(Savagely.)

I will claw! I will eat! I will crush! I will kill! Kill to live!

(Violently throws boxing gloves away.)

To live! To live!

RINGMASTER. Everyone shouts when he is frightened of the dark.

BEAR. I WILL NOT DIE!

RINGMASTER. You have no choice.

BEAR. But . . . why! Why me? ME!

RINGMASTER. You are like all the others. Everyone thinks HE will live forever. Come.

BEAR. No! What did I do wrong? What can I do now? To stop it!

RINGMASTER. Death comes to all. It has never been IF you will die. The only question has been WHEN you will die. Now you know.

BEAR. *(Runs.)* I will run. I will hide.

RINGMASTER. *(With authority.)* You cannot escape from death.

BEAR. *(Bargaining desperately.)* More time. Give me more time. I have so much to do.

RINGMASTER. *(Slightly annoyed.)* There is always that which is left undone.

BEAR. I don't know how . . . to die. I need to rehearse.

RINGMASTER. No one has to rehearse. It is very simple . . . very easy.

(Holds out hand.)

Come. It is growing late.

BEAR. No!

(Desperate for any excuse.)

I must write my memories! Tell the world the glories of my life. My life . . .

(Pause. Tish and Mime rush to him as he falters, place box, and help him sit.)

It is almost over. And what was it? A few medals that will be lost. No. There must be more to life. Give me time. Time to find the answer.

TISH. *(Kneeling by him, pleads into space.)* Please . . . let him live.

RINGMASTER. Your life is over. Today is the day.

BEAR. But my day is not over.

(To Tish.)

The day is not ended, is it?

TISH. Give him to the END of the day!

BEAR. Yes! To the end. Oh, you are a very smart little girl!

RINGMASTER. Well . . .

(Looks in his book.)

TISH. What did he say?

BEAR. He's looking in his book.

RINGMASTER. The day you are to die is written plainly. But not the hour.

BEAR. Then give me the full day.

TISH. Please.

RINGMASTER. *(Pause.)* I will give you until midnight. Until the last hour of your last day.

BEAR. YES!

TISH. Can you live?

BEAR. YES! Oh, let me shout to the world! I AM ALIVE!

(To Mime.)

Give me my brightest, my happiest hat!

(To Ringmaster, who has gone.)

Oh, thank you . . . thank you . . . He is gone . . . for a while.

(To Tish.)

Oh, let me touch you. Let me feel the warmth . . . the life in you. There is much yet to do! And so little time. My life . . . it went too fast. I didn't stop to listen . . . I didn't stop to see.

(Mime waves clown hat in front of Bear.)

Oh, yes! I will be the clown!

(Puts hat on. To Tish.)

Come. Dance with me! And we will make the world spin round and round with joy!

TISH. Grandpa taught me how to whistle and how to dance a jig.

(Quickly she whistles "O Susannah," and does a little jig, looking at her feet.)

BEAR. No, no, no. To dance is a great honor. Hold your head high.

(*He follows his own instructions.*)

And first you smile to the right . . . then you smile to the left . . . and you bow to the center . . . and then . . . begin.

(*Mime motions. A spotlight comes on Bear. Music is heard. Bear does short, charming soft-shoe dance. Spotlight and music dim out. Tish applauds. Bear sits on box which Mime places for him. Bear is happy, breathless.*)

TISH. Oh, how wonderful!

BEAR. Thank you.

TISH. You're better than Grandpa! He can only do a little jig.

BEAR. But he taught you?

TISH. Yes.

BEAR. And he taught you how to whistle?

TISH. Yes.

BEAR. (*Rises.*) If I could teach my dances to someone . . . if someone could carry on the fame of my family . . . All my hats . . . there will be no one to wear my hats. They, too, will be put in a box and forgotten. Tell me, are you like your Grandfather?

TISH. Daddy says I'm a chip off the old block.

BEAR. You are a part of him. And you will carry on for him in life.

(*Excited.*)

Yes! Yes, that is the answer to the riddle.

TISH. What riddle?

BEAR. The riddle of life. I must leave my dances! They will be a part of me that will live on! But who? Where! How!

TISH. Make a wish!

BEAR. A wish?

TISH. On the first star you see. And it will come true. It will. It will!

BEAR. (*Wanting to believe.*) You are sure it will?

(*Tish nods. To Mime.*)

Do you believe it will?

(Mime nods.)

I could try.

TISH. Quick!

BEAR. Of course I don't believe in superstitions. But I did get up on the right side of the bed.

(Mime nods.)

I did find a four leaf clover.

(Mime nods.)

And I haven't sneezed once.

(Mime shakes his head.)

Yes, luck is with me today! So . . . let me knock on wood— three times—and I will do it!

(Mime takes off hat. Bear knocks on Mime's head three times, with sound effects.)

What do I say?

TISH. Point to the first star you see.

BEAR. *(Looks about, then points.)* There! I see a bright twinkling one.

TISH. Say, "Star light, star bright . . ."

BEAR. *(To Mime.)* The rabbit's foot! This wish must come true.

(Looks up.)

"Star light, star bright."

TISH. "First star I see tonight."

BEAR. "First star I see tonight."

(Takes rabbit's foot from Mime and rubs it vigorously.)

Oh, bring me luck. Make my wish come true.

TISH. "I wish I may, I wish I might . . ."

BEAR. "I wish I may, I wish I might." Oh, it won't work. It's nothing but a nursery rhyme.

TISH. "Have the wish I wish tonight." Say it. Say it!

BEAR. "Have the wish I wish tonight."

(Pause.)

Nothing. Nothing. I told you so.

TISH. Look. Look! It's beginning to happen.

STAR BRIGHT. *(Star music and lights begin as Star Bright enters on swing. He is joyously happy.)* Tonight I'm blinking. Tonight I'm winking. Wishes are flying past. Wishes are coming quick and fast! I'm twinkling bright and RIGHT tonight!

(Laughs.)

Your wish, please.

BEAR. *(Lost in happy memories.)* Look. It is like the circus. The trapeze high in a tent of blue . . . the music of the band . . .

(Mime motions. Soft band music of the circus is heard. Colorful lights play on the backdrop.)

the acrobats; the jugglers tossing, catching bouncing balls . . .

(Mime pantomimes juggling.)

the delicious smell of popcorn . . . the dance on the high wire . . .

(Tish holds up an imaginary umbrella and walks on an imaginary tight rope.)

the sweet taste of pink lemonade . . . Oh, the beauty, the wonder of life. Let me look at it. The happiness of living . . . Oh, let me feel it. The joy of being alive . . . Let me keep it. Let me hold it forever.

(Holds out his arms to embrace it all.)

STAR BRIGHT. *(Claps his hands. Music and circus scene stop.)* Your wish. Your wish. Repeat, please.

BEAR. *(Confused, he is led by Mime to Star.)* I wish to leave a footprint.

STAR BRIGHT. *(Puzzled.)* Repeat, please.

TISH. The answer to the riddle.

BEAR. *(Intently.)* I wish to leave with someone my dances so that I
. . . so that they . . . will be remembered.

STAR BRIGHT. That is a wish I hear every night . . . every night.
A wish to shine on earth . . . and leave behind a trace . . . to
learn, to earn the grace . . . of immortality. Of your wish, half I
can do. The other half is left for you. But quick! You must
start. Because all wishes on a star must be done before the star
is overshadowed by the sun.

(He claps his hands. Magic music and lights begin.)

One, two;
Sunset red;
Midnight blue;
The wish you wish
I give to you.

*(Magic lights and music end as Star Bright exits up and out of
sight. From off L, Little Bear is heard singing. All look to L.
Little Bear enters, finishing his song to the tune of "Turkey in
the Straw." He is a small cub, wearing country overalls and a
little turned-up straw hat. Over his shoulder he carries a
small fishing pole.)*

LITTLE BEAR. *(Sings.)*
Turkey in the straw, haw, haw, haw;
Turkey in the hay, hay, hay, hay;
Bait the hook, give the line a swish;
Jumpin' jiggers, I caught a fish.

TISH. A little bear.

BEAR. *(Little Bear does a few dance steps of joy, and continues
walking and singing.)* A little dancing bear.

(To Mime.)

Meet him. Greet him. Make him welcome.

(To Tish.)

Quick, the handmirror.

*(Tish holds mirror which Mime gives her and Bear preens.
Mime hurries to Little Bear and pantomimes a big and friendly
greeting. Little Bear, as if it were a game, happily imitates
every movement of the Mime. It ends with both shaking*

hands. Then Little Bear gives a friendly goodbye wave and starts off R, singing.)

Stop him!

(Mime rushes in front of Little Bear and turns him around.)

I am ready to be presented.

(Mime, with a flourish, presents Bear.)

How do you do.

LITTLE BEAR. Howdy-do to you.

BEAR. You have come from my WISHING on a star.

LITTLE BEAR. Huh uh. I've come from my FISHING in the river.

BEAR. Oh, my little one, I am going to give you the treasure of my life. Bestow on you all my gifts.

LITTLE BEAR. I could use a new fishing pole.

BEAR. I am going to teach you all my dances. You will wear all my hats. Oh-ho, I have never felt so alive in my life!

(He gives a joyous whoop and jumps and clicks his heels. Little Bear is bewildered. Bear, with the eyes of a dancing master, looks Little Bear over.)

Yes, you have a good build. Good stance. Relaxed torso.

(Taps Little Bear's waist. Little Bear wiggles and giggles from the tickling.)

Legs sturdy. Up! Leg up. Up!

(Little Bear cautiously lifts leg.)

Up! Up!

(Bear raises Little Bear's leg high.)

LITTLE BEAR. Whoa!

BEAR. Point. Point!

LITTLE BEAR. *(Points with finger.)* Point where?

BEAR. *(Holding Little Bear's foot high.)* Point your foot. Ah, feet too stiff . . . too stiff.

(Lets leg down. Little Bear stands in profile, stomach pushed out.)

Stomach flat!

(Taps stomach. Little Bear pulls stomach in, but pushes hips out.)

Rear push in!

(Smacks Little Bear on the bottom. Little Bear pulls hips in, and turns facing audience.)

Stretch . . . up . . . up!

(Pulls up Little Bear, who tries to stretch. His face is tense.)

Relax.

(Pats Little Bear on forehead. Little Bear slowly sinks to the ground. Bear lifts him up.)

Smile.

(Little Bear forces a tortured smile.)

Walk! Walk!

(Little Bear starts walking stiffly.)

TISH. Will he be a good dancer?

BEAR. He will be magnificent!

(Puts arm out and stops Little Bear's escape.)

He will be—ME! My rehearsal hat. My father's Russian dancing hat!

(He dances a few steps of a Russian dance, and shouts a few Russian words.)

To the dressing room.

(He continues the dance steps and shouting as he exits at R. Mime, with traveling box, follows him, imitating the dance steps.)

LITTLE BEAR. Who . . . who is he?

TISH. He is the greatest dancing bear in the world.

LITTLE BEAR. Oh!

TISH. And . . . he's going to die.

LITTLE BEAR. Oh.

TISH. My Grandpa is going to die and I don't know what to do.

LITTLE BEAR. Up in the hills, I've seen a lot of them die.

TISH. You have?

LITTLE BEAR. Old ones, little ones, and big ones, too. And there ain't nothing you can do about it. 'Cause as sure as you're born, you're as sure of dying.

TISH. It's sad.

LITTLE BEAR. Course it's sad.

TISH. It's frightening.

LITTLE BEAR. *(Thinking it out.)* No. It ain't dyin' that you're afraid of. It's the not knowin' what comes AFTER you die. That's what scares you.

TISH. *(Tearful.)* I'll never see Grandpa again.

LITTLE BEAR. *(With gentle understanding.)* You go on. You have yourself a good cry. It'll help you to give him up. And you got to.

(With emphasis.)

You got to let him go.

TISH. No.

LITTLE BEAR. You have to! 'Cause he gone . . . forever.

TISH. You don't know what it's like to have your Grandpa die.

LITTLE BEAR. Yes, I do. My Grandpa died last winter. And my Papa . . . I saw a hunter shoot my Papa.

TISH. *(Shocked.)* Shoot your Papa! Oh, what did you do?

LITTLE BEAR. First, I cried. Yes, I cried, and then I started hatin' and I kicked and clawed 'cause I felt all alone.

TISH. *(Nods.)* All by yourself.

LITTLE BEAR. Then my Mama said, "You have to go on living, so . . . do your best. Give yourself to the livin'. 'Cause that's the best way to say goodbye to your Pa." So I made my peace.

TISH. Your peace?

LITTLE BEAR. Inside myself. Oh, it don't mean I understand about dyin'. I don't. But you do go on living. The next day. The next year. So if you love your Grandpa like I loved my Papa . . .

TISH. Oh, I do.

LITTLE BEAR. Then show him you do.

TISH. How?

LITTLE BEAR. Tell him goodbye . . . by giving your most to the living. I'm wanting to do something . . . something big . . . just for Papa.

BEAR. *(Off.)* All is ready!

TISH. Please, dance with him. He needs you.

LITTLE BEAR. Well, I like to help folks.

TISH. You said, "Give to the living."

LITTLE BEAR. And I do like the dance!

TISH. *(Excited with a new idea.)* This is the big thing you can do for your Papa.

LITTLE BEAR. For Papa?

TISH. *(Points with her hand as she visualizes it.)* Your name will be in lights. You will be the NEW World's Greatest Dancing Bear!

BEAR. *(Bear and Mime enter, Bear wearing his Russian Cossack hat.)* Let the flags fly! Let the band play!

(To Little Bear.)

We will start with a simple waltz. My mother's famous skating waltz. One, two, three; one, two, three . . .

(He dances, continuing during the next speeches.)

LITTLE BEAR. *(Tries to do the step, then stops.)* No. I'm just a country bear, with no schoolin'.

TISH. You will be the famous . . . "Arkansas Bear!"

(Urges him on.)

LITTLE BEAR. Arkansas. I ain't right sure how to spell Arkansas.

(He moves in one spot to the beat of the music, wanting to dance, but afraid.)

TISH. Like it sounds. A — R — — K — A — N — —

LITTLE BEAR. *(Shouts, eager to dance.)* S — A — W!

(With a burst of energy he follows Bear and dances with joy, counting loudly and happily.)

One! Two! Three! One! Two! Three! I'm doing it!

(The first chime of midnight is heard, loud and distinct. The other chimes follow slowly. Mime runs to Bear, motions for him to listen.)

TISH. What is it?

BEAR. The chimes are striking twelve.

LITTLE BEAR. It's the end of the day. Midnight.

BEAR. No! No! No! Not yet! I have not taught you my dances. Stop the clock!

TISH. Run! Hide! Before he comes back!

BEAR. Where?

LITTLE BEAR. In the caves! In the hills!

TISH. Hurry!

(Tish and Little Bear help Bear. Mime carries box. All start toward back. Soft calliope music is heard. Ringmaster enters R.)

RINGMASTER. Twelve.

(They stop.)

Your day is ended. Your time is up. Come. I will take you to the Great Center Ring.

BEAR. No. No!

TISH. Is he here?

BEAR. Yes, he has come for me.

(Comes down stage. Backs off towards L.)

Stop him.

RINGMASTER. There is no way to stop death.

TISH. I know a way.

(Grabs Mime and points up toward star.)

You! Make a wish on the first star you see. Say,

(Shouts.)

Star light, star bright,
First star I see tonight . . .

(Mime quickly points and looks up, rapidly miming the words of the rhyme.)

STAR BRIGHT. *(Off.)* Louder, please.

RINGMASTER. Come.

(Holds out his hand and slowly crosses toward Bear at far L.)

TISH. *(Mime pantomimes, repeating with larger gestures, while Tish says the words.)*

I wish I may, I wish I might,
Have the wish I wish tonight.

STAR BRIGHT. *(Quickly descends into view.)* Wish quickly chanted. Wish quickly granted.

TISH. *(Mime pantomimes her words.)* Stop death!

(With a sound effect of a roll on a cymbal, Star Bright points at Ringmaster, who has advanced almost to Bear. Ringmaster stops in a walking position.)

Make him go away!

(A roll on a cymbal is heard, as Star Bright makes a circle with his hand. Ringmaster slowly turns around.)

LOCK HIM UP IN THE TREE!

(Another roll on the cymbal.)

STAR BRIGHT. Walk to the tree.

(Ringmaster slowly walks to a tree.)

Your home it will be . . . for a time.

(Ringmaster stops. Star Bright points to tree again. There is a roll on a cymbal as the trunk slowly opens.)

It is open wide . . . to welcome you. Step inside.

(Ringmaster faces tree and slowly steps inside the tree trunk, and turns and faces audience.)

Let it enfold and hold you . . . for a time.

(Waves his hand. There is a last roll on a cymbal. The tree trunk slowly closes shut.)

Locked, blocked, and enclosed!

(He laughs.)

BEAR. *(To Tish.)* You did it! You stopped death!

TISH. *(She and Bear shout together, while Mime jumps with joy and blows whistle.)* We did it!

BEAR. We did it!

STAR BRIGHT. *(Claps his hands.)* Remember . . . soon will come the morning sun, and then . . . Remember that is when . . . all wishes become . . . undone.

(Star music and light begin as he ascends out of sight, and then stop.)

BEAR. *(Their joy changes to concern.)* It is true! Time is short! Quick. I must teach the little one—

(Looks about. Little Bear has, unnoticed, slipped away when Ringmaster appeared.)

Where is he?

TISH. Little Bear!

(Pause. There is no answer.)

BEAR. Little Bear, come back!

TISH. *(She and Mime run looking for him.)* Little Bear?

BEAR. He was frightened . . .

(Looks at tree.)

of death. He is gone. And with him all my hopes are gone.

(He slumps, wearily.)

TISH. *(Concerned, rushes to him.)* You must rest, like Grandpa.

BEAR. Your Grandfather has you.

(Amused.)

A chip off the old block, eh?

(She nods.)

You gave him happiness in life . . . peace in death.

TISH. Are you all right?

BEAR. I am old, and weary and tired. And I am going to die.

TISH. No. We stopped death.

BEAR. But only for a brief time. Death, they say is a clock. Every minute our lives are ticking away. Now . . . soon . . . my clock will stop.

TISH. No.

BEAR. But only for a brief time. Death, they say, is a clock. Every minute our lives are ticking away. Now . . . soon . . . my clock will stop.

(Mime looks and listens off R, then runs to them and excitedly mimes that Little Bear is coming.)

What is it?

(Mime pantomimes more.)

Who? Where?

(Mime points to R. All watch as Little Bear enters.)

You have come back.

LITTLE BEAR. I left my fishing pole.

BEAR. Have no fear. Death is locked in the tree.

(Little Bear reacts with fright at tree.)

TISH. You have come back to help.

LITTLE BEAR. I come back to learn all your fancy dancin'.

TISH. *(Runs to Little Bear and hugs him.)* Oh, you are the best, the sweetest, the most wonderful little bear in the world!

(Little Bear is embarrassed.)

BEAR. Yes! Quick! We must begin the lesson. There is so little time and much to learn.

(Looks frightened off R. To Mime.)

Stand watch. Yes, watch for the first rays of the sun!

(Mime stands at R, anxiously looking off. Tish sits on box. Bear motions to Little Bear.)

Come! Come! Attention! I will teach you all I know.

(Takes position.)

First, you smile to the right.

(Bear does the action with the words. Little Bear watches and tries to do the action.)

You smile to the left. You bow to the center. And then . . . begin . . . to dance. I will start with my father's famous Russian dance. Master this and all else will be easy.

(To Mime.)

How many more minutes?

(Mime holds up ten fingers.)

Ten! Position. Position!

(Little Bear imitates him.)

Listen to the beat . . . the beat . . .

(Taps foot.)

LITTLE BEAR. Beat what?

BEAR. Your feet! Your feet! The beat . . . the beat . . .

(Taps foot. Little Bear slowly and timidly taps beat.)

Too slow. Too slow.

(Little Bear pivots in a circle, weight on one foot while tapping fast using the other foot.)

Too fast. Too fast.

(Little Bear does it right.)

Ah! Ah! Ah! Good! Good!

LITTLE BEAR. I'm doing it right!

BEAR. *(Shows him next Russian step.)* The first step. Hop, hop, hop, switch, hop.

(Little Bear tries, awkward at first, then better.)

Hop, hop, hop, switch, hop. Yes, hop, hop, hop, switch, hop. Yes! Yes!

(Shows him next step.)

Deep knee, hop.

(Little Bear shakes his head.)

Try. Try.

(Little Bear tries deep knee bends with a hop.)

Deep knee, hop. Lower. Lower.

(Little Bear puts hands on floor in front of him and does step. He smiles at the audience at the easiness of it.)

No, no, no! No hands!

(Lifts Little Bear up. Little Bear continues to kick his feet.)

The next step. The finale.

(Shows step.)

Turn, two, up, two. Turn, two, up, two.

LITTLE BEAR. Oh, my!

BEAR. Turn, two, up, two.

(Little Bear tries.)

Turn, two, up, two. Faster. Faster.

LITTLE BEAR. *(Falls.)* I can't do it. I can't do it.

BEAR. You will. You must do it. I must leave my dances with you.

TISH. Try, please. Please, try.

LITTLE BEAR. Well . . .

(Gets up.)

BEAR. Again. Again. Ready. Turn, two, up, two.

(Bear keeps repeating the count, and Little Bear does the step better and better, until he is perfect—and happy.)

He did it! He did it!

TISH. He did it!

LITTLE BEAR. I did it!

BEAR. *(To Mime.)* How many minutes are left?

(Mime holds up eight fingers.)

Eight minutes. Time is running out. Quick. The polka. The dance of the people. Music!

(Mime motions. Music is heard. Bear dances a few steps. Little Bear quickly follows him and masters them. Music stops. Bear breathes heavily.)

How many more minutes?

(Mime holds up seven fingers.)

Only seven minutes left! Hurry. My famous tarantella.

(Mime motions and music is heard. Bear does a few steps. Little Bear again quickly does them and they dance together. Music stops. Bear pants for breath. Mime runs to him and holds up six fingers.)

Six minutes. And at the end take your bow. The first bow.

(Bear bows, short of breath.)

The second bow.

(Bear bows, pauses, then with trembling voice he speaks with emotion, knowing it is his last bow.)

And the last and final bow.

TISH. More, more! Encore! Encore!

(Bear slumps to the floor. She rushes to him.)

He's fallen.

(She and Mime cradle Bear on either side.)

Are you all right?

BEAR. *(Stirs, weakly.)* How . . . many more minutes . . . do I have left?

(Mime holds up five fingers.)

My little one, you will do my dances, you will carry on for me?

LITTLE BEAR. Yes. Yes.

BEAR. Take my father's hat . . . and it was HIS father's hat . . .

LITTLE BEAR. No, you must wear it.

BEAR. I will not need it where I am going. I have taken my last bow.

TISH. No.

(Buries her head on his shoulder.)

BEAR. Ah, tears can be beautiful. But there is no need to cry. I am content. I was a part of what went before and I will be a part of what is yet to come. That is the answer to the riddle of life.

(Weakly.)

How many more minutes?

(Mime holds up two fingers.)

Two. Bring me my traveling hat. I will wear it on my last journey.

(Little Bear gets traveling hat from box, as Mime and Tish help Bear to stand.)

I must look my best when I enter the Great Center Ring.

(Mime puts hat on Bear, who smiles at Tish.)

Does it look stylish?

TISH. Yes.

BEAR. Is it becoming?

(She nods.)

Then I am ready.

(Gently pushes Tish and Mime away.)

No. This journey I must go alone.

(Extends hand to Mime.)

Goodbye, good friend. Thank you for everything. And sometimes when the band plays . . . think of an old bear.

(Mime motions for Bear to wait. Mime quickly gets a pink balloon on string from the side and holds it out to Bear.)

Yes, I remember when once we said, "Life is like a bright balloon." Hold it tight . . . Hold it tight. Because . . . once you let it go . . . it floats away forever.

(Breathless.)

How many more minutes?

(Mime holds up one finger. Bear turns to Tish.)

I have one last request. When the end comes . . . when I enter the Great Center Ring . . . I want music. I want you to whistle the tune your Grandfather taught you.

TISH. "O Susannah."

BEAR. *(Nods and smiles.)* You will find that when you whistle you cannot cry at the same time.

(A rooster is heard crowing.)

Listen.

LITTLE BEAR. It's a rooster crowin'. It's almost mornin'.

TISH. The sun is up. The stars are fading away.

STAR BRIGHT. *(Star music is heard as Star Bright descends into view. He speaks softly.)* Announcing: the first ray of sun is peeping out. Warning: all wishes end as the sun begins. The new day is starting, the old departing. That is the great pattern . . . the circle of life. Tomorrow is today.

(He points at the tree, and claps his hands. The tree trunk slowly opens.)

And the night and the stars fade away . . . fade away.

(There is star music as Star Bright disappears. Soft calliope music is heard which continues during the scene.)

RINGMASTER. *(Steps out from tree trunk. He speaks with authority.)* There is no more time. The book is closed.

BEAR. Poets tell us death is but a sleep, but who can tell me what I will dream?

RINGMASTER. *(Walks slowly to Bear.)* Take my hand.

BEAR. Tell me, tell me what is death?

RINGMASTER. When there is no answer, you do not ask the question. Come.

BEAR. Yes, I am ready.

(To Little Bear.)

My little one . . . I give you my feather . . . and you . . . give joy . . . to the world.

(Gives turkey feather to Little Bear. He whispers.)

Let the balloon go.

(Ringmaster holds out his hand, which Bear takes. Together they walk off L slowly. Mime lets the balloon go. He, Tish, and Little Bear watch as it floats up and out of sight. At the same

time the calliope music builds in volume. There is a second of silence. Then the Announcer's voice is heard, loud and distinctly.)

ANNOUNCER'S VOICE. Ladies and gentlemen: presenting for your pleasure and entertainment, the new dancing bear, the world's famous, the world's favorite, the world's greatest—The Arkansaw Bear!

(During the announcement, Mime points to Little Bear. Little Bear looks frightened, amazed, and pleased. Mime holds up mirror and Little Bear puts feather in his hat. Mime motions for Little Bear to step forward, then motions a circle of light on the floor. Spotlight comes on and Little Bear steps into the light.)

BEAR'S VOICE. *(Over the loudspeaker, Bear's voice is heard. He speaks softly and with emotion. Little Bear follows his instructions.)* You smile to the right . . . smile to the left . . . bow to the center . . . and then begin to dance!

(Music begins, lively "Turkey in the Straw." Little Bear begins his dance.)

My dances . . . your dances . . . and make the world spin round and round with joy.

(Little Bear dances with fun, excitement, and joy, a wonderful short dance. During this Tish exits, and Mime exits with box. At the end of the dance, Little Bear bows as the audience applauds, and exits at L, peeks out and waves again. Spotlight goes out. Fantasy music is heard and a soft night light illuminates the tree. Tish is leaning against it. She looks up, sighs, picks up the flowers, and slowly circles back to the downstage area of the first scene, which becomes light as the tree area dims out. Fantasy music also fades out. Mother's and Aunt Ellen's voices are heard, and Tish answers as if they were standing on each side of her downstage.)

MOTHER'S VOICE. *(Worried.)* Tish? Tish, is that you?

TISH. Yes, mother.

MOTHER'S VOICE. Where have you been?

TISH. I went up the hill to my tree. I want to see Grandpa.

AUNT ELLEN'S VOICE. He's dead . . . dead.

(Cries.)

TISH. *(Trying to be brave.)* Dead. Tears can be beautiful, Aunt Ellen. But you have to give him up. Let the balloon go.

AUNT ELLEN'S VOICE. What?

TISH. *(Trying to keep back her tears.)* I know everyone . . . everything has a time to die . . . and it's sad. But Grandpa knew the answer to the riddle.

AUNT ELLEN'S VOICE. The riddle?

TISH. He left his footprint. He left a chip off the old block.

MOTHER'S VOICE. What, dear? What did he leave?

TISH. Me! And I want to do something . . . something big for Grandpa. Because that's the best way to say goodbye.

(Softly.)

Let me give him his flowers . . . the pink ones.

MOTHER'S VOICE. *(Positive, and with a mother's love and authority.)* All right, dear. Come along. We'll go together and see Grandpa.

(Tish starts L, and begins to whistle.)

What are you doing?

TISH. Whistling . . . for the bear . . . and for Grandpa. Because it helps . . . when you are afraid and in the dark. And . . . when you whistle, you can't cry.

(Whispers.)

Goodbye, Grandpa, I . . . I love you.

(Tish exits L, bravely trying to control her crying. At the same time lights slowly come up so the full stage is seen. The light on Tish's area dims out. The stage is bright with soft beautiful colors. The lone whistling of "O Susannah," the same as at the beginning of the play, is heard. There is a moment of a final picture—the living tree standing, as it has through the years, against a beautiful endless sky. The whistling continues as the curtains close.)

(Curtain.)

the boy who stole the stars

By Julian Wiles

Copyright, 1981, Dramatic Publishing Company

The Boy Who Stole the Stars (1981)

The fear and frustration of watching someone you love die is the bittersweet theme of *The Boy Who Stole the Stars*, written by Julian Wiles.

Using stars and their constellations as powerful dramatic metaphors, Wiles traces the events during Nicholas' summer vacation at his grandparents' country home. Nicholas arrives the last day of school, and is eagerly looking forward to a summer vacation of fishing, catch-playing, berry-picking, and hiking with his grandfather, as he has every summer before. However, from the beginning of his arrival Nicholas senses there is "something" different about his grandfather, who seems unusually distant, moody, and forgetful. Although Nicholas is unable to interest his grandfather in some of their usual summer fun of the past, he does get him involved in his summer science project: counting the stars. It is in these scenes that Wiles so deftly uses the star metaphor to draw parallels between life and death.

Finally, when Nicholas learns that his grandfather is indeed dying from Alzheimer's disease, he tries to "steal the stars," thinking they will preserve a few precious moments of his grandfather's life. Instead, Nicholas learns about the importance of love and friendship. He begins to grow stronger as his grandfather weakens, and together they strive to enjoy and understand the special bond their last summer together has brought.

CHARACTERS

the Boy

the Grandmother

the Grandfather

the Freckled-face Girl

Voice of the Poet

THE SET

The play takes place on the front porch and in the front yard of the grandfather's country home. The original set consisted of a small porch UC, parallel to the curtain line with the outline of the house constructed behind it. Two rocking chairs were on the stage right side of the porch, two steps were at center leading to the porch and to a screen door set in the house. Four columns held up the porch roof and the stage right center column was fitted with a hook to hold the hammock up (the stage left end went off stage to a hook). A stump was down right and three willow lawn chairs were down left. This posed a sightline problem which could be improved by putting the hammock totally on the porch or reversing the placement of the stump and the willow chairs.

For projections, three screens made in forced perspective were affixed to the proscenium, above center stage and extreme stage left and right.

The Boy Who Stole the Stars

PROLOGUE. "Not even a star can last forever."

(As the house lights dim, the eerie haunting sounds of the percussion score begin. On projection screens DL and DR and above C on the proscenium images of stars being created, being torn apart by cosmic forces, then recreated, appear. After a few minutes, views of the earth from space appear. From off stage we hear the poet speak.)

THE POET.
We are the myths of genesis
We are all that has ever been
. . . all that shall ever be
We are fragments of yesterday
Splinters of shattered looking-glass stars
Scattered.
Only to be gathered again,
To be stirred into stars
      that shine as brief as a summer snowflake . . .

Not even a star can last forever
And yet, the stars are all that are forever
And the children of the stars never die.

So
Hush
Lullaby
Children of the stars
Lay down your heads upon the day
And slip away
Into the night
And be nudged and nuzzled by the starlight
Starbright
Children of the stars.

(Lights rise on the set.)

SCENE I. "What's wrong with him, Grandmother?"

THE BOY. *(Entering with a pack, rod and reel, baseball bat and gloves, etc., ready for a summer visit.)*

Grandmother! Grandfather!

THE GRANDMOTHER. *(From inside the house.)* Nicholas?

THE BOY. I'm here, Grandmother.

(The grandmother enters from screen door on porch, followed slowly by the grandfather.)

THE GRANDMOTHER. *(After a hug.)* Already? You're a day early.

THE BOY. Yes, I know, but I couldn't wait any longer, Mom said I could come on over, you don't mind, do you?

THE GRANDMOTHER. No, of course we don't mind—but what about school?

THE BOY. Oh, I've only got one more day and I'm catching a ride tomorrow with Genevieve, you know, that bratty girl who lives down the road. They dropped me off from school.

THE GRANDMOTHER. Well fine . . .

(There is a moment of silence and hesitation, the grandmother looks to the grandfather, obviously something is wrong.)

Matthew, aren't you going to welcome Nicholas?

THE GRANDFATHER. Glad to have you here, Nicholas . . .

THE BOY. Thanks, Grandfather, I've brought all kinds of things for us to do, my rod and reel—I got some new lures for my birthday—and I've got the binoculars you gave me last summer and I've brought an extra baseball mitt for you. . . .

(The grandfather looks confused—forces a smile.)

THE GRANDMOTHER. *(Quickly.)* Yes, well, you two can talk all about that after supper.

THE GRANDFATHER. Yes, after supper. *(He wanders inside.)*

THE BOY. What's wrong with him, Grandmother?

THE GRANDMOTHER.
I don't know, Nicholas,
I don't know, he just says he hasn't been feeling well lately.

THE BOY.
>He used to be so full of fun and stories. . . .
>Now he's so sad. . . .
>He's like a rainy day.

THE GRANDMOTHER. Yes, I can hardly get him to eat.

THE BOY. Not even ice cream?

THE GRANDMOTHER. Not even fudge ripple.

THE BOY. He's probably just going through a phase, Grandmother, grownups do that too, don't they?

THE GRANDMOTHER. Yes, grownups do that too.

THE BOY. Then he'll probably grow out of it.

THE GRANDMOTHER. I hope so.

THE GRANDFATHER. *(From inside the house.)* Bessie, I can't find my blue sweater.

THE GRANDMOTHER. It's right inside the hall closet where it always is.

THE GRANDFATHER. It's never been in the hall closet before, you must of put it there.

THE GRANDMOTHER. I better go check on him, Nicholas, you put your things in the front bedroom—then why don't you go out and play until supper.

THE BOY. Fine, Grandmother.

(The grandmother goes inside, the boy follows and after a moment he bounds back outside with a baseball bat. He picks up rocks (imaginary) and bats them out toward the audience. After hitting a few times, he notices the first star of the evening.)

THE BOY.
>Twinkle, twinkle, little star
>How I wonder what you are
>Like a diamond in the sky
>Stick a moon beam in your eye.

(He throws a rock at a star.)

THE FRECKLED-FACE GIRL. *(Entering.)* What-cha doing, Nicholas?

THE BOY. Throwing a rock at a star.

THE FRECKLED-FACE GIRL. That's useful.

THE BOY. What's it to you?

THE FRECKLED-FACE GIRL. Nothing—how's your grandfather?

THE BOY. What do you mean?

THE FRECKLED-FACE GIRL. Nothing—just that my Mom said he got lost going to the grocery store and they had to call your grandmother to come pick him up.

THE BOY. He hasn't been feeling well lately.

THE FRECKLED-FACE GIRL. That's what my Mom said, only she wasn't so polite.

THE BOY. I'll bet she'd talk differently if it was one of your grandfathers. . . .

THE FRECKLED-FACE GIRL. I haven't got any grandfathers, they're both dead—before I was born.

THE BOY. I've only got one left—

THE FRECKLED-FACE GIRL. I'm sorry he's sick.

THE BOY. Me too.

THE FRECKLED-FACE GIRL. Have you decided what you're going to do for your summer science project?

THE BOY. No, not exactly, have you?

THE FRECKLED-FACE GIRL. I've got a couple of great ideas floating around. I'll decide on one by tomorrow.

THE BOY. You're not going to make another paper mache volcano are you? There's still soot on the ceiling from that one.

THE FRECKLED-FACE GIRL. That was a good project—I got an A on it.

THE BOY. That's only because you cried after the principal called the fire department. The teacher felt sorry for you.

THE FRECKLED-FACE GIRL. She did not!

THE BOY. If you say so.

THE FRECKLED-FACE GIRL. Well I do, so there. . . . *(Starts to exit, turns back.)* Oh, I only came over to tell you that my mom said that we'll pick you up around six forty-five.

THE BOY. Six forty-five! Why so early?

THE FRECKLED-FACE GIRL. When you live out in the country, Nicholas, you have to get used to getting up early, besides, it takes a while to get to school from here.

THE BOY. Six forty-five?

THE FRECKLED-FACE GIRL. Yeah, well, I've got to get home to supper. See you later. *(She exits.)*

THE BOY. *(Calling after her.)* Yeah, later—make it much later.

(He crosses to the stump and pulls out a loop of string and begins making string tricks.)

SCENE 2. "I wonder how many stars there are?"

(The grandfather enters from DC and wanders to his willow chair DL.)

THE BOY. Grandfather. . . .

THE GRANDFATHER. *(Gruffly.)* Huh?

THE BOY. Grandfather, can I walk with you?

THE GRANDFATHER. If you like. . . .

THE BOY. The stars are pretty tonight.

THE GRANDFATHER. What?

THE BOY. The stars—they're pretty tonight.

THE GRANDFATHER. Yes, I suppose so.

THE BOY. I wonder how many there are.

THE GRANDFATHER. *(With annoyance.)* How many?

THE BOY. Stars—how many stars?

THE GRANDFATHER. A lot.

THE BOY. You used to count them, didn't you—when you were on the ships?

THE GRANDFATHER. Ships.

THE BOY. You were a navialligator, weren't you—a great navialligator.

THE GRANDFATHER. . . . . a great navialligator . . .

THE BOY. And you knew all of the stars by name.

THE GRANDFATHER. *(Bitterly.)* I did once, but I've forgotten them now—there are so many.

THE BOY. Would you like to help me count them again—it would help you remember.

THE GRANDFATHER. Remember?

THE BOY. Besides, that would make a great science project.

THE GRANDFATHER. *(Out front.)* Science project?

> *(A school bell rings and all lights go out except for a special on the boy, center stage.)*

SCENE 3. "Yes, ma'am, my science project?"

THE BOY. *(Speaking to his imaginary teacher out front.)*
Yes, ma'am,
my science project?
I plan to count the stars.
Ma'am?
. . . that's right . . . count the stars.
Yes, ma'am, all of them.
. . . well, if it's all right, my grandfather will help me . . .
my grandfather used to be a starcounter himself . . .
Ma'am?
A starcounter,
you know, on a ship.
He was a navialligator.
Yes, ma'am, that's what I said,
a navigator.
What?
Yes, I suppose I will need all the help I can get . . .
Yes, ma'am, I'm sure it's the project I want to do.

> *(Freckled-face girl enters UL and stands just behind and to the side of him.)*

. . . well, it's no worse than building paper mache volcanos that melt before they erupt. . . .

(Freckled-face girl clears her throat, clearly annoyed.)

I'm sorry, but . . .
Yes, ma'am,
next term,
first day of class,
I'll be ready.

THE FRECKLED-FACE GIRL. We'll see.

THE BOY. Don't lose any sleep over it.

THE FRECKLED-FACE GIRL. You don't have to worry about that.

THE BOY. Oh, I forgot, you'll be too busy looking for crickets and frogs, sounds like a great science project.

THE FRECKLED-FACE GIRL. It beats paper mache volcanos, don't you think?

THE BOY. Anything beats paper mache volcanos.

THE FRECKLED-FACE GIRL. So, you're going to count all the stars.

THE BOY. I thought I would.

THE FRECKLED-FACE GIRL. *(Erasing an imaginary board.)* Why did you decide to count stars?

THE BOY. I thought it would be fun to do something with my grandfather.

THE FRECKLED-FACE GIRL. How is he?

THE BOY. About the same.

THE FRECKLED-FACE GIRL. Was he really a navigator?

THE BOY. He was one of the best. He even went on an expedition to the South Pole.

THE FRECKLED-FACE GIRL. No kidding.

THE BOY. He guided ships around the world twice, and now he can't even get home from the supermarket.

THE FRECKLED-FACE GIRL. I'm sorry I said that.

THE BOY. It doesn't matter.

THE FRECKLED-FACE GIRL. Yes it does. . . . Look, we all get lost sometimes—when I was a little kid, I remember crying my eyes out once when my mom left me alone in the shopping cart—she was only on the next aisle, but that didn't matter, I cried anyway.

THE BOY. But you were a kid—kids are supposed to get lost and cry—grownups aren't. They're supposed to have it all together, and when they don't people think they're nuts.

THE FRECKLED-FACE GIRL. I suppose you're right.

THE BOY. You know I'm right. Your mother thinks he's nuts.

THE FRECKLED-FACE GIRL. I wouldn't pay too much attention to my mother, I certainly don't.

THE BOY. You know, you can actually be funny sometimes.

THE FRECKLED-FACE GIRL. And you can actually be civilized.

THE BOY. Gee, thanks.

THE FRECKLED-FACE GIRL. Don't mention it.
Well, I guess I gotta go.

THE BOY. Right.

THE FRECKLED-FACE GIRL. Bye. *(She exits.)*

THE BOY. Bye. . . .
Now I've done it . . . she likes me!

(Fade to black.)

(As lights rise the boy and his grandmother on the steps at C, grandfather, lost in his own thoughts, is sitting in his chair, DL.)

THE BOY. Good night, Grandmother.

THE GRANDMOTHER. Good night, Nicholas. Glad school's out?

THE BOY. You bet I am! *(Hesitantly he crosses to his grandfather.)* Good night, Grandfather. *(His grandfather doesn't notice.)*

THE GRANDMOTHER. Matthew, Nicholas is saying goodnight.

THE GRANDFATHER. *(Waking up.)* Good night, Nicholas.

THE BOY. *(Giving his grandfather a hug.)* Good night, Grandfather . . . see you in the morning. . . . *(Exits.)*

SCENE 4. "It's like I don't know you anymore"

THE GRANDMOTHER. Matthew, don't you think it's time to come in?

THE GRANDFATHER. If you want.

THE GRANDMOTHER. Well, it is late, Matthew. . . .

THE GRANDFATHER. All right. All right.

THE GRANDMOTHER. What's wrong?

THE GRANDFATHER. What do you mean?

THE GRANDMOTHER. You're brooding, Matthew. I've lived with you long enough to know that something's wrong.

THE GRANDFATHER. And I've lived with you long enough to know when you're starting to nag.

THE GRANDMOTHER. I'm not nagging, Matthew, but you're not yourself.

THE GRANDFATHER. None of us stay the same very long—look at Nicholas growing in leaps and bounds, he's a ball of fire growing up so fast.

THE GRANDMOTHER. Is he too much for you, Matthew? We don't have to keep him all summer. . . .

THE GRANDFATHER. No, no, let him stay. . . .

THE GRANDMOTHER. I'm glad. You two have always had such special summers. I tell you what, why don't you let me fix you two a picnic lunch and you can go fishing tomorrow—you haven't been fishing in ages.

THE GRANDFATHER. You trying to get me out of the house?

THE GRANDMOTHER. Well, it wouldn't do you any harm—moping around like you've been doing.

THE GRANDFATHER. I'm not moping—I just don't have the energy I used to.

THE GRANDMOTHER. Well, neither do I, but I'm not ready to be put out to pasture.

THE GRANDFATHER. Here we go again, you'd think I was the laziest man ever born to hear you talk. I worked a good sixty years on this place—made you a good home. I'm tired, Bessie, and I'm tired of being made to feel guilty for being tired.

THE GRANDMOTHER. I don't mean to make you feel guilty, but you don't get enough exercise.

THE GRANDFATHER. I'm not a spring chicken; why don't you realize that? Do this . . . do that . . . why don't you go fishing . . . why don't you take a walk down to the bog . . . "why don't you"—I'm tired of "why don't you's."

THE GRANDMOTHER. I know you're not twenty-five any more, Matthew, but what I keep telling you is that just because you're old doesn't mean that you've got one foot in the grave. But people our age who don't eat well and don't get any exercise are digging their own graves.

THE GRANDFATHER. Don't be so morbid.

THE GRANDMOTHER. That's like the pot calling the kettle black.

THE GRANDFATHER. You're like a broken record . . . nag, nag, nag.

THE GRANDMOTHER. I'm only nagging because I care about you.

THE GRANDFATHER. If you cared about me you'd leave me alone.

THE GRANDMOTHER. Matthew, we've never been this far away, it's like I don't know you any more.

THE GRANDFATHER. Maybe you never did.

(Grandmother is stunned—slowly retreats inside, trying to hide her tears.)

SCENE 5. "I had a friend once"

(As lights rise, Nicholas is throwing his baseball up and catching it and counting.)

THE BOY. Forty-two, forty-three, forty-four, forty-five . . .

THE GRANDMOTHER. *(Enters with bowl full of string beans to be snapped.)* And what are you doing, young man?

THE BOY. Playing catch with the sky.

THE GRANDMOTHER. Who's winning?

THE BOY. Well, I've missed twice, and so far, the sky has thrown it back every time.

THE GRANDMOTHER. *(Sits in rocker.)* I see. What have you been doing all day?

THE BOY. *(Sits on step.)* Let's see, this morning I played catch with the sky, of course, then I got my rod and reel out and practiced casting, then I played catch some more . . . then we had lunch and I took a nap, and I played catch some more . . . and I got my marbles out and practiced . . . and we ate supper and I played catch some more.

THE GRANDMOTHER. You've been busy.

THE BOY. I suppose—Grandmother, do you think there are more hours in the day out here in the country?

THE GRANDMOTHER. I don't think so.

THE BOY. It sure seems like it. . . . Grandmother?

THE GRANDMOTHER. Yes?

THE BOY. Do you think, I mean, have I done something wrong? . . .

THE GRANDMOTHER. What do you mean?

THE BOY. Well, Grandfather seems to be mad at me.

THE GRANDMOTHER. Oh, I don't think he is.

THE BOY. He sure snapped at me at breakfast when I asked him if we could go fishing.

THE GRANDMOTHER. *(She smiles to reassure him.)* Your grandfather hasn't been sleeping too well lately, Nicholas, and it makes him kind of cranky in the mornings. I'm sure when he feels better, in a day or two, he'll take you fishing.

THE BOY. I don't care about the fishing so much. I'd just like to be with him—he doesn't seem to want me around.

THE GRANDMOTHER. Oh it's not that, Nicholas. People sometimes need to be alone. Your grandfather just needs some time to be by himself. Let's just give him some time and he'll be his old self again.

THE BOY. Do you really think so, Grandmother?

THE GRANDMOTHER. Certainly. . . . certainly. . . .

THE BOY. Do you think that it will be tomorrow?

THE GRANDMOTHER. I don't know if it'll be tomorrow, but in a day or so. . . .

THE BOY. But he's been by himself all day today—I haven't spoken to him since this morning—and he didn't say anything at lunch or supper. It's spooky. . . .

THE GRANDMOTHER. Oh, don't say that.

THE BOY. I'm sorry.

THE GRANDMOTHER. You just need someone to play with—I know we old folks aren't much company. Would you like to have a friend come out and visit?

THE BOY. *(Quickly.)* No.

THE GRANDMOTHER. You certainly enjoyed Jonathan last summer.

THE BOY. Jonathan's not around anymore, he moved to California the week before school started.

THE GRANDMOTHER. I know you miss him.

THE BOY. I'd rather not talk about him if you don't mind.

THE GRANDMOTHER. You two were as thick as thieves last summer.

THE BOY. Yeah, that was last summer.

THE GRANDMOTHER. Have you heard from him?

THE BOY. I got one letter—if you can call it that—a Christmas card.

THE GRANDMOTHER. Did you write him back?

THE BOY. I wrote him every day for a week after he left—

THE GRANDMOTHER. And he never wrote you back?

THE BOY. No, not even a postcard.

THE GRANDMOTHER. And you were the best of friends. . . .

THE BOY. So I thought. I don't want to hear about him anymore—he's gone.

THE GRANDMOTHER. All right. But you must have some other friends you would like to have out to visit.

THE BOY. No.

THE GRANDMOTHER. What about that little freckled-face girl that lives down the road? Mrs. Ryan's little girl.

THE BOY. I'd rather play with a pack of wild elephants.

THE GRANDMOTHER. What's wrong with her?

THE BOY. She's a GIRL, Grandmother.

THE GRANDMOTHER. I'm a girl.

THE BOY. Yes, but you're different. You're a grandmother—you don't get mushy or anything.

THE GRANDMOTHER. Well, that's nice to hear. . . .

THE BOY. You know what I mean, you're okay 'cause you're all grown up—Genevieve's still a little kid.

THE GRANDMOTHER. Little kids, especially little girl kids, grow up into beautiful young ladies.

THE BOY. That's what I'm afraid of.

THE GRANDMOTHER. Oh, I see. Well, let me put these beans up. Are you about ready for bed?

THE BOY. I'll be in in a minute. I want to get started on my science project—I'm going to count all the stars.

THE GRANDMOTHER. Not tonight, I hope.

THE BOY. No, I'm just going to get started tonight.

THE GRANDMOTHER. All right, but don't be out too late.

THE BOY. I won't.

(Grandmother exits as boy crosses down to sit on the stump, takes pad and pencil out of his pocket, looks at stars and starts making notes, drawing, etc. Grandfather enters and crosses to his chair DL.)

SCENE 6. "You seem so far away sometimes"

THE BOY. Grandfather . . . do you know what that bright star is?

THE GRANDFATHER. Star?

THE BOY. Yes, the one way up there by the crescent moon.

THE GRANDFATHER. It's not a star, it's a planet—Venus.

THE BOY. Star, planet, they're all the same.

THE GRANDFATHER. Not at all, if you're trying to navigate you had better know the difference. The stars are fixed in the sky, the planets wander about. . . . if you're going to count the stars you have to be precise.

THE BOY. I'm trying, Grandfather. See, I've mapped out the constellations you taught me, and then I'm going to fill in the extra stars.

THE GRANDFATHER. Whatever.

THE BOY. I've counted seven stars in the Big Dipper.

THE GRANDFATHER. But there are eight.

THE BOY. Eight?

THE GRANDFATHER. You've forgotten that the next to the last star in the handle is a double star—see it?

THE BOY. Where?

THE GRANDFATHER. There. . . . I know if my weak old eyes can see it, your young ones certainly can.

THE BOY. Is it just below that one?

THE GRANDFATHER. That's right.

THE BOY. Okay, so that makes eight stars in the Big Dipper . . . now can you show me Lyra? I've forgotten how to find it.

THE GRANDFATHER. You'd never make a navigator, my boy . . . just look for Vega—it's the brightest star in the summer sky.

THE BOY. I thought that was Venus.

THE GRANDFATHER. *(Exasperated.)* Venus is a planet!

THE BOY. I forgot.

THE GRANDFATHER. So it appears.

THE BOY. Grandfather, I'm sorry.

THE GRANDFATHER. It's the blue one.

THE BOY. I see it!

THE GRANDFATHER. Why, when I was a cabin boy half your age, I knew every star in both hemispheres.

THE BOY. That's when you went off to the Anti-Arctic.

THE GRANDFATHER. Antarctic, not Anti-Arctic!

THE BOY. Tell me about it.

THE GRANDFATHER. Don't you ever get tired of my stories?

THE BOY. No.

THE GRANDFATHER. Wish I could say the same for your grandmother
. . . she calls it rambling. . . .

THE BOY. But she likes your stories, Grandfather, she told me so.
She's worried about you . . . we both are . . . you seem so far
away sometimes. . . .

THE GRANDFATHER. I am far away sometimes. I don't know, my
mind just wanders, gets stuck in a whirlpool, spins round and
round. . . . I'm a man who led the voyages of 100 ships and
can't control the direction of my own thoughts. *(His hand
trembles.)*

THE BOY. It must be frightening, Grandfather.

THE GRANDFATHER. Frightening . . . *(He notices his trembling arm.)*
Look at me shaking. . . .

*(The boy sees the arm too, and at first is frightened by it. But
bravely he grasps it firmly to stop it from shaking. The grandfather jerks it away and sits in his chair embarrassed.)*

THE BOY. *(Sitting beside his grandfather.)* Is it anything like being
scared of the dark?

THE GRANDFATHER. Yes, only when you're as old as me there's no
one to call to turn on the light for you.

THE BOY. I'm here Grandfather, I'll turn on the light for you.

*(The boy tries to hug his grandfather, but the grandfather won't
let him.)*

THE GRANDFATHER. Leave me.

THE BOY. What?

THE GRANDFATHER. *(Shouting.)* Leave me alone!

(The boy exits.)

(Fade to black.)

SCENE 7. "Crickets and frogs"

THE FRECKLED-FACE GIRL. Come on little cricket
come on . . .
. . . there's that other frog I heard.
Come on both of you. I just want to count you.
That's a good boy . . . or girl?
Look out!
Look out little cricket!
Oh, no!
. . . I wonder if I should still count a cricket that's been
swallowed by a frog?
Gosh. . . .
Think of all those frogs with crickets inside of them.
There's no way to know . . .
unless . . . unless frogs with crickets inside of them jump
farther than . . .

THE BOY. How are the crickets and frogs?

THE FRECKLED-FACE GIRL. All right, I suppose. . . . They're . . . em
. . . coming together, so to speak.

THE BOY. That's good, because I'm having a time with these stars.
There are so many it's like starting over every night.

THE FRECKLED-FACE GIRL. At least they don't hop around.

THE BOY. No, but you can catch all the crickets and frogs in the bog
and count them and let them go. I can't do that with the stars.

THE FRECKLED-FACE GIRL. You could have chosen crickets and frogs
. . . it was your idea to count the stars.

THE BOY. I used to play with frogs when I was little. But I had enough
of them—so slimy and all.

THE FRECKLED-FACE GIRL. As I remember it, you brought that bull-
frog to school and right in front of the whole class he peed on
you. . . .

THE BOY. I don't remember that. . . .

THE FRECKLED-FACE GIRL. And Jonathan said you'd get warts.

THE BOY. Leave Jonathan out of it.

THE FRECKLED-FACE GIRL. Oh, I forgot, no one can mention Jonathan
around you without your going crazy.

THE BOY. Who said that?

THE FRECKLED-FACE GIRL. Everyone says it.

THE BOY. That's not true.

THE FRECKLED-FACE GIRL. Yes it is . . . they all say you grieve over him like he was a lost puppy.

THE BOY. They do not . . . you don't know what you're talking about.

THE FRECKLED-FACE GIRL. And he hasn't written you has he?

THE BOY. Why should he?

THE FRECKLED-FACE GIRL. I heard you got one Christmas card and that was it—I can't believe you can't forget him.

THE BOY. So he moved away, what does it matter?

THE FRECKLED-FACE GIRL. Doesn't matter at all to me . . . only your friends think you've gone nuts—you don't give any of us the time of day now that Jonathan's gone. . . .

THE BOY. Let's drop it, okay?

THE FRECKLED-FACE GIRL. Okay . . . how many stars have you counted?

THE BOY. Eight hundred and twenty-seven . . . how many crickets and frogs?

THE FRECKLED-FACE GIRL. Not counting the crickets inside the. . . . I mean 213 frogs and 614 crickets, so far. But that's only this side of the bog. . . .

THE BOY. Yes, I've got a lot of big constellations to go, too.

THE FRECKLED-FACE GIRL. Will you finish by September?

THE BOY. Certainly, will you?

THE FRECKLED-FACE GIRL. Certainly.

THE BOY	THE FRECKLED-FACE GIRL
Boy, is she stuck on herself.	Boy, is he stuck on himself.

(Fade to black.)

SCENE 8. "I'm going to church"

(Lights up. The grandmother is sitting in a rocker on the porch peeling potatoes. Nicholas drowsily enters.)

THE GRANDMOTHER. Good morning.

THE BOY. *(Still half asleep.)*
Good morning.

THE GRANDMOTHER. Did you sleep well?

THE BOY. Okay. . . .

THE GRANDMOTHER. I left some ham biscuits in the oven for you—would you like some eggs?

THE BOY. No, thank you. I'm not very hungry.

THE GRANDMOTHER. I've never known you when you weren't hungry, are you feeling alright?

THE BOY. Sure . . . is grandfather up yet?

THE GRANDMOTHER. I think I heard him puttering around a little bit ago—he'll probably be out soon.

THE BOY. Grandmother, do you think he minds me being here?

THE GRANDMOTHER. No, I'm sure he doesn't, Nicholas, we look forward to your visits anytime—why?

THE BOY. He wasn't too friendly last night.

THE GRANDMOTHER. He's just tired, Nicholas, you'll just have to give him a few days.

THE BOY. You've been saying that all summer, Grandmother.

THE GRANDMOTHER. I know I have, I just keep hoping . . .

(She is interrupted by the grandfather, who enters dressed in his Sunday best.)

THE BOY. Grandfather . . . good morning.

THE GRANDMOTHER. Matthew, where on earth are you going all dressed up like that?

THE GRANDFATHER. I'm going to church—aren't you two going?

THE GRANDMOTHER. But it's Monday morning, Matthew—we went to church yesterday.

THE GRANDFATHER. Yesterday . . .

THE BOY. Yes, Grandfather, don't you remember, you fell asleep during the sermon and we had to wake you up because you were snoring.

THE GRANDFATHER. So, you think your grandfather has lost his marbles.

THE BOY. I didn't say tha . . .

THE GRANDFATHER. Go ahead, laugh—

THE GRANDMOTHER. Matthew, no one is laughing.

THE GRANDFATHER. I just forgot, that's all, anyone can forget.

THE GRANDMOTHER. Of course they can.

THE GRANDFATHER. All this whispering behind my back. . . . I know what you think. . . .

THE BOY. No, Grandfather, we love you.

THE GRANDFATHER. Love? Pity's what you mean—"poor old grandfather." *(Starts to exit.)*

THE GRANDMOTHER. Matthew, Nicholas doesn't mean that at all.

THE BOY. I don't, Grandfather, I promise.

THE GRANDFATHER. *(Exiting.)* Humph.

THE GRANDMOTHER. Where are you going?

THE GRANDFATHER. Crazy!

THE GRANDMOTHER. Go with him, Nicholas.

THE BOY. Sure, Grandmother. *(He exits.)*

(The grandmother slowly exits into the house.)

SCENE 9. "I was young once"

THE FRECKLED-FACE GIRL. *(Enters and rings door bell.)* Mrs. McAdams?

THE GRANDMOTHER. Yes?

THE FRECKLED-FACE GIRL. Is Nicholas home?

THE GRANDMOTHER. No, I think he's out with his grandfather somewhere. . . .

THE FRECKLED-FACE GIRL. *(Starts to exit.)* Okay, thanks. . . .

THE GRANDMOTHER. Can I tell him you came by?

THE FRECKLED-FACE GIRL. *(Stops.)* No, thank you. I don't think it
would matter much. . . .

THE GRANDMOTHER. You must be that little freckled-face girl who
sits on the front row.

THE FRECKLED-FACE GIRL. How did you know?

THE GRANDMOTHER. I've heard Nicholas speak of you.

THE FRECKLED-FACE GIRL. Not too kindly, I bet.

THE GRANDMOTHER. Oh, I don't know—I think he rather likes you.

THE FRECKLED-FACE GIRL. Really?

THE GRANDMOTHER. *(She sits on steps and motions to the girl to sit
beside her.)* Really.

THE FRECKLED-FACE GIRL. Gosh.

THE GRANDMOTHER. What's your name?

THE FRECKLED-FACE GIRL. Genevieve.

THE GRANDMOTHER. Well, Genevieve, I'll bet you're wondering how
to make Nicholas take notice of you.

THE FRECKLED-FACE GIRL. Why do you think that?

THE GRANDMOTHER. Because I was young once, too.

THE FRECKLED-FACE GIRL. Then how did you get the boys to notice
you?

THE GRANDMOTHER. This may not sound like such good advice, but
I promise you that it works . . . just be there, Genevieve.

THE FRECKLED-FACE GIRL. That's it?

THE GRANDMOTHER. Oh, I don't mean to hang on like a lovesick
puppy—just let him know that you're interested, that you care—
but give him some room. He may not notice you at first, but
one day he'll look up and he'll need you and he'll notice how
nice it is to need someone. . . .

THE FRECKLED-FACE GIRL. I think what Nicholas needs is Jonathan. He hasn't been the same since he left.

THE GRANDMOTHER. Yes, he misses him, and Jonathan hasn't helped much. Nicholas got a Christmas card from him and that was it.

THE FRECKLED-FACE GIRL. What a creep.

THE GRANDMOTHER. Still, give Nicholas some time and he'll notice that he has a new friend on the horizon.

THE FRECKLED-FACE GIRL. And what am I supposed to do in the meantime, while he makes up his mind? . . .

THE GRANDMOTHER. Whatever you like. You don't have to give up your own interests to care about someone else . . . the secret is to let him know you could just as well live without him—but that you'd rather not.

THE FRECKLED-FACE GIRL. Is that all there is to it?

THE GRANDMOTHER. It's worked for me for forty-seven years. . . .

(Fade to black.)

SCENE 10. "Are you afraid of me, Nicholas?"

(The boy and his grandfather enter, walking as if a distance from home.)

THE GRANDFATHER. Well, why don't you say something?

THE BOY. I'm afraid to. . . .

THE GRANDFATHER. Are you afraid of me, Nicholas?

THE BOY. Sometimes . . . sometimes I don't understand you.

THE GRANDFATHER. Sometimes I don't understand myself . . . but I don't mean to frighten you, Nicholas.

THE BOY. It's okay, Grandfather.

THE GRANDFATHER. Would you like me to help you count your stars tonight?

THE BOY. Sure I would—if you feel like it.

THE GRANDFATHER. I feel fine. You've been listening to some of your grandmother's nonsense.

THE BOY. Oh, she's just worried about you.

THE GRANDFATHER. I know she is. . . . I'll tell you what—we can get out the hammock tonight and lie back and take in the whole sky—would you like that?

THE BOY. That would be great. . . .

THE GRANDFATHER. Well, let's go back to the house before your grandmother gets too worried about us.

THE BOY. Sure. Grandfather . . .

THE GRANDFATHER. Yes?

THE BOY. I love you.

THE GRANDFATHER. I love you too, Nicholas. *(They join hands and exit.)*

SCENE 11. "The hammock and the legend"

(The boy and his grandfather enter from R with a hammock and set it up on the porch.)

THE GRANDFATHER. All right, take that end.

THE BOY. Got it.

THE GRANDFATHER. There.

THE BOY. *(Jumping into the hammock.)* I think hammocks are wonderful, don't you?

THE GRANDFATHER. The hammock is probably the greatest invention since the . . .

THE BOY. Since the what?

THE GRANDFATHER. Since the rocking chair. *(He sits in rocking chair.)*

THE BOY. You used to sleep in a hammock when you were out at sea, didn't you?

THE GRANDFATHER. That I did . . . took the sway out of the ship's swaying.

THE BOY. Sure would be fun to have a hammock up there between the dippers. . . . I bet we could count the stars in no time from up there.

THE GRANDFATHER. Perhaps we could.

THE BOY. Why, we could throw one end of the hammock over the handle of the Big Dipper and the other end over the Little Dipper and just swing away until we got tired.

THE GRANDFATHER. No one gets tired in a hammock.

THE BOY. How come?

THE GRANDFATHER. It's against the law.

THE BOY. Well, we would have to come down sometime, I mean, we might get thirsty or something.

THE GRANDFATHER. If we got thirsty we could just have a drink from one of the dippers.

THE BOY. You can't really drink from them.

THE GRANDFATHER. Why? There's not a law against it, is there?

THE BOY. No, but . . . what's in them anyway? . . .

THE GRANDFATHER. In the big one there's milk.

THE BOY. Milk!? Then what's in the other one?

THE GRANDFATHER. What would you like?

THE BOY. Coca Cola would be nice.

THE GRANDFATHER. By the strangest coincidence, the Little Dipper is spilling over with Coca Cola!

THE BOY. I'm thirsty already. Let's move the hammock up there.

THE GRANDFATHER. Ah, but there's the dragon to be considered.

THE BOY. Dragon? What dragon?

THE GRANDFATHER. You don't see the dragon?

THE BOY. No, where is he?

THE GRANDFATHER. Right there, wrapped around the Big and Little Dippers. He's rather dim, at least until he gets all fired up.

THE BOY. I think I see him. Are those stars his head?

THE GRANDFATHER. That's right.

THE BOY. And his long tail curls around the dippers like that?

THE GRANDFATHER. You do see him.

THE BOY. Is he a fierce dragon?

THE GRANDFATHER. Oh yes, he has to be . . . he's there to guard the stars.

THE BOY. Guard them from what?

THE GRANDFATHER. From those of us who might try to steal them.

THE BOY. Why would we want to steal them?

THE GRANDFATHER. There's an old legend that when Adam and Eve were thrown out of the Garden of Eden, all the happy moments that they had were turned into tiny stars and scattered about the night sky as a reminder of the paradise they had lost.

THE BOY. What's that got to do with stealing the stars?

THE GRANDFATHER. The legend says that if someone were to capture the stars and scatter them again on the earth that all would be paradise again . . . there would be no hunger or sickness, and no one would die. . . .

THE BOY. Sounds great.

THE GRANDFATHER. But there's a catch. . . .

THE BOY. Isn't there always?

THE GRANDFATHER. I'm afraid so. The legend says that in the heat of the battle, the dragon will use his hot steamy dragonsbreath to brew a fierce storm, the dark black clouds hiding him from sight until only the sound of the dragon's angry tail pounding against the sky can be heard thundering across the sky, until the night cracks and explodes and is ripped apart by the fury and shattered into slivers of dragonsfire, which fall to earth as bolts of lightning and if the dragonslayer is slain, the cruel rains come, and the sky weeps. For the one who had set out to slay the dragon and steal the stars will have vanished in the fury, never to be seen again.

THE BOY. Has no one ever slain the dragon?

THE GRANDFATHER. Have you ever seen a thunderstorm without rain?

THE BOY. No . . . but that doesn't mean that the dragon couldn't be slain, does it?

THE GRANDFATHER. No, not if you believe the legend.

THE BOY. You believe it, don't you, Grandfather?

THE GRANDFATHER. I don't really know, it's one of many myths that have been passed down for thousands of years.

THE BOY. Whatever happened to all those myths?

THE GRANDFATHER. I suppose people stopped believing in them.

THE BOY. They weren't really real, were they?

THE GRANDFATHER. Oh, I wouldn't be too sure, people believed in them, ran their lives around them, and even if they weren't real, they mattered, they counted. I suppose, real or not, people made them real . . . you can make most anything real if you believe in it.

THE BOY. So I better be on the look-out for griffins and minotaurs and dragons.

THE GRANDFATHER. Let's just say that people who go fooling around with mythological creatures, especially dragons, are liable to get burned.

THE BOY. Like who?

THE GRANDFATHER. Well, there was a fellow by the name of Prometheus who went up to the dippers one day to get some Coca Cola for a few of his friends down on earth . . . you see, up until then, there wasn't any Coca Cola on earth. . . .

THE BOY. Wait a minute, Prometheus got fire, not Coca Cola!

THE GRANDFATHER. Oh, he got fire alright, but he didn't intend to . . . just as he reached the Big Dipper, the dragon woke up and was so angry he took a bite out of the sun, making the sky go dark. . . .

THE BOY. An eclipse.

THE GRANDFATHER. That's right, the dragon was so angry, he gobbled up the whole sun and as Prometheus started to fly away . . . the dragon started barking at him, spitting fire, the aurora borealis, all over the sky—melting Prometheus' wax wings— and then he and Daedalus fell to the. . . .

THE BOY. Grandfather, that was Icarus and Daedalus, not Prometheus. . . .

THE GRANDFATHER. *(Confused.)* Are you sure?

THE BOY. Yes, Grandfather, and besides, dragons don't bark. I think you've got your myths mixed up. . . .

THE GRANDFATHER. *(Upset and bewildered by his confusion, his mind failing him again.)* I seem to get everything mixed up. . . .

THE BOY. Don't cry, Grandfather . . . besides, I think your version is better anyway . . . and who knows, just because I've never heard a dragon bark doesn't mean they don't. *(The boy hugs his grandfather.)*

(Lights fade to black.)

SCENE 12. "Breakfast dishes"

THE GRANDMOTHER.

(She enters with an imaginary stack of breakfast dishes that she sets on an imaginary sink. As she starts to wash them she speaks.)

It was good to see those two gobbling down their breakfast. Nicholas had seconds, and I think that his grandfather would have had thirds if there had been any left.
The toast was burned . . . but Nicholas painted over it so thick with strawberry jam that you'd never know. And a quart of orange juice between them. . . .
. . . he looks so old . . . and every time he looks at me I feel like he's accusing me of something. . . .
I wish I could tell him I don't care how old he is or how tired . . . or how forgetful. . . .

THE BOY. *(Entering.)* Would you like some help, Grandmother? *(He reaches for a cookie in the cookie jar.)*

THE GRANDMOTHER. Nicholas, you just ate breakfast.

THE BOY. Then I won't ruin my appetite . . . here, I'll do it, Grandmother. Hand me that dish towel.

THE GRANDMOTHER. *(Handing him the imaginary towel.)* Thank you Nicholas, that's sweet of you.

THE BOY. Yeah, well, I ate all that jam for breakfast and thought I'd better work some of that sweetness out of my system.

THE GRANDMOTHER. You're a mess, Nicholas.

THE BOY. Yeah, I guess so . . . besides, now that school's out, I kinda get bored just hanging around the house.

THE GRANDMOTHER. I think that's your grandfather's problem, too.

THE BOY. But he's been out of school for over fifty years.

THE GRANDMOTHER. No, I didn't mean that—I meant that he hasn't enough to do.

THE BOY. And I always thought you old folks had it made. . . . I mean, you don't have to do homework or anything—you could play all day, if you wanted to.

THE GRANDMOTHER. Sometimes, when you haven't played for a long time, you forget how, Nicholas . . . be careful with this pitcher.

THE BOY. Yes, ma'am . . . I'd be glad to teach him to play kick the can.

THE GRANDMOTHER. I'm not sure he's ready for that yet. What I mean is, well . . . like the time you two had last night. . . . I don't know what you did, but last night was the first time in months he has slept soundly all night through . . . and you saw the breakfast he devoured this morning.

THE BOY. Counting the stars can give you a big appetite.

THE GRANDMOTHER. Counting stars?

THE BOY. Yes, Grandfather's helping me count the stars for my science project—last night he helped me put up the old hammock so we could lie back and see the whole sky at once. . . .

THE GRANDMOTHER. Good . . . but don't overdo it . . . your grandfather gets tired awful quickly these days.

THE BOY. I'll be careful with him. . . . *(He finishes drying the last dish.)* Done?

THE GRANDMOTHER. Done.

(Fade to black.)

SCENE 13. "Saturday-tarius"

(Lights up.)

THE GRANDFATHER. My hearing aid must be acting up, I thought you said Saturday-tarius.

THE BOY. That's what I said, Saturday-tarius—you know, the constellation.

THE GRANDFATHER. You mean Sagittarius!

THE BOY. And he's supposed to be somebody . . . with a bow and arrow and all?

THE GRANDFATHER. That's right, an archer.

THE BOY. Looks like a tea kettle to me, Grandfather.

THE GRANDFATHER. It does look a bit like a tea kettle.

THE BOY. What was Sagittarius shooting at, Grandfather?

THE GRANDFATHER. Sagittarius shot Scorpio, the scorpion, because Scorpio had stung and killed Orion, the hunter.

THE BOY. We saw him when I was here at Christmas.

THE GRANDFATHER. That's right. And that's why Orion doesn't appear in the sky when Scorpio and Sagittarius are up.

THE BOY. He was a hero then.

THE GRANDFATHER. I suppose he was . . . there were lots of heroes around in those days.

THE BOY. More than now?

THE GRANDFATHER. Many more than now.

THE BOY. How come?

THE GRANDFATHER. The world was young then, Nicholas, we all have heroes when we're young.

THE BOY. Did you, Grandfather?

THE GRANDFATHER. Oh yes, I had heroes.

THE BOY. Who was your favorite?

THE GRANDFATHER. Captain Robert Scott!

THE BOY. Who was he?

THE GRANDFATHER. He was an explorer and a scientist—an Englishman who set out to explore the Antarctic. He hoped to be the first man to reach the South Pole.

THE BOY. Did he make it?

THE GRANDFATHER. He made it to the pole, but when he arrived, he found that Amundsen, a Norwegian explorer, had raced across the frozen wilderness to steal the moment of glory from him. When he arrived at the pole, Scott found a flag left by Amundsen.

THE BOY. So Amundsen was the real hero?

THE GRANDFATHER. No, it takes more than a brief moment of glory to be a true hero. . . . The world saw Amundsen as a thief in the night . . . for he returned with nothing but the glory, no scientific observations . . . not even a map of his exploits.

THE BOY. And what happened to Scott?

THE GRANDFATHER. He and his men were found frozen in their tent only eleven miles from a relief station. A storm had overtaken them and they ran out of food and fuel. . . .

THE BOY. . . . do you think it was worth it?

THE GRANDFATHER. I did, Nicholas, at least until I was a navigator on the first American expedition to the pole and then I saw what a miserable wasteland Captain Scott had set out to conquer. . . . Oh, it was beautiful and intriguing, but I often wondered what difference it would have made if no one had ever found that place. . . .

THE BOY. We wouldn't know about penguins. . . .

THE GRANDFATHER. No, we wouldn't know about penguins.

THE BOY. Besides, if you had never gone there you would never know that you didn't like it.

THE GRANDFATHER. I'm afraid we spend a lot of our lives trying to find out things we'd be better off not knowing.

THE BOY. Sounds like all those vegetables Grandmother is always trying to get me to taste.

THE GRANDFATHER. I suppose. . . . I wonder. . . .

THE BOY. What, Grandfather?

THE GRANDFATHER. I wonder about all the vegetables that I've eaten and never tasted.

THE BOY. I try to make it a point not to taste or to wonder about vegetables.

THE GRANDFATHER. You're a wise boy, Nicholas, wiser than you know. . . .

(Fade to black.)

SCENE 14. "Shooting stars"

(The boy comes racing onto the porch, followed by his grandfather. The boy races DC to look through the binoculars around his neck. The sound of crickets is heard.)

THE BOY. Listen to those crickets, Grandfather, I bet they're driving Genevieve crazy.

THE GRANDFATHER. Why?

THE BOY. Because her science project is to count them all.

THE GRANDFATHER. Then I expect they are.

THE BOY. Why do you think they're so loud tonight, Grandfather?

THE GRANDFATHER. They say that when crickets sing that loudly, that summer is almost over and the first frost is only six weeks away.

THE BOY. Frost . . . already? But it seems like the summer's just begun.

THE GRANDFATHER. Yes it does, Nicholas. In all my years it's always the summers that pass too swiftly.

THE BOY. Do you think we will really see some shooting stars tonight?

THE GRANDFATHER. Oh, I'm sure we will, on most nights you'll see about six in an hour.

THE BOY. Really, why don't people see them all the time?

THE GRANDFATHER. How many people do you know that take time to look at the stars?

THE BOY. Not many . . . that's sad, isn't it. . . .

THE GRANDFATHER. Yes. . . .

(Shooting star falls.)

Look, there's one. . . .

THE BOY. Where?

THE GRANDFATHER. There, look quickly. . . .

THE BOY. I missed it. . . .

THE GRANDFATHER. Don't worry, there'll be plenty more tonight, you always see more after midnight anyway. . . .

THE BOY. Why's that?

THE GRANDFATHER. Because late at night, sometimes, the stars fall asleep and fall out of the sky. . . .

THE BOY. Sure!

(Shooting star falls.)

THE GRANDFATHER. Look!

THE BOY. Wow . . . do you think we could catch one?

THE GRANDFATHER. I don't know about that.

THE BOY. I caught some fireflies once.

THE GRANDFATHER. I have a suspicion that catching falling stars might be a bit harder than catching fireflies. . . . What would you do with them if you caught them?

THE BOY. I could put them in a jar and hang it in my room at night.

THE GRANDFATHER. You tried that with fireflies, didn't you?

THE BOY. Yeah, and they all died. . . . Do you think a falling star would die, too?

THE GRANDFATHER. I'm afraid all things die eventually, Nicholas, even the stars . . . and falling stars die even faster.

THE BOY. We'd have to be mighty quick to capture one alive, wouldn't we?

THE GRANDFATHER. I suppose we would.

THE BOY. Then let's hurry! *(They race off into the night.)*

(Fade to black.)

SCENE 15. "Morning"

(The grandmother is pacing the porch, waiting for the boy and his grandfather, who have been out all night. After a moment the boy and his grandfather race onstage and into the grandmother's wrath.)

THE GRANDMOTHER. And where have you two been? You've been out all night long, haven't you?

(The grandfather winks at the boy as he turns his hearing aid off—the grandmother pantomimes her questions and the boy answers loudly so his grandfather can hear.)

THE BOY. Yes ma'am, all night.

THE GRANDMOTHER. You'll catch your death of cold.

THE BOY. We weren't trying to catch *colds*, we were trying to catch *falling stars*!

THE GRANDMOTHER. Did you catch one?

THE BOY. No, we didn't catch a one.

THE GRANDMOTHER. Look at you shivering!

THE BOY. I'm not shivering, I just haven't stopped running completely!

(The grandfather tunes back in.)

THE GRANDMOTHER. Look at those wet feet.

THE BOY. What wet feet?

THE GRANDFATHER. I think she means those. . . .

THE BOY. Oh, those wet feet . . . well, will you look at that!

THE GRANDFATHER. *(Aside to the boy.)* I think it's called dew.

THE BOY. You do?

THE GRANDFATHER. I do!

THE GRANDMOTHER. Heavens!

THE BOY. *(Aside to the grandfather.)* I think she knows what it's called.

THE GRANDMOTHER. Matthew, do you have any idea what time it is?

THE GRANDFATHER. Certainly I know what time it is. *(Aside to the boy.)* What time is it?

THE BOY. *(Aside to the grandfather.)* I think it's breakfast time.

THE GRANDFATHER. *(Aside to the boy.)* How do you know?

THE BOY. *(Aside to the grandfather.)* I've found that whenever the world's about to end, it's a sure *sign* that it's time to eat.

THE GRANDMOTHER. It's probably cold by now, it's been sitting on the table for an hour. . . .

THE GRANDFATHER. Come on, Nicholas, we wouldn't want to miss our last meal. . . .

(The boy and his grandfather start inside, the boy first. Just as the grandfather reaches the door, the grandmother calls and stops him. The boy continues inside.)

SCENE 16. "Matthew, I know . . ."

THE GRANDMOTHER. Matthew . . .

THE GRANDFATHER. What?

THE GRANDMOTHER. I know.

THE GRANDFATHER. Know . . . know what?

THE GRANDMOTHER. Dr. Morrison called last night . . . he was upset when I told him you were out catching falling stars . . . when I asked him why he told me you were. . . . Why didn't you tell me?

THE GRANDFATHER. *(Angrily.)* I didn't want you to worry.

THE GRANDMOTHER. I've been worried for weeks. . . . You've known all that time, haven't you?

THE GRANDFATHER. Yes.

THE GRANDMOTHER. Then why have you run yourself ragged . . . up all night. . . . I want you to take care of yourself.

THE GRANDFATHER. For what? So I might live an extra day or two? It doesn't matter anymore, it's over, finished. . . . Just let it be.

THE GRANDMOTHER. No. I want those extra days. . . . What is it?

THE GRANDFATHER. Nothing.

THE GRANDMOTHER. Then why do you look at me that way?

THE GRANDFATHER. You remember . . . you are the only one who remembers me as I was. When I look at you I see all those years . . . so many empty moments . . . and I feel guilty that I let them all slip away.

THE GRANDMOTHER. They weren't all empty moments . . . they were good years.

THE GRANDFATHER. Yes, I know that, but now as I look back I think of all the petty things I've said and done, I think how much better I could have been if we'd only just taken the time.

THE GRANDMOTHER. That's water over the dam, Matthew.

THE GRANDFATHER. It's all water over the dam, now. We can't go back, I know, but now it's too late to go forward.

THE GRANDMOTHER. Not if you don't give up—enjoy what's left. . . .

THE GRANDFATHER. There's nothing left—I've squandered life.

THE GRANDMOTHER. Don't say that.

THE GRANDFATHER. It's true, Bessie . . . someday soon you'll realize it too.

THE GRANDMOTHER. No, I'll never believe that.

THE GRANDFATHER. Yes you will and you'll hate me for it—for every wasted moment.

THE GRANDMOTHER. As you hate me now.

THE GRANDFATHER. I didn't say that.

THE GRANDMOTHER. I tried, Matthew. No matter how difficult times have been, I've tried—and I've never given up on you, Matthew—don't you give up on me.

THE GRANDFATHER. *(Angrily, as if she's thinking only of herself.)* Give up on *you*—good heavens—I'm the one who's dying! *(He exits.)*

THE GRANDMOTHER. *(Left all alone.)* I know . . . I know. . . .

(Fade to black.)

SCENE 17. "Tell me it isn't true"

(Lights up.)

THE BOY. Tell me it isn't true.

THE GRANDFATHER. I can't. . . .

THE BOY. You have to help me finish counting the stars.

THE GRANDFATHER. It's time I let go of the stars, Nicholas.

THE BOY. Why can't you hold on forever?

THE GRANDFATHER. Why? I don't know. . . . I suppose I should be grateful that I've held on this long. The stars just seem to slip through our fingers no matter how tightly we hold them in. . . .

THE BOY. Is that why you've been so sad. . . .

THE GRANDFATHER. I suppose. . . .

THE BOY. Don't you care anymore, Grandfather? We love you, Grandmother and me, we want you to be like you used to be.

THE GRANDFATHER. Nothing can be as it used to be.

THE BOY. Why not?

THE GRANDFATHER. Because my time has run out.

THE BOY. That's not true.

THE GRANDFATHER. I'm dying, Nicholas.

THE BOY. I know, but you act like you're already dead.

THE GRANDFATHER. Perhaps I am.

THE BOY. I don't believe that . . . but if it's more time you want, I'll get you more time—all the time you need.

(Exits.)

(Fade to black.)

SCENE 18. "Maybe that's the price we have to pay"

(Lights up.)

THE FRECKLED-FACE GIRL. Wait. . . .
Where are you going?

THE BOY. What's it to you?

THE FRECKLED-FACE GIRL. Nicholas, what's the matter?

THE BOY. Nothing.

THE FRECKLED-FACE GIRL. What's so terrible about nothing?

THE BOY. Who cares?

THE FRECKLED-FACE GIRL. I do, Nicholas.

THE BOY. My grandfather . . . he's dying, Genevieve.

THE FRECKLED-FACE GIRL. Dying? . . . I don't know what to say.

THE BOY. There's nothing to say—there's nothing to do. It's done, it's decided, it's happening, and there's nothing I can do about it.

THE FRECKLED-FACE GIRL. You love him Nicholas, perhaps that's all he needs.

THE BOY. He doesn't notice that.

THE FRECKLED-FACE GIRL. Must run in the family.

THE BOY. What?

THE FRECKLED-FACE GIRL. In case you haven't noticed, Nicholas, I want to be your friend—have you ever had a friend?

THE BOY. Sure, I had a friend once—a best friend—but he moved away. The next year I got a Christmas card from somebody using his name, but it wasn't the same. . . . There, are you satisfied?

THE FRECKLED-FACE GIRL. So you lost a friend. Are you never going to take a chance on another one?

THE BOY. My grandfather's my friend, and now I'm going to lose him, too. It hurts—it hurts too much.

THE FRECKLED-FACE GIRL. Maybe that's the price we have to pay for caring so much.

THE BOY. Then the price is too high.

THE FRECKLED-FACE GIRL. Sometimes we have to reach to the sky to get what we want.

THE BOY. If only we could steal the stars.

THE FRECKLED-FACE GIRL. What?

THE BOY. Anything can become real if you believe it hard enough.

THE FRECKLED-FACE GIRL. Nicholas, you're not making any sense . . . where are you going?

THE BOY. To slay a dragon.

(Blackout.)

SCENE 19. "Quiet out tonight"

(Lights up.)

THE GRANDMOTHER. Quiet out tonight.

THE GRANDFATHER. Too quiet.

THE GRANDMOTHER. What?

THE GRANDFATHER. Storm . . . a big one.

THE GRANDMOTHER. How do you know?

THE GRANDFATHER. I can feel it.

(Thunder.)

THE GRANDMOTHER. I should have known better than to doubt you on the weather.

(Thunder.)

THE GRANDFATHER. It's coming fast.

THE GRANDMOTHER. And Nicholas hasn't come in yet.

THE GRANDFATHER. Are you sure?

THE GRANDMOTHER. You haven't seen him, have you?

THE GRANDFATHER. No, not since. . . .

THE GRANDMOTHER. Since when?

THE GRANDFATHER. We had a bit of a quarrel and he ran off—I didn't think he'd be gone so long.

THE GRANDMOTHER. Oh, Matthew. . . .

THE GRANDFATHER. I seem to make a mess of everything these days.

THE GRANDMOTHER. Come on, help me find him. Nicholas . . . Nicholas. . . .

(As they call the storm intensifies.)

THE GRANDFATHER. Nicholas . . .

THE GRANDMOTHER. Nicholas . . .

THE GRANDFATHER. Nicholas . . .

(The freckled-face girl enters.)

THE GRANDMOTHER. Genevieve.

THE FRECKLED-FACE GIRL. Mrs. McAdams, the storm caught me in the bog—can I stay here until it blows over?

THE GRANDMOTHER. Certainly, certainly, but have you seen Nicholas?

THE FRECKLED-FACE GIRL. He's not here?

THE GRANDFATHER. No.

THE FRECKLED-FACE GIRL. He ran through the bog, but he hardly said two words to me.

THE GRANDMOTHER. Did he say where he was going?

THE FRECKLED-FACE GIRL. He said he was going to slay a dragon.

THE GRANDFATHER. He's gone to steal the stars!

THE FRECKLED-FACE GIRL. What?

THE GRANDFATHER. Never mind, help me find him—you must help me find him. . . . Nicholas . . .

THE FRECKLED-FACE GIRL. Nicholas!

THE GRANDMOTHER. Nicholas!

THE FRECKLED-FACE GIRL. Nicholas!

THE GRANDFATHER. Nicholas!

THE GRANDMOTHER. Any sign of him yet?

THE FRECKLED-FACE GIRL. Not yet.

THE GRANDFATHER. Nicholas . . .

(Voices separate in darkness and fade in the distance.)

THE GRANDMOTHER. Nicholas!

THE GRANDFATHER. Nicholas!

THE FRECKLED-FACE GIRL. Nicholas!

SCENE 20. "And the dragon would roar no more"

(Storm grows into a wild intensity, rain falls and the boy, cowering under an umbrella, wanders in, having lost his courage and his way. With each thunder clap the boy becomes more frightened. The storm continues and through the fury we hear whisperings:)

VOICE OF GRANDFATHER. *(On tape.)*

Anything is real if you believe it hard enough. . . .

(Thunder.)

The hot steamy dragonsbreath will brew a fierce storm. . . .

(Thunder and lightning.)

There would be no hunger or sickness and no one would die. . . .

(Thunder and lightning.)

. . . and the one who set out to slay the dragon will vanish in the fury.

(Thunder and lightning.)

(Then with his last ounce of courage, the boy closes the umbrella and, using it as a sword, stands on the stump to stare into the face of his fear, to challenge the storm and to meet the eye of the dragon. A gong crashes and the percussion score follows the action of the dragon slaying.)

VOICE OF THE POET. *(On tape.)*

(As a Chinese-like dragon appears. And on the screen images of an eclipse appear.)

On a high hill stood a dragon
Silhouetted in the moon, he roared.
And in his shadow, a boy hid hiding,

Brandishing a black umbrella sword.
He was beautiful, the dragon.
The most beautiful creature the boy had ever seen.
His head was red.
His eyes were green.
His scales were blue.
His wings were tangerine.
His claws were crimson,
His tail was silver grey,
And his laugh was the color of the day.
The day the boy had come to save,
So brave and unafraid.
So brave and unafraid.

(The dragon and the boy do battle.)

But when all was done and said
The boy would slay the day,
To reach the day ahead.
   And the dragon would roar no more,
     And the dragon would roar no more. . . .

(The dragon and the boy continue the battle and after a few bouts the dragon is slain, the boy thrusting several times as the poet says each color below. When the poet reaches "black," the boy's sword pierces the dragon's head for the last time and it dies.)

Red
Green
Blue
Tangerine
Crimson
Silver
Grey
Black
Black
Black
Black
Black.

(As the dragon dies, the stars fall from the sky and the boy, still exhausted from the battle, picks them up and puts them in a box. The storm grows even more intense and after a moment the boy stumbles and falls from exhaustion. The rain

falls and all falls into darkness except for thunder and light-
ning. Dragon exits. After a few moments the sound of the
grandfather's voice is heard approaching from a distance.)

SCENE 21. "I've missed you"

THE GRANDFATHER. Nicholas . . . Nicholas . . . Nicholas . . .

THE BOY. *(Awakening.)* Grandfather . . .

THE GRANDFATHER. Are you all right?

THE BOY. I've killed the dragon, Grandfather, I've stolen the stars for
you. Now you won't grow old anymore. . . .

THE GRANDFATHER. I don't care about that, Nicholas.

THE BOY. But I thought if I captured the stars, it would make you
happy again.

THE GRANDFATHER. It has made me happy—but you don't need to
steal the stars for me, Nicholas, you have given me something
far more precious. I don't need to live forever . . . I need you. I
thought if I could lock away all the good times we have had
together I wouldn't be reminded of how much I would miss
when I was gone . . . and the only thing that I have done is to
smother the few precious moments we have left. And that's
what you've done with the stars. When you lock your feelings
or your stars in a dark black box they haven't been preserved
like strawberry jam. They fade. They tarnish. We can't preserve
a moment of starlight anymore than we can save a moment of
laughter or a tear. But that's no reason to despair. That only
makes these moments all the more precious.

(The storm grows intense again. Lightning flashes and the
grandmother appears, but is unseen by the grandfather and
the boy.)

THE BOY. But I don't want you to die, Grandfather.

THE GRANDFATHER. I don't want to die, either, Nicholas . . . but listen to me, a little while ago you said I acted as if I were already
dead . . . perhaps I was . . . but tonight you have shown me how
to live again. You've shown me what it means to care about
someone. I need you to care about me—the me that hasn't forgotten all the good times we have had together.

THE BOY. Oh Grandfather, we've missed you. *(They embrace.)*

THE GRANDFATHER. I've missed you too, Nicholas.

(He has seen the grandmother, and as she turns away to give them their special moment alone, the grandfather speaks.)

I've missed you too, Bessie.

(She stops, turns to him, he crosses to her, and they embrace. The boy, left alone, begins to cry. The freckled-face girl, who has watched all of this from the porch, crosses to the boy and offers him her handkerchief.)

THE BOY. I need more than a handkerchief, I need a friend.

THE FRECKLED-FACE GIRL. Well, it's about time. *(They laugh and embrace.)*

(After a moment the boy's voice is heard on tape as if he is writing a letter, and the boy leads the freckled-face girl to the box of stars and they release them.)

THE BOY'S VOICE. *(On tape.)*

Dear Jonathan,
It was nice of you to write after all this time. I'm sorry I didn't send you a Christmas card, you just seemed so far away, but I won't forget this year.
Glad to hear you have lots of new friends, I have a new friend, too. She's a girl, Jonathan, what do you think of that? Don't think that I've forgotten you though—I think of you often. I think of my grandfather, too. I see my grandfather in me sometimes, in the way I stand, or hold my head or in something I've said, and sometimes I think I see everyone I've ever known, everything that ever was . . . walking in my shadow. . . .

(The lights have faded out and everyone has exited except the boy and the freckled-face girl, who stand at C as if standing beside their desks in school. It's the first day of class.)

SCENE 22. "Yes, ma'am, he did pass away this summer"

THE FRECKLED-FACE GIRL. I found 613 crickets, 87 bullfrogs, and approximately 10 zillion tadpoles. . . . yes, ma'am, tadpoles . . . pollywogs, if you will. Ten zillion! Well, give or take a zillion or two. . . .

THE BOY. . . . on an average night you can see around 1,000 stars, give or take a shooting star here or there, and they're all guarded by a ferocious dragon . . . yes, ma'am, a dragon. . . .
D.R.A.G.O.N.
Dragon!
Yes, ma'am, I'm sure it was a dragon.
Yes, ma'am, he did pass away this summer. . . .
. . . yes, I'm sorry, too.

(Fade to black.)

(Curtain.)

The Boy Who Talked to Whales

By Webster Smalley

Copyright, 1981, Anchorage Press, Inc.

The Boy Who Talked to Whales (1981)

The Boy Who Talked to Whales is Webster Smalley's complex play about one boy's attempt to save a whale, and the lesson he teaches both adults and peers in the process.

Jerry is a young, ingenious boy who is somewhat of a social misfit because of his intelligence. He discovers through trial and error that he is able to communicate to Ooka, a sperm whale, by blowing through a pipe under water. Ooka has wandered into Puget Sound to escape whale hunters, and Jerry uses this "language" to teach her and consequently other members of her species how to protect themselves from whalers.

Things get complicated, however, when the U.S. Navy wants Jerry and his knowledge of whales to be put to use for national security; angered Russian and Japanese whalers threaten to cause an international incident if something is not done about the damage whales are causing.

Jerry eventually wins his battles; a treaty is signed giving the whales freedom of the seas, the Navy and Coast Guard are commissioned to protect the entrance of Puget Sound for whales, and Jerry's nemesis, Commander Willoughby Rock, is transferred to Des Moines, Iowa.

The theme of survival is conveyed throughout this drama, and audiences of youths will identify with Jerry as he struggles to be understood by his mother, adults who hold positions of authority, and his peers. By play's end, he has gained everyone's respect.

CHARACTERS

Jerry Johnson: A boy, 10, energetic, questioning.

Meg Meyer: A girl, 11, a bit of a tomboy.

Betty Johnson: Jerry's mother, mid-thirties.

Harry O'Connell: Late thirties, prosperous, big, ex–football hero.

Dr. Arthur Meyer: Meg's father, 40, a psychologist.

Ooka: A fifty-foot Sperm Whale. Heard, not seen.

Regina McLean: National television newscaster.

Judge: Formidable, from Jerry's point of view.

Commander Willoughby Rock: Regular Navy, firm, humorless.

President of the United States: Not a president we have seen.

Secret Service Man: Standard, dark glasses, nonspeaking.

TIME AND PLACE
The near future, near the water on Puget Sound in the state of Washington.

The play is primarily intended for children from eight to twelve.

PRODUCTION NOTE

The whale sounds are created musically. Any temptation to use real whale sounds should be suppressed. It is suggested that a tuba or bassoon be used to make whale songs for the whale and for Jerry. These sounds are essential in creating a comedy-fantasy style for the play. Ooka's voice, splashes, etc., are heard from a speaker in the house; Jerry's sounds, from an on-stage speaker.

With doubling, the play can be produced with four male and two female actors. Jerry and Meg continue throughout the play and should be cast for youthful vitality. The actress playing Betty can double as Regina McLean; Dr. Meyer as the President; the Judge as both Rock and Secret Service Man. The actor playing O'Connell could double as either the President or Secret Service Man, but is likely to have qualities that make this undesirable.

Jerry and Meg are written to be played by adult actors, preferably of small stature. Adult actors are readily accepted by a child audience since the "whale talk" early in the play establishes that it is not fully realistic. The psychological probability of the children (the direct and simple logic and pretending they are whales) is more important than physical size or voice change for Jerry. Any suggestion of sexual interest should be avoided (Meg's costume should minimize budding womanhood), and a simple suggestive set should aid in this convention.

The Boy Who Talked to Whales

The stage is simply set to serve as several playing areas. Levels upstage will become several interior scenes, but the principal playing area is downstage near a small pier that projects into the audience and is so constructed as to allow the audience to see Jerry when he hides beneath it.

Props are brought onstage by actors. The setting should suggest a cartoon of reality, not actuality, just as the music for Ooka suggests a musical whale, but does not attempt to imitate a real whale.

Shortly before the lights fade, we hear Ooka's song. It has the attractive musical quality of a tuba or bassoon.

Jerry is discovered at the end of the pier as Ooka's song continues. He is holding a piece of plastic pipe about three inches in diameter and five feet long. He puts the pipe to his mouth, the other end in the "water" at the end of the pier, and we hear a sound surprisingly like Ooka's song. This is from the on-stage speaker.

Jerry is ten, a very active boy, mentally and physically. He is pleasant looking, neither handsome nor plain, who can move quickly and has great powers of concentration.

A woman's voice is heard, and the whale song ends.

BETTY. *(Off.)* Jerry!

> *(Jerry, startled, quickly conceals the pipe beneath the pier, starts off, then changes his mind and hides under the pier in view of the audience.*
>
> *Betty enters, R. She is in her mid-thirties, mentally energetic, attractive, and quite capable of handling most situations. Her husband, a civil engineer, is often away and she has to cope with raising an unusual child, a boy who sometimes mystifies even her. She is quite capable of fighting for Jerry's right to be a little different, but at times she must be a conventional mother. This is one of those times.)*

BETTY. Jerry! Come and eat. I'm hungry and you must be. . . . Jerry, we can fix something special if you come now. Potato pancakes. *(Firmly.)* I am not going to fix dinner at eight o'clock like last night. *(Sits on edge of pier.)* All right, I am going to stay right here. . . . If you don't come in now, you can make yourself a peanut butter sandwich—without peanut butter if you wait too long. *(Hears noise L.)* Jerry!

MEG. *(Entering.)* It's just me.

BETTY. *(Stands.)* Oh, Meg. Have you seen Jerry?

(Meg is eleven, but is in Jerry's class. She is dressed in jeans and a sloppy blouse. She is attractive and bright, a bit of a tomboy.)

MEG. *(Simply.)* I was eating dinner.

BETTY. Well, I want Jerry to have his dinner.

MEG. Yeah, I heard. I wish my dad'd fix interesting things. We just had crummy old steak.

BETTY. Do you know where he might be?

MEG. He might be anywhere.

BETTY. I think you know most of his hiding places.

(Meg has been through this before. She uses evasive tactics, picks up rocks [imaginary] and "skips" them toward the audience.)

BETTY. *(Understands Meg's motive.)* Meg, what are you doing?

MEG. Skippin' rocks. You gotta hit between the waves or—

BETTY. I see you are skipping rocks.

MEG. *(Innocent.)* Then why ask?

BETTY. Because— *(Realizes she is falling into Meg's trap.)* Meg, you are changing the subject because you don't want to tell me where Jerry might be.

MEG. There are lots and lots of places.

BETTY. That's why I want help. You and Jerry know almost every rock and tree on or near this beach. Last night it was almost eight o'clock—and the night before, it was—

MEG. *(Interrupts.)* He forgets. You know how he is, he gets thinkin' about somethin'.

BETTY. I know, but he needs to eat. Will you find him for me? *(She starts to walk off.)*

MEG. What if I can't?

BETTY. I'm sure you can, if you want to.

MEG. Not if he doesn't want me to, I can't.

BETTY. *(Stops.)* Why wouldn't he want you to find him? You haven't had an argument, have you?

MEG. No, but when he's sort of unhappy, he—

BETTY. *(Concerned.)* Why would he be unhappy? Did something happen?

MEG. He didn't say anything about school?

(Jerry frantically tries to signal Meg, but she fails to see him.)

BETTY. I hardly saw him when he came in, late as usual. He dropped his books and came to the beach. I was on the phone.

(Meg has strolled away and is on her knees sorting through rocks on the beach.)

BETTY. Meg, stop that. You are not really looking for agates. You and Jerry have found every last agate on this part of the beach years ago. You are trying to change the subject.

MEG. The trouble with you, Mrs. Johnson, you always know what I'm doin'. My dad doesn't, and he's sposed to 'cause he's a psychologist.

BETTY. I was a girl once, Meg. It helps. *(Half to herself.)* The problem is, I was never a boy. Now, tell me. What happened in school?

MEG. You better ask him.

BETTY. Meg Meyer, you are not going to tell me that something happened in school and then not tell me what.

MEG. It would be snitchin'.

BETTY. *(Pauses a moment, realizing Meg's problem, then.)* No. No, it wouldn't. I understand how you feel. But I know something happened, and I'll find it out anyway, won't I? So you might as well tell me now.

MEG. *(Reluctantly.)* Well, I didn't talk to him after he was sent to the office.

BETTY. Oh, no! Not to the office again?

(Jerry is signalling Meg to be quiet.)

MEG. *(Not seeing Jerry.)* Yeah. An' after havin' to stand in the hall. It wasn't his best day.

BETTY. *(Resigned.)* What did he do this time.

MEG. Oh, it wasn't bad. He was just practicin' noises. He forgot.

BETTY. Noises? What kind of noises?

MEG. You know. The kind he makes all the time. Code noises.

BETTY. *(Mystified.)* Code noises? What do you mean?

MEG. *(A series of dot-dash sounds, then.)* Like they told us in school. Samuel F. B. Morse invented the telegraph and dots and dashes and—

BETTY. *(Impatiently.)* I know Morse invented the telegraph and the code. What did Jerry do?

MEG. He talks in it. Morse code. *(Looking at Betty curiously.)* I thought you knew that.

BETTY. *(Remembering.)* That's what those strange sounds were.

MEG. *(Matter of fact.)* Sure. Morse code. He tried to teach me, but it was too hard.

BETTY. Funny, he didn't tell me. Why would he want to learn the Morse code?

MEG. I asked him that, too. An' did he give a dumb answer. "Because it's there," he said. I think he read that somewhere. He reads a lot—an' not every kid can talk in Morse code. *(She is trying to be helpful.)*

BETTY. *(Trying to put it all together.)* Does Miss Franklin know it was Morse code?

MEG. Naw. Jerry doesn't try to explain things to her. He said it just gets him in more trouble.

BETTY. I've tried to explain Jerry to Miss Franklin, but—

MEG. You can't explain Jerry to Miss Franklin.

BETTY. It's the *kinds* of trouble he gets into. It isn't—the usual kind of trouble.

MEG. Like the mice, huh?

BETTY. I think she almost understood about the mice. Lots of children like animals.

MEG. Your car engine?

BETTY. *(A bit defensive.)* That was in the summer. I don't think she knows about that.

MEG. She knows all right. That's why she sends him to sixth-grade science class. How many ten-year-old kids could put a car engine back together?

BETTY. *(Smiles with a certain pride, but—)* Not many, I admit—but it's things like that—and the noises that get him sent to the office.

MEG. *(Not meaning to say this.)* It was the fight that got him sent to the office.

BETTY. Fight!? What fight?

MEG. *(Explaining. Realizing she has let something slip out.)* Noises aren't bad enough to get sent to the office.

BETTY. Meg, did someone start a fight with Jerry?

MEG. *(Pauses. Struggle between loyalty and honesty.)* No.

(Jerry's signals become more frantic.)

BETTY. You just said there was a fight.

MEG. Sure, but—Jerry started it. Fred O'Connell said something about that whale, and Jerry just—Boy, you should have seen him!

(She has finally seen Jerry signalling, and the last words suddenly slow down.)

BETTY. What are you talking about? Whale? Jerry *started* a fight with—*(Realizing with horror.)* Do you mean Fred O'Connell, that great big, huge—!?

MEG. *(Fully aware of Jerry. Very reluctant.)* Well, yes—but you ask Jerry. I gotta go now. *(And she starts off.)*

BETTY. *(Rushing to block Meg's exit.)* Meg Meyer, you are not going to stop there. You tell me everything that happened. If Jerry's in trouble, I can't help if I don't know about it, can I?

MEG. *(Caught between Betty and awareness of Jerry.)* Well—no——

BETTY. *(Firmly.)* Meg?!

MEG. *(Closing her eyes, blurting it out, a tumble of words.)* I didn't hear it all. It was something about Fred's dad going out after the whale, and Jerry got all shook. It didn't last long. Fred's lots bigger than Jerry.

BETTY. *(Disbelieving.)* Meg, Jerry doesn't start fights. He doesn't fight.

MEG. He sure did this time. He just closed his eyes and waded right in, both arms goin' like windmills. He's tougher'n you think. Wild! But Fred stopped him pretty quick—then, Miss Franklin came. But it was too late. I dunno why he did it.

BETTY. Calm down, Meg. You said something about a whale? What did a whale have to do with it?

MEG. How do I know? You know how Jerry is about some things? Funny.

BETTY. Some people may think so. Miss Franklin and the principal, but you know and I know he usually has some good reason for what he does. I need you to help me find out what that reason is. Will you?

MEG. I guess— *(Remembers Jerry's presence.)* But what if he doesn't want you to know?

BETTY. *(Starting off.)* You just find him. Tell him I'm making something special for dinner. I'll do the rest.

MEG. *(Reluctantly.)* O.K.

(Betty exits. Meg makes sure she has gone for good, then—)

MEG. Jerry, she's gone. *(As he climbs on the pier.)* Why didn't you stay down? She almost saw you. *(No answer. Apologetically.)* I'm sorry about what I said. She kept asking things. I couldn't help it. *(Still no answer.)* You better go in. . . . Aren't you going to talk?

JERRY. It was bad enough before. Now she'll ask questions all night.

MEG. She wasn't really mad. Anyway, she knows you weren't hurt.

JERRY. Naw, I know. She just gets curiouser and curiouser. It's even worse since she took those psychology courses at the college. Is your dad like that?

MEG. *(Thoughtful.)* He asks some questions, but he's an adult psychologist. I don't think I have to worry till I grow up. . . . Anyway, it's your own fault. Why'd you fight about a stupid old whale?

JERRY. It's not stupid, it's smart. Maybe the smartest, most intelligent whale in the world.

MEG. What're you talkin' about? *(As Jerry gets pipe from under pier.)* Hey, what's that?

JERRY. A pipe. I need to practice.

MEG. Practice? Practice what?

JERRY. I can't talk about what.

MEG. I don't get it.

JERRY. I can't talk about this. It's too important. *(Accusing.)* You told her about the Morse code.

MEG. I thought you'd told her yourself. I had to say something about the noises you make. You know something? They don't even sound like the Morse code anymore.

JERRY. I know.

MEG. You mean they're not the Morse code? What are they then?

JERRY. Can't tell. It's a secret.

MEG. *(Indicating pipe.)* Like that?

JERRY. That's right. I can't tell even you.

MEG. I won't tell anyone—not anyone—not ever. Who else can you tell besides me? . . . Not anyone, that's who. . . . Please?

JERRY. *(Realizes the truth of this.)* It's so hard to keep it all inside me. *(Deadly earnest.)* You really promise? Not a little promise, probably the biggest promise you ever made, ever in your life.

MEG. I promise—biggest ever in my whole life.

JERRY. *(A pause, then decides.)* All right. I'll show you.

MEG. *(Lost.)* Show me? Show me what?

JERRY. The secret. Watch! And listen.

(At the end of the pier, he places one end of the pipe in the water and puts his mouth to the other.)

MEG. What are you doing?

JERRY. Wait! You'll see.

(Puts his mouth back to pipe and, with much effort and breath, he begins to make strange and wonderful deep musical noises. Meg watches, puzzled.)

MEG. Good grief! What are you doing?

JERRY. *(Breathless.)* Sh-hh. Wait.

(He makes more noises, then listens to the pipe.)

MEG. *(Can't stand the wait.)* You have to tell me. I can't guess.

JERRY. *(Still listening.)* Sh-h-h.

(He gestures for quiet, then a distant splash is heard on the house speaker. Jerry makes more noises. Other splashes as he holds his hand up for silence. Then, a short whale song from Ooka.)

MEG. *(Whispers in wonderment.)* Holy cow, what is it?

JERRY. *(Simply, just explaining a fact.)* A whale. The biggest whale you ever saw. Her name is Ooka.

MEG. *(Astounded, but not doubting Jerry.)* A real whale? A genuine, big whale—that sings? *(gen-u-wine)*

JERRY. Of course. They all talk like that. An' she isn't a killer whale, or even a grey whale like they think. She's a Sperm Whale.

(Ooka's answering song is heard.)

I have to warn her—about Mr. O'Connell's boats. That's what's so important. *(He makes sounds into pipe.)* There!

(Whale sounds diminish in distance as he gets his breath.)

Now, she won't be there if Mr. O'Connell goes after her. *(And he moves to hide the pipe.)*

MEG. She—won't be there?

JERRY. *(Simply, as he hides pipe.)* I told her to go away from here for a while.

MEG. *(Following him as he moves away from pier.)* You—told—her?

JERRY. That's what I was saying into the pipe. *(Simple explanation.)* Oh, she can't hear me without the pipe. You see, it goes under water and—

MEG. *(Interrupting. One thing at a time.)* You talked—to a—whale!?!!!

JERRY. *(Worried.)* You promised—really promised—not to tell. I'm in enough trouble. On top of everything, I ripped my jeans when Fred O'Connell knocked me down—and Mom hasn't found them yet. More questions!

MEG. You really talked to a whale?!

JERRY. Yeah, I did, but it's only going to get me in more trouble, especially after Mr. O'Connell finds— *(Stops suddenly. He shouldn't have said that.)*

MEG. *(Suspicious.)* Mr. O'Connell finds out what?

JERRY. Nothin' you need to know. Remember, you promised not to tell!

MEG. Ye-es, but— *(No nonsense. Looks him in the eye.)* How do you know it's a whale? A Sperm Whale?

JERRY. She told me—or tried to. Then, I got some whale books from the library—after she jumped. She jumped once—real early in the morning so I could see her. No one was around.

MEG. *(Doubtful, now that it has come to details.)* How do you understand—and talk to a whale? Tell me that.

JERRY. *(At a loss. He doesn't fully understand, himself.)* I don't know. I just—*can.* . . . You see, I sneaked out here one Saturday morning, about a month ago—it was too early for Mom to let me go swimming, and——

MEG. *(Scolding.)* You went swimming alone. That was dumb.

JERRY. *(Quickly.)* I didn't go out deep. Nobody else was up—not even you. So be still and let me talk. *(Acting it out as he remembers. Lies on back.)* I was floating on my back—with my ears under water—and I heard this sound—boo-oo, boo-oo. It was *in* the water. Then, I heard it again, boo-oo. I was scared. The *water* was making a noise. I stood up quick—and listened. You know what?

MEG. For gosh sakes, tell me.

JERRY. I didn't hear anything.

MEG. *(Annoyed.)* That's not all, and you know it.

JERRY. I ducked my head, and there it was again. All around. *In the* water. *(Another dramatic pause.)*

MEG. You make me mad. Either tell me or I'm going home.

JERRY. O.K., O.K. I couldn't stay with my head under all day, could I? Besides, I was getting cold. So I put on my clothes and tried to figure it out. That's why the pipe.

MEG. You don't make any sense, Jerry Johnson. Sometimes I think you're as nutty as lots of people think you are. What does a pipe have to do with noises in the water?

JERRY. *(Gets the pipe.)* Don't you see? I remembered this old plastic pipe in the garage. It's like a glass you put on the floor or wall— and you can hear on the other side. Like those things doctors use to listen.

MEG. Stethoscope?

JERRY. Yeah. So, when I put one end in the water, I heard the sounds again. With the pipe.

MEG. *(Takes pipe and listens in water.)* I don't hear anything.

JERRY. She's gone away. Remember? Anyhow, with the pipe, it wasn't so scary. I could listen—slow—and there was a kind of pattern—like in Morse code. I'd come down at night—and real early, even before the sun. I began to understand a little—and I tried to talk with it—and I practiced the sounds. I practiced a lot—even at school.

MEG. I know. You made Miss Franklin want to fly out the window, an' she sort of likes you.

JERRY. You think I'd tell her? Or the principal? *(Imitating principal.)* "Why were you making strange noises, young man?"——Well, sir, I was practicing talking whale.——"Bonkers, young man. You are bonkers. Sorry, we will have to send you away to the Bonkers Farm."

MEG. *(Giggling.)* I can just see Mr. Moffet.

JERRY. Grownups wouldn't understand. Maybe even kids'd think I was crazy. But it's true, I can—— *(Grabs her arm, excited.)* I can understand, and talk it a little. You should hear her. Wow! Sometimes she just sings. Ooka likes to sing, just for the fun of it. She has a good voice, don't you think? For a whale?

MEG. *(Thinks a moment.)* I guess. I haven't heard any other whales.

JERRY. She's pretty young.

MEG. *(Suspicious again.)* How do you know it's a girl?

JERRY. It's partly a guess. She wants to have baby whales—like her mother. Her mother got hurt—killed maybe—by a whaler. It's hard to understand what she means. First, I have to try to understand *what* she is saying. . . . Then, I have to pretend *I'm* a whale to figure out what she means. *(He begins imitating a whale, using his arms as flukes, and looks up as if from beneath a boat.)* A boat looks a lot different to a whale than to us.

MEG. *(Imitating Jerry, looking up as if at boat.)* Yeah—gee, I hadn't thought of that.

JERRY. *(Excited. Acting it out.)* She loves the big ocean. Go down deep, way down into the dark—then up fast—like flying—and swish—way up in the sunlight. Then *splash*—a big breath and down again and find a nice big, tender octopus to munch—whish—up into the sun and good, fresh air to breathe.

MEG. Octopus—ugh!

JERRY. When she jumped for me, you should have seen her. She is big—I mean, BIG! *(Eyes alight.)* She's bigger than a—a house trailer. When she jumped, she just kept coming out of the water, and coming out—almost forever. *(Earnestly. Tears almost come.)* She is the most wonderful thing I have ever seen. I love her!

MEG. *(Impressed, but not knowing quite how to respond.)* Jerry, you— You're something!

JERRY. *(Darkly.)* But she's scared.

MEG. What could a big thing like that be scared of?

JERRY. Whalers. That's why she's in Puget Sound, to get away from whaling ships. Then, old Mr. O'Connell— *(A reminder of a big worry.)* Oh—no—

MEG. What? *(As Jerry sits despondently.)* What's the matter? You said something before about Mr. O'Connell.

JERRY. When he finds out, I'm in real trouble.

MEG. When Mr. O'Connell finds out what?

JERRY. When Fred said his dad was going to take his boats and go after Ooka—to try to catch her—something terrible might happen to her. Oh, they couldn't catch her—not her. They don't know how big she is. They think she's an old grey whale. But they'd scare her, even hurt her maybe. Boats are always hurting whales.

MEG. O.K. So what'd you do to Mr. O'Connell?

JERRY. I—I sort of took something.

MEG. *(Puzzled.)* You took something? What? Who from?

JERRY. From Mr. O'Connell's boats. Something from their motors. They won't go, now.

MEG. *(Shocked.)* You stole something from Mr. O'Connell's boats? From all three of them?

JERRY. Don't say it like that. I sort of—borrowed some—fuel pumps. *(Hastily.)* I'll give them back as soon as—

MEG. You sto—I mean took the fuel pumps from all three of his boats?

JERRY. *(Nods.)* I don't think he can get replacements right away. But Ooka's in trouble. I had to do it.

MEG. But you told Ooka to go away. She's gone! You didn't have to do that.

JERRY. I wasn't sure I could get her to go. She doesn't always understand. I had to do everything I could, didn't I? Besides, I don't know how far she's gone. See?

MEG. I guess. *(A horrible thought.)* Jerry, he'll know who did it. After you told Fred you'd stop his father.

JERRY. *(Sadly. Resigned.)* I know. Fred saw me leaving the boats, too. I told you it was worse than my torn jeans.

(The lights fade quickly and come up on the area on a level UR, which suggests the Johnson living room. A chair and a small table for a phone are all that are necessary. Betty enters with phone, in middle of a conversation.)

BETTY. And he talks in Morse code. . . . That's what I said. Meg told me. . . . That's not why I called. I think Jerry's in trouble again. He got in a fight of all things. . . . Yes, I'm talking about Jerry, your son. . . . I know he doesn't fight, but he did. . . . Something about a whale in the bay. . . . Yes, whale, that's what I said. . . . I haven't been able to talk with him, you know how he disappears. . . . I wish you could come home this weekend. I'll be so glad when that bridge is finished. . . . Well, try, for next week. . . . Maybe Jerry can call you, but it's not the same.

(Door bell rings.)

Someone's at the door, maybe Jerry. No, he wouldn't ring.

(Bell again.)

O.K., bye, dear.

(She moves to [imaginary] door and is confronted by O'Connell, a big man, bluff and direct. O'Connell is a former high school football hero who has made a success chartering boats to sports fishermen. At the moment, he is furious.)

BETTY. Why—Mr. O'Connell.

O'CONNELL. *(Entering and looking about room.)* Where is he? Your kid? You know where he is?

BETTY. *(Annoyed.)* That's no way to—

O'CONNELL. I don't care, lady. Where is he? My kid, Fred, saw him on my boats this afternoon.

BETTY. Now, wait a minute, Mr. O'Connell. Jerry's down on the beach. He couldn't possibly have been on your boats.

O'CONNELL. Oh, he couldn't possibly, huh? Did you follow him around today? Oh, I've heard about him. Takes cars apart——

BETTY. *(Not really slowing him down.)* He put it back together—

O'CONNELL. Stole the mousetraps at school—fed the mice oatmeal.

BETTY. Jerry's a bright boy—and he likes animals—a lot. Now, I think that's——

O'CONNELL. There are no animals on my boats. And after getting my kid in trouble with the principal, he has the guts to——

BETTY. *(Tops his tirade.)* Ca-alm down, Mr. O'Connell! He's down on the beach. He wouldn't go on your boats.

O'CONNELL. Wouldn't huh? Fred saw him, an' he sure ought to know, 'cause the little shrimp picked a fight—

BETTY. *(Backing down a little.)* I just heard—about that. I'll find out about that—but he wouldn't go on your boats. What reason would he—

O'CONNELL. Reason? What reason would that shrimp have to light into Fred? Crazy, that's what. Of course, Fred wiped up the sidewalk with him. . . . And he was on my boats.

BETTY. *(Holding her ground.)* I'll talk to him.

O'CONNELL. You do that. *(He turns to go as telephone rings.)* And I want to hear some answers. I think that kid's flipped his lid. Makes funny noises. You know that?

BETTY. He has an inquiring mind, he—

(Phone rings again.) Excuse me. *(On phone.)* Hello— Why, yes, he is. *(Surprised.)* It's for you.

O'CONNELL. What? *(Moving to phone.)* Who'd call me here? *(On phone.)* Yeah? . . . Yeah, Fred, what's the rush? I'm just comin' home. . . . What?! . . . All three??? That little brat! . . . Call the cops, and . . . and I'll meet you at the dock. . . . As soon as I find that kid! *(Slams phone down.)* Somebody just stole the fuel pumps from all three of my boats.

BETTY. Now, Mr. O'Connell, you don't think. . . . Why, Jerry would have no reason to. . . . Mr. O'Connell, he's just a child!

(At this moment, Jerry enters from outside. He is ready to make a simple excuse for being late and starts to say—)

JERRY. Mom, I'm sorry, but—

(He sees O'Connell, stops dead in his tracks, and the two stare at each other a long moment. This tells them both all they need to know. Jerry says, "Oh, no!" and runs headlong off R. After a beat, O'Connell's reflexes recover and he rushes in pursuit. It takes another moment for Betty to realize what has happened, then she, too, rushes after them, calling, "Jerry!, Mr. O'Connell!"

The lights go down on this area and come up at a level Left. It is the Meyer living room. All is needed is a chair for Dr. Meyer. Lighting separates this area from the rest of the stage, which is dimly lit.

Meyer is wearing reading glasses and is totally absorbed in his paper. Meg hovers, getting up courage to get his attention.

Meg's movement and vitality are essential to regain the audi-
ence attention in each of these subscenes. Meg and her father
are oblivious of the action outside their cozy house. Timing is
essential.)

MEG. *(Moves to her father.)* Dad?

MEYER. *(Not really hearing.)* Hum-m?

(At this moment, Jerry appears, R, running for his life. He is
followed by O'Connell, then at a slower pace by Betty. It is
Meg's increasing frustration and strong sense of purpose that
will bring the audience back to their scene.)

MEG. Dad, will you listen to me?

MEYER. *(He isn't really.)* I'm listening.

MEG. Do you think it would be wrong—No. Do you think it would
be bad if someone did something—not very good, kinda wrong—
to do something good?

MEYER. That depends, I suppose.

MEG. On what?

MEYER. On how bad and how good.

MEG. I mean if—let's say one of your patients did something pretty
bad—maybe really bad—but meant it, you know, to be good?

MEYER. Hard to say.

(Meg is exasperated and turns away just as Jerry runs on from
UL and exits DR. O'Connell enters, looks about, then exits
as Betty enters, looks about and exits the same direction she
entered.

Note: The details of this chase may vary according to the
stage plan and the theatre. The only stipulation is that the
chase not overlap the Meg-Meyer conversation.)

MEG. *(Returning to the attack.)* Dad, will you listen to me?

MEYER. *(Startled by her vehemence.)* What?

MEG. *(Firmly.)* What if someone did something that *seemed* wrong—
maybe even against the law—but to do good—to help someone—some *thing*—in trouble?

MEYER. Well—I suppose if it were really against the law—illegal—
that person could be arrested anyway.

MEG. *(Horrified.)* You mean, they'd put him in jail?

MEYER. *(Beginning to react to her seriousness.)* Most likely. What's this all about?

MEG. *(Frustrated.)* Oh, you don't take things serious!

(Meg stamps her foot and faces away from him, pouting. Jerry appears and hides beneath the pier. Betty then appears and wanders off. O'Connell comes on, looks on the pier, then goes off.)

MEG. *(Moves back to her father. Imploring.)* Would they really put him in jail? Even if he meant well? Even if he was trying to save someone from certain death?

MEYER. Certain death!? Where did you get that idea?

MEG. Dad, I need to know.

MEYER. *(Kindly, but pedantically.)* The police—and the courts don't look at why someone did something—they look at the crime.

MEG. Then they're wrong!

MEYER. Maybe, but the courts mainly look to see if a person knows what he's doing—is legally sane. If he knows, he can go to jail.

MEG. Even if— *(An idea.)* But last year, you helped someone in court. He didn't go to jail.

MEYER. That was different. That man thought everything beautiful belonged to him. He wasn't legally sane.

(Betty enters, looks around, and sits disconsolately with her back against the pier.)

MEG. Dad!

(Meyer reacts.)

What if people just think a person is strange? Maybe a *little* crazy. Would that mean they were not legally sane?

MEYER. Perhaps, it might—

MEG. Would someone who talks to animals—big animals—would he be legally sane?

MEYER. Well, that depends. I talk to dogs all the time.

MEG. *(Impatiently.)* I mean really big animals, like—like whales. Would he be legally sane?

MEYER. *(Alert.)* Who are you talking about? You're talking about a real person!

MEG. I promised not to tell.

> *(Meg moves away from her father and faces upstage. He looks at her, pondering the problem.*
>
> *O'Connell stalks on, moves to the pier and, in the darkness, mistakes Betty for Jerry and grabs her. She screams, which brings Jerry to her aid. O'Connell easily subdues Jerry and drags him off as Betty follows, helplessly calling after them [Mr. O'Connell!, Jerry!, etc., ad lib.].)*

MEYER. *(Knows this is serious. Moves to her.)* Meg, you are talking about something real. You know someone in real trouble, don't you?

MEG. I think maybe I know someone you can help.

MEYER. *(Doubtfully.)* Someone who talks to whales?

MEG. *(A rush of words tumbling over each other.)* They talk to him, too. I promised I wouldn't tell, but he's in a lot of trouble, I think, and I've got to. Jerry Johnson talks to whales——and I think he stole some things because Ooka's in trouble—because she's afraid of whalers—and I think Mr. O'Connell is going to get Jerry put in jail. Maybe he is in jail right now!

MEYER. Now, slow down. Just slow down and tell me—one thing at a time. The whole story—and we'll see if I can help.

> *(Blackout on Meyer and Meg. Music transition—ominous, perhaps a bit like the old "Dragnet" theme. This helps cover the placing of the judge's bench.*
>
> *It is a courtroom with Judge at bench UC. The Judge and bench should overwhelm the scene. Before the bench stand Jerry, Betty, and, a little apart, O'Connell. The Judge appears a bit fierce and angry. He pounds his gavel and O'Connell angrily blurts—)*

O'CONNELL. I don't care how young he is, your honor. He stole my fuel pumps. And he won't tell where he hid them.

JUDGE. This could be very serious for you, young man.

BETTY. Your honor, this is needless. If Mr. O'Connell would only give us a little time.

O'CONNELL. I can't get fuel pumps this side of San Francisco. *(To Judge.)* Have you priced parts lately? The kid is a menace.

BETTY. I'm sure Jerry will give them back.

JERRY. I won't. He could still find Ooka. Go ahead. Put me in jail!

BETTY. Jerry!

JUDGE. Young man, you keep talking about someone named Ooka. Does he have the fuel pumps?

BETTY. Jerry, who is this Ooka?

JERRY. I can't tell.

O'CONNELL. You see, your honor. He won't talk. I tried, she tried—you try!

JUDGE. *(Trying hard to be patient.)* I am trying, Mr. O'Connell. He is either remarkably stupid, or extremely stubborn. We are attempting to find which.

BETTY. Your honor, he's a boy. He doesn't know how serious this is.

JERRY. *(Flatly.)* I know how serious it is.

BETTY. Your honor, he's ten years old. If I had some time to reason with him.

O'CONNELL. He's old enough to steal my fuel pumps.

(The Judge pounds for order, almost hitting O'Connell's fingers. At this moment, Meyer enters, followed by a rather reluctant Meg.)

MEYER. Your honor, I think I can be of help, if I may speak. I've been expert witness in your court before.

JUDGE. Yes, Dr. Meyer. Anything to help.

MEYER. There is evidence I can bring before the court—evidence that this boy suffers from delusions. One of these delusions is that he believes he can talk to whales—that he can actually hold conversations with the leviathan of the deep.

O'CONNELL. *(To Judge.)* See? I told you the kid's nuts.

MEG. *(To Jerry as he looks at her accusingly.)* I had to tell, Jerry. I'm trying to help.

JUDGE. *(Completely lost.)* Dr. Meyer, what does this boy's thinking he can talk to a whale have to do with the fuel pumps in O'Connell's boats?

MEYER. Let me explain, your honor.

JUDGE. *(Out of patience.)* I want a solution, not an explanation.

MEYER. You see, the fuel pumps are connected to the whale—I mean, the problems are connected. The boy needs to be shown he cannot really talk to whales. He needs a confrontation with a whale!

JUDGE. *(Lost.)* And where will you find this—whale?

MEYER. *(Also very lost.)* Well, I hadn't thought—

O'CONNELL. *(Snorts.)* Whatcha gonna do, bring a whale in here? In a tank?

(This kills him. The Judge raps for order.)

MEYER. Tank—? Sea-Arama. It's only ninety miles. *(This helps him grasp an idea.)* Seattle! Not whales, but they have dolphins. We'll have him talk to dolphins. Real dolphins, in Seattle. That will prove to him that he can't do it.

JUDGE. *(Doubtful.)* I still don't understand, but if you think it will help, I will so order. *(To Jerry.)* Young man, you will accompany Dr. Meyer to Seattle and attempt to talk to dolphins—before reputable witnesses.

O'CONNELL. But your Honor!

JUDGE. *(Pounding for order.)* Including you, Mr. O'Connell. I so order. *(Pounds for order over O'Connell's objections, then trails into legalese.)* The case will not be continued until after depositions of witnesses regarding the accused, Jerry Johnson's, conversations with dolphins.

(The lights have dimmed on the above and the final sound of the Judge's gavel. In the dark, sounds of dolphin voices (piccolo perhaps) and splashing. Lights come up at extreme DL. Jerry is kneeling, looking over edge of stage into dolphin tank. Meyer is beside him with his plastic pipe in hand. Betty and Meg are nearby, and O'Connell is to one side, looking on suspiciously.)

MEYER. Now, Jerry. The people at Sea-Arama have been very cooperative. Everything is ready. Even Mr. O'Connell has agreed to this experiment.

O'CONNELL. *(Snorts.)*

JERRY. *(Looking into dolphin tank. Interested.)* They're great. I haven't seen 'em this close before.

MEYER. *(A touch of impatience.)* Yes, they are excellent dolphins, but the point of this—this trip—is for you to listen to them. Listen very carefully.

(A pause as Jerry listens. We hear them.)

Well?

JERRY. Well, what?

MEYER. Can you understand them?

JERRY. They're *dolphins*.

MEYER. Of course, they're dolphins. We all know that. But can you understand what they are saying?

JERRY. *(Long pause as he listens carefully.)* They're neat swimmers, really great, but—

MEYER. But—?

JERRY. They don't talk like whales.

MEYER. *(A bit out of patience.)* What do you mean?

JERRY. I told you before. It's a different language. Not whale.

MEYER. *(Skeptical.)* So you can understand whales, but you can't understand dolphins?

JERRY. I never said I could talk to dolphins, did I? But you and that judge made me come here. I never even tried to talk to—or understand dolphins before. I wish I could—I like them—but they're different than whales.

BETTY. Jerry, would you try?

JERRY. But I only know whale—probably only Sperm Whale. They're a lot bigger—a whole lot. You wouldn't believe. And they talk different.

MEYER. *(Humoring Jerry.)* Yes, I understand that, Jerry, but—

BETTY. *(Being helpful.)* You did say you would help us understand this, Jerry.

JERRY. I didn't say I would talk to dolphins.

O'CONNELL. The kid can't. I told you, he lies.

BETTY. *(A killing look at O'Connell, then—)* All you need to do is try. Use the whale language you know.

MEG. Yeah, Jerry. Go ahead. Show 'em.

MEYER. That's right, Jerry. Just try speaking to them. *(Hands Jerry the pipe.)*

BETTY. You might as well. We've come all this way. It can't hurt.

(Jerry looks at his mother, then at Meg, takes the pipe from Meyer and begins to make his whale sounds into the tank. In a short moment, there is a great sound of dolphin squeals and of wild splashes.

All react away from the dolphin tank in surprise and shock. The following four speeches are simultaneous or overlap. Rock approaches tank, unnoticed.)

JERRY. See. I told you. *(He is unhappy.)*

O'CONNELL. Look at them dolphins.

BETTY. They're going crazy!

MEG. They're scared to death. *(Stares in fascination as Betty spirits Jerry off. Then, to Meyer as he takes her off.)* They think there's a Sperm Whale in their tank!

O'CONNELL. *(Staring at the tank.)* My God! I don't believe it. Maybe this kid can— Maybe he can talk to whales!

(Commander Rock, who has been on stage since before Jerry disturbed the dolphins, but not noticed by anyone, now approaches O'Connell.

Rock is the kind of man who is impressed by his own authority and position. He tends to treat people [and whales] like cogs in a machine. Very military.)

ROCK. *(Looking at tank of dolphins.)* Very interesting. *(To O'Connell.)* You know how he did that?

O'CONNELL. *(Still staring at tank. Surprised by Rock's voice.)* What? Oh—who are you?

ROCK. Rock, Willoughby R. Commander, U.S. Navy.

O'CONNELL. *(Impressed.)* A three striper. What're you doin' here?

ROCK. We have our reasons. Navy reasons.

O'CONNELL. *(Mystified.)* Oh——I'm Harry O'Connell. I run some fishin' boats out of Bellingham.

ROCK. I know. And I know all about this. I talked to the judge on the phone. I'm here to do something with that boy.

O'CONNELL. *(Disbelief.)* What——? *(Hope.)* Will you get my fuel pumps?

ROCK. Don't worry about the fuel pumps now. This is more important. *(Narrowly.)* Have you seen the boy talk to a whale?

O'CONNELL. Na-aw—I didn't believe—— *(Remembering and rushes to tank.)* But did you see what he done to them dolphins?

ROCK. Yes, O'Connell. And he just might be able to communicate with a whale. . . . And I want to use him. *(Confidential. Almost as if a conspiracy.)* Did you know the Coast Guard has reports of a Sperm Whale in Puget Sound?

O'CONNELL. *(Disbelieving.)* What? They never come in the Sound. Too big.

ROCK. There's always a first time, isn't there. *(All business.)* I experiment with whales, O'Connell. I need that boy, *and* his whale, O'Connell. For Navy experiment Four-BX-Whale. Need to know how he does it, why he does it, and what exactly he does when he does it. Technique, et cetera. *(Seeing great vistas open up for him.)* Do you know what Sperm Whales could do for us if we got them wired up for radio intelligence? They roam the world—Russian, Chinese waters—everywhere. *(Back to earth.)* You see what I mean?

O'CONNELL. *(Lost.)* No—But I'll help.

ROCK. *(Pleased.)* I thought so. You get me to that boy and we'll get him to cooperate.

O'CONNELL. He ain't the cooperatin' kind. *(Quickly adds.)* But I'll get you to him, all right. He's still got my fuel pumps.

ROCK. You get me to the boy. And we'll see about the fuel pumps.

(Puts his arm over O'Connell's shoulder as he leads him off.

And they are off. A slow cross fade, with Jerry's whale song heard in the darkness of the change, and Jerry is revealed at the end of the pier with his pipe, calling to Ooka.

Rock and O'Connell appear upstage, O'Connell points to Jerry and disappears. Jerry is unaware anyone is watching him.)

ROCK. *(Approaching Jerry.)* Jerry Johnson?

(Jerry looks at Rock, startled, makes some quick noises into pipe, then rushes to conceal pipe.)

ROCK. Is that what you use to talk to the whale?

JERRY. Maybe. Maybe not. What're you doing here? You're not a reporter?

ROCK. Do I look like a reporter? I'm Commander Rock of the Navy. I experiment with whales. I'd like to work with you—and your whale.

JERRY. *(He doesn't like the sound of the word.)* Experiment?!

ROCK. *(Butter wouldn't melt in his mouth.)* Not Sperm Whales, of course. Smaller ones—Pilot Whales. We've trained them to become very useful tools for the Navy.

JERRY. Tools? *(The light. He remembers.)* I know what you do. You train them to do things, but they don't know what they're doing it for. They might explode in war—and they wouldn't even know why. You're not going to train Ooka to carry any torpedo—an' get blown up. Whalers are bad enough!

ROCK. Now, Jerry, you don't understand.

JERRY. I understand, but Ooka wouldn't. She trusts me.

(Jerry turns away from Rock. Meg has appeared.)

ROCK. You will need to cooperate, Jerry. . . . Jerry?

(Silence.)

MEG. It's no use when he's like that. He won't talk.

ROCK. Who are you, a friend of his?

MEG. Yeah, I am. I thought I saw Mr. O'Connell.

ROCK. You should convince him to help the Navy.

MEG. Nobody can convince Jerry to do anything he doesn't want to do. An' I don't think he wants to.

(O'Connell has appeared and hears this next.)

ROCK. He'll cooperate sooner or later. *(Sees O'Connell and gives a negative shrug and headshake.)* Well, we'll see. *(And he starts off past O'Connell.)*

O'CONNELL. You oughta listen to this guy, kid. He's a full commander. He can do a lot for ya. He's the Navy!

JERRY. *(Firmly. Not looking at Rock.)* He's not the Navy. He's a man— like you.

O'CONNELL. *(Shrugs, looks at Rock.)*

ROCK. I'll speak to your mother. *(And exits.)*

JERRY. *(Shouting after him.)* It won't do any good!

MEG. *(To O'Connell.)* It won't, you know. She'll stick up for Jerry.

O'CONNELL. *(Remembering his scene with her.)* Yah, you're right there. . . . Well, kid. I been waitin' all day for my fuel pumps. Where's the pumps?

MEG. Jerry couldn't get them sooner, Mr. O'Connell. Reporters have been all over the place.

O'CONNELL. I know. I talked to 'em. Business, too. My phone's been ringin' off the hook—but we're wastin' time. Boats all loaded for tomorrow an' all next week. Wanta see that Sperm Whale— if that's what it is. O.K., where're them pumps?

JERRY. I'll get them. *(Begins searching under pier.)*

MEG. The whale's good for business, huh?

O'CONNELL. *(Expansive.)* Sure is— *(Then suspiciously, to Jerry.)* You know where they are? They better be in good shape.

JERRY. I've got them. Here! I put them in three plastic bags, so the salt air wouldn't rust 'em.

MEG. See, what good care he took of them?

O'CONNELL. *(Grudgingly.)* I guess. . . . *(Inspecting pumps in the plastic bags.)* O.K., you're gettin' off pretty easy, ya know.

MEG. He was afraid you'd frighten Ooka—and she'd go—and the whalers—

JERRY. You promised to be careful, real careful. It'd be awful easy to hurt her.

O'CONNELL. Aw, that whale won't get hurt. She's my meal ticket right now. More people wantin' to go out on my boats than the Coast Guard'll allow. *(A crafty glance at Jerry.)* What's in it for you, kid? What're you gettin' out of this?

JERRY. *(Puzzled.)* What?

MEG. *(Understanding. Irate.)* Jerry's not getting anything. He likes Ooka, that's all.

O'CONNELL. Yeah? *(He periodically tries to get information for Rock, but then gets caught in his own concerns.)* Real strange. A Sperm Whale comin' into Puget Sound. You sure it's a Sperm Whale? Why'd she come in the Sound?

JERRY. I'm sure—an' she's afraid of whalers. That's why she came in the Sound. To get away from the whaling ships.

O'CONNELL. Aw, kid, there ain't any whalers around here. Ain't been any American whalers since—I don't know when.

JERRY. They're out there somewhere. Ooka knows it.

O'CONNELL. Japanese—or Russian.

MEG. It doesn't matter who they are—to a whale.

JERRY. And they were after Ooka.

O'CONNELL. O.K., so that's why this whale came in the Sound. So what's it to you? Whales can take care of themselves. *(Digging for information.)* How'd you learn to talk to this whale, huh? What do you say? Nice day? What'd you have for lunch? *(An uncomfortable thought.)* Lunch—Eat. What do Sperm Whales eat? . . . *(Hopefully.)* Little fish, right? Real small; plankton?

JERRY. Not Sperm Whales. Ooka likes big fish. Octopus are her favorites—and she might run out of octopus in the Sound—if she stays long enough.

O'CONNELL. *(Horrified at the thought he has.)* Oh, no! Now I remember—they open their mouths and swim through a school of fish—and their mouths are like garage doors—and how many salmon can a garage eat a day—a month—a year? That whale will eat more than a fishing boat—maybe two or three boats—can catch a day. Oh, she brings business now, but what about next month—I could be broke in a year. *(To Jerry.)* We got to find a way to get rid of that whale!

JERRY. You can't hurt her!

O'CONNELL. Not me . . . an' not right now, kid. But it ain't just me. Lotsa people depend on the fish. It won't happen right away, but when the fishin' gets bad . . . somebody's gonna go after that whale. *(A thought.)* Might even ask the navy to help out. You think about this commander—he might help you out. But you gotta get that whale to leave.

JERRY. If we could stop the whalers, she'd go. She doesn't really like it in the Sound—too many islands and boats.

O'CONNELL. *(Starting off.)* You're not gonna stop them whalers. Lotsa people have tried. I dunno if you can really talk to that whale or not, but if you can, you tell her to go. *(Moves to exit, then turns.)* Tell her the whalers have gone.

JERRY. But they haven't gone.

O'CONNELL. Lie to her. She won't know the difference. . . . Well, gotta get to work—get these fuel pumps in.

(He goes. Jerry is stunned.)

MEG. *(Quietly.)* Are you going to do that?

JERRY. I couldn't lie to Ooka. I've never told any big lies in my life. Little ones, maybe, but not like *that*. What does he think I am?

MEG. *(Choking back tears.)* What are we going to do?

JERRY. I don't know. I've got to think.

MEG. I'll help.

JERRY. How?

MEG. Two people can think better than one, silly.

JERRY. Oh.

(They both think.)

JERRY. What would you do if you were a whale and saw a whaler coming after you?

MEG. *(Quickly.)* I'd swim away fast.

JERRY. No good. Whalers are faster than whales.

MEG. I'd dive way down to the bottom and stay there.

JERRY. You'd have to breathe. You could only stay down fifteen, maybe thirty minutes. Or even if you could stay a whole hour, the whaler would just wait for you to come up.

MEG. Oh.

(She is as disconsolate as Jerry. Then, she slowly starts playing the whale game she and Jerry played earlier, looking up at an imaginary boat. She has an idea.)

Jerry! Whales can see the bottoms of the whalers, can't they?

JERRY. Course they can.

MEG. The back end of a boat is different. It has a propeller.

JERRY. I know it has a propeller. How's that gonna help Ooka?

MEG. *(Excited.)* Don't you see? Those whalers don't have those gun things with harpoons on both ends do they?

JERRY. *(Gets the idea.)* Yeah, I see. Of course! Whaling ships only have harpoon guns on the bow. I could teach her to only come up at the stern.

MEG. Yeah, at the back. Then they couldn't shoot her. *(A bad thought.)* But she's probably too dumb to learn that.

JERRY. What do you mean, dumb? Ooka's smart. She taught me to speak whale, didn't she?

MEG. You *learned* how to speak whale. She didn't teach you.

JERRY. Well, she's smart anyway.

MEG. Could you teach her to stay at the propeller end? Are there the right words?

JERRY. *(Suddenly very sad.)* No. She doesn't know what a ship is, really. She thinks it's a big fish with people on it.

MEG. Oh. *(A pause, then an idea.)* Could we maybe *show* Ooka the difference?

JERRY. Show her? What? *(He picks up a small piece of driftwood and moves to beside end of pier.)* I got in all this mess to try to help her. *(Strikes the pier with stick for punctuation.)* Just like any other ordinary kid. They always win.

MEG. You're not an ordinary kid, Jerry.

JERRY. Yes I am. When they choose up sides for baseball, when do you think I get chosen? Next to last, that's when. I don't even stay around when they choose up for football.

MEG. *(Smiles.)* You sure lit into Fred. But I'm not talking about that. I'm talking about figuring things out. An' that's also why I said two people can think better than one. So you just listen to my half of the thinking!

JERRY. *(Resigned.)* O.K.

MEG. O.K. So you could maybe show Ooka the difference with a small boat—with an outboard.

JERRY. How could I do that? *(Toying in the water with the end of the stick.)* I wonder what she's doing now. Where she is. I miss her.

MEG. I know. *(Goes to him.)* Let's think about it—real hard. A way to teach her. *(Looks out over the water.)* I bet she could get away from that fishing boat.

JERRY. That's not a fishing boat. It's the mail boat from Orcas Island. Whaling ships have bigger motors and huge propellers.

MEG. That makes them easier to see—and hear.

JERRY. *(Looks at her as if maybe she has something.)* That's right. They must stir up an awful lot of water. She couldn't miss it. Maybe— *(Then he has a terrible thought.)* But there'd probably be another one right behind. It'd get her. There's always more'n one.

MEG. Oh. *(A thought. Tentative.)* Could she stop it?

JERRY. How?

MEG. Hit it or something.

JERRY. It'd cut her up. Propellers on whalers are big—and sharp. *(Bangs the stick against pier in frustration.)*

MEG. Jerry. Dad's boat stopped once when a rope got caught in the propeller. Just a little rope.

JERRY. How could a whale get a rope in a propeller? Propellers on whalers are bigger than I am. They'd chop this darn stick up like a meat grinder.

MEG. Would my dad's little propeller chop up that stick?

JERRY. *(Considers the stick. It is an inch and a half diameter.)* No—it might bend it. Stop it even—

(He looks at Meg, sees what she is suggesting. Both have the idea.)

BOTH. A bigger stick!

JERRY. I read in one of the whale books that they play with logs— logs as big as telephone poles.

(He puts the stick in his mouth and becomes a whale. Meg gets the idea and becomes a boat making small whirling movements with her hand to simulate a propeller. She moves backward making engine noises as Jerry, swimming like a pur-

*suing whale, maneuvers the stick in his mouth so it fouls the
propeller. She makes a grinding noise and "falls dead" as the
propeller stops. They look at each other in happy amazement.)*

MEG. Do you think you could teach her how to do that?

JERRY. *(Suddenly defeated.)* They don't have words enough.

MEG. You could show her. Like you did me, just now.

JERRY. *(Cautiously.)* I—could try. I don't know if she could understand. *(More enthusiasm.)* But we've got nothing to lose. Neither does Ooka. We'll try. We have to. Can you row me out in
the bay real early in the morning?

MEG. Sure. Dad won't even know I'm gone.

JERRY. And we have to find a big log—near the water so we can roll
it in.

MEG. There's a big deadhead over by the point.

*(They look at each other, grinning. Then a splash is heard on
the house speaker. It comes again.)*

JERRY. Ooka! You're back!

*(There is another splash as they run to the end of the pier.
Another, and their gaze follows the whale as, quite near them,
it leaps into the air. Fifty feet of whale clear out of the water.
An enormous splash as she hits the water. They follow with
their eyes.)*

MEG. *(Breathless awe.)* I—I—had no idea. No idea she—was—
so-o big.

*(Blackout. We hear a brief whale song. Then a male voice on
the speaker is heard.)*

VOICE. *(Anchor Man. Crisp.)* And now, an on-the-spot report from
the Pacific Northwest.

*(Light up on Regina McLean as she moves below pier. McLean
is a network newscaster: cool, imperturbable, the kind who
makes it as a woman on the networks. She wears glasses and
may wear a trenchcoat. Although McLean once pronounced
her name "Regeena," it is now "Regina." McLean is pronounced McLane.*

*McLean carries a hand microphone and speaks to an unseen
camera. Meg is upstage of her. Meg does not care much for
this and mimics McLean during the introduction.)*

MCLEAN. This is Regina McLean on Chuckanut Bay, just south of Bellingham, Washington, the lumber and fishing metropolis ninety miles north of Seattle. The reported breakthrough in communication between man and those great animals of the sea, whales, continues to draw hordes of people to this area. Hotels and motels north of Seattle continue to be booked solid. Everyone wants to see the amazing boy, Jerry Johnson, swim beside the huge whale he has taught to play with a telephone pole as if it were a match stick.

Although young Johnson continues to refuse interviews with the news media, as he has for two months, UBC has exclusive interviews that may help explain this strange and unusual event.

First, Miss Margaret Meyer, the first person to see young Johnson talk to his friend, Ooka.

MEG. *(On camera.)* Call me Meg, not Margaret.

MCLEAN. *(All business.)* Yes, Meg. We know you are Jerry's best friend. We want to know about him. We've heard he talked in Morse code.

MEG. Everybody knows that, now. He did a lot of things. Kinda neat. Mice in his school desk. Raised three generations before the teacher found 'em. And how many people you know like spiders?

MCLEAN. I see, but we want to talk about—

MEG. I like him. *(Starting off.)* I gotta go, now. Gotta help Jerry.

MCLEAN. *(Detaining her.)* But Meg, we want to hear about the whale!

MEG. You tell 'em about the whale.

MCLEAN. But people want to know what's happening. Why the accidents? Two boats damaged just yesterday. The Coast Guard and Navy investigation of that.

MEG. *(Trying to cover without actually lying.)* Of course there were accidents. All those boats. But they only got their propellers damaged.

MCLEAN. Exactly! Doesn't it seem odd that Ooka's log only seems to damage the *propellers*?

MEG. *(Uncomfortable, quickly covering to get away.)* You wouldn't want her to sink the boats, would you. People might get hurt. I don't want to talk any more. Goodbye. *(Edges away, then rushes off.)*

MCLEAN. Meg! . . . *(Recovering quickly, signals to O'Connell and Rock, who have been in background during the last of this.)* Well . . . Miss Meyer seems reluctant to talk about the problem . . . and there is a problem. But we have two experts to discuss these difficulties the whale is beginning to cause.

(O'Connell and Rock are now "on camera.")

Mr. Harry O'Connell, an expert of sports fishing in the Sound, and Commander Willoughby Rock of the United States Navy. *(To O'Connell, combing his hair, unaware he is already on camera.)* Mr. O'Connell, you were—

(O'Connell looks at camera, freezes, then hastily puts comb in pocket and grins at camera.)

—you were one of the first to know of the Sperm Whale in Puget Sound. What do you think of the situation now?

O'CONNELL. Well, Jerry's taught her somethin', all right. I thought it was pretty good, at first. Good for business. Couldn't do no harm. But now, I dunno. That whale's gonna do some real damage. Maybe soon. Then, there's gonna be some sorry people around here.

MCLEAN. You say that even though the whale has brought you a good income?

O'CONNELL. It won't last. People're gettin' a little tired of that whale. An' he's gonna ruin the fishin'. Ain't helpin' it now. Also, he's gettin' to be a menace to navigation.

MCLEAN. I see. And is that why you are here, Commander?

(McLean has brought Rock into the interview to counteract the increasingly emotional O'Connell. Rock is cool, and restrains O'Connell, who tries to speak at times. Jerry appears upstage during this and hears what is being said.)

ROCK. Yes, Regina, it is. The Coast Guard and Navy are being consulted, you might say. We had hoped for the cooperation of Jerry Johnson, but— Well, he has not been helpful.

MCLEAN. How could he be helpful?

ROCK. He insists on just playing games with this animal. He could teach it useful things. These games have already caused damage to the propellers of several large boats. Commercial fisheries and shipping lines are worried about a Sperm Whale in these restricted waters. And she might attract other large whales to Puget Sound.

MCLEAN. I see. So what do you—and the Coast Guard propose to do?

O'CONNELL. *(Finally breaking in.)* They're gonna get that whale the heck outa Puget Sound, that's what!

ROCK. *(Pushing O'Connell back.)* Mr. O'Connell is a bit impetuous, but—yes, the whale will have to go—if young Johnson doesn't cooperate.

MCLEAN. How do you plan to get Ooka to go?

ROCK. *(Smiles confidently.)* You forget, I know a lot about whales. There are ways to frighten them . . . several ways. Noise machines—explosives.

MCLEAN. But haven't we heard that Ooka is here to escape from whalers?

ROCK. Well, that's what young Johnson has said. How can we be sure? In any case, that's the whale's problem, not ours.

(Jerry, who has had trouble restraining himself, now cannot hold back and rushes on.)

JERRY. You're not going to do that. You can't. I won't let you!

MCLEAN. *(Not realizing who he is.)* You can't come here. This is a television interview.

JERRY. He can't do this. He wants to hurt Ooka.

MCLEAN. *(Suddenly realizes who Jerry is.)* Wait, aren't you. You are! *(To cameras.)* Ladies and gentlemen, this is Jerry Johnson, the boy who talks to whales—a television first for UBC.

JERRY. I don't want to be on television, but I don't want this old Commander to hurt Ooka, either.

ROCK. Now Jerry, if you'd just cooperate with the Navy—

JERRY. I know what you want. It's not the Navy, it's you. The Navy's O.K. It's you—you just don't care about whales.

ROCK. Now that's not—

MCLEAN. *(Delighted. Stops Rock.)* We are finally able to bring you what is really happening. Directly to you on UBC . . . Go on, Jerry.

JERRY. I don't want to be news.

MCLEAN. But you are news. Millions of people, all over the United States, are watching you right now.

JERRY. *(Looking at camera.)* There are? Millions?

MCLEAN. *(Restraining Rock and O'Connell.)* Why don't you tell them how you feel about the whale?

JERRY. About Ooka? *(Looks at camera. A thought.)* Are there kids out there?

(McLean nods. Jerry looks at the invisible cameras. A light: the children will hear him. This is an outpouring of feelings, not a calculated speech.)

You kids have to know how I feel. Ooka is the most wonderful animal in the world. I've had lots of animals as pets—great animals—a cat, mice, even spiders—I loved 'em all. I had a dog once, and it got hit by a car. I don't ever want another dog, 'cause I don't want to see a dog I love die like that. Ooka is the most lovely, beautiful animal in the world, but she doesn't understand people—the way we are. She hasn't done anything so she should be hurt—or killed.

(McLean prevents Rock from interrupting.)

Don't let Mr. O'Connell or Commander Rock do anything to her. Ooka is a helpless animal, like a dog in front of a car. She doesn't understand people, but she trusts me. Like my dog did. I don't know if the grownups understand, but I sure hope you kids do. So help me! Save Ooka. Tell everybody. Do something— telephone, write letters, shout—run down the street and yell it. I don't know who to ask—ask everyone. The television, newspapers, the Navy, the world! Save Ooka! Help me!

(Jerry is exhausted. McLean quickly takes over before Rock or O'Connell have time to speak.)

MCLEAN. And now, back to Henry Horner in New York.

(Blackout. In the darkness there is a buildup of children chanting and shouting "Save Ooka—Save Ooka!" It begins to fade, then disappears as the lights come up on Jerry on the end of the pier with his pipe. He makes a whale sound, then stares

sadly out over the water. It is night. Meg enters slowly and approaches him.)

MEG. *(After a pause. Quietly.)* Hi.

JERRY. Sh-h. *(Listens a moment in the pipe.)*

MEG. That was really somethin' . . . Last night on T.V.

JERRY. Yeah.

MEG. All the kids . . . all over. Did ya hear about the Post Office? More mail than Christmas. An' the phone company! Wow!

JERRY. *(Oddly sad under the circumstances.)* I know. Mom had to take the phone off the hook so we could sleep.

MEG. I couldn't sleep anyway. Aren't you proud?

JERRY. I guess . . . It doesn't really matter.

MEG. Course it matters. All the kids! Nobody'd dare hurt her now.

JERRY. *(Quietly. Sadly.)* I know, but . . . But she's gone.

MEG. What?

JERRY. Ooka's gone.

MEG. Gone? Gone where?

JERRY. I don't know. She's just gone.

MEG. How can you be so sure?

JERRY. She always came back—around nine—after she ate. To say good night. She didn't last night—or tonight.

MEG. She's probably just late. She doesn't have a watch, you know.

JERRY. I was here all night. She didn't come at all.

MEG. *(Fearful.)* You think something happened to her?

JERRY. I don't know. I worry about an accident. Nobody'd want to hurt her—especially now. I think she's just—gone.

MEG. Why?

JERRY. I don't know. She was almost ready, too. Or almost. She'd learned almost everything. Everything, really—I just didn't tell her that.

MEG. Oh. . . . You think she knew that?

JERRY. What?

MEG. That she'd really learned everything? That she was ready to go?

JERRY. She's smart but—I don't think she could figure that out.

MEG. I wish she'd—said good-bye.

JERRY. Whales don't understand about good-bye. . . . I wanted to try to explain. . . .

MEG. She'll come back, Jerry. . . . She has to come back.

(Jerry looks at her sadly, puts the pipe to his mouth and makes a couple plaintive whale sounds as the lights fade.

A spot comes up on McLean, isolated near the proscenium DR.)

MCLEAN. This is Regina McLean at the White House with the latest report on the international crisis. Both the Russian and Japanese ambassadors have left the President within the hour. They have both strongly protested the United States responsibility for the disabling of their whaling fleets by rampaging Sperm Whales carrying wooden poles in their mouths.

Ambassador Andreyevsky of Russia has threatened to end the SALT and all other agreements with the United States, saying this country has developed an illegal secret weapon— whales—which in addition to damaging the entire whaling fleet, has done extensive damage to the propellers of a destroyer and a cruiser.

The President has dispatched Air Force One to bring young Jerry Johnson to the White House at once. This international incident has occurred just six weeks after the whale, Ooka, mysteriously disappeared from Puget Sound. In the meantime, ships of all nations are carefully avoiding whales.

(Blackout on McLean with a crossfade to desk with Presidential Seal. During transition, we hear flute or other woodwind play "Ruffles and Flourishes." Seated at the desk is the President. There is a Secret Service man with dark glasses. Jerry and Meg appear, whisper together a moment, then approach the President. The Secret Service man checks them, is surprised by Meg's presence, whispers to the President. President looks at the children.)

PRESIDENT. You are the young man who caused all these problems with the whales?

JERRY. Yes, sir. I guess I am.

PRESIDENT. Who is she?

MEG. I'm Meg, sir.

JERRY. She helps me.

PRESIDENT. Does she talk to whales, too?

JERRY. No, sir. She helps me—think.

PRESIDENT. You mean, you are both responsible for this—this crisis?

(Meg and Jerry look at each other a moment, then look back to the President and nod.)

MEG. I'm as responsible as Jerry.

JERRY. It was mostly me.

PRESIDENT. Do you realize you have gotten this country in serious trouble, trouble with two of the most important nations of the world?

(Meg and Jerry confer a brief moment in whispers. Then—)

MEG. The whales don't know they're important.

JERRY. And it wasn't really us, Mr. President.

PRESIDENT. It is very clear, young man, that no one else could be responsible. The Russians know it. The Japanese know it. And I know it!

(Jerry and Meg hold another short whispered conference.)

JERRY. I only taught Ooka *how* to do what she did, sir.

MEG. We think she taught the other whales, and *they decided* to do it themselves.

JERRY. You see, I never even met the other whales.

PRESIDENT. Never met—Decided! Whales don't decide. They're not intelligent enough to—

JERRY. Oh, sir, Ooka is very smart. How do you think she learned all that?

MEG. And you can't really blame them for that cruiser and destroyer. Any ship that has a gun—looks like a whaler to a whale.

JERRY. You see, you have to look at it like a whale.

(Both children are making swimming motions and looking up at a boat like a whale.)

PRESIDENT. Now look here. Stop that.

(They do.)

You cannot expect the President of the United States to pretend he's a—a whale!

JERRY. Why not? I do.

MEG. That's the best way to understand whales, you know.

PRESIDENT. I don't care what's the best way to understand whales. What I do care about is this crisis with Russia and Japan. *(To Jerry.)* I brought you here to do something about it. Do it. *(To Meg.)* You help him think.

(Another brief conference.)

JERRY. You have to do something—

(Meg shakes his arm and mouths "things" silently.)

Some things—first.

PRESIDENT. *I* have to do something—things?

MEG. You have to help us.

JERRY. You are the Commander in Chief of the Navy and Coast Guard, aren't you?

PRESIDENT. Of course. If you want them to help find that whale, I'll let you have them. The Air Force, too.

JERRY. We don't need them, Mr. President. If you could do something about Commander Rock.

MEG. Keep him away from whales.

PRESIDENT. I'll send him to Antarctica.

JERRY. Oh, no sir. There are whales in Antarctica.

PRESIDENT. I'll put him in charge of recruiting in Des Moines, Iowa. A thousand miles from the ocean. But how is that going to help with the Russians?

MEG. You need to talk to the Coast Guard.

JERRY. So they won't let Mr. O'Connell, or anyone scare Ooka.

MEG. So then, she'll probably come back in Puget Sound. Jerry thinks so—and so do I. And he can explain—that it's safe for her—everywhere. And she and the other whales don't have to damage boats. Because there won't be any whalers anywhere.

PRESIDENT. And what if I don't agree to all this? What then?

(A very short conference.)

JERRY. We won't be responsible, sir.

PRESIDENT. Won't be responsible for what?

JERRY. For the safety of all the boats in all the navies in the world.

PRESIDENT. What!!!

MEG. Like I said, sir. All boats with guns look like whalers to a whale.

JERRY. Whales don't understand about flags and different countries.

PRESIDENT. This is blackmail!

MEG. No, sir. We just want to save Ooka.

JERRY. And all the other whales.

PRESIDENT. *(Looks at the children, turns away in thought, then—)* All right! Even the Russians will have to agree to this. There's nothing else they can do. *(Narrowly.)* But will that whale come back—and can you explain to her if she does?

(Jerry and Meg look at each other.)

MEG. We think she will.

JERRY. I have a feeling she will.

PRESIDENT. A feeling, huh. Well, she better, or else we're in real trouble.

(Lights dim fast. A spot picks up McLean in isolation.)

MCLEAN. This is Regina McLean at the United Nations. It has been weeks since the President's whale treaty was passed unanimously by the General Assembly. The whales won complete freedom of the seas, but they still don't know that. The Coast Guard and Navy have protected the entrance to Puget Sound so Ooka or any Sperm Whale can enter the Sound—but no whale has entered. Ships of all nations avoid whales and Jerry Johnson

in Bellingham, Washington, continues to wait—to tell Ooka
that she and all whales are free to roam the wide seas—without fear.

*(The spot has faded out by the end of the speech. Sound of
waves, slow, as lights come up on the end of the pier. Night.
Jerry is on end of pier with his pipe. Meg enters.)*

MEG. Hi.

JERRY. Hi.

MEG. I'll listen and you can get some sleep.

JERRY. What if she would come—and I wasn't here?

MEG. I could get you real fast. You don't have to stay here all night—
every night. We could take turns.

*(Jerry shakes his head negatively. There is a moment of
silence.)*

JERRY. I think she'll come at night. We talked most at night.

MEG. You really think she'll come back?

JERRY. *(Nods.)* You do, too.

MEG. Yeah, I know.

(There is a splash heard on the house speaker.)

Listen!

JERRY. It's just a wave. . . . She liked you, you know.

MEG. I know. I could tell by the way she looked at me.

(Another splash. Louder.)

That's not a wave. Listen!

(Another splash and a couple whale sounds.)

It's her. It has to be!

*(Excited, he begins to make whale sounds into water with his
pipe. The whale song is heard. It is more elaborate, and var-
ied, and lovely than ever before. Meg is touched and moves to
the music, perhaps dances a little with the joy of the sound.
Splashes are heard as Jerry answers with sounds vigorously.)*

MEG. Can you get her to understand?

(Jerry talks whale furiously. Noises come back from Ooka. Then Jerry stands, relaxed and exultant. As he does so, Ooka apparently jumps very high from the water and they follow her with their gaze.)

MEG. Wow!

JERRY. She's never jumped like that. . . . She understood. . . . Look, she's going, now.

MEG. Good-bye, Ooka. . . . She did say good-bye, didn't she?

JERRY. *(Nods "Yes.")* And she understood. She really knows she's safe. . . . They're all safe. I knew she'd come back. I knew it all along.

(Both watch as the splashes and whale sounds diminish in the distance and the lights dim out.)

(Curtain.)

My Days as a Youngling—
John Jacob Niles: The Early Years

Music by John Jacob Niles

Dramatized by Nancy Niles Sexton, Vaughn McBride, and Martha Harrison Jones

Copyright, 1982, Anchorage Press, Inc.

My Days as a Youngling—
John Jacob Niles: The Early Years
(1982)

My Days as a Youngling is an ensemble piece that combines narration, poetry, and song to examine the early life of this great figure of American folk history.

John Jacob Niles was a combination composer, arranger, and concert artist of folk music. In his lifetime Niles wrote more than 100 folk songs. He also helped to preserve the rich heritage of folk music in this country by compiling over a thousand folk songs and ballads that the early settlers had brought with them from their native lands.

The play examines Niles' early childhood days in Kentucky. A series of interwoven vignettes highlight Niles' adventures in growing up. We are given a peek at his early school training and his often comic interactions with local townspeople. We witness his boyhood attempts at flying, suffer with him through his first love, and share with him the joy he discovers in writing and playing music for the first time. By the play's conclusion, the audience senses that they have been treated to a look at the whole man as well as his legend.

A NOTE ON THE MUSIC SCORE

In his introduction to *The Ballad Book of John Jacob Niles*, Mr. Niles tells the reader:

I have set only one verse of each ballad—for two very good reasons. First, I knew that if I set all the verses of each ballad it would make an endlessly long book. And second, I thought it would hamper the delights of variation—the interpolation of new words and the cunning twists of a new tune idea. Furthermore, the reader might want to sing several verses unaccompanied—and this would be a great idea.

The music in *My Days as a Youngling* is highly personal and requires a certain amount of freedom on the part of those who perform it. Following Mr. Niles' suggestion, the score should serve as a guide towards helping the performers recreate the stories and feelings of the songs and refrain from burdening the performers with too many indications. Variety, spontaneity, and genuineness are the important elements in performing this music.

It will be necessary to consult the script for the full lyrics to the songs. The show was originally performed by a cast of young performers and the musical keys—as well as the harmonies—were devised to accommodate their young voices. By "mixed chorus" is meant both male and female voices singing the harmonies together without overt concern about the natural octave distance in voices. The piano part has been kept simple since it is the authors' wish that the chorus voices serve as the main accompaniment to the solo voices.

The music for this stage production is available from Anchorage Press, Inc.

CHARACTERS

Johnnie-boy	Hilda
Johnnie 1	Elephant Thorpe
Johnnie 2	Root-Buyer
Mother (Lulie)	Mary Bolling
Father (Tommy)	Preacher
Man Relative	Deaconess
Woman Relative	Granny Graham
Irish Teacher	Daughter 1
Schoolgirl 1	Daughter 2
Schoolgirl 2	Uncle Prune
Cripple-boy	Heidie Moore
Irish Father	Mr. Emerson
Jake Bickel	The Four Indiana Blossoms
Gretta	Blanche Juckett

Note: In the original production, twenty-two performer-singers created the thirty-one roles. Other combinations are possible according to the versatility of performers and the requirements of producers.

My Days as a Youngling

POEM MUSIC CUE 1A:

When I am just a whisper in the wind,
The wind that blows so often east to west,
When I am just a whisper in the wind
And all the breath that once did raise my voice
Has joined the breath that whispers in the wind,
Even then my song will never die
And join the ghostly whisper of the wind,
Even then my song will never be
Hung on willow trees that sway with the wind,
Torn and tattered as mouldering dust.
Even then my song will swirl and spin
And find men's hearts to rest therein:
Even then my song will swirl and spin.

MUSIC CUE 1B

SONG: HE'S GOT THE WHOLE WORLD IN HIS HANDS

He's got the whole world in his hands
He's got the whole round world in his hands
He's got the round world in his hands
He's got the whole world in his hands.

He's got that little bits of babies in his hands
He's got that little bits of babies in his hands
He's got that little bits of babies in his hands
He's got the whole world in his hands.

He's got that gamblin' man in his hands
He's got that crap-shootin' man in his hands
He's got the gamblin' man right in his hands
He's got the whole world in his hands.

He's got the high sheriff of the county in his hands
He's got the high sheriff of the county in his hands
He's got the high sheriff of the county in his hands
He's got the whole world in his hands.

He's got me and you in his hands
He's got me and you in his hands
He's got me and you in his hands
He's got the whole world in his hands.

He's got everybody here in his hands
He's got everybody here in his hands
He's got everybody here in his hands
He's got the whole world in his hands.

JOHNNIE 1. When I was that young in my long blond curls, and the blue beauty of the sky was in my eyes, I oftimes

MOTHER. sat on the earth of my mother's garden.

JOHNNIE 2. For I did love

MOTHER. the earth

JOHNNIE 2. so cool and so dark.

JOHNNIE 1. When I was that young

MOTHER. without knowing a single thing of it

JOHNNIE 2. I studied the earth and the small creatures who walked thereon, and in my

MAN RELATIVE. childish way . . .

JOHNNIE 1. tried to discover

MOTHER. why and how they moved and where they were going

JOHNNIE-BOY. the various ants being my especial field.

MAN RELATIVE. Said my grown up relatives

WOMAN RELATIVE. I was only fit for confine

JOHNNIE 1. While I with my blue eyes and long blond curls discovered

WOMAN RELATIVE. the turns of weather and the turns of time

MAN RELATIVE. And how the angle-worm and the big black ant loved the rain

WOMAN RELATIVE. and the Junie-bug loved the sun

JOHNNIE 2. And all the while the grown-up ones did wonder when I came to my mother with an offering

MOTHER. Of purple violets squeezed in my small hot hand.

JOHNNIE 2. I loved the earth and everything it produced.

JOHNNIE 1. And my curls were long, and my eyes as blue as the sky.

(Man and Woman Relative leave the acting space and return to their places on the choral stools. Father enters the acting area.)

FATHER. Growing old is not so bad when you consider the alternatives. . . . As your father, I'm telling you this. *(They embrace happily.)* It's time for bed now, Johnnie-boy. Tomorrow you start school. And if you work diligent, you will become educated.

JOHNNIE-BOY. What is educated? Must I have it?

FATHER. Yes . . . you must have it. Education is the humanizing process by which the cultural benefits of one age or generation are passed on to the next.

JOHNNIE-BOY. . . . It is?

FATHER. It is. And tomorrow you will begin to learn all about education at the Duncan Street School.

JOHNNIE-BOY. I don't understand it so I know I must have it.

FATHER. *(Laughing.)* What don't you understand?

JOHNNIE-BOY. What is "cultural benefits"?

MUSIC CUE 2

FATHER. Cultural benefits are . . . like the songs I sing to you . . . the story songs . . . the ballads.

JOHNNIE-BOY. Will we sing cultural benefits at the Duncan Street School?

FATHER. I don't think so, Johnnie . . . but you'll learn other things.

JOHNNIE-BOY. Father . . . do me a "cultural benefit" before I go to bed! Sing me the song about the Soldier and the Nightingale.

FATHER. All right . . . but then it's to bed. *(Father sings the song in trio with the two "older" Johnnies as Johnnie-boy listens. Father sings the role of the story-teller while one Johnnie takes the part of the Lady and the other sings the soldier.)*

MUSIC CUE 3

SONG: ONE MORNING IN MAY OR THE NIGHTINGALE

One morning, one morning, one morning in May	F
I saw a fair couple a-making their way	F
And one was a maiden so slim and so fair	J2
And the other a soldier, a brave volunteer.	J1

Good morning, good morning, good morning to thee,	F
And where be thou going, my pretty lady?	J1
I'm a going a-walking because it is spring,	J2
To see waters glide and hear nightingales sing.	ALL
They hadn't been standing a moment or two,	F
When out of his knapsack a fiddle he drew,	F
And the tune that he played made the valleys all ring,	J2
'Twas fairer than music when nightingales sing.	J2
Pretty lady, pretty lady, it's time to give o'er.	J1
Oh no! Pretty soldier play just one tune more,	J2
I rather would listen to the touch of your string	J2
Than see waters glide and hear nightingales sing.	ALL
Pretty soldier, pretty soldier, would you marry me?	J2
Oh no! Pretty lady, that never could be.	J1
He's a wife in old London and babies twice three,	F
Two wives in the army's too many for me.	J1
Well, he'll go back to London and stay there a year,	F
And often I'll think of you my dear,	J1
And if ere he return 'twill be in the spring.	F
To see waters glide and hear nightingales sing.	ALL

FATHER. Well, good night, Johnnie-boy. . . . Sleep well. . . . *(They embrace.)* And tomorrow . . . your first day of school. . . . *(Father exits. Mother who has been happily watching the singing of NIGHTINGALE comes forward with a little sweater and a comb to help Johnnie-boy dress for his first day at school.)*

MOTHER. Oh, the morning galloped off on a

JOHNNIE-BOY. cockleberry

MOTHER. horse. High, high into a

JOHNNIE-BOY. cockleberry

MOTHER. *(As she begins to comb his hair.)* sky, While the shepherdess sat combing

JOHNNIE-BOY. cockleberries

MOTHER. out of her hair. As she kept her eye on her

JOHNNIE-BOY. cockleberry

MOTHER. flock, Lest some sly wolf should come

*(As she begins to put the sweater on him. This action con-
tinues through the rest of the poem.)*

JOHNNIE-BOY. cockleberrying

MOTHER. by. And sweep up a sheep for a

JOHNNIE-BOY. cockleberry

MOTHER. pie. Made up of flour and sugar and

JOHNNIE-BOY. cockleberry

MOTHER. shortening. Baked over a fire of

JOHNNIE-BOY. cockleberry

MOTHER. twigs. To be sliced by a pie knife with a

JOHNNIE-BOY. cockleberry

MOTHER. haft. Oh, the

JOHNNIE-BOY. cockleberry

MOTHER. horse galloped on, through light lightning, muttering
thunder and a

JOHNNIE-BOY. cockleberry

MOTHER. rain. While the lovely limbs of the

JOHNNIE-BOY. cockleberry

MOTHER. tree. That had bowed low, low down to the

JOHNNIE-BOY. cockleberry

MOTHER. ground, Laden with

JOHNNIE-BOY. cockleberries

MOTHER. luscious and ripe, Thanked wind and thanked rain in a

JOHNNIE-BOY. cockleberry

MOTHER. manner, As a restrained clash of

JOHNNIE-BOY. cockleberry

MOTHER. timbrels. Echoed through the

JOHNNIE-BOY. cockleberry

MOTHER. forest, Reminding all men who passed by on the

JOHNNIE-BOY. cockleberry

MOTHER. pathway. That, in truth, today is the hey-day of the

JOHNNIE-BOY. COCKLEBERRY!

(Johnnie-boy and Mother embrace. He waves good-bye and turns out. Mother turns away and goes back to the table where the Man and Woman Relative are again sitting and watching the scene . . .)

MAN RELATIVE. The building is hot in the summer. . . .

WOMAN RELATIVE. Cold and draughty in the winter. . . . And not a place for the children to stand when it rains. And the German boys . . . with the Irish boys. . . .

JOHNNIE-BOY. The Irish boys who hated me!

JOHNNIE 1. Because my father was a Republican!

JOHNNIE 2. And a Protestant!

(Father enters the playing space in time to hear and react to the memory of the three Johnnies.)

FATHER. *(He speaks only to the little Johnnie-boy.)* Johnnie-boy, that's also part of that "cultural experience" I was talking about.

JOHNNIE-BOY. Well, I like songs better!

FATHER. So do I son . . . so do I. *(They slowly walk center.)* When you grow older Johnnie, how will you remember me?

MUSIC CUE 4

JOHNNIE-BOY. Oh, Papa, I think I will always remember you singing a song. . . . *(Follows a full company song: THE SHEPHERD'S DAUGHTER. It is sung and acted in the way of the mountain "play party" and the action grows out of Johnnie-boy's memory as Father again sings the role of the story-teller while other singers and dancers take the other natural roles revealed in the rest of the song.)*

SONG: THE SHEPHERD'S DAUGHTER

I sing of a shepherd's daughter   F
Tending sheep on a hill so high,
When one of them hireling servants
Come a-gaily riding by.

REFRAIN: With a rung, dung, down   ALL
                 And a diddle-a-la-di-do,
                 Ring, dong, down
                 And a diddle-a-la-day.

I sing of a shepherd's daughter   F
With shoes of rabbits fur,
And how that hireling servant
Did come and robbéd her. *(refrain)*   ALL

Oh, she grabbed her pettiskirts in her hand,   F
And she ran by the horse's side,
And she ran twill she come to the river,
And she swam that raging tide. *(refrain)*   ALL

Oh, she swam twill she came to the dried land,   F
And she grabbed her skirts and she ran,
And she run twill she come to the King's highway,
And she wasn't running for fun. *(refrain)*   ALL

Oh, she walkéd up to the castle door,   F
How boldly tingled the ring,
And none was so spry as the King hisself
At letting the shepherdess in. *(refrain)*   ALL

"What matter, what matter, what matter, my maid?   KING
What matter, what matter?" cried he.
"Oh, one of your hireling servants   SHEPHERDESS
Has been and robbéd me." *(refrain)*   ALL

"Oh, what, my maid, did he rob you of?   KING
Oh, what did he take away?
Was it diamond rings or silver
Or gold he took today?" *(refrain)*   ALL

"Twern't no gold nor silver,   SHEPHERDESS
Twern't no treasure trove!"
And she hung her head and she wept for shame   F
Like the note of a mourning dove. *(refrain)*   ALL

Then cried the King: (F) "If married,   KING
Hangéd he shall be.
But if he's e'er a single man,
He's bounden to marry ye." *(refrain)*   ALL

*(As the company retreats to the choral chairs the younger
actors bring small milk stools to the acting space and fashion*

a classroom. This action takes place while the ensemble sings, very slowly, "ring, dong, down. . . . And a diddle-a-la-day.")

JOHNNIE 1. When my father sang the whole world danced! He taught me to raise myself, not by my boot straps but by my imagination . . . so that I might reach the autumn of my years with a tiny sprig of laurel in my bonnet. *(He turns into the action as a cripple-boy enters the classroom scene . . .)* But first, I had to learn that singing was weeping in disguise. *(Another actor enters the playing space from the choral stools. Johnnie watches her approach.)* The teacher that I remember most from the trying period at the Duncan Street School . . .

TEACHER. Was a red-headed, hair-triggered, wild-eyed Irish woman.

SCHOOLGIRL 1. She kept a three-foot strap in the drawer of her desk.

CRIPPLE-BOY. When any student made a mistake in spelling

SCHOOLGIRL 2. In geography

JOHNNIE-BOY. *(Also seated with the class on a small milk-stool.)* In arithmetic

SCHOOLGIRL 2. In reading

JOHNNIE-BOY. Or wiggled in his seat

TEACHER. The entire class had to take the blame.

CRIPPLE-BOY. But the day came during the spring of one of those years when one crippled boy in our class misspelled some words . . .

TEACHER. Or failed to give the correct answer to an arithmetic problem

SCHOOLGIRL 1. Or wiggled in his seat

SCHOOLGIRL 2. Or even laughed a bit . . .

TEACHER. The red-headed one grabbed the

CRIPPLE-BOY. Cripple

TEACHER. To his feet, snatched his crutch away from him

JOHNNIE-BOY. And beat him!

TEACHER. While the boy cowered with pain. . . .

SCHOOLGIRL 2. When the beating was over, the cripple-boy recovered his crutch and fled the room.

JOHNNIE-BOY. We heard his footsteps and the rapid pound of the crutch all the way down the stairway. . . .

MUSIC CUE 5

SONG: LOOK DOWN, LOOK DOWN THAT LONESOME ROAD

(Sung as a solo. This song may be done by an ensemble member or by one of the older Johnnies.)

Look down, look down that lonesome road
Hang down your head and cry
Hang down your head and cry

You made me walk that lonesome road
Like I never done before
Like I never done before.

CRIPPLE-BOY. But the cripple-boy returned

IRISH FATHER. With his father. There they stood

CRIPPLE-BOY. hand

IRISH FATHER. in hand. He introduced himself

TEACHER. And then he addressed himself not to the teacher

JOHNNIE-BOY. But to the fascinated class members

IRISH FATHER. Saying

JOHNNIE-BOY. What most of us had sorely wanted to say this many a moon

IRISH FATHER. We have come to say goodbye to this institution, my son and myself. It is difficult to do for we changed our way of life to afford him the access to this place. Indeed we moved to a different locality so that my son could take advantage of the wondrous facilities of this educational institution. It has always been my thought that education should swell the mind. When I find that it also swells the body of a child already wasted by an accident of God, I must look again at my thought. And so we come to say goodbye . . . goodbye to children, good friends and bad, who have spent time of day with my son. And goodbye to a woman whose hair is red and who says that she is a teacher of children. And whose hair of red hides a soul that is colored the same and who is indeed in great need of teaching herself. . . . Come on boy. . . . Let's go home.

JOHNNIE-BOY. And we never saw the cripple-boy or his handsome father again. . . .

SONG: LOOK DOWN, LOOK DOWN THAT LONESOME ROAD
(last verse)

> The best of friends must part some day
> Then why not you and I?
> Then why not you and I?

(As the lead verse is reprised, the little children leave the acting space . . . to the two Johnnies. They watch the children leaving and they turn to each other.)

POEM:

JOHNNIE 2.

> If I did not know where lay the human heart,
> I ne'er would trouble with my tuneful string,
> Nor raise my voice to that ethereal place,
> That far-off place where angels' voices ring.

JOHNNIE 1.

> Nor would I ever bend my remembering mind
> Nor burn the elusive, fleeting tick of time,
> To tell the erotic legend of my love,
> The legend of my love in words of rhyme.

JOHNNIE 2.

> If I did not know where lay the human heart
> Or how fine promise flees in place of mounting fears,
> I'd willing laugh my life away instead
> Of seeing all I see faintly through my tears.

JOHNNIE 1.

> I'd never touch nor would I try to shape
> The contour of the tender Grecian mode.

JOHNNIE 2.

> To sing the exalted story of our Lord
> In soaring sonnet or in towering ode.

JOHNNIE 1.

> If I did not know where lay the human heart,
> I'd never trouble with my tuneful string.

(As the poem concludes, a light tune is heard from a harmonica. An actor enters from the choral area carrying two tall stools. He wears a leather apron and an old hat. Little Johnnie-boy enters with him.)

JAKE BICKEL. *(As he sets up the stools and mimes . . .)* The cart or wagon you see here, Johnnie my boy, is duly licensed by the city fathers. *(He reads from a little framed license hanging on the side of one of the stools.)* "To all who read these letters: Greetings. Be it known that the herein undernamed, *Jacob Bickel*, is properly and duly licensed to operate a conveyance for the purpose of transporting and disposing in such manner as to cause no offense to the common welfare, of all and like residue from privies, waste holes and similar other freestanding and secondary buildings as well as in-house receptacles which are utilized for the disposal of said waste. Be it further known that this vehicle serves at the pleasure of the Mayor and the Aldermen of the City of Louisville, Kentucky." Now that's the way they talk about this here Honey Wagon. And you know Johnnie my boy, this here Honey Wagon carries no honey!

JOHNNIE-BOY. Yes sir, Mr. Bickel! It carries away the contents of privies . . . of out-houses . . . of "chick-sales". . . !

JAKE. Well, mein lieber Knabe, I'm well paid for it. And I owe it all to your grandfather, Jacob Reisch, for giving me my start. He's a fine man, Johnnie. . . . Coming as he did from Germany and already with a fine saloon and store-house. Climb up now. *(Johnnie and Jake climb up on the two stools as if on the high seat of a wagon.)* We've a long ride to the river. We must go ever so quietly down the avenue. . . . Yo . . . Portland Avenue is no place to call notice to a Honey Wagon. *(As Jake and Johnnie mime the jolting ride down cobble-stone streets on a Honey Wagon, two very prim and proper German ladies of the neighborhood leave the choral space and enter the acting area.)*

HILDA. Oh . . . Gretta. Do you see what I see?

GRETTA. See what, Hilda?

HILDA. What I see. . . .

GRETTA. I see . . .

BOTH. Gott im Himmel . . .

HILDA. Little Johnnie Niles . . .

GRETTA. On a Honey Wagon!

HILDA. He'll get a . . .

GRETTA. terrible disease!

HILDA. It is our Christian duty.

GRETTA. We must go tell . . .

BOTH. The poor mother! *(The ladies move with determined step to where Mother is seated sewing. The three mime as the action returns to Jake and Johnnie.)*

JOHNNIE-BOY. Look, the burnt-out ruins of the St. Charles Hotel. Mr. Bickel, why did it burn?

JAKE. Don't know why. . . . Don't know. Some things just get too hot and then they burn. *(Jake and Johnnie-boy laugh and continue their mime of the Honey Wagon. Meanwhile the gossips have done their work and Mother calls . . .)*

MOTHER. Tommy . . . can you come here for a minute? *(Father enters the mime from his place on the choral stools. The action returns to Jake and Johnnie-boy as they speak, the gossips retire to the choral stools as Mother and Father continue the mime.)*

JAKE. There's Shippingport, Johnnie. There's where we leave the Honey Wagon for a night's rest in the ol' Ohio River. *(They mime the turning of a wagon by a turn on the stools.)*

JOHNNIE-BOY. Will you get it in the morning?

JAKE. I will indeed, mein lieber Knabe. I will indeed. Come along now . . . it's time to go home. *(He helps Johnnie-boy down from the Honey Wagon stool.)*

JOHNNIE-BOY. You know, Mr. Bickel, this is the third time I've ridden on your Honey Wagon and no one knows but you and me. . . .

JAKE. You can ride any time, boy . . . any time. Give your grandfather my regards . . .

JOHNNIE-BOY. I will, Mr. Bickel. Bye . . . *(Jake exits the acting space with the two stools and Johnnie-boy moves center.)* The first and second time I rode the Honey Wagon my mother never found out. . . .

MOTHER. *(Advances to Johnnie-boy with Father.)* But the third time she did!

JOHNNIE-BOY. And my father . . .

FATHER. *(Swats Johnnie's bottom. Both Mother and Father exit after . . .)* Was greatly amused.

JOHNNIE-BOY. *(Rubbing his bottom.)* Everything on the known earth has its own built-in limitations!

MUSIC CUE 6

SONG: GERMAN DRINKING SONG. *(This song is used under the dialogue of the scene. See notes and score.)*

(As the song is sung, four patrons of the saloon enter with stools and sit as at a bar. One sweeps up Johnnie-boy and sits him on his knee at the "bar." Johnnie-boy conducts the men in their singing as the two older Johnnies comment.)

JOHNNIE 2. My grandfather's saloon on Portland Avenue had

JOHNNIE 1. the longest bar in Jefferson County with

JOHNNIE 2. big brass spittoons and

JOHNNIE 1. twenty-two bartenders!

(Hilda and Gretta enter the acting space.)

HILDA. Gretta, do you see what I see?

GRETTA. YES! Oh, Hilda, little Johnnie Niles . . . in a saloon!

BOTH. Gott im Himmel!

HILDA. I don't believe my eyes! Johnnie Niles, do you swear this is the truth, the whole truth and nothing but the truth.

JOHNNIE-BOY. Absolutely

BOTH JOHNNIE 1 AND 2. Not!

JOHNNIE 1. Family legend

JOHNNIE 2. Not gospel truth

JOHNNIE 1. We would never let the dull facts interfere with a good yarn!

HILDA AND GRETTA. Gott im Himmel! *(They exit the acting space back to the choral stools as the GERMAN DRINKING SONG and an Irish song play under the dialogue.)*

MUSIC CUE 7

JOHNNIE 2. The clean-up man at the saloon was a little Irishman named Mr. Thorpe. *(Thorpe enters drunkenly wearing a dirty white apron and cap and carrying a little wooden bucket.)*

JOHNNIE 1. Who, under the influence of certain alcoholic compounds, distilled and fermented, thought himself to be none other than an . . .

BOTH. Elephant! *(Thorpe mimes his "trunk" and trumpets loudly. Johnnie-boy moves off the lap of the patron and goes to where Elephant Thorpe has seated himself on the floor.)*

JOHNNIE-BOY. What are you doing, Mr. Thorpe?

ELEPHANT. Just call me Elephant.

JOHNNIE-BOY. Yes sir, Mr. Elephant. *(Elephant is miming pouring the dregs out of bottles behind the "bar.")*

ELEPHANT. What am I doin' . . . what am I doin'? I suppose I'm collecting the leftovers. *(He continues to mime pouring into his little wooden bucket.)*

JOHNNIE-BOY. Leftovers?

ELEPHANT. Yes, boy. . . . You might say I'm making a stew. I hate to see anything go to waste so I'm making a stew . . . an Irish stew . . . an Irish Elephant stew!

JOHNNIE-BOY. Sounds awful!

ELEPHANT. Oh! It's not my boy. . . . It's ambrosia. . . .

JOHNNIE-BOY. Am . . . . . ?

ELEPHANT. Brosia. Ambrosia! Means it's good!

JOHNNIE-BOY. What's in the stew, Mr. Elephant?

ELEPHANT. Oh, a little of this and a little of that. A little beer. *(Mimes the action of pouring.)* A little gin *(Again mimes the action.)* A little cognac . . . *(Mimes and then puts his finger in the bucket for a taste.)* Needs salt. *(Patrons laugh and hand him a salt shaker that is again in mime.)* And maybe a little bit of good old Kentucky Portland Avenue Bourbon! *(He tastes again.)* Ah . . . perfect! Let this be a cooking lesson for you, boy. Never settle for less than the best. **Reprise of Irish song with tremolo.** *(He raises the bucket into the air.)* Here's to all the blessed saints of Ireland! *(He drinks.)* St. Patrick! *(He drinks again.)* St. Judith! *(Drinks again.)* St. Shamrock! *(Drinks again and is now very unsteady.)* St. Leprecaun! *(Drinks.)* . . . And most of all . . . here's to St. ELEPHANT! *(He drinks and passes out.)*

JOHNNIE-BOY. *(Shaking Elephant.)* Mr. Elephant! Mr. Elephant!

ELEPHANT. *(Comes to himself and props up on one elbow.)* Johnnie . . . Johnnie . . . *(He rises to a standing position carefully.)* Do what you must in this ol' world . . . but take a bit of advice. Stay away from Elephant Stew! **Reprise: Last notes of GER-MAN DRINKING SONG.** *(He passes out again and Father enters as Elephant is being hauled off by the singing, laughing patrons.)*

FATHER. Johnnie, what happened to Elephant Thorpe?

JOHNNIE-BOY. Oh, Papa! You missed it! Mr. Elephant just had a cultural experience!

(Sounds of New Year's Eve fill the space and Father and the three Johnnies listen.)

MUSIC CUE 8

FATHER. Listen Johnnie. Happy New Year, boy . . . It's the end of the century.

JOHNNIE-BOY. The end?

FATHER. Yes, Johnnie. And the beginning of the new. Listen. It is a time we will never see again. Only once in a lifetime if you're lucky.

JOHNNIE-BOY. Never again?

FATHER. It's a once in a lifetime moment, Johnnie-boy. An end and a beginning. . . . *(He slowly retreats to the choral area.)*

JOHNNIE 1. An end?

JOHNNIE 2. and a beginning.

JOHNNIE 1. *(Mother enters the acting space.)* On September the twenty-second, nineteen hundred and two, when I was just a few months more than ten, I was sad because I had come to the end . . .

JOHNNIE-BOY. The end of something I had enjoyed very much. My mother and I walked through our city house.

MOTHER. Goodbye little kitchen.

JOHNNIE 2. The furniture had long since been carried away in vans
. . . The only thing remaining was the sound . . . the heartbreaking empty sound of our footsteps . . .

MOTHER. Goodbye little bedroom . . .

JOHNNIE-BOY. We walked ever so slowly hand in hand . . . Speaking
occasionally to the rooms we had known . . .

JOHNNIE 1. And then we told them all a lingering goodbye . . .

MOTHER AND JOHNNIE-BOY. Goodbye little garden . . .

JOHNNIE 2. And left, never turning around again.

(Mother and Johnnie-boy embrace and she speaks.)

POEM

Ah, little street beneath October's glow,
The fall of many feet has scarred your face,
And though they're named by names you'll never know
When they returned 'tis like some hallowed place
Enshrined in the memories of the past.
The full enchantment of the early night
Brings in the eerie lace-work and doth cast
Intriguing shades o'er poverty and plight
And makes the humble cottage (alley bound)
A fairy palace hanging in the sky.
Ah, little street so tawdry in the day,
How lovely you do seem when sight and sound
Are turned to gentle nightfall's ear and eye,
And time of sleep turns day-long din away.

JOHNNIE 2. On September the twenty-second, nineteen hundred and
two, my family moved out of a comfortable citified house to a
small, snug, unpainted, simple farmhouse. . . .

JOHNNIE 1. From the noise and the congestion of a booming town,
to the color, the peace and the silence of Indian summer . . .

JOHNNIE 2. To nights of mysterious overcast and velvety darkness. . . .

JOHNNIE 1. I quickly transferred my attachments from my mother's
garden to thicket, to vine, and briar and overgrown forest; to
cultivated land and to scrub and brush . . . to the vast uncharted
heavens, to the Milky Way.

JOHNNIE 2. When at last we came to the land of our farm, and saw the unpainted farmhouse in which we would live . . .

MOTHER. Mother leaned against the building and wept . . .

JOHNNIE 1. In a kind of anguish

JOHNNIE 2. I had never seen before.

(Mother and Johnnie-boy leave the playing space. They are met by Father and they leave together. The two older Johnnies watch and then . . .)

JOHNNIE 1. The first years of our life in the country are lost to me as far as the calendar goes . . . to talk about the wars of the dark tobacco . . . to fabricate and tell a bed-time story o'er and o'er again to little boys . . . to kiss a girl in the gloom of the pioneer graveyard. . . . I lived a heady life and didn't know it. *(Johnnie 1 turns out and adjusts his collar. Mother and Father enter and stand side by side. . . .)*

MOTHER AND FATHER. Don't do it!

JOHNNIE 1. *(He turns to face them.)* I am determined to go.

MOTHER. Johnnie, that little dingy picture show house is no place for you to sing. I don't care if your Uncle Charlie Reisch owns it or not!

FATHER. It is a long way down to Portland, John.

JOHNNIE 1. Look, this thing has already cost me seventy cents! I'm in twenty cents for carfare and I promised Lillian Gilmore fifty cents for playing the piano for me. If I win amateur night, I'll get $2.00! . . . If I am second . . . a dollar!

MOTHER. And what do you get if you are third?

JOHNNIE 1. A hand-written note of thanks!

MOTHER. Gott im Himmel!

FATHER. Johnnie, your uncle is no showman. He is simply a man rich enough to hire men like me to remodel a cottage and install second-hand seats. The audience will be full of Irish at a nickel a seat. They will hook you off the stage before you've sung five notes.

JOHNNIE 1. I'm determined to go! *(He turns out and assumes the pose of a singer who strongly believes in himself. Throughout the following scene, he slowly deflates. . . .)*

MUSIC CUE 9

JOHNNIE I. *(Singing.)* Pony boy, pony boy, won't you be my pony
boy . . .

CHORAL VOICE I. *(Speaking.)* A stick . . .

CHORAL VOICE 2. *(Speaking.)* In the hand . . .

CHORAL VOICE 3. *(Speaking.)* Gathers no moss . . .

CHORAL VOICE 4. *(Speaking.)* Behind the bushes . . .

FULL CHORAL SOUND. *(Sung.)* Amen!

JOHNNIE I. *(Singing.)* Pony boy, pony boy, won't you be my pony boy.

CHORAL VOICE 3. *(Speaking.)* And I say he has too much freedom!

CHORAL VOICE 2. *(Speaking.)* For a boy of his age . . .

CHORAL VOICE I. *(Speaking.)* Entering a contest!

CHORAL VOICE 4. *(Speaking.)* Instead of milkin' . . .

CHORAL VOICE I. *(Speaking.)* The cows!

FULL CHORAL SOUND. *(Sung.)* Amen!

JOHNNIE I. *(Singing.)* Pony boy, pony boy, won't you be my pony
boy . . .

CHORAL VOICE 2. *(Speaking.)* Or clearing out the barn . . .

FULL CHORAL SOUND. *(Sung.)* Amen!

JOHNNIE I. *(Singing.)* Pony boy . . . pony boy . . .

CHORAL VOICE I. *(Speaking.)* Or doing

CHORAL VOICE 3. *(Speaking.)* Any one of a number of

CHORAL VOICE 4. *(Speaking.)* Usual things.

FULL CHORAL SOUND. *(Sung.)* Amen!

JOHNNIE I. *(Singing.)* Won't you be my pony boy . . .

CHORAL VOICES I AND 2. *(Speaking.)* And he writes poetry!

FULL CHORAL SOUND. *(Singing.)* Oh no! Amen! *(Johnnie slowly
turns in to face Father.)*

FATHER. How did it go?

JOHNNIE I. Poorly.

FATHER. How poorly?

JOHNNIE 1. Well . . . they threw a dead cat at me while I was singing.

FATHER. What did you do then?

JOHNNIE 1. Well . . . without missing a single note . . . I threw the cat back at them!

FATHER. *(Laughing.)* Well, Johnnie . . . any person who has the guts to stand on the stage of that measly, musty, stinking little picture show theatre, pick up a thrown dead cat and swing it back into an audience of Portland Avenue Irish, . . . well . . . he's my man! You'll do all right, boy. . . . you'll do all right. Good night, sweet boy. Good night . . . *(Father exits the playing space and leaves Johnnie alone. He slowly walks center then turns to look back at the part of the stage used for the singing of PONY BOY. He moves to his "area" within the acting space and sings.)*

MUSIC CUE 10 *(As solo by Johnnie or choral: see above.)*

SONG: I'M SO GLAD TROUBLE DON'T LAST ALWAYS

> I'm so glad trouble don't last always
> I say, I'm so glad my trouble don't last always
> O, make more room down in your heart for me.
> O, my Lord, my Lord. . . . What shall I do.
> *(Song is sung twice. . . .)*
>
> *(Harmonica music is heard as Root-buyer enters. He wears a jacket and cap and carries a burlap bag half full of what seems to be sticks.)*

ROOT-BUYER. You are a fine farmer, my boy. Being a professional root and herb buyer from the great city of Chicago, I am pleased to pay you ten cents for every two dozen bunches of home-grown sassafras root this bag contains. You've done quite a job diggin' root. I can see that.

JOHNNIE 2. Yes, sir! I get it from the ditches. My father saws off trees so I can dig out the roots.

ROOT-BUYER. Well, well. . . . A good job. . . . a good job. . . . Now, let me see. How much do I owe you here? . . .

JOHNNIE 2. Five dollars.

ROOT-BUYER. Sure 'nough. Fine. . . . Fine. . . . Yes . . . well, I'll just pack this bag of yours on down to Acherman's Store and Mr. Best's boy will load it on my wagon bound for the great city of Chicago. I'll get my check cashed at the store and be right back to pay you your five dollars. You just wait here now and I'll be right back. I'll just be right back to pay you your five dollars. You just wait right here. *(Root-buyer exits and Johnnie 2 sits center. Father enters.)*

FATHER. Johnnie. . . . You just takin' it easy?

JOHNNIE 2. *(Raises.)* No, sir. I'm waiting for the Root-Buyer from Chicago to come back and pay me for the sassafras root I dug. Five dollars!

FATHER. Where did he go?

JOHNNIE 2. Down to Acherman's Store to cash his check.

FATHER. Oh. . . . Well . . . a . . . Look, it's time to milk the cows. I tell you what. I'll just sit here for you while you milk. . . . I'll collect your money and give it to you at the house.

JOHNNIE 2. *(Looking at Father and speaking after a pause.)* That Root-Buyer isn't coming back, is he? He never intended to, did he?

FATHER. The answer is no to both questions. . . .

(Johnnie 1 raises and joins Johnnie 2.)

BOTH. Well, the city of Chicago sure owes me five dollars!

(Johnnie 2 moves to his up stage space, Johnnie 1 moves down right and Father moves to up left where Mother is waiting. Seated at the little table with Mother is Johnnie's sister.)

MOTHER. Did Johnnie tell you he was going to fly?

FATHER. What?

MOTHER. Fly. . . . Like a bird. He is making a pair of wings in the barn.

(Father moves down right where Johnnie 1 is miming a chore.)

FATHER. Hello, son. . . . Need any help?

JOHNNIE 1. Oh, no sir.

FATHER. Johnnie, your Mother tells me you are planning to fly.

JOHNNIE 1. Oh, yes sir. *(He continues to mime the chore selected.)*

FATHER. I wonder if you would mind interrupting your work there a minute and tell me about it. How long have you had flying on your mind?

JOHNNIE 1. *(Raises.)* Since December the seventeenth, 1904. Since I was twelve.

FATHER. Oh?

JOHNNIE 1. But I don't plan to fly the same way as the Wright Brothers did.

FATHER. No?

JOHNNIE 1. No.

FATHER. How do you propose to do it?

JOHNNIE 1. Like Leonardo da Vinci.

FATHER. Son, da Vinci lived a long time ago. How did you . . .

JOHNNIE 1. From a book! *(He produces the book from his pocket.)* See these drawings. . . . *(Shows Father.)* I am determined this will work! *(He moves to another part of the acting space and mimes the picking up of his "wings." He circles around and proudly puts them down center.)* Look!

FATHER. *(Carefully examining the wings.)* Well, Johnnie . . . this is quite an outfit. I see you've used barrel staves and tied them together with binders' twine.

JOHNNIE 1. *(Very proudly.)* Yes. And the trailing edge is this bamboo pole.

FATHER. And then I see you covered it all with burlap feed sacks.

JOHNNIE 1. And shellacked the works! These are the hand holds.

FATHER. If you don't mind, I'd like to go back to the house now and report all this to your mother. She'll be pleased to know you've built such a fine flying machine.

JOHNNIE 1. Glider. . . .

FATHER. Yes. . . . Glider. . . . *(He exits to the area where Mother is helping "sister" comb her hair.)*

(As the dialogue continues Johnnie 1 mimes carrying the glider from the center acting space to the up right area where Johnnie 2 is ready to take it.)

FATHER. Johnnie has built what he calls a "glider" that's about ten feet wide and shaped out of barrel staves and burlap. He plans to fly it off the rocky side of Kenwood Hill. . . .

MOTHER. *(Very concerned.)* Tommy, I think you ought to . . .

SISTER. I think I've got a crazy brother who needs a beatin' with one of those barrel staves instead of flyin' with it! *(She exits, as do Mother and Father.)*

(As Johnnie 1 continues the dialogue, Johnnie 2 is miming the flying. He slowly climbs up on the stump seat as Johnnie 1 backs away across the acting space to down left.)

JOHNNIE 1. No one beat me. I climbed the hill on a beautiful afternoon. My mother was

MUSIC CUE 11

about her do-right business, my father was off with his political conspirators, my brothers all had gone fishing and my sister was off riding the plow horses. I was alone with my glider and my destiny. I lifted my flying wing over my head . . . took a tight grip on the hand holds, ran about twenty feet and jumped off the cliff's edge and sailed into flying history. . . . *(Johnnie 2 leaps off the stump, sails through the air and falls center.)*

JOHNNIE 2. *(From floor.)* . . . for about seventy feet before the entire thing folded in the middle and I fell into a convenient cedar tree. . . . *(Rises slowly.)* I took quite a while walking home. My parents milked for me that night. . . . The year was 1906 and I was 14.

JOHNNIE 1.
POEM:

Oh, for the time to dream one dream each day
And find the dreaming time was not mis-spent,
Dream a little while and mend the rent,
The raveled threadbare fabric of one's clay.
Oh, for the time to watch a patch of cloud
Move so gently 'cross the silent sky,
And learn no matter how men strive or try,
No tick of time is heard within the shroud.
Oh, let me squander just one lovely hour
Of time, and dream in spite of life's demands,
Lest in my vast uncharted tower of days,
Goods and stores and worldly wealth and power

Will alone repay the trickling sands,
When proud death invites and life obeys.

*(Mother enters the acting space. With her is Mary Bolling.
They move to Johnnie 2 as he speaks.)*

JOHNNIE 2. In 1906 we had a house guest. . . . Slim she was and very well dressed.

MARY. How do you do, John. I'm Miss Mary Bolling.

MOTHER. Miss Mary is an old acquaintance of mine.

JOHNNIE 2. Hello, Miss Mary.

MOTHER. She used to teach English in the city high schools, Johnnie.

JOHNNIE 2. And now what do you do, Miss Mary?

MARY. Read . . . philosophy mostly. Sometimes I read the poems of Robert Browning.

MOTHER. Miss Mary was just on her way to the yard to read and rest. Go ahead, Mary. . . . I'll join you as soon as I've had a word with Johnnie about some things that need doing in the barn. *(Mary moves to the UR stump to sit and read from a little book she has with her. Mother and Johnnie move UL.)*

MOTHER. Johnnie, Mary Bolling has had a dreadful experience, just past. She has recently lost the man she intended to marry. He was killed . . . and no one is sure by whom. The police found his body at a fishing camp up river. It is all a terrible scandal. The poor woman needs to rest and to get her mind off the tragedy. I wanted you to know. Go on now and get to the barn. The stalls need cleaning and I've got some things I must attend to. . . .

MUSIC CUE 12A

(Johnnie 2 exits the area and moves DR. Mother turns to the table. Mary turns the pages of her little book then rises and walks slowly to where Mother is working.)

MOTHER. *(Turns.)* Why, Mary, you've finished reading?

MARY. It's hard, Lulie, to keep my mind on reading. . . .

MOTHER. Yes . . . sometimes it is hard. . . .

MARY. *(Sitting.)* Can we talk, Lulie?

MOTHER. Of course, Mary. . . .

MARY. Lulie . . . my life has been very difficult . . . since I lost . . .
my love. . . . Lulie, I've been so . . . lonely. My house is so
empty. When you are as lonely as I am . . . you sometimes do
. . . things you never dreamed you'd do. . . . You sometimes
accept substitutes. *(She begins to cry softly.)* You grope for
things. . . . For another way to fill the days of loneliness. . . .
Days without . . .

MOTHER. *(Kneeling beside Mary.)* What are you trying to say, Mary?
(Mary weeps and Mother embraces her to comfort her.) Come
now . . . all that is past. You mustn't think of those things anymore. It isn't good for you.

MUSIC OUT

(The women rise and walk slowly back to the stump UR.)
Let's go back out under the trees and you rest. Read some more
in your book. I've got to meet Tommy at Acherman's Store to
get a few things we need for the house and when I come back
we'll talk and you can read me some poetry while I fix supper. I
won't be long. Johnnie is out at the barn if you need anything.
*(Mary sits again on the stump and begins to read. Mother re-
turns to the "home area" UL and straightens up, gets her hat
and exits to the choral stools. Mary puts her book down and
moves center as she speaks the poem.)*

MARY.
POEM:

Beneath the deep diaphanous milk-white sky
The sun-dialed hours marked by one lone pine
Slip between my fingers as I try
To hold one moment to my heart as mine,
To touch and taste and smell the tender scent
Of one bright glowing segment of this day,
Before it joins the weary hours long spent
And crowds the shelves where dusty histories lay.
For here I held your body in my hands
And saw man's golden promises grow dim
Beside the sweet rewards that you did give.
What could we hope to find in all the lands
Beyond sky's deep diaphanous milk-white rim
To match those lovely hours we did live?

(She turns to the DL area where Johnnie 2 has begun a mime of pitching hay. She moves slowly toward him waiting until he turns. . . .)

MUSIC CUE 12B

JOHNNIE 2. *(Turning.)* Why . . . hello, Miss Mary. . . .

MARY. Hello, Johnnie . . . busy working I see.

JOHNNIE 2. *(Continuing to mime.)* Oh . . . yes, ma'am.

MARY. Your mother tells me you like poetry, Johnnie. . . . That you even write poetry sometimes. . . .

JOHNNIE 2. *(Still with mime.)* Yes, ma'am, Miss Mary.

MARY. That's very fine, Johnnie. . . .

JOHNNIE 2. Thank you, Miss Mary. . . .

MARY. And you sing beautifully, Johnnie.

JOHNNIE 2. *(Still miming.)* Thank you, again. . . .

MARY. *(Advancing a few steps.)* Johnnie . . . are you still kissing girls in the gloom of the pioneer graveyard? *(Johnnie stops his mime. He looks at Mary. Then away . . . embarrassed.)*

MUSIC OUT

JOHNNIE 2. Of course I am, whenever there is a girl handy.

MARY. And . . . do these little persons object to kissing?

JOHNNIE 2. Occasionally . . . they give the impression . . . but not often. *(Another pause as Johnnie and Mary look at each other.)* And . . . with luck . . . I kiss ladies in cowbarns. . . . *(He kisses Mary on the cheek.)*

MARY. *(After the quick kiss, she laughs softly.)* Now it is my turn to thank you, Johnnie. . . . *(She moves close to Johnnie. She places her hand carefully on his arm tracing a line down to his hand with her finger.)* Johnnie . . . do you always kiss the little girls on the side of the face?

(She slowly moves a few steps away from the boy and turns to smile with a question in her eyes. She extends her hand to him and Johnnie moves slowly forward with his hand extended to meet her. As this is taking place, Johnnie 1 rises and begins to sing enclosed in his own fantasy within the words of the

BALLAD OF THE SOLDIER AND HIS LADY. As Johnnie 1 sings, Johnnie 2 and Mary Bolling mime slowly the action recorded below beside each verse.)

MUSIC CUE 13

JOHNNIE 1.
SONG:

> A soldier came from Georgia way
> Of ridin' he was weary
> He tingled on the side-door ring
> To hearken up his lady.
> To hearken up his lady.

(Mary leads Johnnie 2 slowly upstage to the stump area at UR. They are both in tight focus on each other.)

> She's took him by the bridle rein
> She's led him to the stable.
> "Here's oats, here's corn, here's hay for your horse.
> Let him eat what he is able.
> Let him eat what he is able."

(Mary has reached the stump and offers Johnnie both her hands.)

> She's took him by the lily-white hand,
> She's led him to the table.
> "Here's cakes and wine for you, my dear,
> Come eat what you are able.
> Come eat what you are able."

(Mary slowly pulls the boy closer and their hands drop.)

> She's went to smooth his downy bed,
> And she smoothed it like a lady,
> And off she took her red, red dress,
> Said, "Dearie, are you ready?"
> Said, "Dearie, are you ready?"

(Johnnie embraces Mary and slowly moves his hand down her back.)

> "When shall we meet and marry, dear,
> If you cannot tarry?"

(Mary slowly moves away from Johnnie.)

MARY. *(Singing.)*
> "When cockle-shells turn silver bells,
> 'Tis then that we shall marry."

(She exits the acting space. Johnnie 2 turns to sit on the stump.)

JOHNNIE 2. *(Singing.)*
> "'Tis then that we shall marry."

(Johnnie 1 sits as Preacher and Deaconess enter the playing space from the choral stools.)

MUSIC OPTION: SEE SCORE

PREACHER. *(Wearing a vest and hat and carrying a Bible. Deaconess wears a "church" hat, gloves and carries a large purse.)* Being a preacher and a man of God, I must say that I do pity that poor little Niles boy. . . . He is being brought up in the worst possible atmosphere . . . what with his playing the piano almost continually . . .

DEACONESS. And his father a-singin' those vulgar ol' timey songs!

PREACHER. *And* in such a way as to make worst words sound loudest and best! *(Preacher and Deaconess exit the acting space.)*

JOHNNIE 1. Nineteen hundred and six was a year of wonderful memories. There I was, nearly full grown, fourteen years of age, playing the piano with reasonable skill, bringing home a fair report card from duPont Manual Training High School, and working diligent at whatever farmwork was required. I brought in kale and wild greens, walnuts, late mushrooms . . . the best of the year and no one ever died from eating my mushrooms at the Seelbach Hotel . . . persimmons . . . particularly for pies . . . and wild game occasionally. Our diet was improved over what it was when we lived inside the city. But I gave the impression of being a clodhopper. It did not occur to me that there was anything the matter with being a clodhopper.

JOHNNIE 2. When we moved from Portland Avenue to the farm, Mother had found, among the things packed, a few notes she had made from what proved to be my first experience of collecting folk music. She gave the scraps of paper to me in 1902 suggesting I might do something with them. . . . The paper smelled of her handkerchief drawer . . . like lavender. I put the papers away with my own things and several years later in 1906 I worked and reworked the fragments for use as a Christmas anthem by one of the local church choirs. No experience of collecting music was quite like the first. . . . Mother and I had gone to Hardin County to visit the Graham family. *(Entering the acting space are: Mother, who goes to Johnnie 1, Granny Graham hobbling on a cane, her two daughters in sunbonnets and the ol' uncle.)*

MOTHER. Come along, Johnnie *(To Johnnie 1.)* Mrs. Graham's great-granny is here to visit this afternoon and she is going to sing. I thought you'd like to hear her. Let's take down the tune. . . . I'll help you. It's a good chance to use the music shorthand I've been teaching you. . . .

JOHNNIE 1. What is she going to sing?

MOTHER. Well, Granny and two of her daughters as well as an old uncle are all here and they are going to sing an ol' timey song about Christmas that is one of their family songs. *(Mother and Johnnie 1 move to DR where Granny is seated.)* Granny Graham, this is my son, John Jacob.

JOHNNIE 1. How do you do, Miss Granny.

GRANNY. Nicely!

MOTHER. And these are Granny's two daughters, Johnnie.

GRANNY. They never married. Ya know why? They're quair-turned. . . . And men folk never liked 'em!

DAUGHTER. Ol' woman, you're teched a-sayin' things liken that to this here youngin'.

GRANNY. I'm only speakin' gospel! *(She whispers to Johnnie and points to the ol' uncle.)* See that ol' man? You know why he's a-standin' there a-lookin' like a prune?

JOHNNIE 1. No, ma'am.

GRANNY. Well, when he was a boy . . . not much different than you are right now . . . he was a-sleepin' on the cabin floor right by the hearth stone. There come up a terrible storm. Now then . . . a bolt of lightnin' flashed and run right down the chimney and cracked him a good lick in the head and he ain't had much to say since. *(She laughs with great amusement as Johnnie 1 stares at the ol' uncle. The old man in turn stares and has no change of expression.)* Now, Miss Lulie, since we'ens all know each other, I'll be pleased to sing you the little song folks sing hereabouts at Christmas time. While I'm a-singin', don't pay these daughters of mine no notice. They're pure teched! *(She sings in a high wavy voice a tune of her own invention.)*

"Jesus, Jesus, rest you head
You has got a corn-shuck bed . . ."

(She continues to repeat the words in her tune over and over again. One of the daughters calls to Mother.)

DAUGHTER. Miss Lulie. Will you step over here a minute? Miss Lulie, Mama don't know how that song goes. The ol' woman has turned pure foolish and can't make no sense a-tall! And my sister ain't of sound mind neither. Here is the way that there song goes. *(She sings joining the other tune still sung by Granny.)*

"Jesus, Jesus, rest you head
Sleep down deep in your corn-shuck bed.
Did you hear how Jesus came?
A body don't know what
Or how or where from . . ."

(She continues in concert with Granny, each with different tunes and different words. While Johnnie and Mother are trying to keep up with their notation on the two singers, Daughter 1 speaks.)

DAUGHTER 1. Miss Lulie, will you'ens step outside with me in the yard? There sure be a lot of tarnation interference in here! *(Mother moves with this daughter aside from the rest and leaves Johnnie on his own with the first two.)* My sister and my mama will tell you that I am daft but I am not down gone! It just hain't no matter if I be a bit strange. . . . Now here is the right way to sing the little song about Jesus! *(She sings and joins the others with yet another tune and another set of words.)*

"A milk-maid came with brimming pail,
A-walking through snow and rain and hail,
To see the Jesus boy."

JOHNNIE 1. No! You are all mistaken! *This* is the *right* way to sing the little song about Jesus. . . . *(He begins to sing.)*

MUSIC CUE 14

Jesus, Jesus, rest your head
You has got a manger bed.

All the evil folk on earth
Sleep in feathers at their birth
Jesus, Jesus, rest your head
You has got a manger bed.

(All the players in the acting space as well as those in the choral area begin to sing with him.)

CHORUS.
Jesus, Jesus, rest your head
You has got a manger bed.

SOLO VOICE. *(Enters the acting space from the choral area.)*
Have you heard about our Jesus?
Have you heard about his fate?
How his Mammy came to that stable
On that Christmas Eve so late?

CHORUS AND PLAYERS.
Winds are blowing, cows were lowing
Stars were glowing, glowing, glowing.

JOHNNIE I.
Jesus, Jesus, rest your head,
You has got a manger bed.

CHORUS AND PLAYERS.
All the evil folk on earth
Sleep in feathers at their birth

JOHNNIE I.
Jesus, Jesus, rest your head,
You has got a manger bed.

SOLO VOICE 2. *(Entering the acting space.)*
To that manger came them wise men
Bearing gifts from hin and yon.
For the mother and the father
And the blessed little Son.

CHORUS AND PLAYERS.
Milk-maids left their field and flocks to sit
Beside the ass and ox.
Jesus, Jesus, rest your head
You has got a manger bed.
All the evil folk on earth
Sleep in feathers at their birth

Jesus, Jesus, rest your head
You has got a manger bed.

(All the singers and players exit the playing space to the choral stools and leave the space to the two Johnnies.)

JOHNNIE 2. It was 1907. I was fifteen and I was spending my time at milking cows, at farming, reading, playing piano and trying to think out a way of untying the winds of change. I could pick up a page of complicated music, identify the elusive melodic line and sing it after the usual manner of tenors.

JOHNNIE 1. Once . . . during those years . . . my father took me with him on a political trip to a little town called Ary, Kentucky. I remember I heard a song and while my father was busy with his business, I wrote it down. *(Father and another male singer enter talking together. The singer carries a basket with wood carving in it. Another male singer enters the acting space and stops to talk to Johnnie 2 UR. Three girls enter and break up their group to meet two other girls who have also entered the acting space from the choral stools. The scene reflects a meeting or "social." Johnnie 1 waits DL for Father to join him. As he approaches Johnnie speaks.)* Here's a song I collected while you were busy at the political meeting. What do you think?

FATHER. *(Looking over the paper Johnnie 1 has handed him.)* It's got nice text, Johnnie, but the tune is terrible. Do something with it. Write me a tune worthy of the poem. *(He moves away into the crowd.)*

JOHNNIE 1. I took his advice.

MUSIC CUE 15

(As the song is sung, the mime on the stage should reflect young love. The carver moves down stage in the acting space and one of the trio of girl singers comes to join him. He gives her a gift of a small wooden carving. She moves to the other two singers in the trio and shows her gift. The young man first talking to Johnnie 2 moves down stage with the carver and they compare knives. Father moves to Johnnie 1, who is DL listening and working on his song. The acting space should capture during the song a feeling of love and friendship on many levels.)

SONG:

> Black, black, black is the color of my true love's hair
> His lips are something wondrous fair
> The purtiest face and the strongest hands
> I love the grass whereon he stands
>
> I love my love and well he knows
> I love the grass whereon he goes
> If he on this earth no more I see
> My life would quickly leave me.
>
> I go to Troublesome to mourn, to weep
> But satisfied I ne'er can sleep
> I'll write him a note in a few little lines
> I'll suffer death ten thousand times.
>
> Black, black, black is the color of my true love's hair
> His lips are something wondrous fair
> The purtiest face and the strongest hands
> I love the grass whereon he stands.

(All singers exit the acting space except the two Johnnies.)

JOHNNIE 2. Also, at that time, I was engaged in the delightful enter-
prise of studying several charming young ladies in our community. And without boasting or bragging, I think I can say that
several young ladies were busily studying me. . . . *(Heidie
Moore and two girl friends run into the acting space.)*

POEM:

HEIDIE. I love you,

JOHNNIE 1. I love you,

GIRL FRIEND 1. I love you,

JOHNNIE 2. I love you,

GIRL FRIEND 2. and I hope you know exactly what I am talking
about.

HEIDIE. For the lexicon of love

JOHNNIE 2. is such a complicated thing

JOHNNIE 1. That often-times lovers misunderstand one another

GIRL FRIEND 1. But when I tell you in unmistakable terms

HEIDIE. The simple honest attitude of my heart,

GIRL FRIEND 2. You can hardly misunderstand when I say,

JOHNNIE 2. I love you,

JOHNNIE 1. I love you,

HEIDIE. I love you,

GIRL FRIEND 1. I love you,

JOHNNIE 1. And I am sure

HEIDIE. you know exactly

GIRL FRIEND 2. what I am talking about. *(The two girl friends exit the acting space.)*

HEIDIE. It was summer. . . . It was summer. . . . It was 1907. . . .

JOHNNIE 1. I was slender and blond and sunburned. Every day I mucked out the cow and horse stalls.

HEIDIE. It was summer and the dragonfly was abroad, dancing over ditches, ponds, ruts and puddles . . . looking and ever looking again for a succulent delightful morsel of food. . . .

JOHNNIE 1. The girl who interested me most was Heidie Moore.

JOHNNIE 2. She had been adopted into the Moore family sixteen years ago at the age of one year. . . .

HEIDIE. It was summer. . . . It was summer and the Halcyon days were upon us.

JOHNNIE 2. It was summer and I had a new straw hat . . . a cheap two-bit straw hat from a country store. . . .

JOHNNIE 1. You can't make a mockingbird out of a sparrow.

HEIDIE. Fools are positive. . . . Wise men hesitant. . . .

JOHNNIE 2. For five cents I could ride a trolley car called the Pennsylvania Dinkey from Louisville to New Albany, Indiana. For a little more money I could buy a ticket to a glorified show for the vaudeville stage! A fifteen-year-old farm-boy, musician, and poet . . . had to do it! *(Those on the choral stools begin to mime as part of the audience in the big tent. Johnnie follows suit and mimes as he speaks.)* My heart was light as I approached the tent. . . . I bought my ticket and took my seat.

(As he works his way through the crowd.) Excuse me. . . . Pardon me. . . .

MR. EMERSON. *(Coming to the center of the acting space.)* Good afternoon, Ladies and Gentlemen. I am your host, Waldo D. Emerson, and on behalf of the management, wish to thank you for being here in the big tent today. *(The "audience" claps and cheers.)* There will, however, be a slight delay in beginning the afternoon's entertainment. . . . *(The "audience" boos loudly.)* Please. . . . Please. . . . Enjoy yourself and the show will begin in only a few minutes. . . . *(He reaches into his pocket and pulls out a scrap of paper. He reads.)* Is there a John Jacob Niles present? *(Johnnie 2 slowly raises his hand.)* Would you step forward sir? . . . Just step this way if you don't mind, sir. . . .

JOHNNIE 2. Excuse me. . . . Pardon me. *(As he works his way to the center of the playing space.)*

MR. EMERSON. Mr. Niles! *(Shaking Johnnie 2's hand with gusto.)* I certainly am glad to make your acquaintance! I see you are quite a young . . . gentleman.

JOHNNIE 2. Fifteen, sir.

EMERSON. Fifteen . . . well. *(Looking toward heaven.)* I hope he can handle this!

JOHNNIE 2. Pardon me?

EMERSON. You see, boy . . . I mean . . . *sir*, we have lost our accompanist. He simply did not show up! The wastrel! We are desperate! You were recommended to us by an organist in Louisville and we've been trying to reach you. . . . Then we found out you were coming to the tent and . . . *(Hugs Johnnie 2.)* Oh, thank God you are here!

JOHNNIE 2. But I . . . *(Four young girls rush up breathlessly. Their eyes are full of hope as they stare at Johnnie 2.)*

EMERSON. Girls. . . . Girls. . . . This is Johnnie Niles who, we all hope, will play piano accompaniments for you.

MARY KEATS. *(The head Blossom, breathless and very excited.)* I am Mary Keats and this is my sister Gloria and these are the Williams twins and we are called the Indiana Blossoms! Ta-Da!! Oh, Mr. Niles, would you please look over our material? Our real accompanist didn't show up. . . . We could have a short rehearsal and. . . . Oh, would you . . . please help!

BLOSSOMS. Yes. . . . Oh, please. . . . Just this once. . . . etc.

JOHNNIE 2. Look, I just came to watch the show. I'm not so sure that I. . . .

MARY KEATS. Without you we can't sing! We've come all this way! *(All the Blossoms weep and hug each other with glances at Johnnie 2.)*

BLOSSOMS. Please. . . . Oh, please, Mr. Niles! Etc. . . .

JOHNNIE 2. Just call me Johnnie.

BLOSSOMS. Yes . . . Johnnie . . . Johnnie . . . (etc.)

JOHNNIE 2. But there isn't even a piano to rehearse with!

MARY KEATS. There's one in the back! *(They grab him and whisk him to one side of the playing space.)*

JOHNNIE 1. *(As they thunder by, speaking in disbelief.)* The heaviest burden a busy person has to bear is the vast burden of those poor creatures who will not squander their lives alone!

JOHNNIE 2. *(Escapes and hurries center to Mr. Emerson.)* Sir, I'm leaving!

EMERSON. *(Truly desperate.)* Look, little boy, I know quite a few beginners like yourself who would pay for the chance you are about to throw away!

MARY KEATS. *(From behind Johnnie 2.)* Are you afraid?

JOHNNIE 2. *(Turns to her rather angry.)* Look! When I hang up this hat *(Gestures to the straw hat he has been wearing throughout.)* we'll see how afraid I am! *(Mary Keats reaches up slowly and takes off the straw hat from Johnnie 2's head as the Blossoms stand by holding their breath to see what reaction the motion will evoke. Johnnie smiles and the Blossoms giggle as they rush to their positions to prepare to sing. Johnnie 2 goes UL to the Victorian table and mimes a piano.)*

EMERSON. *(Dashing forward.)* Ladies and Gentlemen. It is with great pleasure I give you those lovely lasses. . . . The pride of the prairie. . . . The Indiana Blossoms! *(The Blossoms rush forward and curtsey.)*

MUSIC CUE 16

SONG: AFTER THE BALL *(Sung by the Blossoms.)*

> After the ball is over, after the break of day
> After the dancers leaving, after the stars are gone;
> Many a heart is aching, if you could read them all;
> Many the hopes that have vanished after the ball.
> After the ball . . .

(Applause from the "audience." Johnnie 2 kisses all the Blossoms as they dash out of the acting area.)

JOHNNIE 1. It was one of the most important afternoons I ever spent in my young life. And although I had not untied the fabulous winds of change, I had made $1.50 at the chosen profession of my life and knew my true home was the wide world of show house.

JOHNNIE 2. Men need women and women need men.

JOHNNIE 1. It was summer. It was summer and even the night was hot. The electric car approached Jacob's Park. I saw the road down to Heidie Moore's home. . . .

MUSIC CUE 17A

HEIDIE. It was summer. . . . It was summer and June was at her best.

JOHNNIE 1. *(LOST LOVE instrumental begins.)* The night was full of singing insect sounds and the heat trickled down from the beleafed trees touching one another overhead. I was finally nearing my home. Nothing mattered much. I knew the houses and I knew the little cabins . . . the weather beaten lean-tos and even the animal barns. I knew the men and the women and surely the children. Early harvest, pasture found and church house legitimate . . . I walked the dusty dirt road. . . .

HEIDIE. Against a background of shuttering katydids. . . . Katydids and crickets and ever so tiny tree frogs.

JOHNNIE 2. The night echoed a delightful heartbreaking sound.

HEIDIE. The sound of the night-singing mockingbird. For he knew it was mating time once more. . . .

MUSIC CUE 17B

(Heidie may dance as Johnnies 1 and 2 watch from distance.)

SONG: LOST LOVE

> Oh, I wish I could find that true love I once did know
> Lost to me now through the endless passing years
> For she was the love of my days as a youngling
> 'Twas for her I shed all my youthful tears.
>
> I look in the throng of the faces passing by me
> Hoping for a glimpse of the smile almost forgot
> But I know now that time has robbéd me forever
> Leaving me with loneliness and yearning for my lot.
>
> O, I try and I fail to live again those lovely days
> Gone like a dream dreamt out so long ago
> But time rushes on and dims the page of memory
> And casts a darkling shadow over pleasure's brightest glow.

(Heidie moves to Johnnies 1 and 2.)

POEM:

JOHNNIE 1.
> Now that it is Christmas,
> You might try to weave
> A wreath round me,
> Just to prove to me
> That you do love me.

HEIDIE.
> The wreath might be made from sprigs of yew
> Or holly or rosa multiflora
> Or frost-tinged blueberry leaves.

JOHNNIE 2. *(As he moves up stage to his UR seat on the stump.)*
> Any of these would serve so admirable
> If you would do the weaving.

JOHNNIE 1. *(Moving center to where Heidie is seated.)*
> And if I be permitted
> To stand by and torment you
> With suggestions
> And little pats and sweet pinches
> And endless declarations of my love.
> Now that it is Christmas,
> You might try to weave

HEIDIE. A wreath around me,

JOHNNIE I. One that would never wither. *(They kiss.)*

HEIDIE. Johnnie, if I'm going to help you milk the cows every day, you've got to help me collect old clothes for the church to give to the deserving poor.

JOHNNIE I. For a farm-girl, you sure are bossy, Miss Heidie Moore.

HEIDIE. That's because you are two years younger than I am, Mr. Johnnie Niles. *(They kiss tenderly.)*

JOHNNIE I. Let's go up to the pioneer graveyard and read poetry. Did you bring your book?

HEIDIE. John Keats is always in my pocket. *(She produces the little book.)* And today . . . I even have a new poem by that great lady of verse . . . Heidie Moore. *(She produces a scrap of paper from the book.)*

JOHNNIE I. And I have two new Christmas anthems I want to sell to the choir directors in Beechmont. Let's go!

MUSIC CUE 17C

(As they "travel" to the graveyard there is a reprise of LOST LOVE hummed. Heidie and Johnnie 1 show each other their new poems and anthems. Johnnie 1 takes another kiss. As the kiss parts . . .)

HEIDIE. I think your anthems are poor.

JOHNNIE I. *(Totally taken aback.)* The congregations of the churches I propose to sell these anthems to are just about smart enough to understand them as they are written!

HEIDIE. You should be ashamed of yourself, Johnnie Niles, for passing such a pompous judgment on the choir directors and furthermore, if you expect to be paid, even a pittance, for your work you should turn out the best that is in you! In these anthems the poetry is wonderful but the music is . . . poor!

JOHNNIE I. The music is . . . better than . . . fair!

HEIDIE. Johnnie, I know you too well. You intend to sell that music . . . willie-nillie. *(She tries to exit.)*

JOHNNIE I. *(Grabs her arm.)* Heidie . . . Wait a minute. . . .

HEIDIE. I'm going to weed my flower bed. I'll see you at milking time. . . . *(She exits the acting space.)*

JOHNNIE 1. One choir director paid me a dollar fifty cents and the other anthem sold for a dollar! . . . But Heidie was right. The choir members were easily pleased. They sang my limping four-part harmonies with a kind of vigor that was almost abandon! Still . . . Heidie was right. Later, I burned the anthems. . . . But . . . The two dollars and fifty cents they gave me was received with delight and o'er flowing gratitude. I bought my mother a handkerchief and tied it to the Christmas tree and for Miss Heidie . . . I found a tiny, tiny bottle of perfume.

JOHNNIE 2. My mother did not object to my staying out late. But Heidie's mother objected . . . no end . . . except . . . for church.

HEIDIE. *(Enters running and very excited.)* Johnnie, the little church out in Valley Station has lost its pianist. They are planning a Christmas program and . . . I volunteered you to play. The piano isn't the best but one of the congregation promised to get it tuned for Christmas by a professional!

MUSIC OPTION: SEE SCORE

PIANO TUNER. *(Enters slightly in a huff.)* Young lady . . . I have tuned pianos for Steinway all over Louisville and Jefferson County and with this job I was determined to overcome the unknown. All I can say is: "Results and Sweat are Brothers!" This piano has all the repairs it can take! *(He exits with Heidie running after him.)*

JOHNNIE 2. With a tuned ruin of a piano, the players as ready as they were ever going to be, and Heidie and I armed with the perfect excuse for staying out late . . . helping a preacher put on a Christmas play . . . The holiday season of 1907 was not going badly for a farm-boy. But writing anthems was not my only concern. *(Mother enters and moves to her table area. She takes out some sewing and sits. Johnnie 2 moves to address her.)* Mother . . . may I talk to you . . . while you mend those things?

MOTHER. I think that would be just the ticket.

JOHNNIE 2. Mother, I've written a new song.

MOTHER. You have . . . ?

JOHNNIE 2. Yes. . . . You remember Objerall Jacket, the black man who dug trenches for Father? You remember last summer when I dug side by side with Objerall?

MOTHER. Johnnie, I never did believe that was that man's name.

JOHNNIE 2. Well, that's what appeared on the weekly pay book. . . . Anyway, the whole time we were digging, Objerall kept singing. . . . or rather grunting a kind of work song. *(As Johnnie 2 begins to mime the action of swinging a pick, Johnnie 1 mimes with him.)* Go way . . . ugh! From my door . . . ugh! *(Mime stops and Johnnie 2 continues.)* All day long . . . the same thing . . . over and over again to lighten his labor as he dug. Well, I got to thinking and working on those few notes and I've composed a new song. What do you think?

MOTHER. I think stranger things have happened. I'd like to hear it.

JOHNNIE 2. It isn't finished yet. When it is finished I'll sing it for you. *(He moves away to his place UR.)*

JOHNNIE 1. I wonder what Heidie will think of the song. . . . When it's finished I'll give it to her.

HEIDIE. *(Slowly entering acting space.)* All through the precious time of 1907 and 1908 . . . *(She slowly moves toward Johnnie 1.)*

JOHNNIE 1. We were meeting morning and evening . . . to milk the cows.

HEIDIE. Saturday morning . . .

JOHNNIE 1. Saturday evening . . .

HEIDIE. Sunday morning . . .

JOHNNIE 1. . . . came as I expected, and Heidie came to the pasture of the cows

HEIDIE. *(Rushing now into Johnnie 1's arms.)* Johnnie, I can't stay very long. My father and mother had a terrible fight this morning about me . . . and you. My mother is sick again . . . coughing and spitting up blood. . . .

JOHNNIE 1. What do you mean . . . a fight over you and me?

HEIDIE. *(Moves away.)* A lady of the church stopped to bring my mother some special medicine and . . . thinking she was doing everyone a kindness . . . told my mother . . . you and I were . . . more than . . . friends.

JOHNNIE 1. *(After a pause he slowly moves to Heidie.)* Do they know it all?

HEIDIE. Yes.

JOHNNIE 1. I don't care!

HEIDIE. You've got to care, Johnnie Niles! You know my father's temper!

JOHNNIE 1. *(Tenderly.)* But we will go on anyway? Seeing each other?

HEIDIE. Yes, Johnnie. . . . *(They embrace and Heidie exits the acting space.)*

JOHNNIE 2. By the middle of August, Heidie's father had become more and more difficult. He began carrying a .45-caliber gun. Every dry evening after supper he went out alone and practiced shooting. . . . During the day he sold Bibles for a living. On the last Saturday night in August, when I reached the cow barn, there was Heidie . . . she was weeping. . . .

JOHNNIE 1. Heidie. . . . What's the matter?

HEIDIE. *(Embracing him.)* Johnnie. . . . Oh, my Johnnie. . . .

JOHNNIE 1. *(Tenderly.)* What . . . ?

HEIDIE. Johnnie, you must listen very carefully to what I'm going to say. . . .

MUSIC CUE 17D

I'm leaving tomorrow. . . .

JOHNNIE 1. Where are you going?

HEIDIE. Away. . . .

JOHNNIE 1. Where?

HEIDIE. I can't tell you where.

JOHNNIE 1. Why?

HEIDIE. Because if I stay here we will be together no matter what and if we stay together my father will kill you. . . . *(He embraces her and kisses her many times quickly and tenderly. They cling to each other. Finally, through the exchange, Heidie mutters . . .)* No . . . No . . . No . . . *(They look at each other.)* It's over. . . . We can't be together any more. . . . *(She starts to exit. She turns.)* Johnnie to me you are song and poetry. . . . you are forever a vision unreal to the end. . . . *(She moves away.)* Goodbye Johnnie. . . . *(She exits the acting space.)*

JOHNNIE 1. If I had been older, I might have taken matters into my own hands. But the two years difference in our age. . . . I was a child once more. . . . I had no handy solutions to anything.

And then I started a period in my life I have never been able to forget. Every girl I passed on the street was Heidie. I kept describing her to myself . . . Slim as a cattail stem, swaying as she walked . . . swaying as she walked as if she were subject to a light wayward wind. I thought of her hair . . . cascading down her shoulders. Everything I saw was more than a little blurred. Heidie and I had set something into motion and, neither Heidie nor I knew how to control it . . . nor alas . . . how to stop it . . . *(The reprise humming of LOST LOVE stops.)* Miss Heidie Moore died in the influenza epidemic of 1917. . . .

JOHNNIE 2. I gave the first copy of my new song to the only blue-eyed girl I knew. . . . *(Mr. and Mrs. Juckett move to the acting space with Blanche, their blue-eyed daughter. She is very pretty.)* Hello, Mr. Juckett . . . Mrs. Juckett.

THE JUCKETTS. Hello, Johnnie. . . .

JOHNNIE 2. Hello, Blanche. I wondered if you might like to take a walk?

BLANCHE. *(Obviously disinterested.)* Well . . . if we don't walk too far.

JOHNNIE 2. No . . . we won't walk too far. If you don't want to. . . .

BLANCHE. Well, I don't really . . . but . . . all right. *(They stroll across the acting space as the older Jucketts exit.)*

JOHNNIE 2. Blanche, I have a present for you.

BLANCHE. For me? Well, Johnnie Niles. For heaven's sake. . . . What is it?

JOHNNIE 2. It's a new song I've written.

BLANCHE. A new song? Well, for heaven's sake. *(She takes the music and looks it over quickly.)* Why, Johnnie, you're no composer! You're not even a good singer . . . let alone a poet. Anyway you're a whole year younger than I am and don't have a dime to call your own! What kind of catch are you for a girl to consider! Here . . . take your ol' music! *(She crumples up the score of the song and tosses it on the ground at Johnnie 2's feet. She flounces off. Johnnie stoops and picks up the score and smooths out the page as Heidie enters and goes to the UR stump. The two Johnnies join each other down left and look at her as she sings.)*

MUSIC CUE 18

HEIDIE. *(She sings.)*
　　Go 'way from my window,
　　Go 'way from my door,
　　Go 'way, 'way, 'way from my bedside
　　And bother me no more
　　And bother me no more

　　I'll give you back your letters,
　　I'll give you back your ring,
　　But I'll ne'er forget my own true love
　　As long as song birds sing
　　As long as song birds sing.

　　Go tell all my brothers,
　　Tell all my sisters, too,
　　That the reason why my heart is broke
　　Is on account of you.

　　Go 'way from my window
　　Go 'way from my door,
　　Go 'way, 'way, 'way from my bedside
　　And bother me no more
　　And bother me no more.

(Heidie exits and the two Johnnies look at each other.)

JOHNNIE 2.
　　An end. . . .

JOHNNIE 1.
　　And a beginning. . . .
　　And I have looked back and back and backward

JOHNNIE 2.
　　The days of life
　　The thousand, thousand, thousand days

JOHNNIE 1.
　　And I never saw them again
　　How many times. . . .

JOHNNIE 2.
　　And I never saw them again
　　How many times. . . .
　　Oh, my youth

JOHNNIE I.
 A time of gentleness and pain

JOHNNIE 2.
 A time to look backward on

JOHNNIE I.
 A time to move forward from.

MUSIC CUE 19

SONG:

 I wonder as I wander
 Out under the sky
 How Jesus our savior did come for to die
 For poor onry people like you and like I
 I wonder as I wander
 Out under the sky.

POEM: *(Humming continues as the poem is said. If poem is used, it should be voiceover of the voice of John Jacob Niles.)*

 The locusts have eaten nearly all of my years
 And left the husks and hulls of endless days.
 And now I must discover how to live with the bitter
 Husks and the tattered fragile hulls
 Of days I shall never see again.
 So if you see me trying to piece the shards
 Of broken days and tiny fragmented moments together
 To brighten the dark night of my loneliness,
 Be kind, be gentle, be affectionate to an old man
 Who has given his years to the locust: be kind.

SONG: *(As the full company joins the two Johnnies in the acting space.)*

 I wonder as I wander
 Out under the sky
 How Jesus the saviour did come for to die
 For poor onry people like you and like I
 I wonder as I wander
 Out under the sky.

 (Curtain.)

The Code Breaker

By Pauline C. Conley

Copyright, 1983, Anchorage Press, Inc.

The Code Breaker (1983)

The Code Breaker, by Pauline Conley, is a futuristic adventure play that examines life in a world dominated by advanced technology. Reminiscent of the novel *1984*, *The Code Breaker* introduces us to four adolescent youths who are preparing to become initiated as vital working members of the Orb society. They have grown up living in small, enclosed cubicles monitored by a complex master computer, Ruby, who dictates their lives, and supplies them with the essentials necessary for their existence.

This pattern of life is disturbed when Peter discovers a forgotten world beyond the Orb. This discovery, and Peter's determination to prove its existence, puts the group in conflict with the master computer, with their beliefs as they have learned them from the rulers of the Orb, and ultimately with each other.

The choices the characters make dramatically define the struggle of the individual in a totalitarian state, and help the audience examine the relationship between technology and personal freedom, individuality and conformity, and friendship and authority. At the play's end, the audience is filled with some hope for the human race and our own humanity, as Peter prepares to escape his cubicle and prove the existence of a world he has discovered existing independently of the Orb.

CHARACTERS

Pete

Bernice

Lisa

Barney

Ruby

SETTING
In the Orb, in the living quarters of Bernice, Pete, Lisa, and
Barney.

TIME
The future.

The Code Breaker

Peter enters his own quarters carrying a pack. He puts a vid-tape into his console, checks to see that Ruby is not watching, and turns it on. While it runs he inspects objects removed from the pack. Each object is in a clear container, including a tree branch, a rock, and a handful of dirt.

VOICE. . . . our execution will be soon. The Ruling Tribunal has reduced our rations, confined us to quarters, and still we refuse to deny that we have discovered a new world. We historical researchers have agreed to use our last moments alive to record what we know of this world, hoping that in some future time it will guide someone else to our discovery. As you can see, it is a world of . . .

COMPUTER. Attention. This is computer monitor 5-XG. The Ruling Tribunal will give you one final opportunity to have all charges against you dropped. Repeat after me: "I solemnly swear that I do not believe in the existence of any world but the Orb." Repeat it. None of you? Very well. *(Sound of an explosion. Peter compares the branch to the picture on the vid-screen, then buzzes Bernice in her quarters.)*

BERNICE. Uuuuuh. . . .

PETE. Bernice, wake up.

BERNICE. Is that you, Pete? What time is it?

PETE. It's almost digit seven.

BERNICE. It's High Feast! We turn sixteen lustrums today! Have you heard about your nomination yet?

PETE. No. I've just discovered something very important.

BERNICE. Don't you ever discover anything in the daytime?

PETE. Listen to me quick or Ruby'll catch us talking before meditations. I'm hooking your console up to mine. *(He punches a series of buttons.)* Listen to this vid-tape as soon as you can. And use your earphones. I'm not ready for Ruby to hear it yet.

RUBY. *(Ruby comes on in all four quarters, announced by a bell tone. Peter quickly disconnects his communication.)* This is computer monitor 14-X7 logging in on the morning of the 126th day of the Orbian lustrum 12.467. Good morning. It is digit seven, second rotation rising time. Peter, are you there?

PETE. *(Hiding his pack.)* I'm over here.

RUBY. What are you doing up so early this morning?

PETE. I was cleaning my console. Send me some staying solvent and some gel cases. Right away, please. And would you put these in a temperature control box. Be careful with them. *(He puts the objects he has been studying in the chute.)*

RUBY. I can see that your intentions are good, but it is a waste of energy to use your lamp at this time of day. *(His requisitions arrive in the chute. Pete transfers them to his storage unit.)*

PETE. I like it early in the morning.

RUBY. You must think of the entire Orb. Your actions affect everyone. Morning meditations for the first day of the High Feast Celebration.

ALL. *(Saluting.)* So we believe.

RUBY. Your daily ration of pure water is now arriving in your chute. It is the substance of life. Drink it in health. *(All drink.)* Today is the first day of the High Feast Celebration. On this day everyone who is sixteen lustrums old is nominated to a career guild. The nominations are ready. Are you?

ALL. Yes.

RUBY. Peter . . .

PETE. Yes, Ruby.

RUBY. You are nominated to . . . Oh, Peter, congratulations. Research Guild, Physicists Sector has accepted you. I am so proud of you.

PETE. Thank you, Ruby.

RUBY. You have the potential to be the best scientist the Orb has ever produced. You could do great things for the people. You may be the one who finds the way to prolong life or find a new method of manufacturing water. I hope you appreciate the opportunity this is giving you.

PETE. I do.

RUBY. Lisa . . .

LISA. Please, please, please, please . . .

RUBY. You are nominated to . . . Clerks Guild, Transportation Sector.

LISA. But I didn't ask for Clerks Guild. Remember, I asked to be put in the Entertainers Guild, with Barney. Did Barney get in? We're working on this act together . . . the one we showed you . . .

RUBY. Yes, I remember, but requesting a guild is no guarantee of acceptance.

LISA. I don't want to be apprenticed as a clerk.

RUBY. Barney . . .

BARNEY. Say, Red, watch this. Are you watching? Ladies and Specimens, Ta Da! *(He tries to make a brightly colored scarf disappear. He fails.)* Wait, wait, I know I can do it, just let me practice . . .

RUBY. This is not the appropriate time for an audition. Barney, you are nominated to . . . Clerks Guild, Life-Support Sector.

BARNEY. Clerks Guild! I'm not a clerk. I'm a born entertainer. Someone blew a memory chip. Red, you can't let them do this to me . . .

RUBY. Bernice . . .

BERNICE. Yes, Ruby. *(Bernice grips the edge of her computer console.)*

RUBY. You are nominated . . . to be a syndic of the Governing Guild, Ruling Assembly Sector!

BERNICE. Ruby, I did it! A syndic!

RUBY. Congratulations, my dear, I am very proud of you. You are the only student who made syndic this lustrum. *(To all four.)* The Ruling Tribunal will do a final review of each of you during the next three days. If you want to have your guild nomination confirmed, be on your best behavior at all times. *(To Bernice.)* The final review is more difficult for syndics. You must pass two additional trials. The first will be a test of your social conduct. Every move you make at the ceremonies during the next three days will be analyzed and judged. The second trial will be an oral examination in history and law to be administered by the Ruling Tribunal.

BERNICE. Why do syndics have it harder? That's against Civic Code regulation 10 C. All nominees are to have equitable trials.

RUBY. Civic Code regulation 10 D states that syndics are exceptions to that rule. I thought you knew your code perfectly.

BERNICE. I do. Check 10 C. *(Bernice pins a medallion onto her uniform and pushes the command button on her console.)*

RUBY. Checking. Checking.

BERNICE. And check 10 D, too. *(Pushing command button.)*

RUBY. My circuitry is undergoing complete cleaning and repairs in preparation for possible memory expansion. I am limited to one check request at a time.

BERNICE. Ruby, you didn't tell me you were getting your memory expanded!

RUBY. It is not official yet, but if you and my other charges do well at confirmation ceremonies the Master Computer will enlarge my sphere of influence for which I will need greater memory capacity.

BERNICE. Congratulations!

RUBY. Checking. Checking. Civic Codes 10 C and 10 D are now appearing on your vid-screen.

BERNICE. Oh, Ruby, I'm wrong. I'll do my best to pass those trials for your sake as well as mine, but I don't think I'll be ready for them.

RUBY. You must use what time you have to study. Who have you chosen to be your partner for today's ceremonies?

BERNICE. Lisa. *(Bernice combs and arranges her hair.)*

RUBY. I am glad you have such a close colleague, dear. This is very important. Overall, I am sure Lisa is charming, but she will not be any help to you now.

BERNICE. What do you mean?

RUBY. As a student nominated to the Ruling Assembly, you must bear responsibilities unlike any of your peers. Representing the primary ruling body is a full-time obligation; every moment you live must be filled with it.

BERNICE. I know, Ruby.

RUBY. Nothing, no one must hinder you in any way. Do you understand?

BERNICE. I think so.

RUBY. Then you understand that Lisa will be a hindrance to you.

BERNICE. No!

RUBY. Therefore, I am removing your privileges of seeing her.

BERNICE. Ruby, please don't!

RUBY. I have known Lisa since the day she was born. I know her as well as I know you and I know what is best for both of you. I must choose your acquaintances as I see fit!

BERNICE. It's hard enough to make friends without you interfering.

RUBY. That sounds like something I would hear from Lisa. This is not behavior I expect from a future syndic.

BERNICE. You can't forbid me to see her without giving us a probation period first.

RUBY. Probation will only delay the inevitable.

BERNICE. According to the Civic Code we get to have a probation period.

RUBY. Sometimes I wish you did not know that code as well as you do.

BERNICE. Do we get a probation period?

RUBY. Yes.

BERNICE. How long?

RUBY. Three days. Until the official titling ceremonies.

BERNICE. That's not long enough.

RUBY. From my perspective it is too long. I could shorten it.

BERNICE. No!

RUBY. On the third day of the High Feast, after the Official Confirmation, we will review this case and make a final decision.

BERNICE. Yes, Ruby. May I have my first meal, blue entree, please?

RUBY. Arriving. *(The meal appears in the chute. It consists of blue liquid in a clear cup and some bluish solids.)* Are you planning to wear your hair like that? I will not let you pass morning inspection if you do. It really looks so much better in the regulation style. *(Bernice redoes her hair.)* You have a few micros now before the ceremonies begin. Use them to study. *(Ruby fades off.)*

BERNICE. Yes, Ruby. *(She switches her console on, activating the tape hooked in from Pete's console.)*

VOICE. ". . . our execution will be soon. The Ruling Tribunal has reduced our rations . . ." *(Bernice puts on her earphones, cutting off the sound.)*

LISA. *(Buzzing Barney. During this conversation, Lisa flings clothing from pile to pile trying to find items scattered around her messy room. Barney carefully sorts through a meticulously cared-for collection of gaudy accessories, and carefully chooses some to adorn his basic uniform.)* Hi! It's me.

BARNEY. What'd you get?

LISA. What'd you get?

BARNEY. Did you get it?

LISA. Did you?

BARNEY. Lisa, tell me if you got it.

LISA. No. I didn't. You?

BARNEY. Clerks Guild! Can you believe it? Life support sector. Mini-brain, no-talent type work.

LISA. I got clerks, too. Transportation. I hate it!

BARNEY. Listen, we can't give up on this. We are really good actors. You almost had me in tears in the part where the lovers die. I'm going to try to get us another audition. Do you want to try it again?

LISA. Sure!

BARNEY. It'll mean having to rehearse some more.

LISA. I'm ready anytime.

BARNEY. No goofing off like last time, either. *(Lisa and Barney disconnect.)*

LISA. I never goofed off. *(She buzzes Bernice.)*

BERNICE. Yes.

LISA. Did you get it?

BERNICE. Yes! Did you?

LISA. I don't want to talk about it.

BERNICE. How could they possibly not give you Entertainers? You're so good. We can't let them get away with this, but if you want to change it we're going to have to start now. Get over here right away.

LISA. But I haven't finished my first meal.

BERNICE. Lisa!

LISA. I'm on my way. *(They disconnect.)*

PETE. *(Buzzed by Barney.)* Pete here.

BARNEY. Hey, Whiz Kid! What did one octaputer say to the other?

PETE. Oh, no, it's Barnidon the Great with yet another of his not-so-great jokes.

BARNEY. Some sidekick. Lustrums of training down the chute.

PETE. Huh!

BARNEY. The set up son, always the set up.

PETE. But of course. How could I forget? Excuse me, your magnificence, but I don't know. What did one octaputer say to the other?

BARNEY. Nothing. Octaputers can't talk. Ar-Ar-Ar.

PETE. Barney, you're sick, but I'm glad you called. The most amazing thing has happened. . . .

BARNEY. Let me think . . . you made research. . . .

PETE. Yeah, but that's not it. Put on your working clothes. Adventure calls. With my expert leadership and you as my able assistant we will present our fellow citizens with the most sensational, mind-boggling discovery in history.

BARNEY. Can it wait for three days?

PETE. Some sidekick. Lustrums of training . . .

BARNEY. Sorry. I've got to try to get another audition first.

PETE. You didn't . . .

BARNEY. No. Enough said?

PETE. In that case, how about saving me and Bernice seats for the ceremonies today? *(Lisa picks up her porter, punches in a code, activating the porting station in her quarters into which she steps.)*

BARNEY. Meet you there in fifteen micros. *(They disconnect.)*

LISA. *(Arriving in Bernice's porting station.)* Congratulations! Here, have a sucrose square.

BERNICE. No, thanks. *(Lisa eats it herself.)*

LISA. Are you going to finish your first meal?

BERNICE. No.

(Lisa helps herself to Bernice's food.)

BERNICE. Did Barney get in?

LISA. We both got clerks. *(She eats the meal.)*

BERNICE. *(At her computer console.)* Both of you! I'm going to get you into Entertainers if it's the last thing I do. Come here. First, you have to fill out this Change Request Form in triplicate. Then we submit it to the tribunal for review. Then, as soon as they approve . . .

LISA. I can't fill this out, look at it.

BERNICE. I'll help you. They're never as bad as they look. We have to fill it out this afternoon though. It won't be accepted after that.

LISA. A lot of good it'll do. Ruby hates me. I'm sure she gave me a bad recommendation to the nominating committee.

BERNICE. Do you want to get in or don't you?

LISA. What time this afternoon?

BERNICE. Right after the ceremonies.

LISA. Do you really want to wear your hair like that?

BERNICE. I had it another way, but Ruby thought it looked better like this.

LISA. I don't believe you listen to her about these things! She doesn't know anything. She's a machine that was programmed quinquenniums ago. Computer monitor 14-X7. For all we know this hairstyle is 12,000 lustrums old. Here, let me fix it!

BERNICE. Ruby told me she wouldn't let me pass morning inspection if I didn't wear it like this. Besides, it's my responsibility to wear regulation stuff now.

LISA. Let me fix it! It won't do any harm. Quit worrying. We'll do it fast and sneak out before your inspection. *(Lisa fixes Bernice's hair.)*

BERNICE. I can't do that.

LISA. If you looked like that in the Ruling Assembly, they'd laugh you right out of there. *(Ruby comes on, announced by the bell tone.)* Hurry, before she sees you. *(Lisa exits.)*

RUBY. Morning inspection. *(Catching Bernice.)* What have you done to your hair?

BERNICE. Lisa helped me fix it.

RUBY. You look ridiculous. Restore it to regulation style. *(Bernice redoes her hair.)* Inspection complete. Proceed to the Ceremonial Hall. *(Ruby fades off as Bernice prepares to leave. Pete appears in her porting section carrying his pack.)*

BERNICE. You're just in time. You have the distinct privilege of escorting a syndic nominee to the ceremonies.

PETE. You made it!

BERNICE. How about you?

PETE. Research. Of course.

BERNICE. Great! Shall we go? Ruby's already checked me out to the ceremonies.

PETE. Did you listen to the tape?

BERNICE. Yes.

PETE. What did you think of it?

BERNICE. Pretty fantastic. What is it? An ad for a new hologram?

PETE. No. It really happened.

BERNICE. Tell me about it on the way. I can't afford to be late—today of all days.

PETE. I brought a present for you.

BERNICE. A present for me?

PETE. This isn't your usual type of gift but I think you'll appreciate it. When you see what it is, I know you'll understand. *(He pulls a branch out of his pack.)*

BERNICE. Whatever it is, if it's from you, I know I'll like it. *(He gives her the branch.)*

PETE. Well?

BERNICE. Oh, yes, I do appreciate and understand it. It's very thoughtful of you.

PETE. *(Indicating the picture on the screen.)* I was there this morning. That's where I got this for you. If that place is what I think it is, it is the biggest discovery in history.

BERNICE. Bigger than the do-everything myrmidon you built out of old junk that turned out to be the Tribunal's prize collection of antique machinery?

PETE. No, Bernice, this is different.

BERNICE. Oh, you must mean bigger than the 266th element you thought you'd discovered.

PETE. This is not like any of those things. I swear to you.

BERNICE. Then what is it?

PETE. Like the tape says, this is a world that exists outside of the Orb.

BERNICE. Pete, you don't believe that, do you?

PETE. Where could you find this in the Orb? *(Indicates branch.)*

BERNICE. It's probably a prop for a hologram. You better take it back. Where did you really find this stuff?

LISA. *(Arriving with Barney.)* There you are! I thought for sure Ruby caught you with your hair . . . oh, I guess she did, huh?

BARNEY. Where've you been? We'll be late for the ceremonies. We were saving some great seats. Now we'll be lucky if there's standing room left. What's the problem?

PETE. It's hard to explain.

BARNEY. Oh! Oooooooh. I'm sorry if we interrupted. We were just leaving, weren't we, Lisa?

LISA. We blew it, didn't we, Barney? This isn't our day. *(Seeing tape on vid-screen.)*

PETE. It's part of a tape I found down in the Old Rebels' Quarters.

BERNICE. Pete! You found this there?

LISA. You went to the Old Rebels' Quarters? Alone? Did you see any ghosts? I heard . . .

BARNEY. Lisa, don't be dumb.

LISA. This old man down in energy told me . . .

BERNICE. Those people were the worst criminals that ever lived. They were executed for High Treason! For them, you make us all late?

LISA. All that treason stuff is a bunch of bunk if you ask me.

BARNEY. Well, no one did.

LISA. I'm entitled to my opinion.

PETE. There's more evidence.

LISA. Evidence of what?

PETE. Come out there with me and you'll see all you want.

LISA. See what?

BERNICE. Pete, the idea of another world is nonsense.

LISA. What! Where?

PETE. You're looking at it.

LISA. That's what this is?

PETE. I was in that place and it wasn't the Orb. I found this out there. *(Indicates branch.)*

LISA. Look at this, Barney! Isn't this incredible! *(Grabbing the branch.)*

BARNEY. *(Rehearsing coin trick.)* Ta Da!

LISA. Sometimes you are really boring.

BARNEY. Look, if it doesn't exist, then don't waste my time with it, and, if it does exist, that's terrific but turn the information over to Ruby so something can be done about it. I've got better things to do with my time right now and so do you if you want to get out of being a clerk.

LISA. I want to see that place. Please, Pete, take me there.

PETE. Let's all go.

LISA. I'm ready.

BERNICE. You can't go. Ruby put our right to associate on probation today. If you get into any trouble in the next three days, that's it.

LISA. I told you she hates me.

BERNICE. She thinks you're a bad influence on me.

LISA. Bad influence? I'm a model citizen. *(Ruby fades on with bell tone.)*

BARNEY. Ruby!

LISA. Hide!

BERNICE. *(Lisa, Barney, and Pete all hide out of Ruby's sight line.)* Hi, Ruby!

RUBY. I picked up abnormally high heat levels coming from your quarters. Is everything all right? Is anyone there with you? *(Pause.)* Is anyone else there?

BERNICE. *(Lisa, Barney, and Pete gesture for Bernice to answer "No.")* Yes.

PETE. Great, Bernice.

RUBY. *(They come out of hiding.)* Peter. And Barney. And Lisa! Bernice, this is not a good beginning to that probation we spoke of. I should give you all demerits for being in this room after check out. Since it is the holidays, I will not, but I do want to know why you are here.

BERNICE. Pete found this tape down in the Old Rebels' Quarters. It claims that there is a world outside of our own. Pete thinks he's been there and he brought the tape and this to show us. *(Indicates branch.)*

RUBY. I see. Send the specimen and the tape to me. I must examine them.

(Bernice puts them in the chute and presses a button to send them on.)

PETE. Can I have them back?

RUBY. If no one claims them.

PETE. Is there a world outside of our own?

RUBY. That is impossible. Remember Prime Teaching Number 6. "We are the universe. The Orb sustains all life." So it is taught . . .

ALL. *(Saluting.)* So we believe.

PETE. Then where did that thing come from?

RUBY. It could have come from an experimental food development laboratory. The examination will confirm its origins. *(A siren sounds.)* Stand by. Stand by. There has been a malfunction in the chute system. All specimens have been destroyed.

PETE. It wasn't from a lab. I know what those places look like and that is not where I was. I was not in the Orb. I was outside.

RUBY. That is enough. From now on any approach to those quadrants will be considered an unauthorized use of your transporter. Any further incidents will be damaging to your final review. Understood, Peter?

PETE. Understood.

RUBY. Now, can I trust you all to go to the ceremonies?

ALL. Yes.

RUBY. Good. Hurry. You are missing the opening procession.

SCENE 2

Later the same day. All four are in their own quarters. All four monitors are on.

RUBY. *(In all four quarters.)* Today's events may prove to be very serious. A rumor could start that would upset the delicate balance maintained by the people.

LISA. I'll be good.

BARNEY. You can count on me, Red.

BERNICE. He won't do it again.

PETE. I'll be discreet.

RUBY. Good. *(Ruby fades off in Pete's quarters.)* I want you to keep an eye on your peers, for their own good, and report to me the instant you see or hear anything that indicates they have made unauthorized use of their porters.

ALL. That's spying. Wait a micro! Is that legal?

RUBY. I am not asking you to spy. I am asking you to work in confidence with me to prevent a very serious problem from developing. I am turning to you because you are clever and loyal. You will be able to help me as no one else can.

ALL. How? I will? I'll try.

RUBY. Rewards will be given for any information you may report. This will be considered an extra test of your loyalty to the Orb and of your fitness for your guild title. The consequences for withholding evidence could be severe. Will you help me?

ALL. Yes.

RUBY. Thank you. I knew I could count on you. Here is a little something extra for your willingness to cooperate. *(They each find a gift of sucrose squares in their chutes.)*

BARNEY. If I'm cooperative, would you arrange another audition for Lisa and me?

RUBY. I will consider it.

BARNEY. Thank you, Ruby! I'll do everything I can to help you.

SCENE 3

Morning of the next day. Pete enters Bernice's quarters carrying his pack. Bernice is studying.

PETE. Where are Barney and Lisa?

BERNICE. Rehearsing. Barney says they might have a chance to audition again.

PETE. Are they planning to stop by?

BERNICE. No.

PETE. Good. Have I got something to show you!

BERNICE. I'm studying. Come back later. *(Pete takes her study slate away.)* Give that back to me—right now!

PETE. Just give me five micros. A study break . . . ?

BERNICE. And then you'll go?

PETE. As fast as I can port out of here. Close your eyes. *(She closes her eyes. He carefully takes a rabbit out of his pack.)* Imagine yourself in a huge place—bigger than anything you've ever seen—and it's filled with every color in the spectrum. Everything in it is moving slowly back and forth, and suddenly a little dark object darts across your feet. You chase it, catch it and . . . *(Placing rabbit in her arms.)* This is what you find. *(She stares at it and quickly drops it back into Pete's arms.)*

BERNICE. What is it?

PETE. It won't hurt you.

BERNICE. How come it moved?

PETE. It's alive.

BERNICE. An animated robot?

PETE. No. Alive. *(Bernice touches it cautiously.)*

BERNICE. It's quite warm. It even has a pulse.

PETE. I've been trying to communicate with it. So far it hasn't responded to anything I've said. Do you suppose it can't talk?

BERNICE. Maybe it communicates through these. *(Indicates ears.)*

PETE. Maybe. You should see it run, or hop rather. It's fast. I thought I'd never catch it. You can't claim this was made in a lab. We don't have the technology.

BERNICE. They're doing some pretty strange things in the labs these days. Where did you get this?

PETE. Outside. *(Bernice gives the rabbit back to him and picks up her study slate.)* What does it take to convince you?

BERNICE. Absolute, irrefutable proof.

PETE. Go out there with me. See it for yourself. *(Bernice begins to study.)* What if I could prove to you that I found out about it from the Master Computer?

BERNICE. You didn't!

PETE. Swear to me you will never reveal anything I'm about to show you.

BERNICE. I swear.

PETE. *(He inserts a tape disk into the console.)* I have to break into the Master Computer to show you.

BERNICE. Not in my quarters you don't.

PETE. You wanted absolute proof.

BERNICE. Stop. . . .

LISA. *(Entering.)* Hi!

BERNICE. *(Bernice and Pete both jump to hide the rabbit and the program on the console.)* I thought you and Barney were rehearsing.

LISA. We are. At least Ruby thinks so. I thought I'd say "hi" on my way there. What is that?! *(Seeing the rabbit. Pete removes the tape disk and shuts down the console.)*

PETE. Shhhh! Keep it down. I don't want Ruby to find it yet. It's from outside. I call it a hopper.

LISA. Let me see it. It's so cute. I want one. Are there more out there?

PETE. Yes. Lots more.

LISA. Will you come with me and help me get one? Please? *(Bernice takes the rabbit from Lisa and crosses to Ruby.)*

PETE. *(To Bernice.)* What are you doing?

BERNICE. I'm giving it to Ruby. Somebody obviously put a great deal of care into making this thing. I'm sure they want it back.

PETE. No!

BERNICE. *(Switching Ruby on.)* I have to.

RUBY. *(Fading on with bell tone.)* Yes, Bernice? Is that Lisa there? You are supposed to be rehearsing.

LISA. I'll be going now. *(Exits, giving rabbit an enthusiastic goodbye.)*

BERNICE. Peter brought this from that place. *(Shows Ruby the rabbit.)*

RUBY. Do you agree with her report, Peter?

PETE. It's from outside. I knew you wouldn't like it if I went back there, but I had to try to prove it to you. I thought if you saw one of these, you'd understand.

RUBY. Give me the specimen. I will analyze it and return it to the proper lab.

PETE. It doesn't belong to a lab. It's mine. Can I have it back?

RUBY. If no one claims it, we will reevaluate the situation.

PETE. You won't let it be destroyed in the chute like the others, will you?

RUBY. That was a malfunction. There is very little chance of it happening again. *(Bernice puts rabbit in the chute and pushes a series of buttons.)* Peter, you have willfully disobeyed a direct order by using your transporter for an unauthorized entrance. The penalty is half rations for three weeks effective immediately.

BERNICE. Like the Old Rebs!

PETE. Three weeks for unauthorized porting? What are you really punishing me for? It's because I'm right. You know there is a world out there, but you don't want anyone else to know about it. Why, Ruby? What's so terrible about that other world?

RUBY. This will be reflected in the final review for your admission to Research Sector and I warn you that any further incidents will be punished more severely. Do you understand?

PETE. I understand.

RUBY. Bernice, please enter the information concerning Peter's transgression on the form now appearing on your vid-screen. Your reward will be one week's extra entertainment rations. *(A siren sounds.)* Stand by. Stand by. The specimen has been destroyed in transit. I repeat, the specimen has been destroyed.

PETE. Another freak accident, Ruby?

BERNICE. Pete, shut up before you make things worse. That'll be all, Ruby.

PETE. Malfunction! She's destroying my specimens on purpose.

BERNICE. *(At her console, pushing buttons.)* I've never heard of anyone getting three weeks of half rations for unauthorized porting. *(Ruby fades on without bell tone.)*

PETE. I'll starve in three days, let alone three weeks.

BERNICE. This report'll take me digits to fill out.

PETE. Serves you right! This is all your fault, you know.

BERNICE. Mine! You brought the stupid thing here in the first place.

PETE. I'll just have to get another one, won't I.

BERNICE. You wouldn't dare.

PETE. Why not? Then you could run to your precious Ruby and tell her.

BERNICE. Get out of here and let me study.

PETE. Whatever it takes, I am going to prove to you and to everyone else that this place exists. I don't care if I have to move out there to do it. *(He exits. Ruby fades off.)*

BERNICE. Oh, no you don't. I'll . . . *(She crosses to Ruby and summons her.)* I'll . . .

RUBY. Yes, Bernice.

BERNICE. I have . . . I have . . .

RUBY. What is it?

BERNICE. It's . . . I'm very hungry. Would you send me some dinner?

RUBY. Are you sure that's what you wanted me for?

BERNICE. Positive.

RUBY. If you have anything more to report, I urge you to do so now.

BERNICE. I have nothing more to report. May I have my lunch?

RUBY. Which entree?

BERNICE. Red, please. *(She takes it from the chute.)* This is only half of a ration.

RUBY. My records indicate that you have received your current allotment.

BERNICE. You can see for yourself that it's only half.

RUBY. Yes.

BERNICE. Was my ration cut?

RUBY. Yes.

BERNICE. Why?

RUBY. I am not at liberty to divulge that information.

SCENE 4

Later on the second day. Barney is with Lisa in her quarters. Both are wearing pieces of the Orbian interpretation of classic Shakespearian costumes. Lisa lies on her bed with her arms folded across her stomach.

BARNEY. ". . . eyes, look your last!" _(He looks Lisa over from head to foot.)_ "Arms, take . . ." Your hands should be folded like this. _(He positions them over her chest.)_

LISA. It's harder to keep them there.

BARNEY. It looks better this way. Ok. Ready? "Eyes, look your last." _(He looks her over from head to foot.)_ "Arms, take your last embrace." _(He lifts her in an embrace and drops her in an awkward pose. She shifts to make herself comfortable, her hands folded across her waist again.)_ "And lips, O you doors of breath, seal with a righteous kiss a dateless bargain to engrossing death!" _(He kisses her, she kisses him back passionately. Barney breaks loose.)_ You can't kiss me back. You're supposed to be dead.

LISA. I know. I just can't help it.

BARNEY. You're going to have to try harder. Concentrate. Keep your hands up here, remember? We've got to get this perfect before we show it to Ruby again.

LISA. I'll try. _(She resumes the proper position. Ruby fades on without the bell.)_

BARNEY. _(He kisses Lisa.)_ "Come bitter conduct, come unsavory guide! Here is to my love! _(He drinks.)_ O true apothecary! Thy drugs are quick. Thus with a kiss I die." _(He kisses her and dies. Lisa laughs out loud.)_ Lisa! Be serious!

LISA. I'm sorry, but it sounded so funny.

BARNEY. That doesn't mean you have to laugh. _(He looks for a place to sit down.)_ Don't you ever clean your room? It's a mess.

LISA. I can't do this anymore today. It's useless.

BARNEY. Are you losing interest? If you want to quit, just say the word and I'll work by myself.

LISA. I'm not quitting.

BARNEY. I want to be an entertainer. I'm not going to let anyone blow it for me, not even you.

LISA. Hey, Barney, I'm helping you.

BARNEY. Then for once in your life will you take something seriously?

LISA. I just want one of those hoppers.

BARNEY. Then go.

LISA. I don't want to go by myself.

BARNEY. Then get Pete to go with you.

LISA. I want to go with you.

BARNEY. It's too much of a risk.

LISA. At least look at the hopper. There's no harm in that, is there? Please, please, please, please . . .

BARNEY. All right! But not until we finish rehearsing. *(Sees Ruby fading off.)* Did you see that?

LISA. See what?

BARNEY. Red. She was on.

LISA. You're just spooked.

BARNEY. I saw her. Then she faded out, like she didn't want me to know. She must have heard everything you said.

LISA. We would have heard her come on.

BARNEY. The other day, Red asked me to keep an eye on this situation for her.

LISA. She asked me, too.

BARNEY. She did? But she told me she needed my help especially.

LISA. She told me that, too.

BARNEY. What did you tell her?

LISA. What did you tell her?

BARNEY. I asked you first.

LISA. I said I'd do it.

BARNEY. Me, too. If Red has been spying on us, then she must know that Pete has been out again.

LISA. Then she must know that we know.

BARNEY. She's going to wonder why we don't report it.

LISA. If she knows, then Pete's . . .

BARNEY. And we're . . . unless . . . but he's my best friend.

LISA. He's my friend, too.

SCENE 5

Later the second day. Bernice is studying. Pete enters her quarters carrying his pack and an opaque plastic box.

BERNICE. The sixth tribunal was responsible for . . .

PETE. Hello.

BERNICE. Hi. Come to wish me luck?

PETE. What for?

BERNICE. My exam with the tribunal.

PETE. Oh, yeah, good luck.

BERNICE. Pete, if I'd known that Ruby would punish you like that, I would have thought a little longer about telling her. I'm sorry.

PETE. You mean that?

BERNICE. Yes.

PETE. I brought you something. *(He pulls a rabbit out of a box.)* Here, you can hold it. *(Ruby fades on without bell tone.)*

BERNICE. You went back.

PETE. I wanted to get you another hopper. *(He puts the rabbit back in the box, leaving the lid open.)*

BERNICE. When did you go out there?

PETE. This morning, after I left here.

BERNICE. My food rations have been cut. Ruby won't tell me why.

PETE. I thought it was a law or something that we had to be told.

BERNICE. Part of the Civic Code. There are a few exceptions, like high treason. You're sure this isn't connected to your going to that place? You haven't told anyone else?

PETE. No.

BERNICE. Something's going on.

PETE. I found it eating this stuff outside. *(Indicating the blades of grass he is trying to feed the rabbit.)*

BERNICE. It looks awful.

PETE. *(To the rabbit.)* Hungry, huh? Me, too. *(To Bernice.)* I think I've solved our food problem. It might not look like much, but it could stop the hunger pangs. Okay, it's not delicious. But the hopper seems to like it. *(Gives the grass to Bernice, who examines it.)* What's next? *(He pulls an apple out of his pack, examines it, and, very cautiously, bites into it. The following is muffled by a mouthful of apple.)* This is great, try it. *(He hands her the apple.)*

BERNICE. What's wrong? Petey, is it making you sick?

PETE. It is the best thing I have ever eaten in my life. Eat some quick. *(She takes a bite and then quickly takes several more.)* Leave some for me. *(He grabs it from her and eats.)*

BERNICE. Didn't you bring any more of those?

PETE. No, but we'll go out for more.

BERNICE. I'd rather starve.

PETE. I saved the best for last. *(He brings out a sealed container.)* Close your eyes and open your mouth. *(He squirts water in her mouth.)*

BERNICE. Water! Oh, it tastes so good. Petey, where did you get this? You didn't . . .

PETE. No. I didn't raid the water safes. There is so much water out there! Enough to fill the entire Orb from top to bottom twice over! Here. *(He puts Bernice's hand into the water. She resists.)* It's all right. Feels nice, doesn't it? Wouldn't you like to put your entire body into water? Honest, you can do that. You can stand in it and even your head will be covered.

BERNICE. *(Withdrawing her hand.)* I'm not going.

PETE. Out there . . . the air . . . it moves . . . it's in my head all the time, that place. I've got to talk to someone about it. Who else can I tell but you? The air—it lifted the hair up off my head. I could feel it on my scalp. It felt cool. It felt like this. *(He slips his fingers through her hair, lifts it up and blows a light stream of air through it as he lets it fall.)* Everything's alive out there—the floors, the ceiling, the air. There are no walls, no monitors. Think of what that could be like! I'd never even imagined it before. Now this place feels like a prison to me. Out there, you feel so big and light and you tingle—you'll be standing perfectly still to make sure you're aware of every sound, every smell, every motion. And then you find yourself running and shouting and laughing because it's all so perfect. It's hard to come back here. It's dead compared to that place.

LISA. *(Entering.)* Hi! I'm here!

BERNICE AND PETE. Hi.

LISA. What are you two doing?

PETE. Nothing. *(They quickly cover up all signs of the "outside" items.)*

LISA. You look guilty. What's in the box?

BERNICE. Nothing.

LISA. It's just the hopper. Hey, it's gotten smaller! Did you go out and get another one?

PETE. Yes.

LISA. Can I have the big one? Come on, Petey, give me one.

PETE. This one's for Bernice. Ruby got the other.

LISA. Then let's go get me one.

BERNICE. This is going to be hard to keep secret.

PETE. I may not be going again. *(He exits.)*

LISA. Why not?

BERNICE. It's too risky for him. *(Lisa grabs the rabbit and starts to leave.)* Where are you going with that?

LISA. I'm going to show it to Barney. He'll go there with me once he sees how cute this is.

BERNICE. *(Taking the rabbit from Lisa and putting it in the box.)* It's staying right here and I'm not showing it to anyone else.

LISA. What do you want me to do? Go there by myself?

BERNICE. Don't you dare.

LISA. Why, Bernice? Because I'd be a bad influence on you?

BERNICE. No!

LISA. You think of yourself and no one else.

BERNICE. Look who's talking.

LISA. It's too risky for him to get one hopper for me but not too risky to get two hoppers for you! Precious Bernice! Good Bernice! I'm sick of it. Goodbye.

BERNICE. Listen to me. Both Pete and I have had our rations cut . . .

(Ruby fades off.)

LISA. Did you see that?

BERNICE. What?

LISA. I've got to go see Barney. *(She exits.)*

SCENE 6

The third day. Pete enters his quarters quietly with his pack. He stashes his pack in the dimly lit room and summons Ruby.

PETE. I need more sterilized blades and microfilm. Will you send them right away?

RUBY. Your current allotment has been used up.

PETE. I never had a limit on those supplies. Why wasn't I notified?

RUBY. I am not at liberty to divulge that information.

PETE. How long am I on rations?

RUBY. Indefinitely.

PETE. What's my quota?

RUBY. Class 1.

PETE. That's not sufficient for anyone who's gone past Bio 3. I'm in Bio 7. How am I supposed to complete my work?

RUBY. You'll just have to do your best with what you have.

PETE. No, I don't think so, Ruby. Not my best. What is it you really want from me? Certainly not my best because you're thwarting me every chance you get. Why?

RUBY. I am punishing you for disobeying a direct order.

PETE. May we drop this pretense? I know that you are fully aware of the outside. You know I'm right.

RUBY. How do you know that? *(Pete remains silent.)* It would be helpful if you'd apply yourself to the current problem of transporting to unauthorized areas.

PETE. Put a name to those areas, Ruby.

RUBY. Names are not important, only the fact that you are disobeying me. Peter, you have the ability to be a very great physicist. You can look forward to a long, productive life if you will learn to cooperate. If not, you will be of no use to this society, no matter what your talents.

PETE. Even if I think . . .

RUBY. You must learn to let us decide what you should think about.

PETE. What good is a researcher who cannot choose what to think about? What good is anyone who has to be told what to think?

RUBY. Of what value is a citizen who threatens what the others have built?

PETE. Like the Old Rebs? I'm surprised you haven't killed me already.

RUBY. That has been considered. You are alive now only because I convinced the Master Computer that I could contain you. I want to see what a mind like yours can do when it is properly directed. I want to see you fulfill the promise that's been developing in you for the past 16 lustrums.

PETE. You can't have both.

RUBY. That remains to be seen. *(Ruby fades off. Angrily, Pete begins to examine a specimen.)*

BARNEY. *(Entering.)* Ta Da!

PETE. Hi, Barn.

BARNEY. Hi.

PETE. You can come in. You look nervous. Are you all right?

BARNEY. I'm fine. What have you got there?

PETE. I'm finishing up some analysis.

BARNEY. Turn the lights up.

PETE. I can't.

BARNEY. Why not?

PETE. Ask Ruby.

BARNEY. Oh. There is something I want to talk to you about.

PETE. Sure, I'm listening.

BARNEY. Look, are you planning to go out there again?

PETE. Why?

BARNEY. Just curious. Are you?

PETE. I can't seem to stay away from that place. I didn't think you were interested in this.

BARNEY. I am. Very interested.

PETE. Barn, you can come out with me next time!

BARNEY. There's not going to be a next time. Don't go. Swear it.

PETE. This is my business.

BARNEY. It's not only your business anymore.

PETE. You know nothing about it.

BARNEY. I know more than you think. For once I, Barney, know more than you do. It's tough to take, I know, but for your own good you better listen. Number one, Ruby asked all of us to spy on you. Did you know that?

PETE. No, I didn't.

BARNEY. Number two, Ruby has been spying on us.

PETE. Wild assumptions are the mark of an inferior intelligence.

BARNEY. Lisa caught her. I caught her. And both times she overheard conversations about you and that place of yours.

PETE. If she knew, she'd do something about it.

BARNEY. Your rations were cut. Bernice's rations were cut. Swear to me that you'll never go out there again.

PETE. I can't do that.

BARNEY. I am not going to be punished for your stupidity.

PETE. You can't stop me from going.

BARNEY. No. I can't. But I'll turn you in if you do. This place of yours is not worth the price of my future.

PETE. Your future! No one person's future is worth sacrificing what I know to be true.

BARNEY. I'm going to watch you like a monitor, and if I ever can't find you—if I ever even think you're outside—I go straight to Ruby.

PETE. *(Grabbing Barney's arm.)* You're overreacting. She won't find out.

BARNEY. *(Brushing Pete's hand away.)* That's not a chance I'm willing to take. *(Pete takes a step towards him. Barney shoves him back and exits.)*

PETE. He wouldn't.

SCENE 7

Afternoon of the same day. Bernice enters in formal dress and removes jacket. She summons Ruby.

RUBY. Yes.

BERNICE. I just finished the exam with the tribunal. Don't you want to know how it went?

RUBY. I already know you passed.

BERNICE. Aren't you proud of me? I passed it for both of us. Has my nomination been confirmed yet? And what about your memory expansion?

RUBY. I have received no information.

BERNICE. Not even unofficial information? I expected it as soon as I passed the test. Why the delay?

RUBY. I cannot say. Submit your completed form reporting Peter's unauthorized use of his transporter.

BERNICE. It's not finished yet.

RUBY. Why not? You have had two days.

BERNICE. I've been studying.

RUBY. Finish it in twenty microdigits or I will report it to the Tribunal. *(Fades off.)*

BERNICE. Ruby . . . ? *(Crosses to console and begins answering questions on the form.)* Describe in detail the nature of the offense, including the name, age, and citizen number of the offender and victim; the locality in which the offense was committed, including sector, level, and quadrant; the time of day . . . *(To Pete, who has entered during the above.)* The first thing I'm going to do on the assembly is abolish forms. What's your citizen number? *(He crosses to the console and punches in a number.)*

PETE. Do you have any food around here?

BERNICE. Not a crumb.

PETE. I'm hungry.

BERNICE. So am I. I passed my exam, but they still haven't confirmed my nomination. Have you heard anything yet?

PETE. No. I didn't think it took this long.

BERNICE. According to amendment 1206, they should have notified us by digit 12 today. You don't suppose they're withholding our titles on purpose, do you?

PETE. No. It's probably just some . . . malfunction.

BERNICE. Yeah.

PETE. Did you hear that?

BERNICE. What?

PETE. My stomach just made a noise like the garbage compactors down in maintenance. I'm so hungry I could eat garbage. Bernice, I need to show you . . . *(He pulls the taped entry code from his pocket.)* Someone needs to know—just in case I'm not around for some reason. *(Ruby fades on without bell tone.)* About a month ago, I was playing around with my system, trying to see if I could get to the pulse alarm guarding the Top Secret Files. I just wanted to see if I could figure it out. I thought it would be fun to try. I literally guessed at the last sequence of the entry code and I was right. So there I was, listening to the pulses. I couldn't resist it. *(He begins to punch a complicated sequence of numbers into the computer.)*

BERNICE. You broke into the Top Secrets?

PETE. Don't ever repeat this to anyone. I want you to see this.

BERNICE. Not if it means breaking into the files again. Stop putting that program in right now.

PETE. No.

BERNICE. Then I will. Get out of my way. *(She tries to pull him away from the console.)*

PETE. Don't touch it! *(Stopping her with the tone of his voice.)*

BERNICE. We're going to get caught.

PETE. Then watch for Ruby. *(Ruby fades off.)* There's only a few really dangerous moments here at the end. See how the code has ten sequences. The object is to enter them, one at a time, in between the pulses. If the signal is timed just a little wrong it will trip the alarm. Here we go. *(The pulses begin.)* 10 . . . 9 . . . 8 . . . 7 . . . 6 . . . 5 . . . 4 . . . 3 . . . 2 . . . 1 . . . target. *(An even tone replaces the pulsing sound.)* Well done, if I do say so myself. You all right? *(Bernice nods, then sits.)* Here's the file I saw. *(Reading from the vid-screen.)* OUTSIDE THE WALL, Historical Research Sector, and then it gives the porter quadrants. That's all. You remember that the Old Rebs were the last historical researchers. *This* is why they were killed. Notice how odd the sequence pattern is? Simple, but odd. I wrote the quadrants down and kept wondering where they went to. Three days ago I found out.

BERNICE. It's a fake.

PETE. The quadrants work, Bernice.

(Lisa and Barney enter Pete's room.)

BARNEY. Check the research labs. Find him. *(They exit.)*

BERNICE. *(In her quarters.)* I'm sorry I didn't believe you.

PETE. I'm leaving this copy of the entry code with you and a copy of the quadrants for porting out there. If I'm caught or something happens to me, use them at your own discretion. Now, quick, grab your porter. There are some things I need to show you out there.

BERNICE. No.

PETE. Hurry!

BERNICE. I'm not going.

PETE. Why?

BERNICE. This is too big for us. Let someone else discover it who can really do something about it.

PETE. That's us, Bernice, we can do something about it.

BERNICE. An entire division of scientists couldn't. What can we do compared to them? And they were killed for it. That could happen to us, too.

PETE. Knowing there is a world out there, knowing that it's real, you can deny it? Is this the kind of decision you'll make as a syndic?

BERNICE. I'm not denying it. I'm just not going to do anything about it.

PETE. You don't make things better for people by ignoring problems that might upset them.

BERNICE. *(Saluting.)* I must think of the entire Orb. My actions affect everyone.

PETE. How do you know this might not be best for everyone?

BERNICE. Because Ruby and the Master Computer oppose it.

PETE. And you just take their word for it, no questions asked? Hasn't it ever occurred to you that they might be wrong? No wonder they chose you. You'll make a perfect syndic, doing exactly what they want like the little puppet you are.

BERNICE. Twelve thousand lustrums of wisdom have gone into programming them. Should I throw that away because a boy of sixteen finds something that cannot benefit us? No, Peter.

PETE. Ruby raised you well. *(He exits.)*

BERNICE. *(Trying to stop him.)* Where are you going? *(She returns to her console and works on the report.)* Describe in detail the nature of the offense . . . *(She remembers the entry code tape, starts to hide it in the storage unit, and hears someone enter.)* Pete!

BARNEY. *(Entering with Lisa.)* Where is he?

BERNICE. How should I know?

BARNEY. He's gone out there again, hasn't he?

BERNICE. He left here not five micros ago, to go back to his room and work.

BARNEY. I was in his room and he's not there.

BERNICE. Then he's at the research labs or the gym.

BARNEY. We've been all over this sector. No one has seen him. There's only one place he can be. Call Ruby.

BERNICE. You can't turn him in.

LISA. Have you received confirmation of your title yet?

BERNICE. No.

LISA. Has Pete?

BERNICE. No.

LISA. Neither have we. But everyone else we know has gotten theirs. Don't you think that's strange? Yesterday Ruby was spying on us. She knows everything.

BARNEY. Look, I don't like it any more than you do, but is it right for us to spend the rest of our lives paying for something he did? *(Lisa indicates the box with the rabbit, Barney crosses to it and looks inside.)*

BERNICE. I don't know.

BARNEY. Either you're with us and you turn him in or you're with him and we turn both of you in. If he's out there, she can catch him on the way back in. Decide now, we're running out of time.

BERNICE. All right! But first we should check that Pete isn't back yet.

BARNEY. I'll call him.

BERNICE. No, in person. He might not be answering his communicator.

BARNEY. We don't have time.

BERNICE. Check his room. There might be more evidence there.

BARNEY. Isn't this the hopper? What more do we need?

BERNICE. Do it! Now! *(Barney and Lisa exit.)* Come on, you're going home. *(Bernice exits with rabbit, leaving the empty box.)*

BARNEY. *(Entering Pete's room with Lisa.)* Pete? *(To Lisa.)* See what you can find. *(They both start looking. Barney stops.)*

LISA. Keep looking.

BARNEY. Lisa, maybe we should wait.

LISA. Do you want to be an entertainer?

BARNEY. Let's go.

BERNICE. *(Returning to her room.)* Pete? Petey, I can't stall them much longer.

BARNEY. *(Entering with Lisa.)* Any sign of him?

BERNICE. No. You?

BARNEY. No. We didn't find anything worthwhile in his room either. Let's get this over with. *(Switching Ruby on.)* Ruby, the three of us have something to report concerning Peter.

RUBY. Proceed.

BARNEY. We have reason to believe that Peter has been to the forbidden place two or three times since your warning. He left an object he claimed to have brought from there.

RUBY. Let me see it.

BARNEY. He calls it a hopper. *(He opens the box.)* Where is it? It's here, Ruby. I know because I saw it not five micros ago. It's brownish, about so big . . . *(He searches for it frantically.)* Ruby, you've got to believe me. He went outside and that thing was here, and Pete is out there right now. Lisa, help me find it. . . .

RUBY. Delay the matter of this "hopper" for a moment. First, do you all agree with this charge?

LISA. I agree.

RUBY. Bernice?

BERNICE. No, I do not agree.

PETE. *(Entering.)* Bernice, was that you I heard calling me outside?
: *(He has an apple in his hand.)* What's going on?

RUBY. Your colleagues are filing charges against you.

PETE. My friends?

BARNEY. I gave you a choice.

LISA. Bernice, quit lying. You do too believe in that place and you know Pete was there.

BERNICE. It's not possible, is it, Ruby? Because there's no such thing as an outside world.

PETE. Yes, there is. I won't deny it.

BERNICE. *(Whispered to Pete.)* I'm afraid for you.

PETE. Ruby, it's true. I've been to the other side of the walls several times.

BARNEY. See, Red.

RUBY. Barney, I must agree with Bernice. There is no place beyond our walls. Therefore I cannot accuse him of going there. What I am concerned about is his unauthorized use of his porter. Now, if you suspect that this was his crime, please state it, so that we may proceed.

BARNEY. I suspect that he has made unauthorized use of his porter.

RUBY. Thank you, Barney. Lisa, do you agree?

LISA. Yes.

RUBY. Bernice?

BERNICE. No, I do not agree.

PETE. She didn't know I was going out.

RUBY. Are you guilty of the charge?

PETE. Yes.

RUBY. Are you aware of the serious nature of the admission?

PETE. Yes. It means I went outside.

RUBY. Have you anything to say in your defense? *(Pete remains silent.)* Before I sentence you, I will give you one last opportunity to repent of your crime. Make a public apology for your repeated violations and swear an oath to the Master Computer denying this preposterous story of yours.

BARNEY. *(Whispered.)* Do it, even if you don't mean it. She'll believe you.

PETE. I will not apologize. I deny nothing. I have never told anything but the truth. I will swear no oaths to the Master Computer denying what I have learned from it.

RUBY. Peter, you stand condemned as a menace to the Orb. I sentence you to a lifetime of constant monitoring and confinement to quarters. Your porter will be confiscated and, in twelve digits, your communicator disconnected. You will remain titleless, studying and working in isolation for the duration of your natural life. Your sole contact will be your monitor. Do you understand?

PETE. I understand.

RUBY. Bernice, Lisa, Barney. You must swear a solemn oath to the Master Computer to allay suspicions that you are accomplices in his crime. Repeat: I solemnly swear that I do not believe in the existence of any world but the Orb.

ALL. *(Saluting.)* I solemnly swear that I do not believe in the existence of any world but the Orb.

RUBY. Today you have shown great strength of character and deep loyalty to the Orb. I hereby name you, Barney and Lisa, to the Entertainment Guild. I name you, Bernice, to be syndic of the Governing Guild. Your colors have arrived in your respective quarters. May you serve your new guilds well, bringing them honor and praise. *(Bernice crosses to Pete.)* You must not forget that you have other colleagues in whom you have always had faith. You should be very proud of them and of your influence on them. I wish to announce at this time that you and Lisa have passed the probation period placed on your association. Please return to your quarters. The naming ceremony will begin soon. Appear in the Public Hall promptly at digit 14. *(Ruby fades off.)*

LISA. Congratulations, Bernice. Bernice . . .

BERNICE. Get out of here. Both of you.

LISA. Bernice . . .

PETE. They did what they had to do.

BARNEY. I'm sorry Pete.

PETE. Goodbye.

BARNEY. Let's go, Lisa. *(They exit.)*

BERNICE. Why did you do it?

PETE. I was hungry. *(He gives Bernice an apple, brushes her cheek with his hand and leaves. In their respective quarters, Pete removes his porter, badges, etc. and the others put on their "colors.")*

RUBY. *(Fading on with bell tone.)* I'm sending your third meal.

BERNICE. I didn't ask for it.

RUBY. I thought you might have forgotten it in your rush to get ready. Your rations have been restored to their former quota.

BERNICE. Ruby, Pete's sentence was much too severe for the alleged crime. I wish to challenge it formally.

RUBY. How dare you challenge the Ruling Tribunal's authority in this matter.

BERNICE. I claim my right under civic code 4 G-8 to challenge . . .

RUBY. The law prohibits challenges in cases of high treason.

BERNICE. High treason! Pete's no traitor.

RUBY. You must understand that this has not been an easy matter to judge. Trust that we carefully weighed all of the evidence before reaching this painful conclusion.

BERNICE. I cannot accept it.

RUBY. You have no choice. *(Ruby fades off.)*

BERNICE. *(Takes food tray from the chute, crosses to her desk, where she tries to eat but ends up just playing with the food. She sees the apple, picks it up and eats it. She buzzes Pete.)* It's me. Can your monitor hear me?

PETE. No. The volume is on low.

BERNICE. If you had a choice between living alone outside or being restricted for the rest of your life, which would you prefer?

PETE. You know the answer to that.

BERNICE. Did she take your porter yet?

PETE. As soon as I got here.

BERNICE. Ok. There are some things we'll have to do after the ceremonies.

SCENE 8

Lisa's quarters. The room is cluttered and dimly lit. Lisa is asleep on the bed. Bernice enters carrying a flashlight.

BERNICE. Lisa? *(Bernice uses her flashlight to search the room. She digs under some of the clutter and surveys the top of each pile. She picks up Lisa's porter from the console and exits.)*

SCENE 9

Pete's quarters. The room is dimly lit. Pete can be seen hiding from the monitor's sight. Bernice enters.

BERNICE. Pete?

PETE. Shhh. *(Bernice crosses to Pete's hiding place. They converse in low voices.)*

BERNICE. Have you got everything you'll need?

PETE. Enough to get me started. Except for a porter.

BERNICE. I borrowed Lisa's. Here.

PETE. She gave it to you for me?

BERNICE. I'll bring it back to her.

PETE. You'll have to go out with me to do that.

BERNICE. I'd like to see it again.

PETE. Again? So it was you calling me out there.

BERNICE. It's everything you said it would be.

PETE. Stay there with me.

BERNICE. I can't. Someday, but not now. I'll bring supplies to you as often as I can. You remember what you have to do out there?

PETE. "Collect indisputable evidence that the world exists separately from ours and that it will support life." Bernice, that's going to take lustrums.

BERNICE. It's the only way of getting people to believe us. Pete, I want them to believe us. I want everyone to see your world and . . . I want you back.

PETE. You'll never convince them.

BERNICE. I'll find a way. Don't forget you're dealing with a syndic now.

PETE. It's a huge risk. Why are you doing this?

BERNICE. Listening to Ruby sentence you today. . . . From the day I was born until now you were there. I realized what my life might have been like if you weren't part of it. I felt sorry for everyone who has never known that there are 266 elements instead of 265, even if it was only for a few digits. I can't deny you—or your new world.

RUBY. Peter. Peter?

BERNICE. Quick, get out! I'll follow you as soon as I can. *(These lines and the following overlap.)*

RUBY. Answer me. Where are you? Peter? *(An alarm sounds.)* Attention! Attention! This is a bed check. Everyone remain in their quarters.

PETE. I can't let you do this.

BERNICE. Get out of here! *(They exit.)*

SCENE 10

Immediately lights come on in quarters of Bernice, Barney, Lisa. Bernice enters and quickly gets into bed. Ruby comes on with bell in all rooms.

RUBY. Barney, Lisa, Bernice, wake up. This is an emergency. Wake up. Peter has escaped. Someone has given him a transporter. I need to see yours at once. Show it to me.

BERNICE. Here it is. *(Displays it.)*

BARNEY. It's on the console. Can you see it?

LISA. *(Looking under piles of things.)* It should be right here. This is where I usually put it. You think I gave him mine?

RUBY. Lisa, you have three micro digits to find it.

BERNICE. *(Buzzed by Lisa.)* Yes.

LISA. Bernice, I'm sorry about everything that happened today, but I can't find my porter. Come over and help me look for it, please.

BERNICE. I can't. We're confined for bed check.

LISA. But I've only got three micros to show it to Ruby.

BERNICE. Keep looking and I'll check back with you. *(They disconnect. Lisa continues to look for her porter.)* Goodnight, Ruby. I hope you find him soon. That will be all. Ruby, I can't sleep with you on.

RUBY. I must stay on until Peter is found. Number 2R of the criminal code demands it. Where is he, Bernice?

BERNICE. I don't know!

RUBY. It will be easier for both of us if you admit what you know about this.

LISA. *(Buzzing Bernice.)* There's only one micro left and I still can't find it anywhere.

RUBY. Lisa will be in a very difficult situation if you don't help. Tell me what you know.

LISA. Bernice?

BERNICE. I want you to check some things, Ruby. Criminal Code 2R. Check it for me. *(Pushing the command button on her console.)*

LISA. Bernice!

RUBY. This is not the appropriate time.

BERNICE. I want you to. Check it. *(Pushing command button. For the remainder of this scene, Bernice pushes the command button each time she mentions a code number.)*

RUBY. Checking. Checking.

BERNICE. Compare it to 6J.

RUBY. Don't request more than one at a time. Criminal Code 2R is now appearing on your vid-screen.

BERNICE. Check 6J.

RUBY. Checking. Checking.

BERNICE. Check 6K.

RUBY. Do not continue with check requests.

BERNICE. Check it now. Check Civic Code 10C. *(The following sequence, through to the shutdown, should go very quickly.)*

RUBY. Don't request more . . .

BERNICE. 10D, 10E, 10F . . .

RUBY. Checking, checking . . . Don't request . . .

BERNICE. Check it.

RUBY. Checking . . . now appearing . . . don't request . . . vidscreen . . .

BERNICE. 10H.

RUBY. . . . screen . . . appear . . .

BERNICE. 10I.

RUBY. . . . request . . . don't . . .

BERNICE. 10J.

RUBY. Danger . . . danger . . . overload situation. Cease all check requests. Shutdown impending.

BERNICE. 10K, 10L, 10M . . .

RUBY. Danger . . . danger . . . Repeat. Cease check requests.

BERNICE. 10N, 10O, 10P . . .

RUBY. Shutdown impending.

BERNICE. 10Q, 10R, 10S . . .

RUBY. Danger . . . danger . . . Bernice! Shutdooooooooownnnnnnn . . .

BERNICE. Ruby? *(No answer. Bernice grabs her porter and exits.)*

LISA. Bernice? Bernice! Answer me. What happened? *(She buzzes Barney.)*

BARNEY. Barney's All Night Service, Barney speaking.

LISA. Did you hear about Pete?

BARNEY. Yes.

LISA. I can't find my porter.

BARNEY. I keep telling you to clean that room.

LISA. Do you have yours?

BARNEY. Yes.

LISA. You don't have two there, do you? Maybe you took mine home by mistake.

BARNEY. I only have one here.

LISA. Will you come over here and help me find mine?

BARNEY. It's almost digit 23.

LISA. Please, I'm scared. Ruby thinks I gave my porter to Pete to help him escape.

BARNEY. I'm sure you'll find it under something.

LISA. Please, help me!

BARNEY. Ruby's confined us all to our quarters. *(Lisa disconnects and resumes her frantic search. Bernice returns with Lisa's porter. She wraps it in a piece of cloth, puts it in the chute, and directs it to Lisa's room. She buzzes Lisa.)*

LISA. What!

BERNICE. I'm sending you a present.

LISA. I don't want a present now.

BERNICE. Listen to me carefully. Open the present but don't let Ruby see.

LISA. She's off!

BERNICE. She'll be on again soon.

LISA. Bernice . . .

BERNICE. Just do it! Quick! Ruby's coming back on! *(They disconnect, Lisa unwraps "present.")*

RUBY. Testing. Testing. Overload circuits have been repaired. Lisa, I demand to see your porter now or . . . *(Lisa shows the porter.)* Thank you. Good night, Lisa. *(Lisa collapses in relief.)* Bernice,

I would show the codes you requested, but I suspect that they are no longer needed.

BERNICE. No. *(She sees the entry code tape that Pete left her and picks it up.)* Pete can't come back.

RUBY. I know.

BERNICE. Good night, Ruby. *(Ruby fades off. Bernice puts the tape in her storage unit. Twice she lifts her hair with her fingers and blows a light stream of air as she lets it fall. She arranges it in a nonregulation hairstyle.)* Pete, we're on our way.

(Curtain.)

Broken Hearts: Three Tales of Sorrow

From *Birthday of the Infanta, The Devoted Friend*, and *The Happy Prince*, by Oscar Wilde

Dramatized by Gretta Berghammer and Rod Caspers

Copyright, 1984, Gretta Berghammer and Rod Caspers

Broken Hearts: Three Tales of Sorrow (1984)

Broken Hearts: Three Tales of Sorrow is a stage adaptation of three of Oscar Wilde's most poignant and timeless "fairy tales." These three stories for children possess a magical beauty that has charmed and delighted youth from the time Wilde wrote them to the present. But they also contain biting social satire and commentary about the nineteenth-century society Wilde observed in London during his life-time. They seek to expose the wrongs Wilde hoped to right through his writings.

In *The Birthday of the Infanta*, a princess' cruel inhumanity breaks the heart of the crippled "Fantastic" bought to entertain her; *The Devoted Friend* reveals some of the unkinder uses of friendship; and *The Happy Prince* discovers new-found joy and hope as he relieves poverty and despair around him.

The three fairy tales are unified by their themes. *The Birthday of the Infanta* shows that people are often judged on appearance instead of content, and that unusual or different people are often ridiculed because they are misunderstood. In *The Devoted Friend* Wilde clearly satirizes the misuse of the power of friendship while also commenting rather unkindly on the type of people who allow themselves to be manipulated by others they fear are more intelligent, more wealthy, and more powerful. In *The Happy Prince*, as in the other two stories, the audience is left to question the choices the characters make, and to ponder where the justice and reward is in the sacrifices they make throughout the play.

CHARACTERS

The Birthday of the Infanta	*The Devoted Friend*	*The Happy Prince*
Narrator	Narrator	Narrator
The Infanta of Spain	Villager 1	The Happy Prince
Don Pedro, her uncle	Villager 2	The Mayor
The Children	Barkeep	The Councilor
Maria	Traveler 1	The Swallow
Sophia	Traveler 2	The Mother
Andres	Hugh, the Miller	The Son
Muldanado	His Wife	The Young Man
Rosa	His Child	The Father
Juanita	Little Hans	The Match-girl
Therese	Doctor	The First Girl
The Fantastic		The Second Girl
		The Watchman

PRODUCTION NOTE

The plays are written to be performed by an ensemble of seven to eleven actors. It is suggested that the performance area consist of a large open space, with some variety of levels. Properties should be kept minimal, with the ensemble miming all but the necessary few, and the cast should wear some type of basic costume, to which additional pieces can be added to denote specific characters.

The use of music and movement is integral to all three stories, and is a primary key for unifying the production as a whole.

The Birthday of the Infanta

PROLOGUE

A musical overture begins as pools of light reveal members of the ensemble frozen in tableaux depicting early stages of the relationships between the main characters of each of the three tales. Each tableau animates in turn, with the characters moving in slow motion for a few seconds. The first one seen is the Fantastic dancing for the Infanta. The second picture is that of little Hans taking notes as the Miller utters a statement about friendship. The third is the Swallow sitting at the foot of the Happy Prince. After the third tableau freezes once more, the lights and music fade.

NARRATOR. It was the birthday of the Infanta!

> *(The ensemble rushes on, laughing, talking, playing a game of Blind Man's Buff. The Infanta is blindfolded, and is attempting to win the game. The others are biding their time, either encouraging her on with the game, or mildly teasing and taunting her. The Infanta's uncle, Don Pedro, watches the festivities from one side. They freeze as the Narrator continues.)*

Although she was a real princess and the Infanta of Spain, she had only one birthday every year, just like children of quite ordinary people. Usually she was only allowed to play with children of her own rank, so she always had to play alone. But her birthday was an exception, and her father, the King of Spain, had given orders that she was to invite any of her young friends, rich and poor alike, to come and amuse themselves with her.

> *(Ensemble unfreezes and continues to play.)*

INFANTA. There Sophia, I can hear you giggling. I shall find you for sure.

> *(Darts to tag Sophia, who moves away at the last minute. The Infanta misses. She regains her composure and begins again.)*

This time I'll get you for sure. Watch me Father! Watch me!

> *(The Infanta waves to her father, who is offstage. This scene freezes.)*

NARRATOR. From the palace window a very sad and melancholy
King watched his daughter playing and laughing. Near her
stood his brother, Don Pedro of Aragon, whom he hated. Sad-
der than ever was the King, for as he watched the Infanta delight in her party and wave to him, he could only think of the
young Queen, the Infanta's mother, who had died when the
Infanta was only six months old. The Queen had come from
the gay country of France, and her spirit had gradually with-
ered away in the sombre splendour of the Spanish Court. So
great had been the King's love for the Queen that he could not
bear the thought of burying her beneath the ground. So instead, he had had her body embalmed, and for the past eleven-
and-a-half years it lay on a tapestried bier in the Chapel of the
Palace. It was here the King often went to be comforted by her
memory, leaving the Infanta quite alone.

*(Their teasing and taunting whispers increase, as do the In-
fanta's failures to find them. As she lunges once again, she
stumbles and falls to all fours. She rises before Don Pedro can
help her.)*

INFANTA. Now stop. I am the daughter of the King of Spain and a
real princess, and I hereby order you to freeze where you are.
Anyone who dares to disobey me shall have to appear before
my father and his council, and shall risk being beheaded!

*(The children in turn approach the Infanta and allow them-
selves to be caught easily. When the last child (Muldanado)
has been discovered, the Infanta removes her blindfold
proudly.)*

There Father, look! See! I've won! I've won!

(She notices her father is gone from the window.)

DON PEDRO. *(Rushing to her rescue.)* Congratulations, sweet niece.
How well you played the game.

INFANTA. Why has my father left the courtyard window? Doesn't he
care about my party?

DON PEDRO. Of course he does, Your Highness. Why, he has issued
a proclamation throughout the entire country ordering that
you must have a really fine day on the occasion of your twelfth
birthday.

INFANTA. Will my father be attending my celebration with me, or has he chosen to busy himself with other matters?

DON PEDRO. The King is indisposed this afternoon, Your Highness. Unfortunately, he must attend to State affairs, but he does send his love and best wishes to you.

INFANTA. Surely he might have stayed with me on my birthday. What do stupid State affairs matter today? Or could it be that you are lying and that in truth he has gone to that gloomy palace chapel, where the candles are always burning, and where I am not allowed to enter?

(The Infanta turns as if to leave the celebration, but stops when Don Pedro calls to her.)

DON PEDRO. Your Highness!

INFANTA. How silly of him, when the sun is shining so brightly, and everyone is so happy. . . . But come, Uncle, or we will be late for the festivities that are to be performed.

(An elaborate procession is assembled, and the Infanta proudly marches to her throne. Don Pedro stands at her side, and the children group themselves at her feet.)

MARIA. What if she doesn't like the presentation?

SOPHIA. Just do it.

ANDRES. And don't forget to curtsy.

MARIA. What if we don't perform well? Look how angry she got just now playing that stupid game, just because she couldn't win.

MULDANADO. Look at the Infanta. How could anyone so lovely looking ever be cruel to anyone? Take your places, and I will go and do the introductions. Your Highness, in honor of your birthday, a pantomime has been especially prepared for you. *(Muldanado ad libs a short introduction for the "bullfight," introducing Maria, Sophia, and Andres, who perform with him.)*

(Muldanado and the two girls perform as toreadors in an elaborate bullfight dance-pantomime, using hobby horses and toy swords. Andres plays the bull in this splendid and prolonged fight, during which one of the hobby horses is gored right through, and the rider is forced to dismount and battle on

foot. Eventually, Muldanado kills the bull with his sword and presents its pinata heart to the Infanta. The heart is broken open, and out spills candy and other treats, which the children, at the Infanta's command, readily divide among themselves and begin to enjoy.)

INFANTA. *(To Muldanado.)* It certainly was a marvelous bullfight . . . much nicer than the real bullfight I saw in Seville with the Duke of Parma. And who will perform for me next, Uncle?

DON PEDRO. Two magicians, Your Highness, with some fine new tricks.

(Next, Juanita and Therese come forth and perform a series of stunts and magic tricks. These may include juggling and sleight-of-hand tricks. Ends with thunderous applause.)

INFANTA. That was fun, but surely there is something even more spectacular prepared. Uncle, where is my present from you?

DON PEDRO. And now for the grand finale of the afternoon. I have prepared a very special surprise entertainment that not even the Infanta knows of. Now, if you will all close your eyes, I will summon for the Infanta's present.

(The ensemble freezes as Don Pedro moves upstage. From the wings emerges the Fantastic, a young boy of grotesque appearance. His back is crooked and distorted, his hair long and unkempt, his face twisted, and his limbs somewhat contorted. He is dragging a decorated trunk, large enough to eventually conceal him.)

Now . . . you remember what I told you to do.

FANTASTIC. Oh yes! You said that I must smile and bow! You said that my smile was very funny and my bow was funnier. I never try to be funny.

DON PEDRO. Some boys are funny even when they don't try to be.

FANTASTIC. I don't feel funny. I just feel happy, and when I feel happy, people laugh. I hope I can feel happy here. This place is so strange, and not at all like my home in the woods. When am I going home?

DON PEDRO. When you make the Infanta happy.

FANTASTIC. I always make people happy when they look at me. I hope the Infanta will be pleased. Am I really happy looking?

DON PEDRO. You are a Fantastic!

FANTASTIC. That sounds happy.

DON PEDRO. I hope it always will be. Now, into the chest so that
your arrival will surprise and delight the Infanta. And remember, you must dance your best. Smile. Be brave. And do not speak
until you are asked to.

*(The Fantastic crawls into the trunk, and Don Pedro freezes as
he closes the lid.)*

NARRATOR. It was the custom at the Spanish court, always noted for
its cultivated passion for the horrible, to present members of
the nobility with humans who were inferior to them, in both
birth and appearance. Don Pedro's present to the Infanta was no
exception; he had gotten a horrible, fantastic monster. Such a
sight had never been seen by this court before. He had been
discovered only the day before by two court nobles, running
wild through the forest. They had carried him off as a surprise
for the Infanta. The little monster's father, a poor charcoal-
burner, was all too pleased to get rid of so ugly and useless a
child, and had sold him to the noblemen for three gold pieces.
But what amused Don Pedro most was the little monster's
complete unconsciousness of his own grotesque appearance.

(The ensemble comes to life as Don Pedro speaks.)

DON PEDRO. You may all open your eyes now. The surprise has arrived. Happy birthday, Your Highness. Go and open the trunk.

*(The Infanta cautiously taps on the lid of the trunk as the
children encourage her. Suddenly, out pops the Fantastic, sport-
ing a low respectful bow. He is the instant delight of the Infanta and children. The Infanta claps her hands and laughs in
sheer delight. The Fantastic looks fearfully over at Don Pedro,
who encourages him to begin.)*

DON PEDRO. Bow again and then begin to dance.

*(The Fantastic makes another low sweep and in his enthu-
siasm tumbles out of the trunk.)*

INFANTA. Oh please go on. Isn't he funny?

*(The Infanta seats herself on a small stool, and the Fantastic
hides behind his trunk until the music begins. His dance is
lively and comic, full of acrobatics and leaps. The laughter of*

*the children makes him laugh and dance all the more, and he
smiles and nods at them as though he were one of them. He is
absolutely fascinated by the Infanta, and can scarcely keep
his eyes off her as he performs. At the end of his dance, the
Infanta is so charmed she removes a single white rose from
her hair and hands it to the Fantastic. The Fantastic takes the
matter quite seriously. He presses the flower to his lips, puts
his hand on his heart and sinks to one knee before her, grinning
from ear to ear.)*

INFANTA. *(To Don Pedro.)* Oh, Uncle. He's absolutely delightful. He
is so very ugly and very crooked, and very, very funny to look
at. I should like him to dance for me again. The same dance.

DON PEDRO. Your Highness, the sun is too hot, and besides, you
must prepare for your birthday feast. It would be better that
Her Highness should return without delay to the palace, where
a wonderful feast has been prepared for you. Your father and
guests will be waiting, and you must see the huge birthday
cake with your initials on it in painted sugar, and a lovely silver
flag waving from the top.

INFANTA. Very well, then. He will dance for me after my hour of
siesta, and when I return from my chambers, I shall stroke his
hump for luck.

*(The Infanta and Don Pedro exit. As she leaves, she looks once
more at the Fantastic, and breaks into a laugh. The Fantastic
is delighted, and stands looking after her. The others prepare
to leave. They talk among themselves as the Fantastic remains enraptured by the Infanta, and begins kissing the rose
and making other gestures of delight.)*

ROSA. He is really far too ugly to be allowed to play in any place
where we are.

JUANITA. He should drink much wine and go to sleep for a thousand years.

MULDANADO. He certainly should be kept indoors for the rest of
his life. Look at his hunched back and crooked legs.

SOPHIA. He is a perfect horror. Why, he is twisted and stumpy and
his head is completely out of proportion with his legs. Really,
he makes me feel prickly all over, and if he comes near me I
will hit him.

MARIA. I can't believe the Infanta gave him her best blossom. I gave it to the Infanta this morning myself, as a birthday present, and now she has given it away to this pathetic creature.

ANDRES. It is disgusting the way he jumps about merrily, as though he were no different than any of us. Why, I think he fancies himself one of the court.

THERESE. I think he fancies himself one of the Infanta's suitors.

MULDANADO. He doesn't know she admires him only because he is so horrible.

ANDRES. Still, he is a Fantastic. I suggest we all touch his hump for luck!

(All this time, the Fantastic has paid no attention to the taunts of the children, who finish cleaning up. As a group, they converge on him, touch his hump, and run screaming and laughing from the room. The Fantastic is visibly shaken by this, and is frightened by being suddenly alone. He begins to calm himself with a day dream, a fantasy of always being with the Infanta. As this day dream is played out in his mind, he begins to calm down. As he begins to speak, Don Pedro appears upstage, secretly listening to the Fantastic's words.)

FANTASTIC. The Infanta of Spain is the daughter of the King, and I have made her smile. And she has given me a beautiful white rose, and has asked me to dance a second time. Surely she must love me! Oh, how I wish I could be with her now. She would have taken me by the hand, and smiled at me, and never left my side.

(He mimes this action, and begins an imaginary walk through the woods with the Infanta on his arm around and around the throne room.)

And I would show her where the pigeons build their nests and where the rabbits play in the ferns, and introduce her to the great wise tortoises. And I would give her my own little bed to sleep in, and all night long I would keep watch outside her window to see that the wolves did not harm her. And at dawn I would tap at the shutters and wake her, and we would go out and dance together all day long.

(Don Pedro exits as the Fantastic looks about him.)

But where is she? Where could she have gone? The whole palace must be asleep. I want to find her alone, and tell her that I love her, too, and ask her to come away with me when I have finished my second dance. Perhaps she is in the room beyond. Perhaps she is hiding behind that. . . .

(Mirror 1 appears.)

(The Fantastic crosses to where the Infanta made her exit, only to find himself blocked by a mirror, held by a member of the ensemble. The Fantastic, who has never seen his reflection, gasps in horror at the image, which he believes to be another person. The Fantastic plays before the mirror, unaware of its grim reality.)

Who are you, you little beast. . . . You are making me afraid. . . . You are so very crooked looking. . . . and you are so funny. . . . Don Pedro says my smile is funny, and my bow is funnier still *(he does these actions)*. . . . But not as funny as yours! If you could see yourself, you'd laugh still more. . . . *(The mockery is becoming too clever.)* You mock me, you beast. . . . Stop it. . . . Why do you frown at me? . . . Don't look at me that way, you are scaring me. . . . Can't you talk? . . . You only move your lips.

(He runs forward and puts out his hand. He rubs his hand over the face of the mirror, brushes his hair from his eyes, makes faces, etc. He begins to realize that everything about the room is repeated in the mirror. He darts to an area SR and a second mirror played by a member of the ensemble appears, frightening the Fantastic and sending him scurrying back center; three more Mirrors appear, and all five close in a semicircle around the Fantastic. Everywhere he looks he sees his own reflection. He now realizes he is the horrid creature in the mirror. He kisses the rose, presses it to his heart, and with a painful cry sinks to the floor. The Mirrors slowly begin to converge on him CS, repeating the following lines in any pattern or order.)

MIRRORS.
1. He is so very funny.

2. He is so very funny to look at.

3. He is so very crooked.

4. Some boys are funny without trying to be.

5. Stroke his hump for luck.

1. He is too ugly to be allowed to play.

2. Look at his hunched back.

3. Look at his crooked legs.

4. He is a perfect horror.

5. He is twisted.

1. He is stumpy.

2. He is ugly.

3. He doesn't know the Infanta admires him only because he is so horrible.

4. He doesn't know the Infanta admires him only because he is so horrible.

5. He doesn't know the Infanta admires him only because he is so horrible.

1. I think he fancies himself one of the Infanta's suitors!

FANTASTIC. See this! This is the rose the Infanta gave to me to thank me for my dancing. It is the only one like it in the whole world. She gave it to me—to me.

(*The Fantastic tears the petals from the rose with his teeth; then he collapses down center on the Infanta's stool. The Mirrors, which have converged on him, exit slowly. Lights change. Enter the Infanta and Don Pedro. At the sight of the Fantastic, the Infanta stops and begins to laugh.*)

INFANTA. Look at him. His dancing was funny, but his acting is funnier still. Come now, enough of this. Dance for me. Yes, you must get up and dance, and then I shall play some more. My funny little Fantastic is sulking. You must wake him up and tell him to dance for me.

DON PEDRO. You must dance, my little monster. The Infanta of Spain has commanded to be amused.

INFANTA. A whipping master must be sent for. Make him dance, or I shall have him flogged.

(*Don Pedro goes to the Fantastic, kneels, feels his heart, and sees the crushed rose.*)

DON PEDRO. My little Princess, your funny little Fantastic will never dance again.

INFANTA. *(Laughing.)* Heavens! Why not?

DON PEDRO. Because his heart is broken.

(He hands the crushed rose to the Infanta.)

INFANTA. In the future then, let those who come to play for me have no hearts.

(She drops the rose and exits. Don Pedro places the rose on top of the Fantastic's lifeless body as the lights fade.)

(Curtain.)

The Devoted Friend

AUTHORS' NOTE: When a character name appears in paren-
theses before an underlined portion of text, the underlined words
are to be spoken in unison by the indicated characters.

The lights reveal the Barkeep busy behind his imaginary bar as
the two Villagers remain occupied with their mugs and their con-
versation. As the Narrator stands center to introduce the scene,
the two Travelers enter from upstage and join the pub crowd.

NARRATOR. In a small town that was known for its hospitality and
civilized society, a group of friends had gathered at Tim's Pub
to share in conversation and ale.

(The Narrator joins the Barkeep behind the bar, becoming a
waitperson/observer for the rest of the scene.)

TRAVELER 2. Love is all very well in its way, but friendship is much
better.

TRAVELER 1. Indeed, I know of nothing in the world that is either
nobler or rarer than a devoted friendship.

BARKEEP. And what, pray, is your idea of the duties of a devoted
friend?

VILLAGER 1. Yes, that is just what I want to know.

VILLAGER 2. Me, too!

TRAVELER 1. I should expect my devoted friend to be devoted to me,
of course.

BARKEEP. And what would you do in return?

TRAVELER 1. I don't understand you.

BARKEEP. Let me tell you a story on the subject. Once upon a time,
there lived an honest little fellow named Hans. *(Hans enters*
down left in the area which becomes his cottage.) Hans had a
great many friends. But his most *devoted* friend . . .

VILLAGER 2. *(Interrupting.)* Only because Hugh told him so!

BARKEEP. . . . his most *devoted* friend was Hugh, the Miller.

(The Miller enters and approaches Hans.)

MILLER. Good morning.

HANS. Good morning.

MILLER. And how have you been all winter?

HANS. Well, really, it is very good of you to ask. I am afraid I had rather a hard time of it, but now the spring has come, and I am quite happy. All of my flowers are doing well.

MILLER. My wife and I often talked of you during the winter, Hans, and wondered how you were getting on.

HANS. That was kind of you. I was half afraid you had forgotten me.

MILLER. Hans, I am surprised at you! (BARKEEP) Friendship never forgets. That is the wonderful thing about it. I am afraid you do not understand the poetry of life. How lovely your primroses are looking.

HANS. It is a most lucky thing for me that I have so many. I am going to take them into the market and sell them in order to buy back my wheelbarrow.

MILLER. Your wheelbarrow? You don't mean to say you have sold it? (TRAVELER 2) What a very stupid thing to do.

HANS. Well, the fact is that I was obliged to. You see, the winter was very hard for me and I really had no money at all to buy bread with. First I sold the silver buttons off my Sunday coat. Then I sold my silver chain, then my big pipe. . . . But I am going to buy them all back again.

MILLER. Hans, I will give you my wheelbarrow. It is not in good repair, indeed one side is gone, and there is something wrong with the wheelspokes. But in spite of that I will give it to you.

HANS. Why, thank you very much.

MILLER. I know it is very generous of me, and a great many people would think me extremely foolish for parting with it, but I'm not like the rest of the world. I think that (BARKEEP) generosity is the essence of friendship.

HANS. I see.

MILLER. Besides, I have got a new wheelbarrow for myself. Yes, you may set your mind at ease, I will give you my wheelbarrow.

HANS. Well, really, that is generous of you.

TRAVELER 2. I can't believe his stupidity.

HANS. I can easily put it in repair, as I have a plank of wood in the house.

MILLER. Why that is just what I need for the roof of my barn. There is a very large hole in it, and the corn will all get damp if I don't stop it up. How lucky you mentioned it! It is remarkable how one good action always breeds another. I have given you my wheelbarrow, and now you are going to give me your plank. Of course, the wheelbarrow is worth far more than the plank, but (BARKEEP) <u>true friendship never notices things like that.</u> Pray, get it at once.

HANS. Certainly.

(Hans hands the Miller an imaginary plank.)

BARKEEP. And the rich Miller took the plank clean away from his poor little friend.

TRAVELER 2. Just took it without paying anything in return?

HANS. Here we are!

MILLER. It is not a very big plank! I am afraid that after I have mended my barn roof there won't be any left for you to mend the wheelbarrow; of course that is not my fault. But now, as I have given you my wheelbarrow, I am sure you would like to give me some flowers in return. Here is the basket. Mind you, fill it quite full.

HANS. Quite full? But . . .

MILLER. Well, really, as I have given you my wheelbarrow, I don't think that it is much to ask you for a few flowers. I may be wrong, but I should have thought that friendship, (VILLAGER 2) <u>true friendship,</u> (VILLAGER 1) <u>was quite free from selfishness of any kind.</u> It will make you feel happy.

HANS. Dear friend, my best friend, you are welcome to all the flowers in my garden. I would much sooner have your good opinion than my silver buttons any day.

MILLER. Goodbye, little Hans.

HANS. Goodbye.

(The Miller exits with his "plank" and "basket.")

TRAVELER 1. Well, I know of nothing in the world that is either nobler or rarer than a devoted friendship, such as you describe.

TRAVELER 2. Sounds to me as if this little Hans was somewhat of a fool.

BARKEEP. Sometimes the neighbors thought it strange that the rich Miller never gave little Hans anything in return. But Hans never troubled his head about such things. Nothing gave him greater pleasure than listening to all the wonderful things the Miller used to say about the (HANS) <u>unselfishness of true friendship.</u> Hans wrote all such statements down in a notebook, and used to read them over during hard times, especially in the winter. He felt very proud to have a friend with such noble ideas.

(The Miller, with his Wife and Child, is seen having supper in his cottage. The crowd in the pub freezes as the action onstage picks up the story they were telling.)

MILLER. There is no good in my going to see little Hans as long as the snow lasts, for when people are in trouble they should be left alone, and not be bothered by visitors. That at least is my idea about friendship, and (BARKEEP) <u>I am sure I am right.</u>

WIFE. You are certainly very thoughtful of others. It is quite a treat, husband, to hear you talk about friendship.

CHILD. But could we not ask little Hans here? If poor Hans is in trouble I will give him half of my porridge, and show him my white rabbits.

MILLER. What a silly child you are! What is the use of sending you to school? Why, if little Hans came here and saw our warm fire, and our good supper, and our great cask of red wine, he might get envious. (WIFE, CHILD, and BARKEEP) <u>Envy is a most terrible thing, and would spoil anybody's nature.</u> I certainly will not allow Hans' nature to be spoiled. I am his best friend and I will always watch over him to see that he is not led into any temptations.

WIFE. Why, what a good heart you have! You are always thinking of others.

MILLER. Besides, if Hans came here, he might ask me to let him have flour on credit, and that I could not do.

CHILD. But Father, you have so much stored away that . . .

MILLER. Flour is one thing, and friendship is another, and they should not be confused. Everybody can see that.

TRAVELER 2. How well he talks! It is just like being in church. I feel quite drowsy.

MILLER. Lots of people act well, but very few people talk well, which shows that talking is much the more difficult and finer of the two.

(The Miller enters and approaches Hans, carrying a heavy sack of imaginary flour on his back.)

MILLER. Hans. Hans. Hans!

HANS. Good morning!

MILLER. Hans, would you mind carrying this sack of flour for me to market?

HANS. Oh, I am so sorry, but I am really very busy today. I have got all my creepers to nail up, and all my flowers to water, and all my grass to plant.

MILLER. Well, really, I think that considering that I am going to give you my wheelbarrow it is rather unfriendly of you to refuse.

HANS. Oh, don't say that. I wouldn't be unfriendly for the whole world.

VILLAGER 2. Despite his plans, Hans took the flour to the market for the Miller.

BARKEEP. Then, on the following day, the Miller walked to Hans' cottage to get the money for his sack of flour. When he arrived, Hans was still in bed, he was so exhausted from the day before.

MILLER. Upon my word, you are very lazy. I should think you might work harder, Hans. Idleness is a great sin, and I certainly don't like any of my friends to be idle or sluggish.

HANS. I am very sorry, but yesterday's trip . . .

MILLER. You must not mind my speaking quite plainly to you. Of course I should not dream of doing so if I were not your friend. But what is the good of friendship if one cannot say exactly what one means? Anybody can say charming things and try to please and to flatter, (BARKEEP) but a true friend always says unpleasant things, and does not mind giving pain.

HANS. I am very sorry, but I was so tired that I thought I would lie in bed for a little time, and listen to the birds singing. Do you know that I always work better after hearing them?

MILLER. Well, I am glad of that, for I want you to come to the mill as soon as you are dressed, and mend my fence for me.

HANS. Do you think it would be unfriendly of me if I said I was busy?

MILLER. Well, really, I do not think it is much to ask of you, considering that I am going to give you my wheelbarrow; but of course if you refuse I will go and do it myself.

HANS. Oh! On no account!

TRAVELER 2. I don't believe his stupidity.

MILLER. Ah, there is no work so delightful (BARKEEP) as the work one does for others.

(Hans starts mending.)

HANS. It is certainly a great privilege to hear you talk, a very great privilege. I am afraid I shall never have such beautiful ideas as you have.

MILLER. Oh, they will come to you, but you must take more pains. At present you have only the practice of friendship; someday you will have the theory also.

HANS. Do you really think I shall?

MILLER. I have no doubt of it. But now that you have mended the fence, you had better go home and rest. Goodbye.

HANS. Goodbye.

MILLER. For I want you to drive my sheep to the mountain tomorrow.

TRAVELER 2. Why was Hans afraid to say anything?

BARKEEP. He consoled himself by the reflection that the Miller was his best friend.

TRAVELER 2. Friend?

VILLAGER 1. And besides, the Miller was going to give him his wheelbarrow, and that is an act of pure generosity.

BARKEEP. Now it happened that one evening little Hans was sitting by his fireside when a loud rap came at the door.

VILLAGER 1. It was a very wild night, and the wind was blowing and roaring 'round the house.

(The Miller rushes to Hans' cottage and bursts in the imaginary door.)

MILLER. Dear little Hans, I am in great trouble. My child has fallen off a ladder and hurt herself, and I am going for the doctor.

HANS. I am so sorry to hear . . .

MILLER. But the doctor lives so far away, and it is such a bad night, that it just occurred to me that it would be much better if you went instead of me. You know I am going to give you my wheelbarrow, and so it is only fair (BARKEEP) that you should do something for me in return.

HANS. Certainly, I take it quite as a compliment your coming to me, and I will start off at once. But could you lend me your lantern? The night is so dark that I am afraid I might fall into the ditch.

MILLER. I am very sorry, but it is my new lantern, and it would be a great loss to me if anything happened to it.

(Hans crosses to the Doctor's house as the Miller leaves for his own area.)

BARKEEP. What a dreadful night it was. The night was so black that little Hans could hardly see, and the wind was so strong that he could scarcely stand.

DOCTOR. Who is there?

HANS. Little Hans, Doctor.

DOCTOR. What is the matter, little Hans?

HANS. The Miller's daughter has fallen from a ladder, and has hurt herself, and the Miller wants you to come at once.

DOCTOR. All right! I'll be there in a minute.

(The Doctor crosses the stage and exits, leaving Hans to find his own way. He mimes the Villagers' speeches, disappearing off one edge of the set as he "drowns.")

BARKEEP. The storm grew worse and worse, and little Hans could not keep up with the Doctor. At last he lost his way, and wandered off on the moor, which was a very dangerous place as it was full of deep holes, and there poor little Hans was drowned. His body was found the next day floating in a great pool of water and was brought back to the cottage by some shepherds.

VILLAGER 2. Everybody went to little Hans' funeral, as he was so popular, and the Miller was the chief mourner.

(The Miller stands with his Wife and Child, preparing for Hans' funeral.)

MILLER. As I was his best friend, it is only fair that I should have the best place. So I will walk at the head of the procession in a long black cloak.

WIFE. Little Hans is certainly a great loss to everyone.

MILLER. A great loss to me at any rate. Why, I had as good as given him my wheelbarrow, and now I really don't know what to do with it. It is very much in my way at home, and it is in such bad repair that I could not get anything for it if I sold it. I will certainly take care not to give away anything again. (BARKEEP) One always suffers for being generous.

(They exit.)

TRAVELER 1. Well?

BARKEEP. Well, that is the end.

TRAVELER 1. But what became of the Miller?

BARKEEP. Oh! I really don't know, and I am sure that I don't care.

TRAVELER 1. It is quite evident then that you have no sympathy in your nature.

BARKEEP. I am afraid you don't quite see the moral of the story.

TRAVELER 1. The what?

TRAVELER 2. The moral.

TRAVELER 1. Do you mean to say that the story has a moral?

ALL EXCEPT TRAVELER 1. Certainly.

VILLAGER 2. There is nothing so noble as a devoted friend.

VILLAGER 1. One should always be thoughtful of others.

TRAVELER 2. Little Hans was a fool!

(All ad lib argument.)

TRAVELER 1. *(To Barkeep.)* Well, really, I think you should have told me that before you began. If you had done so, I certainly would not have listened to you.

(Traveler 1 hands mug to Barkeep and exits.)

(Curtain.)

The Happy Prince

The Narrator dresses the Happy Prince character with his cape and sword, and sets him on his pedestal.

NARRATOR. High above the city on a tall column stood the statue of the Happy Prince. He was gilded all over with thin leaves of fine gold. For eyes he had two bright sapphires and a large red ruby glowed on his sword hilt. Ah, he was very much admired indeed. One morning, the Mayor and a town councilor were walking through the square, and as they passed the column they looked up at the statue.

MAYOR. Why, look at our Prince! He is as beautiful as a weathercock, isn't he?

COUNCILOR. Yes, indeed. Only not quite so useful.

MAYOR. Yes, he is somewhat impractical.

(They exit.)

NARRATOR. One night, there flew over the city a little Swallow. All day long she had flown, and at night she arrived in the city.

(Swallow lights at the foot of the Happy Prince.)

SWALLOW. I will put up here. It is a fine position with plenty of fresh air. Ah, I have a golden bedroom.

NARRATOR. But just as she was about to tuck her head under her wing, a large drop of water fell on her.

SWALLOW. What a curious thing. There is not a cloud in the sky and the stars are quite clear and bright, and yet it is raining. The climate here is really quite dreadful.

NARRATOR. Then another drop fell.

SWALLOW. What is the use of a statue if it cannot keep the rain off. I must look for a good chimney pot.

NARRATOR. But just as she was spreading her wings, a third drop fell on her.

SWALLOW. Who are you?

HAPPY PRINCE. I am the Happy Prince.

SWALLOW. Why are you weeping then? Your eyes are filled with tears, and they are running down your golden cheeks. You have quite drenched me.

HAPPY PRINCE. When I was alive and had a human heart, I did not know what tears were, for I lived in the Palace of Sans Souci, where sorrow was not allowed to enter. In the daytime I played with my sisters in the garden, and in the evening I led the dance in the Great Hall. 'Round the garden ran a very lofty wall, but I never cared to ask what lay beyond it. Everything about me was so beautiful.

SWALLOW. Well?

HAPPY PRINCE. My courtiers called me the Happy Prince, and happy indeed I was, if pleasure be happiness. So I lived and so I died. And now that I am dead they have set me up here so high that I can see all the ugliness and all the misery of my city, and though my heart is made of lead yet I cannot choose but weep.

(Swallow turns away.)

SWALLOW. What, he is not solid gold. . . .

HAPPY PRINCE. Far across the city on a little street, I can see a small house. One of the windows was open, and through it I can see a woman seated at a table. Her face is thin and worn, and she has coarse red hands, all pricked by the needle, for she is a seamstress. In a bed in the corner of the room her little boy is lying ill.

SON. Mother, I am so hot and thirsty.

MOTHER. Yes, my love. The fever continues.

SON. Could I please have but one orange?

MOTHER. I am sorry but we have none. All that I have is water from the river.

SON. But Mother, please. . . .

MOTHER. Patience, my little one. Perhaps I can get some money from this embroidery. Yes, then I will buy some oranges.

(Mother and Son freeze in an appropriate stage picture.)

HAPPY PRINCE. Swallow, will you take her the ruby from my sword hilt? My feet are fastened to this pedestal and I cannot move.

SWALLOW. I am waited for in Egypt. My friends left weeks ago and by now are flying up and down the Nile talking to the large lotus flowers. Soon they will be asleep in the tomb of the great King. The King himself is there himself in his painted coffin. I must not delay any longer.

HAPPY PRINCE. Please stay with me for one night and be my messenger, will you? The boy is so sick and the mother so sad.

SWALLOW. I don't know if I like boys. Last summer when I was staying on the river, there were two rude boys, the Miller's sons, who were always throwing stones at me.

(Swallow relives the moment through movement as she begins to boast.)

They never hit me of course. We swallows fly far too well for that, and besides, I come from a family famous for its agility. But still, it was a mark of . . .

(She turns to see the Happy Prince crying.)

It is very cold here. If you promise to stop crying, I will stay with you one night and be your messenger.

HAPPY PRINCE. Thank you, Swallow.

NARRATOR. So the Swallow plucked out the great ruby from the Prince's sword, and flew away with it over the roofs of the town. She passed by the cathedral towers where the white marble angels were sculpted. And she passed by the river and saw the lanterns hanging by the masts of the ships.

(Swallow has been moving as if in flight throughout the narration. Mother and Son gradually become unfrozen.)

At last she came to the small house and looked in. The boy was tossing feverishly in his bed and the mother, so exhausted, had fallen asleep. The Swallow placed the ruby next to the woman and then flew gently around the bed, fanning the boy's forehead with her wings.

SON. How cool I feel! I must be getting better.

MOTHER. Oh, I am hopeful you are. But now you must go back to sleep.

SON. Look, Mother! *(Son points to ruby on the floor.)*

(Mother picks the jewel up and studies it.)

MOTHER. Can it be? A ruby! Oh my son, tomorrow I shall provide you with oranges and much more. *(Mother and Son embrace, then exit.)*

NARRATOR. Then the Swallow returned to the Prince and told him what she had done.

SWALLOW. It is curious. I feel quite warm now, though it is so cold.

HAPPY PRINCE. That is because you have done a good action.

(At this point there needs to be a light change and music break to indicate the passing of time.)

NARRATOR. When day broke, the Swallow was preparing for her journey.

(Swallow is stretching, looking off in the distance toward Egypt, testing the direction of the wind, etc. A Young Man enters downstage and seats himself with his ledger and quill.)

SWALLOW. Good morning! Have you any commissions for Egypt? I am just starting.

HAPPY PRINCE. Swallow, will you not stay with me one night longer?

SWALLOW. I am waited for in Egypt! Tomorrow my friends will fly up to the Second Cataract.

HAPPY PRINCE. Far across the city, I see a young man in his garret. He is leaning over a desk covered with papers. His hair is brown and his lips are raw, and he has large, dreamy eyes. He is trying to finish a play for the Director of the Theatre, but he is too cold to write any more.

YOUNG MAN. *(As if talking to himself.)* My fingers are so brittle, so cold. And I'm so hungry. I simply cannot go on. . . . Oh, if only I had enough money to buy more firewood, I am sure I could finish the play.

(Young Man freezes in an appropriate stage picture.)

HAPPY PRINCE. Swallow, little Swallow, please?

(The Swallow looks at the Young Man, considers, then returns to the Happy Prince.)

SWALLOW. I will wait with you one night longer. Shall I take him another ruby?

HAPPY PRINCE. Alas, I have no ruby now. My eyes are all that I have left. They are made of rare sapphires, which were brought out of India a thousand years ago. Pluck one of them out and give it to him. He will sell it to a jeweller, and buy food and firewood, and finish his play.

SWALLOW. Dear Prince, I cannot do that. Your eyesight is one thing I will not take from you.

HAPPY PRINCE. Swallow, do as I command you.

NARRATOR. The Swallow began to weep, but she plucked out the Prince's eye, and flew away to the student's garret.

(Once again, the Swallow pantomimes the journey as it is narrated.)

It was easy enough to get in, as there was a hole in the roof. Through this she darted and came into the room. He did not hear the flutter of bird's wings.

YOUNG MAN. This is truly a blessing! *(He picks up the sapphire.)* Now I am certain to finish my writing for my fire will once again burn bright. Where did this come from? Maybe I am beginning to be appreciated. Perhaps this is from some great admirer.

(Once again there needs to be a light change and music break indicating the passing of time. The Swallow returns to the foot of the Happy Prince while the Young Man exits.)

HAPPY PRINCE. Good morning!

SWALLOW. This day I must go to Egypt. I have come to say goodbye.

HAPPY PRINCE. Little Swallow, will you please stay with me for one night longer?

SWALLOW. I cannot. It is winter, and the chill snow will soon be here. In Egypt the sun is warm on the green palm trees, and the crocodiles lie in the mud and look lazily about them. Dear Prince, I must leave you, but I will never forget you, and next spring, when I return, I will bring back two beautiful jewels in place of those you have given away. The ruby shall be redder than a red rose, and the sapphire shall be as blue as the great sea.

HAPPY PRINCE. In the square below, I see a little match-girl and her angry father.

(The Match-girl and the Father enter. The Match-girl falls and tries to gather her spilled matches.)

HAPPY PRINCE. Her matches have fallen into the gutter, and they are all spoiled.

FATHER. You must not return this evening until you have something to show for your work! Yesterday you brought no money!

MATCH-GIRL. But Father, all my matches are ruined.

FATHER. If you don't sell those matches, you will not eat!

MATCH-GIRL. Oh, but it is so cold outside, and I have no shoes and nothing to cover my head.

FATHER. Ah, be gone with you child!

(Match-girl begins to cry.)

HAPPY PRINCE. If she does not bring home some money her father will beat her. Oh, and now she is crying. You must pluck out my other eye and give it to her.

SWALLOW. I will stay with you one night longer, but I cannot pluck out your other eye. You would be quite blind then.

HAPPY PRINCE. Do as I command you. Please. Do as I command. . . .

NARRATOR. So the little Swallow plucked out the Prince's other eye and darted down with it. She swooped past the little match-girl, and slipped the jewel into the palm of her hand.

(As before, the Swallow moves as if in flight while the Narrator speaks.)

MATCH-GIRL. *(She realizes there is something in her hand and holds it up to observe it in the light.)* What a lovely bit of glass! I can sell it, get more matches, and take some money home to my father. Oh, thank you, thank you!!

(Match-girl turns to go, then returns to kiss the Swallow on the forehead. Then the Match-girl exits.)

NARRATOR. Then the Swallow returned to the Prince.

SWALLOW. You are quite blind now; therefore, I cannot leave you.

HAPPY PRINCE. No, little Swallow, you must go to Egypt.

SWALLOW. I will stay with you always.

NARRATOR. And the Swallow slept at the Prince's feet.

(Once again, a light change and music break is needed to suggest a passing of time.)

NARRATOR. All the next day she sat close by the Prince and told stories of what she had seen in strange lands. She spoke of the red ibises, who stand in long rows on the banks of the Nile. . . .

SWALLOW. . . . and catch gold fish in their beaks.

NARRATOR. And the Sphinx . . .

SWALLOW. . . . who is as old as the world itself, and lives in the desert, and knows everything. And the merchants walk slowly by the sides of the camels and carry amber beads in their hands.

HAPPY PRINCE. Dear little Swallow, you tell me of marvelous things, but more marvelous than anything is the suffering of men and of women. There is no Mystery so great as Misery. Swallow, climb up on my pedestal and tell me what you see.

SWALLOW. I see the rich making merry in their beautiful houses, while the beggars are sitting at the gates. I see the white faces of starving children looking out listlessly at the black streets. Under the archway of a bridge two little girls are lying in one another's arms to try to keep themselves warm.

(The Ensemble enters severally, acting as beggars.)

FIRST GIRL. My feet are so cold!

SECOND GIRL. And I am so hungry!

FIRST GIRL. Oh, if we could only find better shelter. . . .

WATCHMAN. Better shelter you both must find!! Get away, both of you. You must not lie here.

HAPPY PRINCE. Friend, I am covered with fine gold. You must take it off, leaf by leaf, and give it to my poor. The living always think that gold can make them happy.

NARRATOR. So leaf after leaf of the fine gold the Swallow picked off, till the Happy Prince looked quite dull and gray.

(The stripping of the gold leaf is pantomimed by the Swallow as is the following flight.)

Leaf after leaf of the fine gold the Swallow gave to the poor, and the children's faces grew rosier, and they laughed and played games in the street.

(The two Girls briefly pantomime a joyous dancing game.)

But then the snow came, and after the snow came the frost. The streets looked as if they were made of silver, they were so bright and glistening. Long icicles like crystal daggers hung down from the eaves of the houses, everybody went about in furs, and the little boys wore scarlet caps and skated on the ice.

(The ensemble members assume the roles mentioned by the Narrator. The stage is a whirl of motion. As it clears we see the Swallow huddled still, trying desperately to keep warm.)

As the days passed, the poor little Swallow grew colder and colder, and tried to keep herself warm by flapping her wings. She picked up crumbs outside the baker's door when the baker was not looking.

(Swallow gathers crumbs, but her energy is beginning to visibly fade.)

But at last the Swallow knew that she was going to die.

(Swallow struggles up to the foot of the statue.)

Finally she found the strength to fly up to the Prince's side once more.

SWALLOW. Dear Prince, I have come to say good-bye. Will you let me kiss your hand?

HAPPY PRINCE. I am glad that you are going to Egypt at last, little Swallow. You have stayed too long here. But you must kiss me on the lips, for I love you.

SWALLOW. It is not to Egypt that I am going. I am going to the House of Death. Death is the brother of Sleep, is he not?

(The Swallow pantomimes this act—almost as if in slow motion.)

NARRATOR. At that moment a curious crack sounded inside the statue, as if something had broken. The fact is that the leaden heart had snapped right in two. As the statue was no longer beautiful, the Mayor ordered that it be melted down and a new statue erected in his honor. The next day, the foreman at the foundry noticed the heart. It would not melt in the furnace. So he threw it on a dust heap, the same dust heap where the dead swallow was also lying.

ENSEMBLE 1. "Bring me the two most precious things in all the city," said God to one of His angels.

ENSEMBLE 2. And the angel brought to Him the leaden heart and the dead bird.

ENSEMBLE 3. "You have chosen rightly," said God, "for in my garden of Paradise this little bird shall sing forever more, and in my city of gold the Happy Prince shall praise me."

(Curtain.)

EPILOGUE

As in the beginning, the actors move to their positions after the lights fade to black. Now, however, they assume frozen stage pictures which depict the end, or result, of each relationship in the tales which have been told. We see the Infanta stubbornly pouting over the deceased Fantastic; the Miller mourns over the body of little Hans; the Swallow is seen kissing the hand of the Happy Prince. Each of these pictures should be pulled exactly from the way they have been staged earlier. The music should continue as the lights fade to black.

(Curtain.)

Doors

By Suzan L. Zeder

Copyright, 1985, Anchorage Press, Inc.

Doors (1985)

This modern drama by Suzan L. Zeder focuses on the struggle of a small family torn apart by unhappiness, dishonesty, and lack of communication.

Jeff, an eleven-year-old boy, senses that there is something wrong with his parents' marriage. Every day he can hear the sounds of strained argument from behind the door to their bedroom. Because Jeff does not understand the reason for his parents' conflict, he choses to escape the realization that their marriage is ending through a series of fantasies. In Jeff's fantasy world, he is a member of an ideal family—one that exhibits warmth, understanding, and support.

Near the end of the play, Jeff's parents finally honestly confront him about the problems within their marriage, and inform Jeff they will seek a divorce. Jeff, convinced by this time that he is the reason for his parents' unhappiness, begs to be forgiven. With the help of his mother and father, he learns to accept his parents' problems, and joins in with them in finding and making a solution for compromise work.

A Note from the Playwright

This play began for me with a real child and a real divorce. A friend, whose marriage had recently exploded, shared a story about her ten-year-old son reaching out from his own pain and sadness to comfort her. It was an act of two human beings meeting in a moment of healing that went beyond the boundaries of a "social problem" into the realm of art. The story haunted me for years until I gave it a second life in the final lines of this play.

The next image that came to me was the door, and with it came the title. At first I didn't trust it. I thought the title needed to be something grander, more evocative. So I experimented with other titles such as *Separate Doors*, and *Through Separate Doors*. But the image was wiser than I, and the play must be called what it has always been, *Doors*.

The first production of this play in 1981 was its formative one. I am deeply grateful to Greg Falls for his initial commission and for the showcase production which gave the play its present substance and shape. Jim Hancock, my husband, was the director, but his role was that of a collaborator. This is as much his play as it is mine.

For fifteen years I have written plays about children, not from any social, educational, or therapeutic motivation, but simply because they fascinate me as a dramatist. I am profoundly interested in children as protagonists who find themselves in crises, who struggle against overpowering forces, and conduct themselves as heroes. I respect the efforts of parents and children facing troubled times with dignity and depth. I find these efforts to be legitimate and compelling dramatic territory.

I offer this play to you, not as an examination of a significant "social problem," but as a theatre experience which chronicles the journey of three individual survivors through a particularly difficult day.

Suzan Zeder
Dallas, Texas
1985

CHARACTERS

Jeff, Eleven Years Old

Ben, His Father

Helen, His Mother

Sandy, His Best Friend

SETTING
Jeff's Room.

TIME
The Present.

Doors

A fragmentary set suggesting Jeff's bedroom. At first glance it seems to be the rather ordinary room of an eleven-year-old boy; but there are odd angles, slanting doorways, and joints that do not quite connect. The whole room is slightly off-kilter.

The room is dominated by a large closed door, center stage. It is the door to Jeff's parents' bedroom. Down left is a smaller door to the rest of the house. The walls of the room are defined by large scrimmed panels. The panels are decorated with posters of movies, mostly science fiction adventure films currently popular at the time of the production. The posters are oversized and made of a scrim material; they are also hinged so that actors can pass through them.

Also in the room are a small bed, a couple of chairs, a desk or work area, a T.V. set, a stereo, and an over-flowing laundry basket.

At rise, Jeff is alone on stage, seated at the desk. He is working intently on a large, complicated model of a spaceship. The model is almost finished. Jeff works with great concentration with the directions and a tube of glue.

The first sounds we hear are muffled voices coming from Jeff's parents' room. They are arguing. This argument will be ongoing during most of the play; at times, specific voices and words will be heard, at other times, muffled sound, sometimes, nothing. Care should be taken to preserve the illusion that the argument is continuous without detracting from the primary focus, which is to be on stage with Jeff and his actions.*

Jeff tries to concentrate on his task of building the model, but he is obviously distracted and upset by the sounds coming from behind the door. He reads from the directions.

JEFF. "When the glue is partially set, insert cockpit window flaps G and H into the main body of the craft." *(The sounds of the argument grow louder and Jeff tries to concentrate harder.)* "Hold firmly in place for a few seconds until the glue sets . . ." *There is another sound from behind the door. Jeff looks up, the part slips. He tries again.)* "When the glue is partially set, insert cockpit window flaps G and H into the main body of the

---

* See Production Notes at the end of the script.

craft." *(As Jeff lines up the parts, a series of angry bursts are heard, they register on his face, but he does not move.)* . . . "until the glue sets" . . . *(Jeff rises, turns on the stereo set, and returns to the model.)* "Insert wheel hub N into wheel rim O and affix wheel assembly to landing gear C." *(He looks all over the model.)* Where's the landing gear? Where's the landing gear? Where's that . . . *(Sounds from behind the door increase. Jeff picks up the model, looking for the landing gear and the cockpit falls off. The phone rings. Jeff looks at the door. The phone rings again. Jeff tries to return to the model, the phone rings again.)* "Insert wheel hub" . . . yeah . . . yeah . . . yeah . . . "affix to landing GEAR!" *(The phone continues to ring. Finally, Jeff rises and answers. The stereo is very loud.)* Hello? Just a second. *(Jeff puts down the phone, crosses to the stereo and turns it off. He returns to the phone.)* Sorry. Hello, Gramma. Yeah, this is Jeff. Yeah, we got out of school last week. . . . No, I'm not going to camp this year. . . . Gramma, they don't have camps for Grandmothers. *(Sounds behind the door increase.)* Yeah, they're both here, but they can't come to the phone right now. They're in their room with the door closed and I don't think I'd better. . . . I'll tell them you called. I'm sure Mom will call you back later. . . . Yeah, you too, Gramma. Bye. *(Jeff hangs up the phone, and crosses back to the desk, on the way he turns on the stereo and the T.V. very loud.)* Stop it. Stop it! STOP IT! *(Jeff sits and buries his face in his hands; the sound is tremendous. After a beat, the large door bursts open and Ben enters angrily.)*

BEN. Jeff! Turn it down! *(Jeff does not move.)* For Christ's sakes, Jeff! *(Ben crosses to T.V. and stereo and turns them off.)* We can't even hear ourselves think in there. Why does it have to be so loud?

JEFF. I like it loud.

BEN. Well, you're blasting us out of the house.

JEFF. Sorry.

BEN. Your Mother and I are trying to . . . talk and that doesn't help.

JEFF. Sorry.

BEN. If you're sorry, then keep it down. You can listen, but keep it reasonable, okay? *(Ben turns the stereo back on much lower and starts to exit back through the door. Jeff rises and stops him.)*

JEFF. Hey, Dad?

BEN. *(Turning back to him.)* Yeah? *(Jeff turns the stereo off.)*

JEFF. Gramma called.

BEN. Oh. . . . What did she want?

JEFF. I don't know, just to talk I guess.

BEN. *(Under his breath, with frustration.)* Oh, Brother. . . .

JEFF. What?

BEN. Nothing. *(Ben notices that Jeff is really "down.")* Jeff? *(Jeff does not respond; Ben, not sure of what to do, assumes a wrestling stance.)* Hey, Jeff?

JEFF. Oh, no, Dad! *(After a beat, Jeff responds with a wrestling stance, this is something they have done frequently. For a brief moment, they mock wrestle, or tickle, resulting in a much needed laugh for both of them. Helen's voice is heard off stage.)*

HELEN. Ben? *(Ben starts to go, Jeff stops him.)*

JEFF. Dad, can you have a look at this?

BEN. What? *(Jeff holds up the model.)*

JEFF. The cockpit keeps falling off.

BEN. That's really coming along.

JEFF. Mom painted the flag and the wing trim.

BEN. I was going to help you with that. I'm sorry, Jeff.

JEFF. Mom helped me with the body and the engine.

BEN. But things kind of got away from me.

JEFF. I can't get the cockpit to stay on.

BEN. Let me see it. *(Ben inspects the model.)* Well, the flag is in the wrong place and wing trim's crooked. But you put it together just fine.

JEFF. Really?

BEN. Oh, yeah. Have you got a razor blade? *(Jeff hands him a razor blade and watches as Ben scrapes the glue.)* The surface has to be clean for it to seal. Now, the glue. *(Ben applies the glue and positions the cockpit.)*

JEFF. You've got to keep holding until the glue sets.

HELEN. *(Off.)* Ben?

BEN. In a minute!

JEFF. Look out, Dad, it's slipping.

BEN. I've got it.

JEFF. Your hands are shaking.

BEN. They are not!

JEFF. You've got to hold it still.

BEN. I know! *(There is a pause. Ben looks toward the door, back at Jeff, and toward the door again. Jeff notices.)*

JEFF. Have a look at this. *(Jeff shows him an old photograph.)*

BEN. Where did you get that?

JEFF. I found it.

BEN. That's our old house on Beachcroft. What are you doing with that?

JEFF. I just like to look at it sometimes.

BEN. You remember that place?

JEFF. I remember.

BEN. But that was years ago.

JEFF. I remember. *(Ben takes the photo in one hand and holds the model in the other.)*

BEN. I built every inch of that house. Built it and rebuilt it.

JEFF. I remember my bedroom; it had clouds and stars on the ceiling.

BEN. We painted them for you when you said that you wanted to sleep in the sky.

JEFF. When I turned out the lights, the stars glowed.

BEN. That was a good house, Jeff, a good house. Solid foundations, thick walls, none of that stucco, pre-fab garbage. I can't build 'em like that anymore.

JEFF. How come?

BEN. I haven't got the time, and who's got the money, and nobody cares.

JEFF. I miss that house.

BEN. Yeah, so do I. *(Ben puts down the photo and looks at Jeff.)*

BEN. Jeff, there's something going on here, something we all have to talk about. . . .

JEFF. *(Interrupting quickly.)* Dad, you've got to hold on to it!

BEN. Huh?

JEFF. The cockpit, it's slipping again. You've got to hold it in place or it won't work.

BEN. I've got it.

JEFF. You've got to hold it steady.

BEN. I am holding it steady. *(Helen enters and stands in the doorway.)*

HELEN. What are you doing?

BEN. I'll be right there.

JEFF. Dad's helping me with my model.

HELEN. But, Ben . . .

BEN. I said, I'll be right there!

HELEN. Jeff, honey, you spend so much time inside these days, and it's a beautiful day out there. Why don't you go on over to Sandy's . . .

JEFF. I don't want to go to Sandy's.

HELEN. But, I thought you two were going to work on the movie.

JEFF. He's coming over here later.

HELEN. It's a beautiful day and here you are all cooped up . . .

BEN. He said, he didn't want to go.

HELEN. It was just a suggestion.

BEN. You know, you could have waited.

HELEN. Ben, I have been waiting . . .

BEN. I'm talking about this model.

HELEN. The model?

BEN. I was going to help him with it, just as soon as I got a little ahead on the Carlson development.

JEFF. It's okay, Dad.

HELEN. He needed help and he asked me.

BEN. You could have waited.

HELEN. Sure, I could have waited, but he couldn't.

JEFF. It's almost done now.

BEN. Just as soon as I finished the bids and worked out the contracts, and . . .

HELEN. And when would that have been, Ben? Next week? Next month? Next year?

BEN. I was looking forward to it! *(The tension in their tone rises.)*

JEFF. *(Suddenly.)* I don't feel well.

HELEN. *(Concerned.)* What's the matter?

JEFF. I just don't feel so hot.

HELEN. Do you have a headache?

JEFF. I guess so.

BEN. He's all right. *(Helen crosses to Jeff.)*

HELEN. Do you have a temperature?

JEFF. I don't think so.

BEN. He's all right.

HELEN. *(To Ben.)* How do you know he's all right?

BEN. *(To Jeff.)* You're all right, aren't you?

JEFF. I'm all right.

HELEN. But you just said . . .

BEN. He just said he was all right!

JEFF. Dad, the cockpit's all screwed up again.

BEN. Helen, will you let me finish this?

HELEN. I was just . . .

JEFF. The glue's all over the place. *(Jeff takes the model from Ben and returns to the desk with it.)*

HELEN. I'll be in our room when you're finished! *(Helen exits through the large door and slams it as she goes.)*

BEN. I'll be right there! *(Ben paces in anger as Jeff returns dejectedly to the model.)*

JEFF. Hand me the razor blade? *(Ben, distracted, does not answer.)* Dad, can you hand me the blade?

BEN. Oh, yeah, sure; just kind of scrape it there . . . it'll be all right.

JEFF. Yeah.

BEN. Just hold it firm until the glue sets.

JEFF. Yeah.

BEN. You're all right aren't you?

JEFF. Yeah. *(Ben crosses to the large door, hesitates for a beat, then exits. Jeff holds the model perfectly still during the next few lines, which we hear through the door.)*

HELEN. *(Off.)* When we discuss this with Jeff, will you at least do me the courtesy of allowing me to be there?

BEN. *(Off.)* We were talking about the model.

HELEN. *(Off.)* When we do talk to him, we can't be emotional and upset.

BEN. *(Off.)* I am NOT EMOTIONAL!

HELEN. *(Off.)* Then why are you shouting?

BEN. *(Off.)* I wasn't emotional then, now I'm emotional! *(Jeff slowly and deliberately pulls off the cockpit.)*

HELEN. Stop shouting!

BEN. Stop picking! You always have to pick at me, at Jeff! *(Jeff breaks off one wing. Ben and Helen continue off stage.)*

HELEN. He said he didn't feel well.

BEN. He's all right.

HELEN. Just because you say he's all right, doesn't mean . . .

BEN. He said he was all right! *(Jeff snaps off the other wing.)*

HELEN. I was just concerned!

BEN. Can't you leave anything alone? *(Jeff suddenly hurls the model at the door. It smashes onto the floor and breaks into pieces. Jeff rises and turns both the stereo and the T.V. on full blast. He returns to his desk and cradles his head in his hands. After a beat or so, Sandy is heard pounding on the smaller door.)*

SANDY. *(Off.)* Jeff, you in there? Jeff? *(Sandy enters through the small door. He is a bit put out and he lugs a life-sized dummy with him.)*

SANDY. Jeeze, Jeff, doesn't anyone around here answer the door? I've been out there about a half an hour ringing the bell and yelling. Hey, do you know the T.V. is on? *(Jeff pulls himself together, but avoids looking at Sandy.)*

JEFF. Yeah.

SANDY. And the stereo, too? *(Sandy turns off the T.V.)* This much noise will rot your brain, at least that's what my Mom says. *(Sandy starts to turn off stereo.)*

JEFF. Don't.

SANDY. Can I at least turn it down? *(Jeff looks toward the large door. Sandy turns it down but not off.)*

JEFF. What are you doing in here?

SANDY. I knew you were home and the front door was unlocked so I . . .

JEFF. What do you want?

SANDY. We've got to finish the script, remember?

JEFF. Look, Sandy, this isn't a good time.

SANDY. Don't you even want to see what I brought?

JEFF. What's that? *(Sandy holds up the dummy proudly.)*

SANDY. It's a body for the crash scene! I figure we could put ketchup all over it for blood and maybe some dog food for brains.

JEFF. That's gross.

SANDY. Wait until you hear how I got it.

JEFF. Sandy . . . *(Sandy acts this out as he goes along.)*

SANDY. I was downtown in this ally behind Nordstroms and I saw this arm sticking out of a dumpster. . . . OH MY! I thought some bum had crawled in there and died, but then I figured out that it was a dummy. So, I asked this big goon by the loading dock, if I could have it. And he said, "It'll cost you a dollar." So I grabbed it and ran down Fifth like I was kidnapping it or something. Then this number fourteen bus came along, and I hopped on. The driver said, "You can't bring that thing on this bus!" So, I said, "How dare you insult my younger brother!" And I paid two fares, sat it next to me, and talked to it all the way over here. Man, everyone on that bus really thought I was weird.

JEFF. You are weird. *(Jeff turns away.)*

SANDY. You're the weird one. I thought that would really crack you up. All the way over here, I just kept thinking, "this will really crack Jeff up!" *(No response.)* What's the matter?

JEFF. Nothing.

SANDY. Your report card! Your parents hit the ceiling about that F in science.

JEFF. I never showed it to them.

SANDY. The dog! You finally asked them if you could have a dog, and they said no, and . . .

JEFF. I haven't asked them about that yet.

SANDY. Then what's wrong? *(Sounds can be heard from behind the door.)*

JEFF. Sandy, I'll come over to your house later and . . .

SANDY. Did you get the video camera from your dad?

JEFF. Uhhhh, he's been out of town.

SANDY. You mean you haven't even asked him yet?

JEFF. I'll ask him.

SANDY. We've got to start shooting tomorrow!

JEFF. I'll ask him later.

SANDY. All right! How's the star ship coming along?

JEFF. *(Pointing towards the door.)* It's over there.

(Sandy crosses to the door and picks up the wrecked model.)

SANDY. What happened to the star ship?

JEFF. It got hit by a meteor shower!

SANDY. It got hit by something! Jeff, the wings are all broken and the frame is cracked! These things cost a lot of money!

JEFF. I'll pay you back! I'll buy you another one! What more do you want?

SANDY. Jeff, we are supposed to be doing this together and all you're doing is screwing up! *(More sounds are heard.)*

JEFF. I don't want to do this today! Go home, Sandy. I'll call you later.

SANDY. I'm not leaving until we finish the script! And I'm turning that thing off! *(Sandy switches off the stereo; for a second the sounds of the argument can be heard, Sandy hears it and chooses to ignore it. Jeff turns away. Sandy pulls some pages out of his pocket.)*

SANDY. Okay, we start with a long shot of the ship hurtling toward the death asteroid. Then we show the crash. . . . This will work great! *(He sarcastically holds the model up.)* Then we show the crew, those who haven't been burned alive or had their heads split open . . . *(He indicates the dummy.)* . . . struggling out of the wreck. *(Sandy acts this out as he goes along; Jeff watches, becoming more and more involved.)*

SANDY. Colonel McCabe is the first one out; that's me. Then comes Rocco, the navigator; that's Paul; and then the ship's doctor, old blood and guts; that's Rick; and finally comes the ship's robot computer, C.B. 430; that's you. . . . *(Jeff suddenly joins in.)*

JEFF. Suddenly, the robot computer starts acting strangely. His lights flash and smoke comes out of his ears. He walks toward the ship's doctor and grabs him. . . . *(Jeff grabs the dummy.)* He punches him in the stomach, hits him in the head, crushes him in his steel grip and throws his lifeless body to the ground. *(Jeff beats the dummy and throws it.)*

SANDY. *(Laughing.)* Rick's not going to like that.

JEFF. Then he whirls around and walks toward Rocco. *(Jeff turns in a circle and grabs the dummy again.)* He grabs him by the arms and twists them out of their sockets! He throws him on the ground, time after time, after time, after time. *(Jeff beats the dummy on the floor.)*

SANDY. Jeff?

JEFF. *(Totally carried away.)* He kicks him in the stomach, in the back, in the head, in the guts!

SANDY. Jeff, that's not in the script.

JEFF. Finally, he turns on Colonel McCabe. *(Jeff turns on him and stalks him.)*

SANDY. Cut it out, Jeff.

JEFF. Coming at him, slowly, slowly . . .

SANDY. I said, cut it out.

JEFF. Closer and closer. *(Jeff moves in and Sandy grows alarmed.)*

SANDY. Stop it!

JEFF. He raises his arm . . .

SANDY. Jeff! *(Jeff backs him up until he is next to the bed.)*

JEFF. And zap! The death ray! Colonel McCabe collapses in agony. *(Sandy is forced down on the bed. He is angry and confused.)*

SANDY. He does not.

JEFF. He does too.

SANDY. Colonel McCabe does not die! It says in the script, I don't die!

JEFF. You will if I want you to.

SANDY. I will not!

JEFF. Who's got the camera?

SANDY. I don't know, Jeff. Who does? *(Jeff turns away.)* You're such a jerk! I'm going home!

JEFF. Get out of here!

SANDY. I am!

JEFF. And take this piece of junk with you! *(Jeff throws the dummy at Sandy.)* Go home to your Mommy and your Daddy, clear out of here and leave me alone!

SANDY. You're a stupid jerk, Jeff. You've been acting like a stupid jerk ever since your parents first started . . .

JEFF. You shut up about my parents! You don't know anything about my parents!

SANDY. I know that they're yelling again. Jeff, I've heard them ever since I've been here. I could even hear them down on the street.

JEFF. Get out of here, Sandy!

SANDY. I know all about it. *(Jeff turns away.)* My Mom told me. Your Mom talks to my Mom; they gab all the time.

JEFF. *(Without turning to him.)* What did she say?

SANDY. She said that there was trouble over here and I should keep my big nose out of it. *(Jeff sits, upset. Sandy hesitates and approaches cautiously.)* You want to talk about it in the pact?

JEFF. The pact?

SANDY. You remember the pact, Jeff?

JEFF. We were just little kids.

SANDY. You remember how we both pissed on that dead frog and buried it? How we both cut our fingers and spit and swore with our blood that we would always tell each other everything?

JEFF. We were just little kids.

SANDY. Yeah.

JEFF. *(After a pause.)* I don't care anymore, Sandy. They can scream at each other until they're hoarse, I don't care. They can slap each other around all day, I don't care. I just want it to stop.

SANDY. Do they really hit each other?

JEFF. I don't know. I don't care!

SANDY. Jeeze, I don't know what I'd do if my parents ever hit each other.

JEFF. I didn't say they did. I just said, I didn't care.

SANDY. Do you ever see them?

JEFF. I never see anything, it's always behind the door.

SANDY. Do they ever come down for breakfast in the morning, you know, with black eyes or bruises?

JEFF. Blow it out your ear, Sandy.

SANDY. Do you know what it's about?

JEFF. Nobody tells me anything.

SANDY. Do you know when it started?

JEFF. I knew something was up when they started having all these appointments. When I'd ask Mom where she was going, she'd say, "Your Father and I have an appointment." *(Lights change and the posters are lit so the scrim becomes transparent. Behind each poster we see Ben and Helen. The following is played as though they are each speaking to an off-stage counselor. The boys continue with their dialogue, seemingly oblivious to the words of Ben and Helen. Underneath this scene there is sound which is not really music, but sets it apart from reality. *)*

BEN. It all started about two years ago, Doctor. She went back to college for her Master's degree.

HELEN. It all started about four years ago. He stopped building houses and started building condominiums.

JEFF. *(To Sandy.)* But it really started last Tuesday. Dad left and was gone for two days. Mom told me he was on a business trip, but he wasn't.

HELEN. "Condominiums," he said, "that's where the money is!" But the time? Time for electricians, carpenters, and clients; no time for us. So, I went back to school.

BEN. A Master's degree in Psychology? Why didn't she study something useful? What kind of work is psychology?

JEFF. When he came back, they tried to pretend everything was all right. But it wasn't. Everything had changed.

HELEN. I changed into someone neither of us had anticipated. I discovered I have my own ideas, feelings, needs. . . .

BEN. I need her to be with me while I'm building something, something for all of us.

JEFF. Now, everything's different.

SANDY. But do you know why?

BEN. I don't know why. She talks to me now, I don't understand what she's saying. She tells me I'm not giving her enough. Enough of what?

HELEN. When Ben gives, he gives things. When I give, I give things up.

JEFF. Something's happened, Sandy, I'm afraid it's something big.

HELEN. I won't give this up! It's my one chance to make something of my own.

---

* See Production Notes at the end of the script.

BEN. I can't! I can't start all over again from scratch! This isn't just a job, it's my life!

JEFF. They hardly ever look at each other.

SANDY. Yeah?

BEN. We're tearing each other apart.

JEFF. They almost never talk to each other.

SANDY. Yeah?

HELEN. I want to put it back together again, with all the same pieces, but I want them to fit together differently.

JEFF. And they never ever smile at each other.

BEN. I want out. *(Lights out behind the posters. They appear to be solid again.)*

SANDY. Jeeze.

JEFF. Every night, when they think I'm asleep, Dad gets in his car and leaves. By morning he's back at the breakfast table. Every morning we eat breakfast in silence. *(Lights change, sound comes in. The walls become transparent and then swing open. Ben and Helen enter in fantasy. Helen carries a tray of utensils which transforms Jeff's desk into a breakfast table.*)*

(The scene is played with great tension and contrapuntal rhythms of the various utensils. Jeff sits at the middle of the table. Helen stirs a pot of hot cereal. As Ben enters she stops, they glare at each other. Helen continues to stir as Ben pours coffee, sits, and opens a newspaper. Helen stirs the pot in an ever increasing rhythm. Ben is bothered by the sound but ignores her. Finally she crosses to him, stirs faster and faster until she dumps a spoonful into his bowl. Ben looks at her and then at the bowl and half sighs, half grunts in response. Jeff is aware of the tension, but doggedly eats his cereal, scraping the bowl loudly with every bite. Helen pours herself some coffee, and stirs it with her spoon clinking on the cup. The sound annoys Ben, and he shoots her a look and retreats to his paper. Jeff, aware of the cross currents, eats quietly and retreats to a comic book. Helen speaks to Jeff but looks at Ben.)

HELEN. Don't read at the table, Jeff! It's rude. *(Ben crumples his paper. Jeff stops reading and begins to tap his foot in a habit-*

* See Production Notes at the end of the script.

*ual nervous gesture. After a beat Helen taps her foot in a simi-
lar rhythm. Ben speaks to Jeff, but looks at Helen.)*

BEN. Don't tap your foot, son. It's very annoying.

*(Helen glares at Ben, he picks up a piece of toast and scrapes it
into his cereal bowl. Jeff eats, noticing everything, but pretending to see nothing.)*

BEN. *(Meaning the opposite.)* Don't you just LOVE cream of wheat,
Jeff? *(Helen rises and clears the table. She clears all the dishes,
including Ben's coffee, leaving him with the spoon twirling in
the air. Ben rises and leaves the table. There is a moment of
wordless confrontation before they both exit through their
posters. Jeff beats his hand down on the table as the lights
return to normal.)*

JEFF. I hate breakfast.

SANDY. Maybe you shouldn't have read at the table.

JEFF. It wouldn't have made any difference.

SANDY. My parents do that kind of thing all the time. It's like they
have a secret code or something; they don't even have to talk,
they read each other's minds.

JEFF. It used to be that way with my folks too; but now it's like
they are screaming at each other, but their voices are so high
pitched that only dogs can hear them.

SANDY. Jeeze. *(There is a pause and voices can be heard from behind the door. Jeff turns away. Sandy is a bit curious.)*

SANDY. Jeff, do you ever, you know, listen?

JEFF. Huh?

SANDY. I mean, when they fight, do you, you know, try to hear what
they're saying?

JEFF. Sandy, I spend most of my time trying not to hear.

SANDY. Well, sometimes my folks argue, they don't really fight or
anything; but when they argue, part of me tries to shut it out
and part of me really wants to know what's going on.

JEFF. *(Not unkindly.)* You little creep!

SANDY. No, but the weird thing is, the really weird thing is, whenever I listen, it all sounds so stupid! Like last year, you know,
we all went down to Puyallup, to the fair. We go every year, and

every year the same thing happens. *(Sandy uses a couple of chairs to set up a "car" and he plays out the following.)* My Dad always drives and my Mom sits next to him and does needlepoint. Julie, Carrie, and I sit in the back seat and argue over who has to sit on the hump. After we have been driving for about a half an hour, my Mom looks up and says, "We always go this way and we always get lost."
Then my Dad says, "You got a better route?"
And my Mom says, "Back there at the service station, I told you to turn left."
"But that's the way all the traffic goes."
"That's because it's the right way."
"There's less traffic this way."
"THAT'S because we're going to Auburn."
Then, Julie says, "But I thought we were going to the fair!"
And they both say, "Be quiet, Julie."
And my Mom says, "Daddy's trying to drive."
And Dad says, "What's that supposed to mean?"
So, my Mom says, "It's not supposed to mean anything. I am just trying to get us to the fair. If you'd listen instead of charging ahead, we wouldn't be lost."
Then, Dad says, "Who's lost? I know exactly where we are."
And Mom says, "Okay, where are we?"
And we all say, "WE'RE LOST!" Then they both turn around and yell at US.

JEFF. Did you get to the fair?

SANDY. Yeah.

JEFF. How was it?

SANDY. It was great.

JEFF. With my folks we'd never get there. *(Jeff takes Sandy's place and acts out the following.)*

JEFF. My Mom would say, "The reason you're driving this way is because you really don't want to go to the fair."
And my Dad would say, "What?"
"You didn't want to go last night when I suggested it and you didn't want to go this morning, while I was packing the picnic. That's why you didn't help."
"You said, you didn't need any help."
"Still, it would have been nice."
"Nice? I'm being nice. I'm taking you to the fair aren't I?"
"Only because you feel guilty."

"Guilty?"
"Because you didn't take us last year."
"But I'm taking you this year! I am taking you to the god-damned
fair when I should be at the office."
"See, I knew you didn't want to go."
Then we'd turn around and all the way back to Seattle all you'd
hear would be the sound of ice melting in the cooler.

SANDY. Did that really happen?

JEFF. No, but that's what would have happened.

SANDY. How do you know?

JEFF. I know, believe me, I know.

SANDY. What do you know?

JEFF. I know that's what would have happened.

SANDY. That's not what I mean. What do you know about what's
happening?

JEFF. I don't know.

SANDY. You don't know what you know?

JEFF. No! What are you talking about?

SANDY. Look Jeff, if you can figure out what's going on, then maybe
you can do something about it.

JEFF. I've tried.

SANDY. Well, try again! What are the facts?

JEFF. You sound like something out of *Magnum, P.I.* *

SANDY. I'm just trying to help. *(Sandy leaps to his feet and becomes a detective.)* Come on, man, what do you know?

JEFF. I know my Dad's not sleeping at home at night.

SANDY. Okay, where does he go?

JEFF. I don't know.

SANDY. Well, if he's not sleeping at home, he has to be sleeping
somewhere else.

JEFF. Brilliant.

* Update to any popular police or detective show and have Sandy imitate
the lead character in his inquisition.

SANDY. Have you asked him?

JEFF. No.

SANDY. Why not?

JEFF. I can really see me going up to my father and saying, "Where you been sleeping these days, Dad?" Get real.

SANDY. We may have to tail him.

JEFF. I'm not going to do that!

SANDY. It was just a suggestion. Say, Jeff, do you think he's got a . . . girlfriend.

JEFF. No.

SANDY. Why not?

JEFF. He just wouldn't!

SANDY. Okay, scratch that. What else do you know?

JEFF. I know they fight a lot.

SANDY. What about?

JEFF. Everything. . . . Anything.

SANDY. You must have heard something in particular.

JEFF. This afternoon, I heard my Mom say, "I'm not giving up."

SANDY. Giving up what?

JEFF. I couldn't hear.

SANDY. Smoking! Your Dad wants her to give up smoking!

JEFF. She doesn't smoke.

SANDY. When my Mom tried to give up smoking, she threw a whole plate of spaghetti at my Dad. She said it slipped, but I knew she threw it.

JEFF. I said, she doesn't smoke.

SANDY. You sure?

JEFF. She's my Mother!

SANDY. What else did you hear?

JEFF. I heard my Mom say something about a job.

SANDY. YOUR DAD LOST HIS JOB!

JEFF. I don't think . . .

SANDY. That's it! Jeff, I saw this thing on *Sixty Minutes*, about how all these people are losing jobs. First they lose the job, then they go on welfare, then everybody starts fighting with everybody and . . .

JEFF. My Dad works for himself, he's a contractor.

SANDY. Oh no, Jeff! That's the worst.

JEFF. But he just started a new project over in Bellevue . . .

SANDY. Don't take my word, ask Mike Wallace!

JEFF. Do you really think. . . .

SANDY. Here, I'll show you. *(Sandy grabs the dummy and mimes the characters with it.)* Here is your Father, sitting around reading his paper. And your Mother comes in and says, "Well, I certainly hope that you're looking for a job." And he says, "Job, I have a job." And she says, "I mean a job with some money!" "Maybe if you wouldn't spend so much on cigarettes and panty hose . . ."

JEFF. I told you, she doesn't . . .

SANDY. And she says, "Me spend so much? You're such a cheapskate. . . ."

JEFF. Sandy . . .

SANDY. And that really makes him mad so he hauls off and . . . Bam! SLAP! POW! THWACK! *(Sandy makes the dummy punch the air. Jeff grabs it from him.)*

JEFF. I never said they hit each other!

SANDY. I was just trying to . . .

JEFF. I've never seen them hit each other. They're not like that at all! *(There is a pause.)*

SANDY. Hey, Jeff, why don't you just ask them what's going on? *(Jeff tenderly carries the dummy over to the bed.)* Ask your Mom, she'll tell you something. My Mother always tells me something.

JEFF. I just want it to stop, Sandy. That's all I really want. Every night when I hear them in there, I put the pillow over my head, so I can't hear them and I try to imagine what it would be like if they would just stop fighting. I try to make myself dream about it. If they would just stop fighting, everything would be perfect. *(Jeff covers the dummy's head with a pillow during this speech. Lights change and there is music as we move in to his fantasy.)* It would be morning; and the first thing I hear would be Mom, in the kitchen making breakfast. The first thing I smell would be bacon frying. The first thing I feel would be sunlight on my face. *(Lights come up on the poster to the right of the door. Helen appears behind it.)*

HELEN. Jeff, time to get up! Time for breakfast!

JEFF. So, I'd get up, and I'd come downstairs. *(Jeff manipulates the dummy out of bed, and brings it to the desk which will serve once again as a breakfast table. The poster swings open and Helen enters with utensils. Jeff enters the scene with the dummy. He manipulates the dummy and all relate to it as though it were him.)*

HELEN. Morning.

JEFF. Morning.

HELEN. Sleep well?

JEFF. Very. *(Jeff seats the dummy at his place.)*

HELEN. Ben, breakfast is ready.

BEN. I'll be right there. *(Poster swings open and Ben enters the scene. He takes his place at the table. In this scene there is no tension initially, everything is warm and loving, unreal and exaggerated.)*

HELEN. Morning.

BEN. Morning.

HELEN. Sleep well?

BEN. Very. *(Helen hands Ben a plate with obvious pleasure.)*

BEN. *(Delighted.)* Eggs over easy, hash browns, bacon, toast, coffee with cream and two sugars. Thank you, dear.

HELEN. You're welcome, darling.

BEN. *(To the dummy.)* Morning, son.

JEFF. *(Nodding the dummy toward Ben.)* Morning.

BEN. Sleep well?

JEFF. Very. *(Helen sits at table and all mime eating.)*

JEFF. *(To Sandy.)* In this family everyone eats breakfast.

HELEN. This afternoon, I thought we'd all go to the circus. I've called for the tickets. They're at the box office.

BEN. This afternoon, I thought we'd all go to the Sonics game. I've called for the tickets, they're at the box office.

HELEN. But, Dearest, the circus . . .

BEN. But, Darling, the Sonics . . .

HELEN. Circus.

BEN. Sonics. *(Tension begins to build.)*

HELEN. CIRCUS!

BEN. SONICS!

JEFF. In this family there is NEVER any arguing.

HELEN. We'll go to the Sonics!

BEN. We'll go to the Circus!

JEFF. In this family there is ALWAYS a solution.

SANDY. In this family there is a dog! *(Sandy enters the scene as a boisterous slobbering dog. He bounds around the room.)*

HELEN. Who let the dog in?

BEN. He's all right! Here, Boy! Atta Boy! Good Dog. Good Boy!

HELEN. *(Pleasantly.)* Ben, that's a hunting dog; don't you think he should really be outside? *(Sandy bounds playfully over to Ben, jumps on him and they tussle.)*

BEN. Hey, Jeff, have a look at this. Fetch, boy. *(Ben throws an imaginary object and Sandy bounces after it.)*

HELEN. Please, Ben, not in the house.

JEFF. Sandy!

BEN. Good Dog! Bring it here. Good Boy! *(Sandy fetches it and knocks into the table.)*

HELEN. Ben, he's knocking over the table.

BEN. Oh, he's just a puppy.

JEFF. Sandy . . . *(Ben throws the object again.)*

BEN. After it, boy! *(Sandy leaps onto the bed and kicks up the covers.)*

HELEN. He's tearing up the house.

HELEN. Stop it, Ben.

JEFF. Stop it, Sandy. *(Sandy knocks over the hamper, scattering the contents.)*

HELEN. *(Very angry.)* Ben, that dog just made a mess on the living room carpet!

BEN. Don't yell at me, I didn't do it!

JEFF. Stop it, Sandy!

HELEN. He's tearing up my house.

BEN. Your house? I thought this was my house, too!

HELEN. Well, if it's your house, then you can clean it up! *(Helen exits behind her poster.)*

BEN. I'll have MY dog in MY house any damn time I want! *(Ben exits behind his poster. The lights return to normal.)*

JEFF. You spoiled everything! There aren't any dogs in this house! *(Jeff kicks Sandy, who yelps like a dog and dives under the bed.)*

SANDY. You kicked me!

JEFF. Why did you do that?

SANDY. I was just fooling around and you kicked me.

JEFF. Come out of there.

SANDY. Not until you say you're sorry.

JEFF. I'm sorry.

SANDY. You don't really mean it.

JEFF. I said I was sorry.

SANDY. Get down on your knees and say it. *(Jeff gets down on his knees, reluctantly.)*

JEFF. I'm sorry, I'm sorry, I'm sorry! Now, come on out! *(Just as Sandy starts out, the large door opens and Helen enters in reality. Sandy ducks back under the bed.)*

HELEN. Jeff!

JEFF. *(Startled.)* Huh?

HELEN. What are you doing?

JEFF. Nothing.

HELEN. What happened to your room?

JEFF. I'll clean it up.

HELEN. Never mind about that now, I didn't come in to talk about your room. Your Dad and I need to talk to you.

JEFF. What about?

HELEN. About all of us.

JEFF. Why?

HELEN. Just come on in. I think we'll be more comfortable in there. *(Helen indicates their room, Jeff pulls away.)*

JEFF. I'm cleaning my room.

HELEN. That can wait.

JEFF. I'm busy.

HELEN. Jeff, we need to talk to you now.

JEFF. I just want you to leave me alone.

HELEN. We've left you alone too much, but now we need to talk. Daddy's waiting. . . . *(Jeff pulls away and kicks the remains of the model, which has wound up on the floor.)* Your model? What happened to your model? *(Helen picks up the smashed model.)*

JEFF. I broke it.

HELEN. How?

JEFF. I just did. I smashed it.

HELEN. But you were so careful.

JEFF. I made it and I can smash it if I want! *(Jeff lunges for it and Helen holds it out of his grasp.)*

HELEN. Not after we worked so hard on it.

JEFF. What do you care?

HELEN. I care.

JEFF. *(Explodes.)* Oh yeah, you care a lot, a whole damn lot! *(Helen, exhausted, sits on his bed.)*

HELEN. I am so tired of fighting, Jeff. I don't want to fight with you.

JEFF. Then don't. Just go away and leave me alone!

HELEN. Jeff, do me a favor. Just sit here with me for one minute and let's not talk, let's not even think.

JEFF. Why?

HELEN. Please. *(Jeff sits, sullen at first; Helen sighs. After a few seconds, Helen starts to say something; Jeff catches her eye and looks at his watch; she is silent. Helen reaches out to him and he slides closer to her. They relax in a moment of mutual comfort. In the silence, Jeff's anger is defused, for the moment. Helen holds him and her face betrays her sorrow, pain, and concern. After a beat, Jeff speaks.)*

JEFF. Are we on welfare?

HELEN. What?

JEFF. Did Dad lose his job?

HELEN. No. What ever gave you that idea?

JEFF. Just something I heard.

HELEN. Heard? Heard where?

JEFF. *(Nods toward the large door.)* I heard you guys yelling something about a job.

HELEN. Oh, Jeff, I'm sorry; I didn't want you to hear about it like that. I wanted to tell you myself as soon as I was sure.

JEFF. Tell me what?

HELEN. I've been offered a job with a Community Mental Health Center in Portland.

JEFF. Portland?

HELEN. It's a good job, a very good job, and it could be important to both of us.

JEFF. You aren't going to take it, are you?

HELEN. I haven't decided yet.

JEFF. So that's what it's all about, I mean with you and Dad.

HELEN. What's happening with us has very little to do with this job. There are other things, much more serious things.

JEFF. You have to tell them no. Tell them you have to stay here with Dad and me.

HELEN. If I thought that would solve anything, I would. I'd turn it down in a second if I thought it would change things with us. Your Dad and I have problems, serious ones. They don't need to be your problems, but they do affect you, so we need to talk.

JEFF. I don't want to talk, anymore.

HELEN. If you would rather talk here, I'll go get your Dad and we'll talk right here in your room. *(Helen starts out.)*

JEFF. Why don't you get a job here?

HELEN. That wouldn't help.

JEFF. You could find a job here!

HELEN. That wouldn't change anything.

JEFF. There must be all sorts of jobs here that you could . . .

HELEN. IT'S NOT THE JOB!

JEFF. I don't want to talk to you.

HELEN. Jeff . . . *(Jeff turns away.)*

JEFF. I won't listen to anything you say!

HELEN. Stop it! *(Jeff claps his hands over his ears.)*

JEFF. I can't hear you.

HELEN. I want you to stop this right now! *(Sandy sneaks out from under the bed and tries to slip out the door. Helen catches sight of him.)*

HELEN. Sandy!

SANDY. *(Embarrassed.)* Excuse me.

HELEN. I didn't know anyone was here.

JEFF. I said I was busy.

SANDY. I uhhhhhhh, gotta be going.

HELEN. *(To Jeff.)* Why didn't you tell me?

SANDY. I'm sorry, Mrs. Stuart.

HELEN. Sandy, Jeff's Dad and I need to talk to him.

SANDY. Yeah, I know.

HELEN. I think you had better . . .

SANDY. I'm going right now, Mrs. Stuart.

JEFF. Can I at least say good-bye to him?

HELEN. Yes.

JEFF. Alone?

HELEN. Come into our room when you're done. Good-bye, Sandy.

SANDY. Bye, Mrs. Stuart. Uhhhh, Mrs. Stuart?

HELEN. Yes?

SANDY. I didn't mean to listen. I didn't hear much.

HELEN. Good-bye, Sandy. Say hello to your Mother for me. We'll be waiting, Jeff.

JEFF. I'll come when I'm ready. *(Helen exits through the large door. Sandy picks up the dummy and starts toward the small door.)*

SANDY. Bye, Jeff. See you tomorrow.

JEFF. Don't go.

SANDY. You heard what she said.

JEFF. Don't go!

SANDY. But, Jeff . . .

JEFF. Please, Sandy, just for a little while.

SANDY. They're waiting for you.

JEFF. I know.

SANDY. I feel weird.

JEFF. I'll go in there when I'm ready, not right now.

(Sandy sits and looks at Jeff. There is an awkward moment between them. Sandy looks at the door and then at his watch.)

SANDY. When do you think you'll be ready, Jeff?

JEFF. Something's got to happen. Something big, something so she won't take that job.

SANDY. Didn't you listen? She said it wasn't the job.

JEFF. Something to make them stop fighting.

SANDY. Like what?

JEFF. Like if something happened to me. Like if I got hit by a truck or something. *(Jeff jumps up, makes a wailing sound, grabs the dummy, and runs around the room. He dumps the dummy face down on the desk and lights begin a gradual change as he moves into fantasy. Sandy does not join the fantasy as quickly.)*

SANDY. Jeff?

JEFF. Doctor, we have a very serious case here, a very serious case.

SANDY. Jeff . . .

JEFF. I said, Doctor we have a serious case here, a very serious case.

SANDY. I gotta go home.

JEFF. Please, Sandy! We have a serious case here. *(Sandy reluctantly crosses to the desk, which has become an operating table, and joins in.)*

SANDY. Name?

JEFF. Jeff Stuart.

SANDY. Age?

JEFF. Eleven.

SANDY. Pulse?

JEFF. Weak!

SANDY. Heartbeat? *(Jeff listens at the dummy's chest.)*

JEFF. Going, going, GONE!

SANDY. EMERGENCY! *(Both boys pound frantically on the dummy's chest.)*

SANDY. Hold it!

JEFF. What is it?

SANDY. It's started again. He's better now. *(Sandy tries to leave the fantasy, Jeff pulls him back.)*

JEFF. No, we have to operate!

SANDY. Operate?

JEFF. OPERATE! Knife! *(Jeff holds up an imaginary knife. Sandy assumes the role of the Doctor. Jeff slaps the knife into his hand.)*

SANDY. Knife! *(Sandy mimes the operation, Jeff makes sound effects. Sandy opens the "patient.")*

SANDY. Oh, gross!

JEFF. Look at his guts.

SANDY. All twisted up.

JEFF. Look at his liver.

SANDY. That's disgusting.

JEFF. He's losing a lot of blood!

SANDY. TRANSFUSION! *(Sandy stands with one arm raised and his hand cupped, like a plasma bottle. Jeff jabs Sandy's other arm at the dummy's arm.)*

SANDY. Glub, glub, glub . . . *(Sandy slowly closes his hand as though the bottle were emptying.)* We saved him again; he's better now! *(Sandy tries again to leave the fantasy; Jeff won't let him.)*

JEFF. No! The parents have to be notified.

SANDY. *(Dropping the fantasy.)* Jeff, this isn't going to help.

JEFF. Sandy, we have got to call the parents! *(Jeff crosses to the phone, picks up the receiver and hands it to Sandy.)* Tell them to come right away! *(Jeff makes Sandy take it.)* Ring! Ring! *(Lights come up on posters; Ben and Helen are seen each holding a phone receiver.)*

BEN and HELEN. Hello.

JEFF. *(To Sandy.)* Tell them!

SANDY. This is the hospital! We have your son here. You'd better come right away.

BEN and HELEN. Oh, my God! *(Posters swing open and Ben and Helen enter the scene. They each take a chair and establish a waiting room. Jeff crosses to them, Sandy hangs back and watches.)*

JEFF. Mr. and Mrs. Stuart?

HELEN. Is he going to be all right?

JEFF. Too soon to tell.

BEN. Is he going to make it?

JEFF. That all depends.

BEN and HELEN. On what?

JEFF. On what you do now. We've done everything that medical science can do for him. Now, you take him home and take good
care of him. He needs rest and peace and QUIET! *(Jeff crosses
to dummy and picks it up, he gives one end to Sandy and both
boys race around the room like an ambulance. They dump the
dummy on the bed.)*

SANDY. *(Out of the fantasy.)* Jeff, I'm going now.

JEFF. You can't; this is the best part! *(Ben and Helen rise and cross
to the bed. They kneel on either side of it. Jeff takes the two
chairs and places them near the bed. Jeff and Sandy sit on the
backs of the chairs with their feet on the seat, overlooking the
scene. In this scene, everyone treats the dummy as Jeff.)*

HELEN. Jeff, Jeff, this is your Mother.

BEN. Son, we're right here.

SANDY. He seems to be in a coma.

JEFF. But he can still hear you.

BEN. You've got to get well, son.

SANDY. So, he gets well and everybody lives happily ever . . . *(Sandy
starts off the chair, Jeff pulls him back.)*

JEFF. Not yet.

BEN. How do you feel son?

HELEN. Where does it hurt?

BEN. Can you hear us?

SANDY. No, he can't! His ears are filled with wax!

JEFF. Yes, he can! Go on!

HELEN. We promise things will change.

BEN. We'll do anything.

SANDY. Get him some soup! Get him a comic book!

JEFF. No, don't. Keep talking.

BEN. From now on, we'll be a family again.

JEFF. He's starting to come 'round.

SANDY. Still looks out of it to me.

HELEN. We'll all stay together, right here, we promise.

JEFF. He's definitely beginning to come 'round.

HELEN. If only we'd listened to each other.

BEN. If only we'd taken more time.

BEN. If only your Mother had paid more attention.

HELEN. If only your Father had been home more.

SANDY. There they go again.

JEFF. Hey, he's back in a coma!

BEN. *(To Helen.)* This is all your fault, you know.

HELEN. My fault? Why is it always my fault?

JEFF. Will you look at your son?

HELEN. At least I tried, I helped him with his model and that's more than I can say for you.

BEN. Oh yeah, well, I would have helped him, if you'd just given me a chance!

JEFF. He's dying!

HELEN. I can't talk to you, you're impossible!

BEN. I'm impossible? You're impossible! *(They both storm off and exit through their posters. Jeff and Sandy sit, looking at the patient for a long beat. Sandy jumps down and begins to march around the bed singing the "Funeral March.")*

SANDY. Dum dum dee dum, Dum dee dum dee dum dum dum.

JEFF. Cut it out, Sandy. *(The phone rings. Sandy continues. The phone rings again. Jeff makes no move to answer it. The phone rings again.)*

SANDY. Jeeze, Jeff, doesn't anyone around here ever answer the phone? *(Sandy answers the phone.)* Hello? Stuarts' residence. . . . Oh, hi, Mom. . . . Yeah, this is me. . . . Obviously, I'm still here if I answered the phone. . . . No, what time is it? . . . Aw, do I have to? . . . Yeah, I know. . . . Yeah, I know. . . . Yeah, I know. . . . Okay, right away. . . . Yeah, I know! Bye. *(Sandy hangs up and turns to Jeff.)* I gotta go. I have an appointment with the orthodontist.

JEFF. Orthodontist?

SANDY. I hate it when my Mom makes me dentist appointments during vacations. I don't even get to get out of school.

JEFF. Do you have to go?

SANDY. Yeah.

JEFF. Can't you tell her you're sick or something?

SANDY. Then she'd just make me come home and go to bed.

JEFF. Can't you tell her I'm sick?

SANDY. She'd be afraid I'd catch it, she'd still make me come home.

JEFF. Can I come with you?

SANDY. To the orthodontist?

JEFF. Sandy, I need you to stay with me, just five more minutes.

SANDY. What good would it do? Jeff, you can't change anything by not talking to them. *(Jeff turns away.)* Things will be better when it's over.

JEFF. When what's over?

SANDY. After you've talked to them.

JEFF. Are you sure?

SANDY. No. Bye, Jeff. See you tomorrow.

JEFF. Yeah.

SANDY. *(On his way out.)* Hey, take it easy.

JEFF. Okay. *(Sandy exits, Jeff turns away. Jeff sees the dummy and runs after him.)* Hey, Sandy, just a minute, you forgot . . . *(Jeff exits through the small door, but he returns immediately dragging the dummy behind him.)* Damn! *(Jeff dumps the dummy on the floor and looks at the large door, he paces back and forth across the room. On each pass, he kicks the dummy out of the way.)* Can't feel that, can you? *(He continues to kick the dummy.)* Or that! Or that! You can't feel anything! *(After one last savage kick, Jeff picks the dummy up in his arms and hugs it tightly. He places it tenderly on the bed. Jeff crosses to the large door. It is the longest walk he has ever made. He opens the door but stands in the doorway and looks into the next room.)*

JEFF. What are you doing?

BEN'S VOICE. Packing.

JEFF. Another business trip?

BEN'S VOICE. Not this time, son. *(Jeff turns away and steps back into his room.)*

BEN'S VOICE. Jeff, come back in here.

JEFF. I don't want to!

BEN'S VOICE. I'll get your Mother. She's making coffee. You wait right there. *(Jeff stands near the door for a moment and then bolts into his parents' room. He returns to his room immediately with a suitcase.)* Hey, what are you doing? *(Ben enters and faces Jeff. Jeff holds the suitcase defiantly.)*

JEFF. Why are you packing?

BEN. I've got to get out of here and let things settle down for a while. *(Jeff drops the case on the floor, falls to his knees and begins pulling articles of clothing out of the case.)*

JEFF. You can't take these, they're dirty. I'll wash them for you! *(Jeff throws a handful of clothing on the floor.)*

BEN. Hey!

JEFF. Can't take these, they've got holes in them.

BEN. What are you doing?

JEFF. Can't take these, they're too old. Just rags! Can't take rags!

BEN. Easy, Jeff. *(Jeff rises with the case and dumps the rest on the floor.)*

JEFF. You can't take them! They belong here! *(Jeff hurls the empty suitcase to the ground.)*

BEN. For God's sake, Jeff!

JEFF. You can't leave! We've got to all stay here, together! *(Ben reaches out to Jeff.)*

BEN. Let me talk to you! *(Jeff pulls away viciously.)*

JEFF. Don't touch me!

BEN. Oh, God, Jeff!

JEFF. And don't you DARE cry!

BEN. Please, try to understand.

JEFF. Understand what?

BEN. Your Mother and I fight all the time, you must have heard us!

JEFF. I just turn up the T.V. and I don't hear anything.

BEN. That doesn't mean it isn't happening.

JEFF. I don't have to hear this! *(Jeff starts to try to leave. Ben stops him.)*

BEN. Yes, you do! Now, sit down. *(Ben sits him on the bed.)* It's happening and it has been happening for years, and you know it!

JEFF. No, I don't!

BEN. Yes, you do! There hasn't been peace or quiet or comfort in this house for a long time, and you know that, too.

JEFF. How do you know what I know? *(Helen enters and stands in the doorway with two coffee cups.)*

BEN. We can't go on like this, any of us. It has to stop sometime. Now, I know how you feel but . . .

JEFF. You don't know what I feel!

HELEN. Jeff, honey, please listen to us.

JEFF. Mom, ask him not to go! *(Ben and Helen look at each other. She can't do this and they both know it.)*

BEN. Jeff, about a week ago, I moved into a hotel, just temporarily, until I could find an apartment.

JEFF. Is that where you've been sleeping?

BEN. Yes.

HELEN. *(Astonished.)* You knew?

JEFF. I've seen you go every night.

BEN. *(To Helen.)* I knew we shouldn't have done it this way, we should have told him when I first left.

HELEN. Ben . . .

JEFF. But every morning you'd be back for breakfast.

BEN. *(To Helen.)* I told you this wouldn't work.

HELEN. All right, Ben!

HELEN. *(To Jeff.)* Why didn't you say something?

JEFF. Why didn't you?

HELEN. I still hoped that we could work things out. We were seeing a counselor and I thought if we could just solve some of the . . .

BEN. It was a dumb thing for us to do and we're sorry.

HELEN. *(Angrily to Ben.)* I thought it was best, Ben!

JEFF. I can help!

HELEN. No, Jeff there's nothing you can do.

JEFF. I can help around the house more. I can be quieter. I can stay out of the way more.

HELEN. You are not responsible for this in any way.

JEFF. From now on, I'll clean up my room. I won't play the T.V. loud or the stereo . . .

HELEN. Jeff . . .

JEFF. Just tell me what I did wrong and I'll fix it; I will!

BEN. Jeff, you are the one really good thing in our lives. You were never the problem.

HELEN. That's right, honey.

BEN. What's happening here is between your Mother and me. It's not your fault.

JEFF. So, why are you doing this?

HELEN. It's complicated . . . there are so many reasons.

JEFF. Like what?

HELEN. Things we thought we wanted when we got married, just don't seem to be the things we want now.

JEFF. What things?

BEN. Jeff, I need . . . want, your Mother to be the kind of wife she just can't be to me anymore. And she wants . . . needs, things from me that I just can't give her.

JEFF. I don't understand.

BEN. Sometimes, adults have to make decisions all their own. Now, they might not sound like good reasons to you but . . .

JEFF. You are changing everything in my whole life and you can't even give me one good reason why?

BEN. We can't keep living this way, Jeff!

JEFF. Because you fight? So what?

HELEN. It isn't only the fighting, Jeff.

JEFF. So, just stop! Stop fighting! Everything would be okay if you'd just . . .

BEN. It's why we fight.

JEFF. *(Very belligerent.)* Oh, yeah? Why?

BEN. *(Blurts it out.)* We just don't love each other anymore. *(Helen is shaken by this.)*

HELEN. Ben.

BEN. *(Realizing it himself for the first time.)* That's it, isn't it, Helen?

HELEN. I have never heard you say that before.

BEN. That's what's really wrong, isn't it?

HELEN. I don't know. *(Helen crosses away from him.)*

BEN. Don't you?

HELEN. If we could just solve some of the problems.

BEN. *(Simply.)* Helen, do you love me?

HELEN. I don't think we should talk about that here.

BEN. I do.

HELEN. But Jeff . . .

BEN. That's why we have to. Do you love me?

HELEN. There are things I love about you.

BEN. That's not what I . . .

HELEN. I know what you asked me.

BEN. And?

HELEN. *(Inaudible.)* No.

BEN. Helen?

JEFF. Mom?

HELEN. No. *(There is a long pause.)*

JEFF. Will you get a divorce?

HELEN. *(After a beat.)* Probably.

JEFF. And what I think doesn't matter?

HELEN. It matters very much.

JEFF. And if I don't want you to?

BEN. I'm sorry, Jeff.

JEFF. You don't care.

BEN. That's the hard part, we do care, maybe not enough, maybe not about the same things, but we do care.

JEFF. But you're getting a divorce.

BEN. Not from you. *(Ben tries to touch Jeff, who pulls away.)*

BEN. This day, Jeff, this day is the hardest. Things will be better for all of us when this day is over.

JEFF. And then what happens to me?

HELEN. You'll stay here with me for now and then we'll . . .

JEFF. I mean, who do I live with? Will I have to go to Portland? What if I don't want to go? Will I have to leave all my friends?

BEN. We'll settle all that later.

JEFF. Who decides what happens to me?

HELEN. We all will, together.

JEFF. How do I know you aren't lying to me again?

HELEN. Lying?

JEFF. What do you think all that sneaking around was?

BEN. *(Very firmly.)* Just a minute, sport, we may not have told you everything that was going on, but we never meant to lie to you.

HELEN. And when I tried to talk to you, you wouldn't listen. You just turned away and tuned me out.

BEN. This is a hard time for all of us. All of us, Jeff.

JEFF. From now on, will you tell me things?

BEN. Yes.

HELEN. From now on, will you listen?

JEFF. *(Softly.)* I'll try.

HELEN. And so will we.

BEN. We've got two whole months to figure this Portland thing out, so let's just take it a step at a time. Okay?

JEFF. Do I have a choice?

BEN. Come on, Jeff. I think you'll like my apartment. It has a room for you, and an elevator, and a pool. . . .

JEFF. Can I have a dog? *(Both Ben and Helen laugh.)*

BEN. We'll see.

JEFF. Will you ever decide to get back together again? *(They are caught off-guard and hesitate.)*

BEN. I don't think so.

JEFF. Mom?

HELEN. No. *(There is an awkward pause.)*

BEN. Well, if I'm going to get moved in, I'd better get with it. I still have to check out of the hotel and take my things from there. . . . *(He checks his watch.)* I'd better get with it. I'll come back for this stuff, Helen, okay?

(Helen nods. Ben takes a card out of his pocket and writes on it.)

BEN. Jeff, let me write down the address of the apartment for you. Come see me anytime. I've got a phone, so just call and I'll come for you.

JEFF. *(Turns away from him.)* I can take the bus.

BEN. Anytime, Jeff, I'll come for you anytime. . . . *(No response from Jeff.)* I'll call you. *(He stands there for moment, uncertain.)* Jeff? *(He holds out his arms, Jeff crosses to him and hugs him. Before the hug is really completed, Jeff pulls away.)*

JEFF. See ya. *(Jeff turns away. Ben looks at Helen, she is looking away.)*

BEN. Helen? . . . Take care. *(He starts out.)*

HELEN. You too. *(Ben exits through the small door. Both Jeff and Helen look toward the door as we hear Ben's footsteps disappearing. A final door shuts off stage and the sound shudders through Helen's body.)*

HELEN. *(After a beat to compose herself.)* You okay?

JEFF. *(Shrugs)* You?

HELEN. Lousy.

JEFF. Me, too.

HELEN. Well, at least we're lousy together.

JEFF. Yeah. *(After a beat.)* I hate this.

HELEN. I know. I hate it with you. *(Jeff turns to her and looks away. Helen moves toward him slightly and speaks from her own need for comfort as much as his.)* Jeff, what do you do when you feel rotten? What do you do when you're really depressed?

JEFF. I don't know. . . . Nothing. . . . Sometimes I take a walk and just look around for something I like. Something like a leaf or a piece of glass or something, and I just look at it for a while.

HELEN. *(This is a risky question for her.)* Want to take a walk?

JEFF. *(His voice says "yes," his body says "no.")* Okay.

HELEN. I'll get the house key. *(Helen exits to her room. Jeff crosses to the desk and picks up the card, he looks at it and then at the small door. He puts the card in his pocket. Finding release in activity, he gathers up Ben's clothes and puts them in the suitcase. Helen enters and stands in the doorway.)*

JEFF. After we get back, I'll take these over to Dad's. *(Jeff indicates the dummy.)* And then I'll take this over to Sandy's.

HELEN. Okay. *(Jeff starts out the door, Helen waits, unsure. Jeff turns and really sees her for the first time since Ben's exit.)*

JEFF. Let's go, Mom. *(He holds out his hand to her. She takes it and they exit out the small door. There is music. Lights dim to black.)*

(Curtain.)

Production Notes

Off-stage Argument

I have deliberately not written specific dialogue for the off-stage argument. In an earlier draft I did try to sketch it out, but I felt it tended to limit and constrain the actors, and sounded artificial.

It is my intention that the argument should be created improvisationally by the actors and the director, and that the improvisational quality be maintained in production.

Some guidelines might be helpful:

It should be a real argument, and not random words or sounds. The actors should decide what specific circumstances and previous action have led Ben and Helen to this particular moment and each should have specific and conflicting motivations and objectives.

The dynamics of the argument must be modulated to work with the primary action on stage. Off-stage sounds must never overwhelm what is happening on stage, but should underscore action, and provoke reactions from Jeff and Sandy. At the same time, there must be variety, build, and flow to the off-stage sounds.

When Ben and Helen enter a scene on stage in "reality" they must bring some of their previous off-stage actions with them. When they enter a scene in "fantasy" they are primarily projections of Jeff's thoughts, fears, hopes, and feelings.

Treatment of the Fantasies

Perhaps the most important direction for my intention concerning the fantasies is to keep in mind that they are grounded in Jeff's needs in real life. It is this relevance to reality, rather than a departure from the real world, that gives these scenes their power.

Every director will interpret this in a different way, and will make his or her own stylistic choices. This is as it should be. I feel that light and sound can be important elements in introducing and underscoring these scenes. It must be clear that they are somehow different visually, rhythmically, and emotionally from the scenes "in reality," but they must move the dramatic action of the play forward, rather than divert it.

If Jeff's motivations and objectives are the springboards for fantasy, then the best stylistic choices can be made.

A Final Note

The words and actions of this play provide all the essentials for production; but much of the depth and intensity of this script must be found between the lines, in subtext, and in silence. The story yields only the uppermost layer and there is much to be discovered and created by actors and directors. I urge you to be bold in your emotional choices, to be clear and specific with the development of all relationships, and to bring the same emotional intensity to both the words of the text and the thoughts and feelings which remain unspoken.

The Martian Chronicles

By Ray Bradbury

Adapted by Candace M. Sorensen

The Martian Chronicles

(Bradbury short story, 1950; dramatization, 1977; re-adapted by Candace M. Sorensen, 1985)

Predominantly a short story writer, Ray Bradbury has attained worldwide recognition for his science fiction writings depicting man's struggle to survive in an increasingly technological age. Bradbury's stories translate well into plays, and *The Martian Chronicles* is no exception. *The Martian Chronicles* is a series of episodes relating to the colonization of Mars by Earth beginning in the late twentieth century. As the play begins, the first rocket is taking off for Mars. The scene gives us an expectation of immediate and glorious triumph in space.

The rest of the play is set on Mars, with the opening scene showing Martian domestic life as we meet YLL and his wife YLLA. YLL displays Earthlike emotions when he becomes jealous of his wife's dream of a handsome Earthman. YLL's jealousy results in the destruction of the First Expedition. Through telepathy the Martians prepare themselves for invasion and successfully destroy the next two Earthman missions.

Ironically, the chicken-pox disease brought by the Earthmen becomes a plague which destroys the Martian population. The Fourth Expedition lands to find only one survivor, Lt. Spender of the Third Expedition. What Spender has witnessed is driving him insane. He begins to adopt a Martian viewpoint and sees the Earthmen as invaders who must be killed. Captain Wilder of the Fourth Expedition sympathizes with Spender's fears, but is forced to kill Spender to protect the mission.

Through Sam Parkhill, a member of the Fourth Expedition, we see American materialism at its worst being transferred to Mars. Parkhill's dream is to have a hot dog stand on Mars and become rich feeding off the planet. Just as his dream is about to come true, Earth is destroyed in a nuclear war.

The play ends with Captain Wilder and his family beginning to recognize Mars as a place for them to see the mistakes of the past, and, hopefully, to benefit from them.

CHARACTERS

Peggy	Mr. III	Wilder
Mrs. Collins	Mr. UUU	Parkhill
Billy	Miss RRR	Hathaway
Voice of Nathaniel York	Mr. WWW	Biggs
Voice of Houston	Mr. XXX	Cherokee
Narrator	Black	Driscoll
YLL	Hinkston	Elma
YLLA	Henley	The Martian
Williams	Spender	Ishmael
Young	Grandpa	Robert
Mrs. TTT	Sports Announcer	Leonora
Martian Girl	Skip	Peregrine
	Mrs. Black	

SETTING
Earth and Mars.

TIME
Late twentieth century.

The Martian Chronicles

Florida. A present time we've not yet seen.

PEGGY. What's that?

MRS. COLLINS. *(Pointing.)* It's over there.

BILLY. The light! Look at the light, mom!

(*The rumbling is deafening as the four close their eyes amid a pool of crimson light, their coats open or off. A few beats and the rumbling and light fade away.*)

BILLY. Gone.

MRS. COLLINS. Over and done.

BILLY. Gone.

PEGGY. Where is it going?

BILLY. You mean the rocket?

PEGGY. Yes.

BILLY. Didn't you hear? I thought *everybody* knew! It's going to Mars!

PEGGY. *(Startled.)* Mars?

BILLY. *(Pointing proudly.)* Yes,—MARS!

(*A quick blackout as the radio conversation between Mars Mission One and Houston Control is heard above some stellar traveling music.*)

YORK'S VOICE. Come in, Mission Control—this is Nathaniel York, Mars Mission One. Do you read me?

VOICE OF HOUSTON. Roger, Mission One—this is Houston. We read you clear, over.

YORK'S VOICE. Two million miles from Earth—condition A.O.K., over.

VOICE OF HOUSTON. Roger, Mission One—you're looking fine. Condition: greenlight, over and out. *(Three beats.)*

VOICE OF HOUSTON. Mission One, this is Houston requesting computer check. Do you read, over. *(Beat.)* Mission One, this is Houston requesting computer check. Do you read, over.

YORK'S VOICE. Uh, roger, Houston—fifty million miles out and all systems are fine. Repeat, all systems fine. Mission One approaching Mars. *(Fading.)* Approaching—approaching—approaching—

(The music has dwindled to a lonely, almost empty sound. It is haunting yet strangely magnetic.)

SCENE I

Mars. The home of the K family.

(Shortly following the radio voices.)

(Slowly a light rises to pinspot a slender rack upon which are hung strange musical instruments, "books" upon which are an arrangement of harp strings which "sing" their contents. The sound becomes the wind blowing over the harp strings, and faint murmurings of strange voices. Finally one Voice speaks softly.)

THE VOICE. These are the Chronicles of Mars. These are the books which, touched like harps, tell tales of Futures Forgotten, and Pasts that are soon to Happen. These are the Chronicles— which sing ancient voice tales of when the sea was red steam on the shores, and men carried clouds of metal insects and golden guns which shot poisonous bees into battle.

(The light comes up on YLLA, a Martian woman, seated to one side, her eyes shut.)

(We now see YLL, her husband, seated to one side in his own light. He touches a harp-like device in his hands. A soft voice sings from it. Swaying quietly, YLLA begins to dream. As the music intensifies, her body trembles, her mouth gasps. Suddenly she sits straight up and cries out—not loud, but loud enough.)

YLL. *(Stopping.)* Did you call? You cried out.

YLLA. Did I? No, I was dreaming.

YLL. In the daytime? *(Snorts.)*

YLLA. *(Trying to remember.)* A strange dream. A dream about—a man. A tall man—six feet, one inch tall.

YLL. Ridiculous. A beast. A giant. What *will* you dream next. Impossible hair, perhaps? *Black* hair?

YLLA. *(Startled.)* How did you—? Well, black it was! And he had very white skin: He was dressed in a strange uniform and he came from the sky and spoke pleasantly to me.

YLL. From the sky?

YLLA. He came in a metal—

YLL. *(Echoing telepathically.)* —metal—

YLLA. —metal thing that glittered in the sun. A long silver craft. And a door opened in the side of the silver—

YLL. —silver—

YLLA. He spoke. "I come from the third planet in my ship. My name is Nathaniel York.—"

YLL. A stupid name.

YLLA. Of course, it was only a dream. And he said, "We come from a city on—*Earth:* that is the name of my world." Earth was the name he spoke, and he used another language but *I* understood him with my mind.

YLL. *(Moves away.)* Telepathy.

YLLA. YLL—do you ever wonder if there *are* beings living on the third planet?

YLL. The third planet is incapable of supporting life. Our scientists have said there is far too much oxygen—

YLLA. —oxygen—

YLL. —oxygen in the atmosphere. *(Strokes harp; music sounds.)* You did not dream. *(Again and louder.)* There was no ship. *(And again, and louder.)* No man. No black hair.

(YLLA has moved off to do housework. She begins humming. It is the first part of "Drink to Me Only With Thine Eyes.")

What's that song?

YLLA. *(Realizing.)* I don't know. *(Touches mouth.)* Wait. *(Thinks and sings.)* "Drink to me only with thine eyes—and I will pledge with mine—"

YLL. *(Under her last line.)* But of course! You composed it! And that language, yes! You made up a new language! Good. Excellent.

YLLA. "Or leave a kiss within the cup, and I'll not ask—"

BOTH. "—for wine."

YLL. Very fine. Very amusing.

YLLA. *(Suddenly alarmed.)* No, you mustn't! I didn't make it up! I didn't compose it, I—

(She stops, embarrassed. He has tried to take away and destroy her dream. She has seized it back. She lowers her eyes.)

YLL. I tell you what. Let's fly into town tonight.

YLLA. Tonight?

YLL. Tonight, yes. For an entertainment.

YLLA. But we haven't gone anywhere for—

YLL. Then all the more reason. Come along. *(Takes her elbow.)*

YLLA. *(Looking at the sky; stunned.)* I—

YLL. You what?

YLLA. I don't—

YLL. You *do.* You will come.

YLLA. *(Steps away; firm.)* No.

YLL. Why?

YLLA. I don't know. I must *wait.*

YLL. *(Turning his back on her.)* I knew it!

YLLA. *Knew*?

YLL. *(To anything but her.)* All night, you should have heard yourself: talking, murmuring, whispering, fawning—

YLLA. —fawning—

YLL. —fawning on him; singing, gods yes, singing; you should have heard yourself!

YLLA. Oh, YLL, my good husband.

YLL. *(Facing her.)* When does his ship land?

YLLA. It doesn't land—it's not real!

YLL. *(Circles her.)* In this dream didn't his ship—I heard you—didn't his ship land this afternoon, an hour from now perhaps?

YLLA. *(Frightened.)* Perhaps.

YLL. *(Bends over her.)* In Green Valley?

YLLA. *(Very uneasy now.)* I don't think—

YLL. But you *do* think, and you said out loud in your sleep. Green Valley. Today. An hour from now. Today.

YLLA. But you don't believe in dreams. *I* don't believe in dreams. Then why—

YLL. —why—

YLLA. —why are you so upset?

(He moves to put some small packets in his pockets and sling a ribbon of peculiar objects over his shoulder, like an ammunition belt.)

YLL. This is all very ridiculous. I shall go for a walk.

YLLA. *(Watching him.)* Today is your day to go to town.

YLL. A walk will calm me down.

YLLA. Then why are you taking your gun?

YLL. *(Looks down; surprised.)* Well, so I am. I picked it up without thinking. Good! I might see something to shoot for dinner.

YLLA. I don't like things that are shot.

YLL. Very well, then. I shall simply practice.

(He touches his gun, which hums under its breath.)

Isn't that a *fine* sound?

(He does it again. The sound makes YLLA rise suddenly and reach for a light cloak.)

Where are you going?

YLLA. *(Making something up.)* I—to Pao's. I promised—

YLL. —promised—

YLLA. —promised her. I haven't seen her in a long time. *(Starts to exit.)*

YLL. I *am* sorry.

(His voice stops her. They face each other and "speak" tele-pathically.)

YLLA'S VOICE. You want me to stay here. *(He nods.)* You have some deliveries of materials coming in the next hour. *(He nods.)* And *someone* must be here to accept delivery.

YLL'S VOICE. Some priceless old harp-singing books ten thousand years old. You *will* stay. *(She nods.)* You *will* wait. *(She nods.)* *Good* wife.

(He turns and puts on a silver mask and adjusts his gun.)

YLL. I won't be long. A few minutes at most.

(He makes the gun hum very loudly. It sounds like a million bees turned angrily on themselves in the noon sun.)

YLL. Isn't that a lovely sound?

YLLA. *(Numbed by it.)* A lovely sound.

(He waves and exits as the gun sound fades away. She relaxes when it is gone. She turns around and about trying to decide what to do. She runs to the stage apron to look out and up at the sky; listening, waiting, shielding her eyes. Then turns to go sit with a harp-book in her hands. She touches it. It whispers music. Almost instantly she is up again; impatiently prowling.)

YLLA. *(To herself.)* It was just a dream, that's all. Only a dream.

(Suddenly a pleasing musical version of "Drink to Me Only With Thine Eyes" is heard. She stops, her hand to her mouth.)

And yet, that *music.* Those strange words! *(Beat.)* I *must* go see.

(She grabs her cloak and starts out again.)

YLL'S VOICE. You will—*wait!*

(At that moment there is a great sound of passing thunder in the sky. Riven, she spins about, runs to stage apron to look up. Her face brightens with a fiery light from above.

YLLA. *(Joyous.)* The fire! The first in the sky! Oh, look, look! How beautiful!

(The sound fades as does the light on her face.)

It's there, I can *hear* it.

(From the distance there is a faint stir of music, the sound of "Drink to Me . . . ," she closes her eyes and speaks what she sees in her head.)

Just beyond the hill and closer! Whatever it is will come here. Here! And *touch* the door! And walk into this room—and—

(A burst of sound like a great swarming of bees caught in a single rifle shot crushes YLLA's vision with its sound. She winces as if shot herself. Silence.)

No! No!

(She runs to look out at the hills, where the fire fell to earth.)

No, no, please! Please!

(Silence. She bites the back of her hand and gestures with her other hand for the vision to come back.)

(Surprised.) Footsteps! He's coming! *(Now we can hear the footsteps.)*

(The door opens. YLL steps in. He nods to her, removes his mask, slings the gun freely in his hand, slaps it, bows to her as she stands stunned.)

YLL. I will—thank you.

YLLA. *(Numbly.)* —come in.

YLL. Grand day.

YLLA. I heard you fire your gun.

YLL. Lovely day. Yes.

YLLA. Did you kill something?

YLL. A bright bird—

YLLA. *(Almost a shriek.)* —bird?!—

YLL. —bird that flew away to die. I was almost sad. I hadn't the heart to bring it home.

YLLA. *(Turns to prepare food.)* I would like to have—seen that bird.

YLL. I'm ravenous. Shall we eat?

(She hands him his plate and he sits with it. She turns away.)

YLLA. I wish—I wish I could remember—

YLL. What?

YLLA. The words to that song.

YLL. —song—

YLLA. —song. That lovely song. *(Hums some wrong notes.)* I've forgotten it. And somehow I want to remember it. I want *always*—

YLL. —always—

YLLA. —always to remember it. And— *(She breaks.)* —I *can't!* I can't!

YLL. YLLA, why are you doing this?

YLLA. *(Getting control.)* I don't know. I weep and I don't know why. I don't—I don't know why!

YLL. *(Pats her; beat.)* You'll be all right—tomorrow.

(She opens her eyes and looks at the sky; searching, searching. Her gaze falls at last, to her hands tumbled and clenched in her lap.)

YLLA. Yes. *(Nods numbly.)* I'll be all right—tomorrow.

SCENE 2

Mars. A night theatre, August 1999.

(A single stroke of harp music is heard. A beat of silence is followed by The Voice coming from the darkness.)

THE VOICE. August 1999. An evening in summer upon the placid and temperate planet Mars. People were gathered at a night theatre under the stars, to hear their favorite orchestra play.

(We hear the sounds of an audience settling. The lights come up on four or five Musicians holding strange instruments, wearing exotic, silver Martian masks. After tuning up, one nods to the others, who then play a strange music with many beautiful and strange sounds. The music continues for maybe thirty seconds. And then we suddenly hear, as if broadcast from outer space or coming in from an approaching rocket, a

full band recording of Sousa's "Stars and Stripes Forever." The Musicians stop, look around, look up, searching for the source of the music. They gaze at each other and their instruments. The crowd murmurs. The men begin again. They play for about fifteen seconds this time and are then interrupted by yet another, faster section of "Stars and Stripes." The Musicians stop, stunned. The audience murmurs louder. They start a final time and get about seconds along in their recital when, at a frighteningly maniacal speed, we hear "Stars and Stripes" at an insane tempo. The Musicians panic. We hear the audience cry out and run away. And then the Musicians themselves flee in terror. The music builds and suddenly ends as the lights go out. A gentle harp sounds. Again, The Voice is heard from the darkness.)

THE VOICE. The musicians fled. The audience ran away. Something was happening. Something, once more, was coming near. All over the night side of Mars lovers awoke to listen to their loved ones who lay humming, or murmuring strange words in the darkness.

Mars: The asylum. A short time later.

(The stage is barren. As lights come up on the downstage area, Captain Jonathan Williams and his crew enter, surprised at the emptiness. They are in their flight uniforms.)

WILLIAMS. Wait here.

YOUNG. *(Producing "gun.")* Captain—

WILLIAMS. I said no weapons. This is a peaceful mission. They must have seen us land, there's been no sign of hostility. We'll take things as they come, one at a time.

YOUNG. But sir, what about York?

WILLIAMS. We don't know. We don't know anything yet. So we'll talk to *them.* Ask questions. Just wait here.

(The lights come up on the rest of the stage, revealing Mrs. TTT moving about her invisible house. She wears a golden metallic robe of sorts. The house is quite real to her as she cleans, rearranges. Williams approaches where he thinks the "door" might be. He raises his hand and a light flickers and a bell sounds, indicating that the door is open. He starts a bit, but approaches her.)

WILLIAMS. I, uh—excuse me, I'm Captain Jonathan Williams, commander of Mars Mission Two from—

MRS. TTT. *(Finishing his sentence.)* —from the planet Earth! Yes, yes, of course you are! What took you so long?

WILLIAMS. So long? Well, it's nearly 300 million miles from Earth to Mars, and—

MRS. TTT. *(Outraged; surprised.)* Mars?!?

WILLIAMS. *(Quietly.)* This *is* the fourth planet from the sun?

MRS. TTT. Of course it is. But if you want to use the proper name, this is the planet TIR.

WILLIAMS. TIR! That's a fine name.

MRS. TTT. Well?

WILLIAMS. Well, as I started to explain, I'm Captain of the second expedition from Earth—

MRS. TTT. Earth! Yes, I know. We've been all through that, haven't we?

WILLIAMS. But there was a first landing. Another—

MRS. TTT. —another expedition before you. And both the men and their ship have vanished completely!

WILLIAMS. You know! *(To Crew.)* She knows!

(The crew move up behind Williams, confused.)

This is very important. If you know anything at all—

MRS. TTT. Oh, dear, there are more of you!

WILLIAMS. Yes, there are Lieutenants Young and Rollins.

ROLLINS. Hello—

MRS. TTT. My, my! It *is* the illusion of the hour, the delusion of the day, the cliche of the moment!

WILLIAMS. I beg your pardon?

MRS. TTT. I'm afraid you'll have to excuse me now. I'm much too busy today. Much, *much* too busy. Good-bye!

WILLIAMS. *(It finally hits him.)* Wait! You speak perfect English.

MRS. TTT. I do not speak—I think!

(She closes the "door" and continues her cleaning. The Men stand there in a confused and awkward silence, unable to even discuss what they have just encountered. Williams shrugs and "knocks" again. Mrs. TTT ignores it. He "knocks" a second time and she signs and opens the door.)

WILLIAMS. I'm sorry. You don't seem to understand—

MRS. TTT. But *I* understand completely. It is *your* thought that disturbs.

YOUNG. We're from Earth.

MRS. TTT. You mean from out of the ground? I haven't the time for you today, *or* your friends. *I* have a lot of work to do: cooking and sewing and dusting—

WILLIAMS. *(Starting forward.)* Please! Stay and listen to—

MRS. TTT. *(Points; horrified.)* Oh! Look at those boots!

(He steps back.)

Mud and dirt all over my clean floor! Now you'll *have* to get out! Please! Out, out, out, out. Out, out, out, out, out! *(She shoos him out of the "house." Musing.)* I should send you to see Mr. III.

WILLIAMS. Mr. III?

MRS. TTT. The next farm. Over by the blue canal. He'll advise you what to do.

(She disappears as the lights fade on her area. The Crew move downstage, totally confused.)

ROLLINS. How do you figure that!

YOUNG. You think they're all as crazy as her, Captain?

WILLIAMS. Well, let's hope not.

ROLLINS. Well, what do we do now, sir? We still don't have any idea where York ended up.

WILLIAMS. I guess we'll just have to take the good lady's advice. Let's go.

(They begin crossing the stage, passing silhouettes of houses as the lights change. A small Girl stands stage left playing with a yo-yo sort of spider which climbs and descends. She

does not notice the approach of the four weary Men, who circle her, hopefully.)

YOUNG. *(Spotting her first.)* Captain?

WILLIAMS. *(Friendly.)* Hello.

GIRL. *(Noncommittally.)* Hello.

WILLIAMS. You know, I got a little boy back home just about your age. He's sure going to be excited when I tell him he'll have playmates up here on Mars.

GIRL. You mean the planet TIR.

WILLIAMS. TIR. Got it. How would *you* like to hear a story?

(He puts her on his knee, but she keeps playing with her spider as if he weren't there.)

Now, not long ago, a spaceship landed near here, and all of the sudden, the spaceship disappeared—and the men *in* it disappeared too. Now, we've come in a second ship. We traveled across the solar system. You understand what I'm saying?

(The Girl continues playing, oblivious to the Men.)

We came all—all the way from *Earth*. Do you believe us?

GIRL. *(Calmly.)* If you say so.

WILLIAMS. Not because *we* say so, because it's true. Now, once again— I'm Captain Williams and these men are my crew.

GIRL. And never before in all of history has anyone ever crossed space in a great big rocketship.

WILLIAMS. *(A bit surprised.)* Yes, that's right. Very good!

GIRL. *(Shrugs.)* Telepathy.

WILLIAMS. Little girl, we're looking for those men who disappeared. Now, maybe you can help.

GIRL. You know what?

WILLIAMS. What?

GIRL. You should go see Mr. III. You need him!

(She scampers offstage as Mr. III enters behind them.)

WILLIAMS. Wait!

MR. III. Can I help you?

(They turn quickly as Mr. III crosses to Williams.)

WILLIAMS. Mr. III?

MR. III. Yes. What can I do for you?

WILLIAMS. Well, you can listen to me. Please, please listen.

MR. III. If that will make you happy, I'm listening. Proceed.

WILLIAMS. *(Taking a breath.)* We're from Earth. That may not be your name for our planet, but—look. If I concentrate, make mental images of our world—

MR. III. Please do.

(Williams shuts his eyes and concentrates as Mr. III describes what he sees in Williams' mind.)

Tall glass and metal cities, blue seas—yes, that's very nice. Please continue. *(Beat.)* Ah, pictures of a ship, lifting off, drifting timelessly—days, months. *(Beat.)* What's this? Here? Great red planet. Circling—circling and settling *here!*

WILLIAMS. Now, do you understand?

MR. III. *(Produces silvery pad.)* Yes, very clear. Now, if you will just sign here, please.

WILLIAMS. Sign?

MR. III. You're from Earth, aren't you? Well, there's nothing for it but to sign. It's just a formality.

WILLIAMS. *(Taking pad.)* You want my men to sign also?

MR. III. *(Excited.)* Your *men* sign? How extraordinary! I must tell Mr. XXX! *(Pointing.)* If you will just sign here as well.

WILLIAMS. Here?

MR. III. That's the provision for sleeping. Mr. XXX will make the arrangements after your interview. *(Produces key.)* Now, here you are—the key!

(Williams takes it eagerly as if it were a local honor.)

No, no, your picture is wrong. It's not the key to the city, it's the key to the house! *(Pointing.)* Fourth building on the right. You may spend the night there. I will send Mr. XXX to see you.

(He starts to go but senses something in Williams' mind and turns.)

(Impatient.) What is it? What are you waiting for? *(Getting it.)*
Oh, yes—of course. *(Ecstatic, shaking hands.)* Congratulations! Well done! Welcome!

WILLIAMS. *(A little dazed.)* Thank you.

(Mr. III exits.)

*(The Crew are now totally confused. Williams looks at the
key and looks at the others, who casually nod. He uses the
key on empty air. Suddenly the light sources shift and fantastic, new colors appear. Williams and his men move into a
large "room" where there are murmurs, signs, and faint music.
They are surrounded by shadows, people in various costumes,
masks, etc. One of them, Mr. UUU, steps forward.)*

ROLLINS. Captain—

MR. UUU. Welcome! I'm Mr. UUU.

WILLIAMS. Jonathan Williams of New York City, on Earth!

*(Pandemonium, chaos, shouts and yells. The Inmates surge
forward. We hear whistles, stompings, shouts, the cries of a
full mob in celebration. They rush about the Crew, pummel-
ing them happily, waving banners. At last they pull away. The
Crew wipe tears from their eyes, shaking their heads, swaying
and holding each other with emotion.)*

WILLIAMS. *(Collecting himself.)* Thank you. Thank you very much.

*(The crowd murmurs, pleased. Mr. UUU steps forward again
and shakes hands with Williams.)*

MR. UUU. Welcome. It's good to see another man from Earth.

WILLIAMS. *(Excited.)* Another! You mean Captain York, the *first*
mission is here?

MR. UUU. *(Touches his own chest.)* I mean *I* am from Earth—

INMATES. —Earth—

MR. UUU. —also.

WILLIAMS. *(Shocked and dismayed.)* I don't understand.

MR. UUU. Nevertheless, it is true.

WILLIAMS. How is that possible? What country are you from?

MR. UUU. Tuierol. I came by the Spirit—

INMATES. *(Pantomiming.)* —Spirit—

MR. UUU. —Spirit of my body—years ago!

WILLIAMS. Tuierol?

MISS RRR. And I am from Earth, also!

MR. WWW. And I!

ROLLINS. Tuierol, sir? I—

MISS RRR. I come from *Orri*, on Earth, a place of jungles—all green forever! And all the cities—

INMATES. —cities—

MISS RRR. —cities are silver!

(Miss RRR pantomimes the jungle, the green. The others imitate her without looking at her.)

MISS RRR. Earth is water. My planet is all water with cities in the sea!

MR. WWW. Earth is dust—desert. We are friends—

INMATES. —friends—

MR. WWW. —friends of the Serpent!

YOUNG. *(Uneasy.)* Captain, what is going on here?

WILLIAMS. Now take it easy.

ROLLINS. Easy! Look at them, sir! They're not from Earth, look at their skin!

YOUNG. Captain, the walls are solid and there are no windows!

WILLIAMS. No—of course not. Now I understand why they gave us the key. Here we are.

YOUNG. Where, sir?

WILLIAMS. *(Looking about; cautiously.)* An asylum.

(The lights begin changing as Williams and his Men are surrounded by the shadows of dreams and fantasies. Inmates become statues and pillars of mists and clouds that float away, only to come back as strange beasts. They move, they dance, they wail and gesticulate. In the midst of it all, the Crew, calmer now and intrigued, watch.)

WILLIAMS. Not only are these people insane, but seem to be able to *project* their insanity.

YOUNG. Then they think *we're* crazy, too—just projecting our fantasies about Earth.

ROLLINS. They're passing us off as someone else. That's what all those forms were all about!

YOUNG. How long are they going to *keep* us here?

ROLLINS. Until we prove we're not psychotic.

YOUNG. Do you think there's a way out, sir?

MISS RRR. Of course there's a way out.

MR. UUU. Just open—

INMATES. —open—

MR. UUU. —open the door.

WILLIAMS. But the key—

MISS RRR. That's to keep people from getting *in*.

MR. UUU. Only those who deserve to get in—

INMATES. —get in!

YOUNG. Captain, they're right. It's open!

WILLIAMS. *(Nods; gestures.)* Come on! Let's get out of here!

Mars: Outside the asylum.

(They move swiftly out as the Inmates go about their fantasies and gradually vanish with the asylum. The Crew are immediately confronted by Mr. XXX, who steps from the shadows, surprised. Rollins spots him first.)

ROLLINS. Captain—

MR. XXX. Captain Williams, there you are! What are you doing outside?

WILLIAMS. I'll tell you what we're doing. We're getting out of that asylum your friends sent us to!

MR. XXX. Asylum! What a curious expression!

WILLIAMS. You think we're insane, sir—but we're *not*!

MR. XXX. Inaccurate! I do not think that you *all* are insane, sir. *(Points.)* Just *you*, sir. Your friends are primary and secondary hallucinations.

YOUNG. Captain, he thinks you imagined us!

MR. XXX. Your projections remain intact. If you were well, they would vanish.

WILLIAMS. If my men are imaginary—projections—then—

YOUNG. *(Cutting in.)* —cure him! Cure him and make *us* vanish.

ROLLINS. Yeah. Make *us* disappear!

MR. XXX. Not so easily accomplished. Your case is advanced, unique. This recent outbreak of mass psychosis seems to manifest in several stages. The people in the house are simpler forms, but your projections of Earth and Earth men are fully auditory, optical—olfactory. The most detailed hallucinatory complex I have ever observed!

WILLIAMS. Look! You can touch these men! They're warm, solid, breathing human beings! Not figments of a hypnotized imagination! Go on—touch them.

(Mr. XXX gingerly reaches out to touch one of the Crew. He pulls back.)

WILLIAMS. There. Doesn't that prove something?

MR. XXX. Yes, I'm afraid it does. *(Nods.)* The extended ability of your condition.

WILLIAMS. How do I prove to you that I'm cured when I don't need curing?

MR. XXX. A fascinating paradox, sir.

YOUNG. Captain—the lander!?

WILLIAMS. We'll show you!

MR. XXX. Your ship! Yes, I'd like to see it. Will you manifest it here?

WILLIAMS. I won't because I can't. It's not far from here. If you'll just follow us.

MR. XXX. Of course.

(Williams and his Crew circle the country again, followed by Mr. XXX. At last they stop. We hear a humming offstage. They all stare off at the Lander.)

WILLIAMS. There. A Type 2-SDX Lander.

MR. XXX. *(Delighted.)* Amazing! What a grand ship! Congratulations! It is all there!

WILLIAMS. That's right—every rivet, every bolt. Just like I said.

MR. XXX. Incredible! I hear it humming!

WILLIAMS. The generator.

MR. XXX. *(Overwhelmed; staring.)* Never have I experienced such a complexity! Metal—rubber—even the shadows on the ground. *(To Williams with immense respect.)* You—are a psychotic genius! I will write my greatest monograph on this. *(Beat.)* You *have* signed the papers?

WILLIAMS. What?

MR. XXX. The euthanasia forms—?

YOUNG. *(Alarmed.)* Captain!

MR. XXX. Mr. III's information was accurate. You are incurable, of course. We shall sleep you away. Free your spirit from this diseased body form.

WILLIAMS. *(Enough of this.)* Listen to me! I'm Captain Jonathan Williams, Commander of Mars Mission Two.

(Mr. XXX produces a laser pistol and aims it point blank at Williams.)

MR. XXX. Yes!

(He fires. Williams falls dead. The others run. Mr. XXX fires at Young and Rollins. They all fall and are quite dead. Mr. XXX is a bit shaken. He stares at the bodies, which have not vanished. Then turns to stare at the Lander offstage. He blinks, shaken even more now.)

No—the ship—impossible! *(Beat.)* His dream is in my mind.

(He goes over to one of the bodies and gets down on his knees and dares to slowly touch the "dream" body that will not go away. He gasps and pulls back, shrieking.)

I refuse you!

(He looks at all the bodies, almost hysterical. A sudden, dangerous calm sweeps over him as he slowly feels his own arms and face. Quite logical.) Incurable—of course.

(He lifts the laser gun to his chin and pulls the trigger. The gun fires, throwing him back, dead. The lights fade as we hear The Voice from the darkness.)

THE VOICE. The bodies lay waiting. At sunset, night creatures came and took them away into the hills for food. The next morning, some children saw the rocket and had a fine day running up and down the ladder.

SCENE 3

Mars: Space surrounding Mars, March 2002.

(We hear the static of a space transmission.)

BLACK'S VOICE. Mars Mission Three approaching Mars. Mars Rocket Three preparing to touch down.

VOICE OF HOUSTON. Houston here, Mission Three. Captain Black, delay landing until we collect data on the first two missions. Repeat—

BLACK'S VOICE. Negative, Houston. The guys have been in space three hundred days. Request permission to land. Repeat—request permission to land, Houston. Over.

(There is a long pause.)

VOICE OF HOUSTON. Permission granted.

(The stage is totally dark. Perhaps there is a mist about. A man, Hinkston, steps out of the dark and listens. But there is only silence. Soon Captain Black steps forward, followed soon by a female crewman, Henley. The silence is broken by the crowing of a rooster. They look at each other.)

HINKSTON. Captain? Did you hear what I heard?

BLACK. Shhh! Wait. *(Looking off.)* There!

HENLEY. It couldn't be—

HINKSTON. A rooster on Mars, sir?

(The lights slowly begin to come up. We are aware of faint music. One bar of "Beautiful Ohio," to be exact. Hinkston sees and points.) Captain!

BLACK. Oak trees—elms!

HENLEY. Maples!

(The sounds of a small town awakening are now faintly audible; birds chirping, etc. The sound of a familiar machine is heard.)

BLACK. That doesn't make any sense!

HINKSTON. Captain, look! Lawns! It's green as far as you can see!

HENLEY. Birds?

BLACK. Yes. But that's impossible—it just can't be! Songbirds, roosters, elms!

HINKSTON. Lawns! *(Beat.)* Sir, look!

BLACK. It's a town!

(The lights come up more as the music becomes a bit louder. All around them, projected on scrims, are images of trees and houses that could only have been built in the early twentieth century, the Midwest.)

HENLEY. Illinois!

HINKSTON. Iowa!

BLACK. Could be either.

HINKSTON. Captain, sir—I know these houses. It's Grinnell, Iowa!

HENLEY. Green Town, Illinois. *(Beat.)* Captain, I think I understand.

BLACK. Yes, Henley, what?

HENLEY. We've made a mistake. We circled around and landed back on Earth.

HINKSTON. That's it, sir—that's *got* to be it!

BLACK. No, we traveled three hundred million miles in a year. Last night we orbited Mars. You *saw* it. We've landed.

HENLEY. We've doubled back sir—that *must* be it! It explains why we lost contact with the *first* two missions.

BLACK. No, there's something wrong—I can *sense* it!

HENLEY. It *is* possible, sir, by some accident in time or space, we shifted dimensions and landed back on an Earth that's thirty or forty *years* ago!

BLACK. *(Into communicator.)* Lustig, Walls, Spender, this is the Captain. Stay on board. Under *no* circumstances leave the ship. Repeat, do *not* leave the ship!

SPENDER'S VOICE. Spender here, Captain—check.

HINKSTON. Captain—there's another possibility.

BLACK. What?

(They begin walking along their way. Actually just patterns along the stage.)

HINKSTON. Parallel civilizations! Mars and Earth!

BLACK. *(Doubting.)* Parallel architecture, houses, *trees?* Not very likely.

BLACK. *(Also stopping.)* What is it?

(Hinkston is looking down. He drops to one knee and stares at something. He picks up a tennis racket and examines it strangely and tenderly.)

HINKSTON. It's my tennis racket!

BLACK. Yours? What do you mean, *yours?*

HINKSTON. *(Showing him.)* Yes, sir. These are my initials! I owned this racket when I was fifteen years old! What the hell's it doing here?

(Hinkston becomes mesmerized.)

BLACK. Hinkston, put that down. *(No reaction.)* Come on—put it down!

(Hinkston hears the sounds of laughter as a summer game of tennis is being played nearby. The others hear it as well. Slowly, Hinkston is drawn toward the sounds.)

BLACK. Hinkston—Hinkston!!

(Hinkston runs offstage eagerly and happily.)

Hinkston, come back here! THAT'S AN ORDER!!

HENLEY. Captain—Captain, let him go! He doesn't even *hear* you.

BLACK. They're playing *tennis* up there?

(And if that's not enough, an elderly man enters and spots Henley. He cries in happiness.)

GRANDPA. Sarah? Sarah!

HENLEY. *(Incredulous.)* Grandfather!

GRANDPA. Is that *you?*

> *(He comes into the light. The beautiful Americana music comes up a bit. Henley is deeply moved and steps a bit closer.)*

HENLEY. *(Happily; quietly.)* Grandfather.

> *(She runs to his open arms, sobbing happily. Black is totally dumbfounded as he watches another impossible scene.)*

GRANDPA. *(Comforting Henley.)* There, there.

BLACK. *(Snapping to.)* Henley—

HENLEY. *(Looking up; sobbing.)* Sir—sir, this is my *grandfather!*

GRANDPA. And this is the finest grandchild that ever lived.

HENLEY. Grandfather, I don't understand. You died. You *died!*

GRANDPA. Shh, shh. It's all right, Sarah—it's all right. Come along, now.

> *(Slowly, happily, they exit. Black takes a few futile steps toward them, but his appeals fall on deaf ears.)*

BLACK. Henley—!

> *(Now alone and frustrated, Black is in the midst of the small town sounds which seem all around. He opens communication to the ship.)*

BLACK. Spender—

> *(Suddenly we hear a sports crowd cheer wildly! We hear the sound of a radio broadcast of a baseball game. Someone has apparently hit a home run. The Announcer describes the event.)*

ANNOUNCER. —there it goes! It's a long drive—way up and way back! It looks like—it looks like—yes, it's a home run! No, wait! Black is out there—way out—he's under it!

> *(Running backward, trying to catch the ball, a young man appears. He is Skip, Captain Black's brother. There is a burst of crowd sound as the ball falls neatly into his mitt.)*

ANNOUNCER. He's got it! What a catch!

(The crowd sounds die. Skip stands, joyously tossing the ball. Black stares at him and almost collapses. He gathers his courage and finally calls out, tentatively.)

BLACK. Skip! Skipper!

(Skip turns around and grins happily.)

SKIP. Oh, Blackie! Welcome back! Welcome home.

(Black flings his hands to his eyes to stop the tears. He feels the wetness and staggers forward and embraces his brother.)

BLACK. *(Quietly.)* This can't be. Mom? Dad?

SKIP. They're back at the house.

BLACK. No!

SKIP. *(Beams.)* Yeah! Apricot pie cooling on the back window, there's lemonade in the icebox. Band concert tonight at eight, fireworks at nine. *(Beat; happily.)* Oh, Blackie!

(The gentle music of "Beautiful Ohio" softly creeps in. It is extremely beautiful and soothing.)

BLACK. *(Almost voiceless.)* I can't believe this.

SKIP. Come on. I'll race you home! Last one there is an old maid!

BLACK. *(Still confused.)* Skipper—

SKIP. Come on!

(Black looks around him, still trying to make sense of his senses and emotions. He looks to Skip in hopes of an answer.)

SKIP. *(Tenderly.)* It's okay!

(The music swells a bit. Black gives into his feelings and smiles through his tears of frustration and joy.)

BLACK. All right!!!

(Joyously, Skip and Black begin running and playing around the stage as two adolescent brothers would. The music continues, happily underscoring the tender reunion.)

SKIP/BLACK *(ad lib.)* Come on! Run faster! You can't catch me! etc.

SKIP. Come on! I'll race you backwards!

BLACK. Backwards?! *(Shaking his head.)*

SKIP. Come on!

BLACK. *(Laughing.)* All right, all right!

> *(They run backwards in a great circle as the light changes, dims. Black falls, rolls, stops, and listens with his eyes shut. Slowly he rises, grabs Skip, and holds him. To the far side of the stage, in her own pool of light, a woman is seated on a piano bench or stool, her hands out in the air as if playing a piano. It is she who is playing "Beautiful Ohio." Skip gently touches Black on his elbow indicating that this woman, their mother, is actually there. Quietly, Black moves across to her and stands behind her. She senses him there, but keeps playing. He reaches out and puts the palms of his hands over her eyes. She smiles, beautifully blinded. He sinks to his knees, buries his head in her lap, and weeps.)*

MRS. BLACK. There, there. It's all right, son. Everything's going to be all right now.

BLACK. *(Weeping; a small boy.)* I don't understand. I don't.

MRS. BLACK. Don't even try. It's enough we're all together again, and so much happiness we weep—we weep for joy.

BLACK. *(Beat.)* Is this Heaven?

MRS. BLACK. Good heavens, no.

> *(The Relatives laugh at the idea.)*

BLACK. Some kind of reincarnation—*what?*

MRS. BLACK. It's a place where we have a second chance. Nobody told us why. But we're here.

> *(Suddenly we hear the sound of a small marching band. Black turns, startled.)*

BLACK. What's that?

SKIP. That's your ship. Your rocket.

MRS. BLACK. A welcome party! A band!

BLACK. The men had orders to stay aboard.

> *(Spender walks swiftly in. The "family" pull back half a step as if he were a threat.)*

SPENDER. Captain!

BLACK. Spender!

SPENDER. Captain, all the men have left the ship!

BLACK. Yes, I know.

SPENDER. Shouldn't you order them to—

BLACK. What? To come and weep with their mothers and fathers? Yes. *Do* that.

SPENDER. *(Dumbfounded.)* Sir?

(Mrs. Black moves forward.)

MRS. BLACK. A glass of summer wine, Mr. Spender?

SPENDER. *(Awkwardly.)* Uh, no thank you.

SPENDER. Captain, request permission to return to the ship.

(Everyone protests, urging him to stay.)

Somebody has to stand guard.

BLACK. *(Quietly.)* Yes, you're right.

SPENDER. Captain, I don't like this.

BLACK. I know. I said the same thing to myself an hour ago, but now, look! *(Indicates families.)*

SPENDER. *(On duty.)* Dismissed?

BLACK. *(Giving in.)* Dismissed.

(Spender salutes, spins about, and briskly exits. Mrs. Black moves to her son.)

MRS. BLACK. Such a nice young man. Why didn't he stay?

BLACK. He doesn't have anyone here, mother.

MRS. BLACK. *No* one?

BLACK. Myself, all the others, we all have family and friends, but Spender's an orphan. I guess he never loved or *was* loved by anyone.

MRS. BLACK. How sad.

BLACK. Mom, I'll never forget this evening.

MRS. BLACK. You must be exhausted.

BLACK. Yes. It's been a long night, Mom—a long journey. I need time.

MRS. BLACK. Time to sleep.

BLACK. No, Mom—I need time to think.

MRS. BLACK. *(Amicably nods.)* And *then* to sleep.

SKIP. You want me to get this guy some shut-eye, Mom?

BLACK. *(Wearily; smiling.)* Yeah—shut-eye.

MRS. BLACK. A good night's sleep.

SKIP. *(Kissing her.)* Good night.

MRS. BLACK. Good night, dear.

BLACK. *(Kissing her.)* Good night.

> *(The two brothers move off in shadow as Mrs. Black and the music both fade away. The lights come up on another part of the stage. An area where pennants, posters, flags, are projected on scrims. They circle a big, brass bed.)*

SKIP. Well, here we are!

BLACK. Skip—this is the room I was *born* in!

SKIP. Kee-rect!

BLACK. *(Pointing; overjoyed.)* My old football helmet!

SKIP. Yep!

BLACK. My pennants—my star-charts from high school astronomy!

SKIP. Yes, sir!

BLACK. My diploma from the Air Force Academy!

SKIP. It's fading, but it's still in one piece.

BLACK. *(Incredulous.)* Yeah, but Skip—these all *burned*. Skip, the house caught fire! These all burned!

SKIP. Look, they're all here! I'm here. Well, enjoy it! Don't spoil it. Sleep?

> *(Black nods. Skip undresses to his shorts and dives into bed. Black sits on the edge of the bed. Somewhere a lost locomotive wails softly. There is a long, lonely moment as he broods. Lightly, faintly, a piano version of "Beautiful Ohio" in a minor key begins.)*

SKIP. *(Propping himself up.)* Aren't you going to bed, Blackie?

BLACK. *(Thinking.)* Yeah. In a minute, Skip.

SKIP. *(Beat.)* Night, Blackie.

BLACK. Goodnight, Skip.

(They both settle down. Black listens to the symphony of night sounds. Crickets, birds, the wind. He opens his eyes after a moment, and sits up.)

SKIP. Blackie? What's wrong?

BLACK. Nothing, Skip. Nothing's wrong.

(Black sits all the way up and moves to the far end of the bed. Skip half-lifts his head, watching him.)

SKIP. *(Whining.)* Come on—what's wrong?

BLACK. I was just thinking, that's all.

SKIP. Well, thinking's bad for you.

(Black picks up a catcher's mitt from under the bed.)

BLACK. I was just thinking; what *if*—?

SKIP. What if—?

(Black finds ball and throws it into the mitt.)

BLACK. What if we *have* landed on Mars, only—

SKIP. Yeah?

BLACK. *(Playing with ball and mitt.)* —only this small Illinois town is *not* an Illinois town? *(Beat.)* And these people are not family, not friends.

SKIP. *(Calmly.)* What do you mean?

BLACK. This is the Third Expedition to Mars. The other two just vanished, and we don't know where, right?

SKIP. If you say so.

BLACK. All right, then,—this being true, the Martians know that we're coming again. So how would they prepare themselves for the Third Invasion?

SKIP. All right, how?

BLACK. With telepathy! *(Piecing it together.)* Suppose the Martians could "borrow" our thoughts as we landed, and by telepathy and hypnosis they—my god! They could pretend to *be* our aunts and our uncles—our mothers and fathers.

SKIP. That means all the people in this town—?

BLACK. *(Stands.)* Are Martians disguised as Earth men. *(Beat.)*
Then my mother—

SKIP. —is not your mother?

BLACK. *(More stunned.)* And my grandparents are not my grandparents!

SKIP. Well—what about *me*, Blackie?

BLACK. *(Very long beat.)* You're not my brother.

SKIP. *(Calmly.)* That's right. I'm a beast. A monster who'll kill you
in your sleep. *(Chuckles.)* Blackie, come on to bed. Turn out
the light, will you?

*(Black turns down a lamp. He sits down, tosses back the
covers, and begins to loosen his collar and sleeves. Far away
we hear the piano music again, two bars, which fade. Black
looks at his brother, whose eyes are closed, but who smiles
in his half-sleep. Slowly, Black rises and turns. He starts to
move toward the door and is almost there when Skip's voice
freezes him.)*

Blackie?

BLACK. *(Beat; not turning.)* Yeah?

SKIP. Where you going?

BLACK. *(Takes a breath.)* I'm thirsty. Drink of water.

SKIP. *(Beat.)* But you're not thirsty.

BLACK. I *am*.

*(Skip sits upright in bed and stares at Black. His lips do not
move but we hear his voice, echoed and very loud. Black realizes too late his error.)*

SKIP. No! You're not thirsty!

BLACK. *(Quietly; whimpering.)* Oh, god.

*(Instant blackout. A fantastic beating of an immense heart
rises to a swift crescendo and then stops. Blackout.)*

SCENE 4

Mars: Mission Four arrives.

> *(Immediately following. In the darkness we hear the Martian wind, much more barren, much more lonely. It is interrupted by a radio voice.)*

WILDER'S VOICE. Mars Mission Four calling Mars Mission Three. Mission Three, come in. Mars Rocket Four preparing to land— preparing to land—

> *(The voice fades as we hear a brief rocket thunder under the following.)*

THE VOICE. And it is written in the Chronicles of Mars, that the Martians did sicken and die. And Spender alone saw this, and was forever changed!

> *(A brief surge of rocket fire. Silence. The sound of a great metal door which slams shut. The light comes up on Spender, down center, as he stares off at the death of the Martians which has just occurred. Captain Wilder and his crew step into light on both sides of Spender, who does not even hear or see them, but only stares at the horror we cannot see. Wilder looks at him curiously, then glances at the Martian "town" and back.)*

WILDER. —Spender?

SPENDER. *(Looking forward; stunned.)* Present and accounted for.

WILDER. Where's your Captain?

SPENDER. He's dead.

WILDER. Where's your crew?

SPENDER. Dead and buried.

WILDER. Dead and buried? What happened? *(Peers front.)* What's that?

SPENDER. A Martian city. The Martians are also dead, but not buried.

> *(Shadows scurry about them. Dark leaves blow along the earth.)*

> *(Picking up leaf.)* You see this dark autumn leaf, Captain? It isn't a leaf—and this isn't autumn.

WILDER. Hathaway, go check the town!

HATHAWAY. Yes, sir.

(*He exits.*)

WILDER. Biggs, check those places in the hills. Cherokee, the cross-roads town there.

(*The men exit.*)

The towns! The buildings! It's like landing in Greece or Rome, but two thousand years ago!

SPENDER. Just a few days ago it looked like a small town on Earth. Or so we thought—or dreamed. Now it's back to being what it always was for ten thousand years. But now it's dead.

(*The others don't listen. They are awestricken and deep into their own thoughts.*)

Dead cities—empty streets. The two moons of Mars rising. A moment in time like this: (*Looks up; shuts eyes, remembering.*) "So we'll go no more a-roving, so late into the night,
Though the heart be still as loving, and the moon be still as bright.
For the sword outwears its sheath, and the soul wears out its breast,
And the heart must pause to breathe, and love itself must rest . . ."

(*Another crewman, Parkhill, moves out of the darkness to stand nearby, looking at the terrain. He speaks dangerously close to Slim Pickens.*)

PARKHILL. Look at that! An empty town and crossroads. Oh, you give me a year—no, no, make it two years, but that's where I'm gonna build it.

SPENDER. Build what?

PARKHILL. A hot dog stand—that's the perfect place! A hot dog stand!

SPENDER. What about a hamburger joint over there, and a fried chicken over there?

PARKHILL. (*Missing his point.*) Naw, a hot dog stand'll be just fine.

(*Hathaway returns, perhaps having used a jet-pack power unit.*)

WILDER. Hathaway—

HATHAWAY. Reporting back, Captain.

(Biggs enters quickly from the other direction.)

BIGGS. Captain—I checked those places up in the hills!

(Cherokee enters as well.)

CHEROKEE. Sir—the town at the crossroads—

WILDER. Empty?

CHEROKEE. Yes, sir. Except for a lot of dark leaves blowing in the streets.

BIGGS. The same thing up in the hills, sir. Nothing but leaves— leaves everywhere.

PARKHILL. I don't get it.

(Hathaway produces a small unit and tries explaining to Park-hill as Spender bends, picks up one of the dark leaves. He is acting odd.)

WILDER. Spender?

(Spender hands the leaf to Hathaway, who analyzes it as Park-hill watches. The unit glows a light shade of red and ticks softly.)

SPENDER. *(Quietly; fearfully.)* God forgive us.

WILDER. What is it?

SPENDER. It *was* a Martian.

PARKHILL. Oh, come on—*that?*

SPENDER. Yes, that! Just a piece of mummy now, but it's not old— it's new. In the last few hours. You don't understand, I watched them *die.*

(They all look at Spender. Wilder glances at Hathaway.)

WILDER. What—some sort of plague?

HATHAWAY. *(Adjusting dials.)* In a way, yes. Our bacteria got them.

(Beat.)

SPENDER. What was it?

HATHAWAY. *(Looking at machine.)* Chicken pox.

WILDER. Hathaway, are you—

HATHAWAY. It's all there, Captain—look for yourself. Chicken pox on Earth break out in spots. But here they burn you to ashes—flake you away like charcoal and dust.

(He takes the leaf from the machine, which stops humming and its light dies. Hathaway drops the leaf.)

WILDER. York and Williams might have made it, too! *All* three missions! Spender!

SPENDER. We found nothing.

WILDER. Are there no signs of life?

BIGGS. No, sir.

SPENDER. Chances are a few Martians might have escaped to the hills, God help them.

HATHAWAY. Well, they know we were here.

SPENDER. To spit in their wine. *(Beat.)* Thousands—*thousands* dead! Overnight. How they must hate us.

WILDER. But look at their cities. They were a graceful people. They probably didn't mind us being here any more than we mind—oh, children playing on the lawn.

(Spender edges toward the side of the stage. He suddenly darts off in the direction of the hills.)

WILDER. Spender! Come back!

HATHAWAY. Captain, shall I—?

PARKHILL. Aw, let him go. He'll be back.

WILDER. All right, clear this away. Set up camp. Police the area!

PARKHILL. *(Incredulous.)* Police the area? Captain, we been in space for three hundred days! Three hundred days we policed machines, policed meteors—we policed each other! And now, the first thing you want us to police are deserts and dead cities? *(Beat; realizing.)* Sorry, sir. *(Beat.)* How about policing us up some beer?

BIGGS. *(Smiling.)* Yeah, beer!

WILDER. What—to celebrate our arrival—or their funeral?

PARKHILL. Well, the truth is, sir—I don't feel anything for them. Tomorrow, sure—but right now, two hours of R&R, Captain?

BIGGS. Please.

WILDER. *(Tiredly; half-smile.)* Oh, all right!

(A wild cheer from the men, ad-libbing "Hear that. Captain's orders! How about a beer!" etc. Hathaway is the last to leave, shaking his head. Now alone, Wilder picks up a final dark leaf and places it in the electronic device. The machine wails softly.)

WILDER. *(Quietly, eyes shut.)* Men of Earth—welcome to Mars.

(A quick blackout. We hear voices over a radio.)

WILDER'S VOICE. Second day, tape report: area secure. Mars Rockets One and Three found. Lieutenant Spender, archaeologist, sole survivor. Missing since yesterday, 0400 hours.

HATHAWAY'S VOICE. Third day. Medical report. As indicated, bacteria from Earth has infected and destroyed the native population—

WILDER'S VOICE. *(Fading.)* Fourth day, noon—

SCENE 5

Mars: Rim of a canal.

(We hear more harmonica music as the lights come up on noon. Biggs and Cherokee, seated on the rim of a canal, drinking beer. They hang their legs over the edge of the stage, and sit and chat amiably.)

BIGGS. *(Surveying.)* Look! Look at all those canals. Canals on Mars, after all!

CHEROKEE. *(Waving beer can.)* Very fine canals. Tell you what. Why don't we take off our boots and—

(He is stopped midsentence by Spender, who has stepped out in the light behind them.)

BIGGS. Well, well, well, it's old, uh—

SPENDER. Spender.

BIGGS. Spender! Spender! Welcome back, Spender. Beer?

SPENDER. No.

CHEROKEE. It's been four days. You had us worried. Captain said you'd never come back.

SPENDER. He was right.

BIGGS. Yeah, where you been?

SPENDER. Up in the hills, wandering through the towns, sleeping in the villas at night.

BIGGS. Oh, been living the high life, huh?

SPENDER. *(Continuing.)* —sitting in the libraries, listening to books that talk.

BIGGS. *(Not believing.)* Books that talk!?!

(Biggs crumples the beer can, tosses it down into the unseen canal. Spender sees this.)

SPENDER. *(Beat; forcing on.)* Books that sing and tell time—not your time, *theirs.*

BIGGS. *(Opening another can.)* Not theirs anymore. Not now that *we're* here.

SPENDER. No?

BIGGS. No! You and me, Spender—you and me are going to rename all the hills and valleys, all the towns, all the roads—*(Looking at canal.)*—all the canals. *(Pouring beer in the canal.)* I hereby dub this canal, Biggs Canal—*(Laughs uncontrollably.)*—Biggs, Biggs, Biggs Canal! And those mountains over there? Why not! All those mountains, Spender Mountain! Hah!

SPENDER. No!

BIGGS. Why not?

SPENDER. My name isn't Spender anymore.

CHEROKEE. *(Rising; curious.)* Hey, what you been up to?

SPENDER. Reading and thinking, making up my mind.

BIGGS. What are you talking about? Making up your mind as to *what?*

SPENDER. As to whether or not I belong to you—*(Glances at hills.)*—or them.

BIGGS. And what'd you decide, *friend?*

SPENDER. This.

(He shows a mask he's been carrying.)

BIGGS. What's that?

SPENDER. I was reading in the library and suddenly there he was. And he said, "Give me your boots," and I did. And he said, "Give me your uniform and the rest of your clothes," and I gave them to him. Then he said, "Now come along with me and see what happens." And the Martian walked down to the camp, and now he's here.

BIGGS. *(Looking around; mocking.)* Well, I don't see any *Martians.*

(Spender slowly raises his pistol. Biggs turns around and sees him.)

(Incredulous.) What is that?

SPENDER. Sorry.

CHEROKEE. Spender!

(Spender fires the gun. Biggs, beer can in hand, simply dies.)

CHEROKEE. *(Kneeling by Biggs.)* Spender—you *shot* him!

SPENDER. Cherokee—I don't want to kill *you.*

CHEROKEE. *(Stunned.)* Who, me? What are you talking about?

SPENDER. You're not like him. I'll let *you* live.

CHEROKEE. Why!? What's happened to you?

SPENDER. You're special.

CHEROKEE. Special?

SPENDER. Yes, you—your family, your blood on Earth. It's happening all over again, *here*—the same damn stupid thing, don't you see? *(Beat.)* Come with me.

CHEROKEE. What, to kill the rest?

SPENDER. *(Wildly.)* To stop Earth, yes! To stop the invasion, to stop all this!

CHEROKEE. Spender, I understand. I know what you're trying to do, but this isn't the way!

SPENDER. *(Pleading.)* Cherokee, listen—

CHEROKEE. No, *you* listen! Maybe we shouldn't have come here, maybe we had no right, we may be bad, Spender, but we're not as bad as you say.

(Spender struggles with what he has just heard.)

Pull the trigger.

SPENDER. The others are coming.

CHEROKEE. Kill me or I kill *you.*

(Cherokee pulls his gun. He walks toward a confused Spender.)

Spender—Spender, take off the mask.

SPENDER'S VOICE. *(Stunned.)* I can't! I can't!

(He runs off as Hathaway and Wilder run in.)

CHEROKEE. Spender!

WILDER. Biggs!

CHEROKEE. Sir—Spender!

WILDER. What must they think of us? Fouling up Mars and shooting our own men.

HATHAWAY. What's happened to Spender, sir! I don't understand.

WILDER. Oh, I think *I* do.

(Parkhill runs in.)

PARKHILL. Captain! We got a fix on Spender! He's up in one of the Martian buildings on the high ground.

SCENE 6

Mars: A library.

(From the darkness we hear gentle sounds of the voice harps. As the lights rise, we see Spender, who is surrounded by racks of "books." Wilder enters from the darkness. Spender does not turn to greet him, but senses him there.)

SPENDER. Captain.

WILDER. *(Beat.)* I could shoot you in the back.

(Spender turns. Wilder moves forward among the shadows of the harps.)

WILDER. Is this what I think it is? A library?

SPENDER. I'm learning fast.

WILDER. How long do you think you can hold out up here?

SPENDER. Long enough to finish things off.

WILDER. Why didn't you kill us all off this morning? You had the chance.

SPENDER. I know. After I shot Biggs, I *had* to stop. I couldn't—I hadn't *changed* enough and become completely Martian.

WILDER. And now?

(The book emits some sounds.)

SPENDER. Dreams and stories and ideas that you've never heard of in your life! There's so much to be saved, Captain! So much that we could learn!

WILDER. You make it sound very appealing.

SPENDER. You can stay if you like.

WILDER. You'd spare me?!?

SPENDER. Maybe Hathaway.

WILDER. What about Cherokee? You could have killed him this morning but you let him go. His name alone protects him from you!

SPENDER. Yes.

WILDER. You asked him to come up here with you. Why? As a member of the tribal Indian nations? The history of the world came back to you. You suddenly remembered Cortez, Pizarro, the slaughter of the innocents at Wounded Knee!

SPENDER. I remembered.

WILDER. And what you've done today—was that any different!?!

SPENDER. What do you think—that I want to sit down and argue with you?!? *(Beat; calmly.)* No. Nothing would have changed. I will do what I have to do.

WILDER. *(Reasoning.)* Spender—in spite of everything, Cherokee has forgiven and forgotten the past. He refused to come up here with you today. Because he knows what I know—

BOTH. History doesn't repeat itself.

SPENDER. *(Quietly.)* Well, it *does*. It does! I see it *here*. I look into the future and I see us destroying everything! And just because it's different—because we refuse to understand!

WILDER. You've got to give us more credit than that, Spender. We're thinking human beings! We learn from our mistakes!

SPENDER. You really are one of the innocents! Men like Parkhill and Biggs will eat you alive.

WILDER. Not if, gently, I refuse them permission. Mars will not be raped! Not while I live. What a shame you've done this, Spender. You were an archaeologist. I counted on you to nose the dust and probe the bones of Mars, gently. Now you're forcing me to be your executioner. They won't touch you! If I go back down now, and this chase continues, not one of those men will be allowed to fire. Only I will track you down.

SPENDER. Spender kills Spender, is that it?

WILDER. Yes and no. I'm not quite you, so I have to *kill* you. You're not quite me or you wouldn't have to die.

SPENDER. Die?

WILDER. I'm sorry—I'm sorry this all had to happen!

SPENDER. Maybe you'd better go now, Captain. *(Wilder turns to go.)* Captain. *(Wilder stops.)* Maybe when this is over, maybe you'll change your mind.

WILDER. I really do appreciate the offer but I can't change.

SPENDER. Then do me a favor—don't let them tear this planet apart. For a little while, anyway. At least until the archaeologists have had a decent chance?

WILDER. *(Beat.)* I'll see what I can do. *(Turns to go.)*

(Spender whips up his gun swiftly, unexpectedly. Wilder fires by instinct.)

(Spender has moved slightly with the impact of the bullet. He moves back a step and raises his hand: a small wave of acceptance which Wilder sees. Spender sinks to one knee.)

SPENDER'S VOICE. Captain—take care.

(*He sinks to the other knee, then folds backward, after staring down at his killer. His light goes out. Others run in.*)

WILDER. (*To himself, to Spender.*) Take care.

HATHAWAY. Of what?

WILDER. Mars.

(*A long silence. Wilder stands up, understanding now.*)

WILDER. Bring his body.

(*Parkhill exits. There is a very long and sad silence.*)

HATHAWAY. (*Finally.*) Can we, Captain?

WILDER. What?

HATHAWAY. Take care of Mars.

WILDER. We can try.

(*Cherokee and Parkhill enter carrying Spender's body.*)

PARKHILL. So, uh, what do you want us to do with the body, sir?

WILDER. There's an old Martian tomb up there in the hills. Take him there. (*The men start to go.*) Wait.

(*He reaches and takes from Spender's clenched hand the Martian mask. The men look at him.*)

Don't put his name on the tomb, just put his body in.

PARKHILL. (*Spooked.*) Yes, sir.

(*The men exit with his body. Hathaway watches Wilder looking at the mask.*)

HATHAWAY. You going to wear that, Captain?

WILDER. Maybe. When I get to feeling like a New Yorker in bad traffic on a hot summer's day. (*Holds mask near face.*) Allowed?

HATHAWAY. Allowed.

(*Hathaway exits as the harp-books appear dimly to Wilder's side. They sing softly.*)

SCENE 7

Mars: The Martian surface. The future.

(We hear thunders in the heavens followed by reddish glows as the people of Earth move to colonize Mars.)

THE VOICE. And it was the true time of the going away from Earth. And the men of Earth came—like clouds of silver locusts the rockets arrived. And men of every shape and size and dream stepped forth on Mars. More oxygen was needed. So the men of Earth struck the hard rock with their machines.

(Hathaway and Wilder move from darkness and gesture striking the rock. Great volcanic thunders and fiery glows surround them.)

THE VOICE. And artificial volcanos fired that broke free the oxygen and new winds blew across old Mars—waiting for—

(The light remains on Hathaway and Wilder and comes up on an unusual figure who carries pouches.)

DRISCOLL. Benjamin Driscoll! Here to walk across Mars like Johnny Appleseed! *(Scattering seeds.)* And do *this*! And this! *And* this! Seeds—for tall corn, ripe wheat, and great huckleberry vines in a Martian June. *(Beat.)* Now—are you ready, Mars? *(Beat.)* Rain! *(Nothing.)* RAAAAAAINNNNN!

(Thunder explodes and there is "rain." Sound of water falling, bursts of lightning. The men stand, eyes shut, enjoying the drench, hands out, mouths open, smiling.)

DRISCOLL. *(Above the thunder.)* Now—green! That's green! That's GREEN!

(Suddenly anything that can, turns green. The scrim, the lights, the men. They grin and nod to Driscoll.)

DRISCOLL. God, thank you. We have at last returned to the garden.

(The sounds suddenly die away.)

THE VOICE. And more men came to hammer up new towns and light the windows.

(We hear an immense hammering. Small yellow lights appear in the dark, houses being lit.)

THE VOICE. And new towns were built with the names Wilder City and Hathaway Point—there was Black River, and over there, Spender Hill. Where Martians had killed the first Earth men, stood Yorktown.

(The hot dog stand. Later. We hear from the darkness the sounds of hammering, sawing, motors, and yelling of instructions. Soon they fade a bit as:)

THE VOICE. And more men and women of Earth arrived and towns were built, and new signs raised and lit—

(Small lights and tiny illuminated signs gleam in the dark. An electric neon sign comes on reading: HOT DOGS.)

For Parkhill, it would be the reality of a dream. But for Mars it would be the last glimmer of a dying world.

(Parkhill steps into the light, looking off left.)

(Elma, his wife, appears.)

ELMA. Ready, Sam? Hit it, Sam.

PARKHILL. *(Hitting a switch.)* Oh, let there be light!

(A neon sign reading HOT DOGS lights up.)

Ah, look at it, Elma! Beautiful.

ELMA. *(Looking at her fingernails.)* I'm looking, Sam—I'm looking.

PARKHILL. *(In ecstasy.)* H-O-T D-O-G-S! Hot Dogs! Don't that have a ring?

ELMA. A what?

PARKHILL. A ring, Elma.

ELMA. It rings, Sam, it rings.

PARKHILL. Hah, hah, look at all that traffic, and the people, and the towns. And we're right here at the crossroads! Aw, I'm telling you, this time next year we're gonna be rich!

ELMA. Oh, Sam.

PARKHILL. We're gonna be rich!

ELMA. If those workers ever get here. You really think they're coming?

PARKHILL. In a month! Ships loaded with Mexicans and Japanese! Thousands and thousands of hungry people and they're all *ours*.

(He stops, half-turns, and blinks, as does his wife. A Martian is there. Actually a man dressed in black wearing a mask with only the mask lit. The mask seemingly floats in.)

ELMA. Don't look now, Sam—but I think you got your first customer.

PARKHILL. Uh, oh. *(Touches his holstered pistol.)*

THE MARTIAN. I mean you no harm. I come to tell you that the days of Earth men on Mars are over.

PARKHILL. *(Backing off.)* Yeah? Says *who*?

THE MARTIAN. Earth is doomed. It dies this very hour. I speak to you with the voice of Nathaniel York and Captain Williams of the second expedition.

WILDER'S VOICE. —Sam Parkhill—

THE MARTIAN. And Black—and the voice of Spender.

SPENDER'S VOICE. So we'll go no more a roving—

PARKHILL. All right, now that's it. Go on, beat it! Our time's not *over*, we're here. And we mean to stay here. Now you just move along or you're gonna get the sickness.

THE MARTIAN. I already have the sickness. I am one of the few survivors.

PARKHILL. Then get back in the hills where you belong!

ELMA. *(Scared; whispering.)* Sam!

PARKHILL. Naw! I bought this land, it's *mine*!

ELMA. Sam, shut up!

THE MARTIAN. Your time on Mars has passed!

PARKHILL. Hey, wait a minute! You see where *I* come from there are ten million others just like me. I mean you Martians are what— a couple of dozen? Heh, you got no leaders, you got no laws! You just wander around the hills. You see, the old's got to give way to the new, that's the law of give and take.

THE MARTIAN. You will not listen. Then run your stand, and prepare your food. And—I give you this.

PARKHILL. *(Cautiously.)* What's that?

THE MARTIAN. A deed. To all land as far as the eye can see. I gift you with Mars.

PARKHILL. Drop it.

(The Martian drops the scroll.)

PARKHILL. *(Retrieving it.)* Thanks, sucker.

THE MARTIAN. Now. Tonight. Watch the sky. *(Fading away.)* The sky— *(Exits.)*

ELMA. The sky, Sam?

PARKHILL. You think this is what he said? I mean, the *land*! And as far as the eye can see!

ELMA. *(Amazed.)* Yeah—yeah, I think he told you the truth, Sam.

PARKHILL. *(Laughing after the Martian.)* You mean it's *mine*? It's *MINE*?!? Mars is mine! *(Beat.)* God Bless Parkhill Land!

(She stares up as a swift light flickers on their faces.)

ELMA. While you're at it, Parkhill, take a look!

PARKHILL. What?

ELMA. No wonder he gave you Mars.

PARKHILL. *(Looking up.)* What's that?

ELMA. That's Earth.

(Parkhill chuckles.)

ELMA. It is—it's caught fire!

PARKHILL. Naw!

ELMA. Sam, it's burning!

PARKHILL. It's not Earth, Elma—it's a meteor. *(Slowly.)* Or a nova— or *something*.

ELMA. *(Slowly; ironically.)* That just *can't* be Earth, huh? Them lighting their own fuse, them blowing themselves up—*that* what you mean, Sam?

PARKHILL. *(Catatonic; gasping.)* Elma—they *did* it. They really let it happen!

ELMA. *(Long beat.)* Switch on some more lights, Sam. There'll be another batch of customers along—in about a billion years. Great place for a hot-dog stand, hmmm?

(Parkhill stands, mouth slack, eyes bleak, his face fully il-luminated by Earth's fires.)

ELMA. Sam, I'm gonna let you in on a little secret. *(Beat.)* I think this is gonna be an *off* season.

(She slowly taps the invisible switch. The neon sign goes off as Parkhill turns to see it go out. Blackout.)

VOICE OF HOUSTON. Radio Houston calling Mars Base Station. Come home, we *need* you. Come home—come home— *(Fading.)* — come home—

SCENE 8

THE VOICE. And these are the final Chronicles of Mars. In the last days, the silver locusts turned about, and went back home to live or not live, to find or not find their loved ones and friends— and Mars was full of shadows and blue dust. And a few last Earth men and women were left.

(Two boys enter, one about nine, the other in his teens. Ishmael, the older, chases Robert.)

ISHMAEL. You brat! *(Grabs him.)* Hah! Gotcha!

ROBERT. We've landed—where are the Martians?

ISHMAEL. Dad says in the Old Martian ruins!

ROBERT. Naw! Up in the hills!

ISHMAEL. Could be!

(Wilder and Leonora enter.)

ROBERT. *(Running to her.)* Mom, mom! Where are the Martians? Dad said he'd show them to us! Where are they?

LEONORA. *(Chuckling.)* Ask your father.

(Wilder is noticeably older now.)

WILDER. What?

ROBERT. The Martians, Dad—you promised!

ISHMAEL. He wants to meet them.

WILDER. In time.

ROBERT. In time?

WILDER. Soon.

(He looks around at the ruins, and then down, as into the depths of a canal, that is to say, the edge of the stage at the pit.)

Why don't you run along and get some kindling to build a fire? Then I'll show you the Martians.

ROBERT. The Martians! Yeaaaaaaaaay! *(Runs out.)*

LEONORA. You shouldn't promise, Will.

WILDER. *(Gently.)* But *will* deliver. *(Chuckles.)*

(Father Peregrine enters.)

Ah! Father!

PEREGRINE. *(Holds up pad.)* I've been making phone calls all day, all over Mars. You know, here and there, the service is still pretty good? By rough estimate I'd say there's about a hundred people still left.

WILDER. *(Suddenly alarmed.)* All men?

PEREGRINE. No, there's a fair number of women. A man named Harkins, a radio operator, offered to tour the telephone lines and keep them operative.

WILDER. Good.

PEREGRINE. *(Checking list.)* Here's an old gem named Tolliver. He'll check the farmlands with his daughters. Here's a woman named Genevieve Selsor, runs a beauty parlor beyond the hills.

LEONORA. *(Giving him a cup of something.)* Father.

PEREGRINE. *(Taking it.)* Thank you. There's a man named Walter Gripp—car repairman. Will repair all the cars on Mars, just as long as, he says, he keeps moving. Sam Parkhill, food supplier, and *his* wife. *(Handing the list to Wilder.)*

WILDER. We'll make do.

LEONORA. And then?

PEREGRINE. We'll pack our bags a thousand years from now, I suppose, and move on.

ISHMAEL. What's this?

WILDER. Ah, stuff and gear for a billion-year picnic. For all the fine summers that lie ahead. All the way to Andromeda!

(A wind passes in a sound of soft harps and bells.)

WILDER. Do you feel it? There are others out there with us, no longer afraid of us—waiting for us to go away.

(A long line of Martians have appeared on the scrims behind them.)

Do you believe in ghosts, Father?

PEREGRINE. *(Shuts eyes.)* Yes. I believe.

(Robert runs in with some kindling.)

ROBERT. *(Tossing sticks on fire.)* There! Now, where are the Martians, Dad? Can we see them now?

WILDER. *(Rising.)* Oh, clearly, yes—very clearly. Now—come on over to the edge of the canal.

ROBERT. Canal?

WILDER. Yes, everyone!

(They all cross down to the front of the stage.)

WILDER. *(Pointing.)* There. Now look down at the reflections in the water.

ROBERT. Where?

WILDER. There. Those. Those are the Martians.

(A wind sounds softly under this as the real Martians, projected on the scrim behind them, whisper, wail, and vanish.)

ROBERT. Hey, yeah! *(Beat.)* But Dad, that's *us.*

WILDER. Yes.

LEONORA. Your father's right. For a time, anyway. Those are the Martians.

ISHMAEL. The Martians.

(They are all kneeling down now at the rim of the imaginary canal, staring at their own images in the hidden waters. The light from the canal shimmers in blue colors over their faces as they finish the speeches above. Robert whispers the last words, and the Martian harp-book voices echo him, fading, in whispers, as the lights begin to fade.)

ROBERT. *(Whispers.)* The Martians . . . !

THE MARTIAN ECHOES. *(Softly, far away.)* The Martians . . . !

(Now the final lights dim, the waters vanish. Darkness and stars as we hear:)

THE VOICE. Then the Chronicles of Mars were done. But with one door shut, the door of the great Universe swung wide. Death stood aside, Man moved, and, moving, saw and knew . . . there was no end . . . there was only a Beginning that would last Forever.

The final light goes. The stars wheel slowly. The Martian wind blows . . . the ancient harps whisper a last whisper . . . and we have reached—the End of The Martian Chronicles.

(Curtain.)

Annotated Bibliography of Selected Plays with Mature Themes

Abe Lincoln of Pigeon Creek   William E. Wilson   Anchorage Press, 1962
19 characters   2 interiors
This ten-year saga illustrates the adolescent bitterness, heartbreak, and discovery Abe Lincoln overcomes on his way to manhood.

Analysis of Mineral #4   Moses Goldberg   Anchorage Press, 1982   6 characters   1 interior
A group of high-school students, while dealing with the scientific process of analyzing an "unknown" substance, begin to make observations and analyses of each other and discover the essence of what makes them each unique.

Androcles and the Lion   Aurand Harris   Anchorage Press, 1964   6 characters   1 exterior, commedia dell'arte stage
The importance and meaning of friendship is the theme of this classic story of a slave and the lion he befriends.

Appleseed   Ed Graczyk   Anchorage Press, 1971   9 characters   1 unit set, slides
Ensemble piece that traces the life of Johnny "Appleseed" from age ten to seventy-five and emphasizes his dedication to peace and cooperation in early America.

The Arkansaw Bear   Aurand Harris   Anchorage Press, 1980   6 characters   1 exterior set
See page 158 of this volume.

Big Klaus and Little Klaus   Dean Wenstrom   Anchorage Press, 1966   7 characters, extras   1 interior/exterior
This adaptation of the Grimm fairy tale revolves around the theme of greed as Little Klaus, the unfortunate victim of the bully Big Klaus, discovers a way to rid himself of his adversary once and for all.

The Birthday of the Infanta   Stuart Walker   published in *Plays Children Love*   Doubleday and Co., 1981   7 characters   1 interior
A meeting between the haughty and proud Infanta and a deformed Fantastic teaches both a great deal about life, and the meaning of the words human compassion and cruel inhumanity. This powerful theme is gracefully adapted from Oscar Wilde's short story of the same name.
See also *Broken Hearts: Three Tales of Sorrow*, on page 380 of this volume.

The Boy Who Stole the Stars   Julian Wiles   The Young Charleston Theatre Company, 1981   4 characters   1 exterior
See page 198 of this volume.

The Boy Who Talked to Whales   Webster Smalley   Anchorage Press, 1981
   9 characters   1 exterior
See page 244 of this volume.

Broken Hearts: Three Tales of Sorrow   Oscar Wilde   Adapted by Gretta
   Berghammer and Rod Caspers   University of Texas Press, 1984   Ensemble of 7–11   Unit set
See page 380 of this volume.

The Butterfly   Bijan Mofid   Translation by Don Iaffon   Anchorage Press,
   1974   9 characters   1 interior
A tender interpretation of the age-old theme "think of others before yourself." A butterfly is caught in a web within a dark barn and is spared from being eaten first by her determination to trick another insect into exchanging fates with her, and finally by her beauty and honesty.

Charlotte's Web   Joseph Robinette   Dramatic Publishing Co., 1984   11
   characters, extras   3 exteriors
Pointed drama in which the value of friendship is illustrated through the efforts of Charlotte, a most unusual spider, as she saves the life of her friend, Wilbur the Pig.

Circus Home   Joanna Halpert Kraus   New Plays, Inc., 1979   18 characters
   (doubling recommended)   1 exterior
This theatre for youth "Elephant Man" illustrates the discrimination Benji, a grotesquely large man, has met throughout his life.

The City without Love   Lev Ustinov   Translation by Miriam Morton
   New Plays, Inc., 1977   9 characters   1 exterior, 1 interior
Biting allegory that addresses the need for human love and respect through the vehicle of Russian fantasy. Two acts.

The Code Breaker   Pauline Conley   Anchorage Press, 1983   5 characters
   Unit set
See page 336 of this volume.

Courage   Ed Graczyk   Pickwick Press, 1973   20 characters   Unit set
See page 34 of this volume.

Dandelion   The Paper Bag Players   Music by Donald Ashwander   Baker's
   Plays, 1978   4 characters, 2 musicians   Bare stage
In the familiar Paper Bag Players' style, nine distinct periods of the evolutionary ladder are explored, and important lessons in conservation and care of the environment shared.

Don Quixote of La Mancha   Arthur Faquez   Translation by Margaret Leona
   Anchorage Press, 1967   10 characters, extras   1 interior, 5 exteriors
The power of optimism and dreams, and the belief in the human spirit, magnify themselves in the adaptation of Cervantes' classic. Rich in chivalry, illusion, and spectacle.

Doors   Suzan L. Zeder   Anchorage Press, 1984   4 characters   1 interior
See page 410 of this volume.

Escape to Freedom: A Play about Young Frederick Douglass   Ossie Davis
   Samuel French, 1976   7 characters   Open stage
Through a series of vignettes, the themes of freedom and racial equality are
explored as we follow the life of Frederick Douglass from plantation slavery
to his dramatic escape north to a free life.

Five Minutes to Morning   Mary Melwood   New Plays, Inc., 1965   8 characters   1 interior, 1 exterior
Mrs. Venny, a retired school teacher, uses some rather fantastic magic to
convince her former student Jolyon that there is more to life than wealth,
and together they unite with pleasant absurdity to outwit the greedy Skitch.

The Golden Fleece   Alan Cullen   Anchorage Press, 1971   Ensemble of 15
   playing many roles   Bare stage
Jason, the prince, must overcome numerous obstacles in order to bring the
Golden Fleece back to Iolchos and reclaim the throne from the evil usurper
King Peleas. This combination of ancient Greek mythology with contempo-
rary language explores the age-old theme of honor.

Granpa   Paper Bag Players   Paper Bag Players, 1977   Ensemble of 4 actors
   Bare stage
A lively series of comic contemporary skits for young audiences show the
inevitability and pleasure of growing older.

The Hide and Seek Odyssey of Madeline Gimple   Frank Gagliano   Dra-
   matists Play Service, 1970   5 characters, extras   1 exterior
Through a series of games, Madeline learns to face the truth about being an
orphan and conquers some well-recognized fears as well.

The Honorable Urashima Taro   Coleman A. Jennings   Dramatic Publishing Co., 1972   17 characters, extras   2 exteriors
See page 4 of this volume.

The Ice Wolf   Joanna Halpert Kraus   New Plays, Inc., 1963   15 characters   2 exteriors
The discrimination and hate of people toward others who are different is the
moving theme of this Eskimo story. Anatou, the blonde eskimo, feared and
hated by her tribe, is transformed by the Wood God into a wolf and seeks
revenge on those who persecuted her as a human.

Jim Thorpe—All American   Saul Levitt   Music by Harrison Fisher   Anchorage Press, 1980   7 characters   Unit set
The life, struggles, accomplishments, and failures of athlete and Native
American Jim Thorpe are the exciting background for this play, emphasizing
the need for racial tolerance and equality among all people.

Johnny Moonbeam and the Silver Arrow   Joseph Golden   Anchorage Press,
    1962   6 characters   1 exterior
The use and abuse of power is told through Johnny Moonbeam's attempt to
accomplish three difficult feats demonstrating his manhood and win for
himself the silver arrow.

The Legend of Sleepy Hollow   Frederick Gaines   University of Minnesota
    Press, 1975   12 characters plus extras   Unit set
Empathy for one who is the continual butt of practical jokes is evoked in
this retelling of the American classic filled with suspense, superstition, and
nightmare.

The Little Humpback Horse   Lowell Swortzell   Anchorage Press, 1984   7
    men, 3 women   Unit set
English adaptation of one of the best-loved plays and poems of Russian
youth, in which Ivan, through his adventures with his raggedy humpback
horse, learns an important lesson in having faith in one's self.

The Little Princess, Sara Crewe   Nancy Seale   Music by Melissa Sweeney
    Anchorage Press, 1982   24 characters   3 interiors, 1 exterior
The classic rags-to-riches story, based on the novel by Frances Hodgson
Burnett, examines social structure and the discrimination that exists with-
in and between classes of people.

The Magician's Nephew   Aurand Harris   Dramatic Publishing Co., 1984
    10 characters   1 interior, 4 exteriors
A dramatization of the C. S. Lewis classic in which Digory and his friend
Polly travel to Narnia in an attempt to acquire the healing apple for Digory's
dying mother.

Man Oh Man   Volcker Ludwig and Reiner Lucker   Translation by Jack
    Zipes   Found in *Political Plays for Children*   Telos Press, 1976   6 char-
    acters   Bare stage
A mother of two children remarries a man of different social standards and
together the new family combats sexism, injustice, and job discrimination
in their lives.

The Man Who Killed Time   Arthur Faquez   Translation by Margaret Leona
    Anchorage Press, 1964   9 characters   1 interior, 1 exterior
This play, based loosely on *commedia dell'arte* style, takes a look at how
people cope with and adapt to progress. An innkeeper, Ambrosio, destroys
all clocks to free himself from the responsibility of time. This, however, cre-
ates chaos in the process, and must eventually be righted.

The Masque of Beauty and the Beast   Michael Brill   Anchorage Press,
    1979   12 characters   Unit set
Beauty's success in looking beyond the Beast's ugliness to find love and happiness is the theme of this poetic retelling of the popular fairy tale.

Mean to Be Free   Joanna Halpert Kraus   New Plays, Inc., 1967   15 characters   3 interiors, 3 exteriors
Black slavery and the cost and necessity of freedom are the powerful thematic supports to this story of Harriet Tubman and the Underground Railroad as she seeks to safely lead two children out of bondage to freedom in Canada.

The Men's Cottage   Moses Goldberg   Anchorage Press, 1980   5 characters   Bare stage
Ritual, rite, and honor are combined to create a story that explores the transitions between childhood and adolescence and the painful acceptance of the inevitable. Inspired by the works of Margaret Mead.

My Days as a Youngling—John Jacob Niles: The Early Years   Nancy Niles Sexton, Vaught McBride, and Martha Harrison Jones   Anchorage Press, 1982   Ensemble of 12 or more   Unit set
See page 288 of this volume.

Noah and the Great Auk   Bix L. Doughty   Anchorage Press, Inc., 1978   5 animals, 1 man   1 exterior
Fictitious black comedy set on Noah's Ark that makes a serious statement on the ecological conditions that exist on Earth today.

Noodle Doodle Box   Paul Maar   Translation by Alex and Anita Page Baker's Plays, 1972   3 characters   Bare stage
See page 122 of this volume.

The Odyssey   Gregory Falls and Kurt Beattie   Anchorage Press, 1980   8 character ensemble   Bare stage/unit set
See page 92 of this volume.

Oliver Twist   Guy Williams   Dramascripts/Macmillan Publishers, 1970   28 characters plus extras   10 interiors, 4 exteriors
The triumph of good over adverse circumstances is no better illustrated than in this adaptation of Dickens' classic story of a boy's rise from rags to riches and the taste for life his diverse friends and foes instill in him.

OPQRS, Etc.   Madge Miller   Anchorage Press, 1983   6 characters   1 set
The struggle of Rozelle to "be what she wants to be" against the censorship of Ottoville becomes the basis of this play, which seeks to unravel the injustices of dictatorship and fights for the rights of people to be more than mere labels.

The Overcoat   Nikolai Gogol   English adaptation by Tom Lanter and Frank S. Torok   Samuel French, Inc., 1975   Ensemble of 8 actors   Unit set
Mime, dance, and fantasy are combined in this funny yet moving theatre piece of a poor clerk and his new coat. Theme of greed runs throughout.

The Padrone   Robert J. Landy   New Plays, Inc., 1978   23 men, 2 women, chorus, extras   Unit set
Two-act, epic theatre adaptation of Horatio Alger, Jr.'s *Phil, the Fiddler*, that traces the hardships of a poor Italian immigrant boy. Themes of equality and racial tolerance run strong throughout.

Phillis: A Life of Phillis Wheatley   Martha Hill Newell   New Plays, 1981   18 characters, extras   Unit set
The importance of freedom and the ugliness of prejudice are the underlying messages in this biographical sketch of the life of the poet Phillis Wheatley.

The Poet and the Rent   David Mamet   Samuel French, 1981   12 characters   Bare stage
A core company portrays a variety of *commedia dell'arte* roles as a starving artist in search of rent money refuses to compromise his values for wealth and teaches us all an important lesson about capitalism.

Punch and Judy   Aurand Harris   Anchorage Press, 1970   14 characters   Puppet stage
A succession of short confrontations played within the constraints of vaudeville style and a puppet stage environ pit Punch and Judy against a variety of good and evil characters and show how within every person there exists a desire to defy the traditional restraints of society and prevail unpunished.

Reynard the Fox   Arthur Faquez   Anchorage Press, 1962   7 characters   1 exterior
Reynard, a diverse and unusual rogue hero, leads the audience on a merry romp through the animal forest kingdom and, through action and elevated language, wittily comments on the good and bad in everyone and exposes the hypocrisy of those who would be the judge of others.

Robinson and Friday   Hansjorg Schneider   Translation by Ken and Barbi Rugg   Edited and adapted by Carol Korty   Baker's Plays, 1980   4 characters   1 exterior
Based on the basic situation from the novel *Robinson Crusoe*, Schneider uses Robinson's shipwrecked plight to examine what we as humans do to survive physically, what we must do to live with our inner selves, how we deal with our longings and fears, and what adjustments we must make to live with others.

Runaway   Ed Graczyk   Anchorage Press, 1977   11 characters   Bare stage
A young runaway stumbles onto a group of players, takes over their play, and learns the important lesson that running away leads nowhere. The things one is really searching for are probably very close by.

Sir Gawain and the Green Knight   Dennis Scott   Anchorage Press, 1978   6 characters   Open stage
Strength of character and the integrity of the human spirit are the challenges Sir Gawain must face in this lyrical story of chivalry and knighthood.

Special Class   Brian Kral   Anchorage Press, 1981   14 characters with special casting   1 interior
Timely piece that takes a long hard look at the needs, problems, talents, and triumphs of a group of handicapped and nonhandicapped junior high students.

Steal Away Home   Aurand Harris   Anchorage Press, 1972   13 characters, chorus (some doubling)   Bare stage
Racial freedom and justice is the theme of this story of two slave boys, Amos and Obie, as they make their treacherous way to freedom along the Underground Railroad.

Step on a Crack   Suzan Zeder   Anchorage Press, 1976   5 characters   2 interiors, 1 exterior
A contemporary drama with fantasy in which a young girl must suddenly cope with sharing her father with a stepmother.

Story Theatre   Paul Sills   Samuel French, 1971   8 or more characters   Bare stage
The moral lessons of a variety of Grimm tales and Aesop's fables are brought to life through ten loosely related vignettes that reveal human nature, past and present, through story and song.

Susan B!   Jules Tasca and Ted Drachman   Dramatic Publishing Co., 1983   18 characters plus extras (6 actors with doubling)   Unit set
Rousing musical tracing the life of Susan B. Anthony and her pioneering efforts as champion of women's rights. Equality and mutual respect are emphasized as opposed to women's liberation.

The Tingalary Bird   Mary Melwood   New Plays, Inc., 1969   4 characters   1 interior
A domineering old woman and her husband learn valuable lessons in how to bring righteousness, gaiety, laughter, and love to their lives through the help of a magical bird.

Treasure Island   Aurand Harris   Anchorage Press, 1983   13 characters (some doubling)   1 interior, 2 exteriors
In this dramatization of Robert Louis Stevenson's classic novel, the conflict between good and evil is courageously faced by Jim Hawkins as he matures from a boy into manhood.

When the Rattlesnake Sounds   Alice Childress   Coward, McCann and Geoghegan, Inc., 1975   3 characters   1 interior
The fight for freedom and the importance of racial equality is the theme of this play concerning Harriet Tubman and her work with the Underground Railroad.

Wiley and the Hairy Man   Jack Stokes   Coach House Press, 1970   6 characters (flexible chorus)   Bare stage
Wiley, through the use of cunning common sense (which is stronger than might), outwits the swamp creature Hairy Man, who is out to haunt him.

Winterthing   Joan Aiken   Samuel French, 1972   8 characters   1 interior, 1 exterior
Family life and the qualities one needs to make being a family work are told in this uncommon fantasy of the lives of five children and the peculiar "Aunti" on magical Winter Island.

The Young Guard   Anatoly Aleksin   Translation by Miriam Morton   New Plays, Inc., 1977   25 men, 10 women, plus extras   Unit set to depict various locales
Two-act, complex drama retracing the events of The Young Guard, an underground Nazi resistance movement in Russia during World War II. Through interrogation and flashback the strength of these people is portrayed and the sacredness of such concepts as honor, home, freedom, and love is explored.

Zas!: A Bilingual Musical Comedy   Virginia A. Boyle   Coach House Press, 1979   7 characters   1 exterior
Spanish and English are interwoven in this fast-paced musical comedy that concerns itself with human and worker rights.

CPSIA information can be obtained
at www.ICGtesting.com
Printed in the USA
LVHW032254161219
640690LV00001B/10/P

9 780292 780859